Alexander Michie

The Siberian overland route from Peking to Petersburg

Through the deserts and steppes of Mongolia, Tartary

Alexander Michie

The Siberian overland route from Peking to Petersburg
Through the deserts and steppes of Mongolia, Tartary

ISBN/EAN: 9783337146832

Printed in Europe, USA, Canada, Australia, Japan

Cover: Foto ©Andreas Hilbeck / pixelio.de

More available books at **www.hansebooks.com**

PAGODA AND GARDENS OF THE EMPEROR'S SUMMER PALACE, YUEN-MIN-YUEN

THE

SIBERIAN OVERLAND ROUTE

FROM PEKING TO PETERSBURG,

THROUGH THE DESERTS AND STEPPES OF MONGOLIA,
TARTARY, &c.

BY ALEXANDER MICHIE.

TOMB AT THE DEPOT, PEKING.

LONDON:
JOHN MURRAY, ALBEMARLE STREET.
1864.

PREFACE.

THE following work has but moderate claims, I fear, to public attention; and it would probably not have seen the light at all but for the urgent request of friends, who think better of it than the author does. It has no pretensions to any higher merit than that of being a plain narrative of the journey, and an impartial record of my own impressions of the people among whom I travelled.

Although some portions of the route have been eloquently described by Huc and others, I am not aware that any continuous account of the whole journey between the capitals of China and Russia has appeared in the English language for nearly a century and a half. Important changes have occurred in that period; and, if I may judge of others by myself, I suspect that many erroneous notions are afloat respecting the conditions of life in these far-off regions, and more especially in Siberia. Observation has modified my own pre-conceived opinions on many of the subjects touched on in the following pages, and I am not without a hope that they will be found to contain some information which may be new to many people in this country.

If I have indulged in irrelevant digressions, I can only say that I have limited myself to those reflections which naturally suggested themselves in the course of my travels; and the subjects I have given most prominence to are simply those which happened to be the most interesting to myself.

My thanks are due to various friends for useful hints, confirming and correcting my own observations; but I am especially indebted for some valuable notes on Siberia, its social phenomena, gold mines, &c., to Edwin E. Bishop, Esq., whose long residence in the country, and perfect acquaintance with the language and customs of the people, constitute him an authority on all matters connected with that part of the world.

22, BERKELEY SQUARE,
October 28th, 1864.

CONTENTS.

CHAPTER I.
SHANGHAI TO TIENTSIN.

JOHN BELL—"Overland" routes—Peking a sealed book—Jesuits—Opening of China—Chinese jealousy of Mongolia—Errors of British policy—Their results—Preparations for journey—Leave Shanghae—Yang-tse-kiang—Changes in its channel—Elevation of the delta—Chinese records of inundations—The Nanzing—Shantung promontory in a fog—Chinese coasters—Advantages of steam—Our fellow-passengers—Peiho river—Intricate navigation—Sailors in China—Tientsin—New settlement—Municipal council—Improvements—Trade—Beggars—Health—Sand-storms—Gambling 1

CHAPTER II.
TIENTSIN TO PEKING.

MODES of travelling—Carts, horses, boats—Filthy banks of the Peiho—Voyage to Tungchow—Our boat's crew—Chinese distances—Traffic on the Peiho—Temple at Tungchow—Mercantile priests—Ride to Peking—Millet—Eight-mile bridge—Resting place—Tombs—Filial piety—Cemeteries—Old statues—Water communication into Peking—Grain supply 23

CHAPTER III.
PEKING.

WALLS of Peking—Dust and dirt—Street obstructions—The model inn—Restaurant—Our boon companions—Peking customs—Rule of thumb—British legation—Confucian temple—Kienloong's pavilion—Lama temple—Mongol chants—Roman and Bhuddist analogies—Mongols and Chinese—Hospitality of lay brother—Observatory—Street cries—Temple of Heaven—Theatres—European residents—Medical mission under Dr. Lockhart—Chinese jealousy of Mongolia—Russian diplomacy—Reckoning with our host—Ice—Paper-money . . . 32

CHAPTER IV.

Peking to Chan-kia-kow.

PAGE

RETURN to Tuugchow—Disappointment—Priest conciliated by Russian language—Back to Peking—Negotiations—Ma-foo's peculation—Chinese honesty and knavery—Loading the caravan—Mule-litters—Leave Peking—Sha-ho—Cotton plant—Nankow—Crowded inn—Difficult pass—Inner "great wall"—Cha-tow—Chinese Mahommedans—Religious toleration—Christians in disfavour—Change of scene—Hwai-lai—Ruins of bridge—Bed of old river—Road traffic—Watchtowers—Chi-ming-i—Legend of monastery—the Yang-ho—Pass—Shan-shui-pu—Coal—Suen-wha-fu—Ride to Chau-kia-kow. . . 56

CHAPTER V.

Chan-kia-kow.

ARRIVAL at Chan-kia-kow—Focus of Trade—Mixed population—Wealth—Mongols—Russians—Name of Kalgan—Chinese friends—Russian hospitality—Disappointment—Proposed excursion to Bain-tolochoi—Camels at last procured—Noetzli returns to Tientsin—The pass—Mountains—Great Wall—The horse-fair—Dealers—Ox-carts—Transport of wood from Urga—Shoeing smiths—Our Russian host arrives—The "Samovar"—Tea-drinking in Russia—Change of temperature—Elevation of Chan-kia-kow—Preparations for the desert—Cabbages—Warm boots—Camels arrive—Leave Chan-kia-kow—The pass—Superiority of mules, &c., over camels 72

CHAPTER VI.

Mongolia.

LEAVE China—Mishap in the pass—Steep ascent—Chinese perseverance—Agricultural invasion—Our first encampment—Cold night—Pastoral scene—Introduction to the Mongols—The land of tents—Our conductors—Order of march—Mongol chants—The lama—Slow travelling—Pony "Dolonor"—Night travelling—Our Mongols' tent—Argols—Visitors—Mongol instinct—Camels quick feeders—Sport—Antelopes—Lame camels—Scant pastures—Endurance of Mongols—Disturbed sleep—Optical illusions—"Yourt," Mongol tent—Domestic arrangements—Etiquette—Mongol furniture—Sand-grouse—Track—Wind and rain—A wretched night—Comfortless encampment—Camels breaking down—The camel seasons—No population—No grass—Mingan 83

CHAPTER VII.

Mongolia—*continued.*

PAGE

VISITORS at Mingan—Trading—Scene with a drunken Mongol—Good horsemen—Bad on foot—Knowledge of money—Runaway pony—A polite shepherd—Gunshandak—Wild onions—Halt—Expert butcher—Mongol sheep, extraordinary tails—A Mongol feast—Effects of diet—Taste for fat explained—Mongol fasts—Our cooking arrangements—Camel ailings—Maggots—Rough treatment—Ponies falling off—Live in hopes—Dogs—The harvest moon—Waiting for Kitat—Lamas and their inhabitants—Resume the march—Meet caravan—Stony roads—Disturbed sleep—Gurush—Negotiations at Kutul-usu—Salt plains—Sporting lama—Ulan-Khada—Trees—Reach Tsagan-tuguruk—Lamas and black men—Small temple—Musical failure—Our new acquaintances—Horse-dealing—Greed of Mongols—Fond of drink—A theft—The incantation—Kitat returns—Camel lost—Vexatious delay—Start from Tsagan-tuguruk 102

CHAPTER VIII.

Mongolia—*continued.*

MARSHES—Camels dislike water—Chinese caravan—Travellers' tales—Taryagi—Looking for cattle in the dark—Butyn-tala—An addition to our party—Russian courier—Water-fowl—Bad water—Kicking camel—Pass of Ulin-dbabha—Mongols shifting quarters—Slip 'tween the cup and the lip—Mountains—The north wind—Guntu-gulu—An accident—Medical treatment—Protuberant ears—Marmots—Ice—Dark night—Bain-ula—Living, not travelling—Charm of desert life—Young pilgrim—Grand scenery—Steep descent—Obon—Horror of evil spirits—Mongol and Chinese notions of devils—Dread of rain—A wet encampment—Snow—The White Mountains—The Bactrian camel—Capability of enduring cold—Job's comforters—Woods appear—The yak—Change of fuel 122

CHAPTER IX.

Urga to Kiachta.

MAIMACHIN in sight—A snow storm—Hasty encampment—Tolla in flood—Delay—Intercourse with Mongols—The night watches—Tellig's family—Rough night—Scene at the Tolla—Crossing the river—the "Kitat" redivivus—His hospitality—How Mongols clean their cups—Maimachin—The Russian consulate—Russian ambition—Its prospects—The Urga, or camp—Kuren—Fine situation—Buildings—

Horse-shoeing—Hawkers—The lamaseries—An ascetic—The Lama-king—Relations between Chinese emperors and the Lama power—Urga and Kara Korum—Historical associations—Prester John and Genghis Khan—Leave Urga—Slippery paths—More delays—The pass—A snow storm—Fine scenery—Rich country—Another bugbear—The Boro valley—Cultivation—Khara-gol—The pass—Lama courier—Shara-gol—Winter quarters—The transmigration—Iro-gol—Forced march—Kiachta in sight 141

CHAPTER X.

Mongols—Historical Notes.

EARLY history of Huns—Wars with China—Dispersion—Appear in Europe—Attila—His career—And death—Turks—Mixture of races—Consanguinity of Huns and Mongols—Genghis—His conquests—Divisions of his empire—Timour—A Mahommedan—His wars—And cruelties—Baber—The Great Mogul in India—Dispersion of tribes—Modern divisions of the Mongols—Warlike habits—Religions—The causes of their success in war considered—Their heroes—Their characters—And military talents—Superstition—Use of omens—Destructiveness and butcheries of the Huns and Mongols—Antagonistic traits of character—Depraved moral instincts—Necessity of culture to develop human feelings—Flesh-eating not brutalising—Dehumanising tendency of war—Military qualities of pastoral peoples—Dormant enthusiasm of the Mongols 166

CHAPTER XI.

Mongols—Physical and Mental Characteristics.

PHYSICAL characteristics—Meanness—Indolence—Failure in agriculture—Hospitality—Its origin—Pilfering—Honesty—Drunkenness—Smoking—Ir'chi or Kumiss—Morality—Of lamas—Women fond of ornaments—Decency of dress—Physique—Low muscular energy—A wrestling match—Bad legs—Bow-legged—Its causes—Complexions—Eyes—Absence of beard—Comparison with Chinese and Japanese—Effect of habits on physical development—Animal instincts in nomads—Supply the place of artificial appliances—Permanence of types of character—Uniformity in primitive peoples—Causes that influence colour of skin—Mongol powers of endurance—Low mental capacity—Its causes—Superstition produced by their habits—Predisposed to spiritual thraldom—The lamas and their practices—Prayers—Knaveries of lamas—Vagabond lamas—The spread of Bhuddism—Superior to Shamanism—Shaman rites—Political result of Bhuddism—The Mongol kings—Serfs 185

CHAPTER XII.

KIACHTA.

APPROACH Kiachta—Maimachin—Chinese elegance—The frontier—Russian eagle—The commissary of the frontier—"Times" newspaper—Kiachta—Troitskosarfsk—Meet a countryman—Part from our Mongols—Their programme—A Russian bath—Siberian refinement—Streets and pavement—Russian conveyances—Aversion to exercise—Semi-civilisation—Etiquette—Mixture of peoples—Wealth of Russian merchants—Narrow commercial views—The Chinese of Maimachin—Domestic habits—Russian and Chinese characters compared—Chinese more civilised than the Russians—The Custom-house—Liberal measures—Our droshky—Situation of Kiachta—Supplies—Population—Hay-market—Fish—The garden—Domestic gardening—Climate salubrious—Construction of houses—Stoves—Russian meals—Commercial importance of Kiachta—Inundation of the Selenga—Travelling impracticable—Money-changing—New travelling appointments—Tarantass—Passports—Danger of delay—Prepare to start—First difficulty—Siberian horses—Post-bell 203

CHAPTER XIII.

KIACHTA TO THE BAIKAL.

LEAVE Troitskosarfsk—Hilly roads—Bouriats—The first post-station—Agreeable surprise—Another stoppage—A night on the hill-side—Hire another carriage—Reach the Selenga—The ferry—Selenginsk—A gallery of art—Cultivation—Verchne Udinsk—Effects of the inundation—Slough of despond—Fine scenery—A dangerous road—A press of travellers—Favour shown us—Angry Poles—Ilyeusk—An obsequious postmaster—Tidy post-house—A night at Ilyeusk—Treachery suspected—Roads destroyed—Difficult travelling—An old Pole—Baikal lake—Station at Pasoilské—A night scene—The Selenga river—And valley—Agriculture—Cattle, sheep, pigs, dogs . 223

CHAPTER XIV.

LAKE BAIKAL TO IRKUTSK.

MORNING scene at Pasoilské—Better late than never—Victimised—Russian junks—Primitive navigators—Storms on the Baikal—Scene at the shipping port—Religious ceremony—A polite officer—Inconvenience of the Baikal route—Engineering enterprise—More delay—Fares by the Baikal steamer—Crowing and crouching—The embarkation—The General Karsakof—A naval curiosity—The lake—Its depth—And area—The "Holy Sea"—The passage—Terra firma—Customhouse delay—Fine country—Good roads—Hotels Amoor and Metzgyr 234

CHAPTER XV.

IRKUTSK.

IN sight of Irkutsk—Handsome town—Wrong hotel—Bad accommodation—Suffocation—Bad attendance—The cuisine—Venerable eggs—Billiards—Meet a friend—Beauties of Irkutsk—Milliners—Bakers—Tobacconists—Prison—Convicts—Benevolence of old ladies—Equipages—Libraries—Theatre—Population—Governor-Generalship—The levée—Governing responsibilities—Importance of commerce—Manufactures insignificant—Education—Attractions of Siberia—Society—Polish exiles—The Decembrists—The sentence of banishment—Its hereditary effect—Low standing of merchants—Discomforts of travelling—Engage a servant—The prodigal—A mistake—Early winter—The Angara—Floating-bridge—Parting view of Irkutsk 246

CHAPTER XVI.

IRKUTSK TO KRASNOYARSK.

LEAVE Irkutsk—Roads and rivers—Capacity for sleep—Bridges—Breakneck travelling—Endurance of Russian ponies—Verst-posts—Appalling distances—Irregular feeding—Tea *versus* grog—River Birusa—Boundary of Irkutsk and Yenisei—Stoppage—The telegraph wires—Improved roads—River Kan—The ferrymen—Kansk—A new companion—Prisoner of war—Advantages and disadvantages of travelling in company—Improved cultivation—A snow-storm—Cold wind—Absurd arrangement of stations—The river Yenisei—Mishap at the ferry—The approach to Krasnoyarsk—The town—Population—Hotel—Travellers' accounts—Confusion at the station—The black-book—The courier service 262

CHAPTER XVII.

KRASNOYARSK TO TOMSK.

SLEDGES—Sulky yemschiks—Progress to Achinsk—Limit of Eastern Siberia—Game—The Chulim—Difficult ferry—Government of Tomsk—Bad roads again—Job's comforters—Mariinsk—An accident—And another—Resources of a yemschik—A drive through a forest—Ishimskaya—A day too late—A sporting Pole—Disappointment—Annoying delay—Freezing river—A cold bath—Sledge travelling—A night scene—Early birds—Arrive in Tomsk—Our lodging—Religion of Russians—Scruples of a murderer—Population and situation of Tomsk—Fire Insurance—Climate of Tomsk—Supply of water—Carefulness and hardiness—Skating—Demure little boys—An extinct species—The gold diggings—The Siberian tribes 273

CHAPTER XVIII.

Tomsk to Omsk.

REFITTING—The optician—The feather-pillow question — A friend in need—A dilemma—Schwartz's folly—Old Barnaul leaves us—We leave Tomsk—A weary night—A Russian dormitory—Construction of houses—Cross the Tom—And the Ob—Enter the Baraba steppe—Kolivan—The telegraph—The ladies of Baraba—Game—Windmills—A frozen marsh—Kainsk—Reach Oms—Outbreaks on the Kirghis steppe—Russian aggression—Its effects on different tribes . . 290

CHAPTER XIX.

Omsk to Ochansk.

LEAVE Omsk—Recruiting—Cross the Irtish—Tukalinsk—Yalootorofsk—Reach Tumen—Improved posting—Snow roads—Ekaterineburg—Mint—Precious stones—Iron works—Englishmen in Siberia—Iron mines—Fish trade—A recruiting scene—Temperature rising—Game—The Urals—Disappointing—A new companion—The boundary between Europe and Asia—Yermak the Cossack—Discovery and conquest of Siberia—Reach Perm—Too late again—Progress of inland navigation—Facilities for application of steam—Water routes of Siberia—Railways—Tatars—Cross the Kama to Ochansk—Dissolving view of snow roads 305

CHAPTER XX.

Russian and Siberian Peasantry.

SIBERIAN and Russian peasantry—The contrast—Freedom and slavery—Origin of Siberian peasants—Their means of advancement—Exiles—Two classes—Their offences and punishments—Privileges after release—Liberality of the government—Its object—Extent of forest—One serf-proprietor in Siberia—Exemptions from conscription—Rigour of the climate on the Lena and Yenisei—Settlers on Angara exempted from taxes—Improvement of Siberian peasants—A bright future—Amalgamation of classes—Slavery demoralising to masters—The emancipation of the serfs—Its results 320

CHAPTER XXI.

KAZAN.—POLISH EXILES.

ROAD to Kazan—Polish prisoners—Arrive at Kazan—More croaking—Temptations to delay—Sell our sledge—View of Kazan—The ferry at the Volga—Ice-boats and icebergs—The military—Tatars—Polish exiles—Kindly treated by their escort—Erroneous ideas on this subject—The distribution of exiles in Siberia—Their life there—The Polish insurrection—Its objects—Imprudence—Consequences—Success would have been a second failure 331

CHAPTER XXII.

KAZAN TO PETERSBURG.

A DAY lost—The moujik's opportunity—Return to Kazan—Hotel "Ryazin"—Grease and butter—Evening entertainment—Try again—The ferry—A term of endearment—Ferrymen's devotions—A Jew publican—"Pour boire"—Villages and churches—The road to Nijni—Penance—A savage—A miserable night—Reach Nijni—"Sweet is pleasure after pain"—The great fair—Nijni under a cloud—Delights of railway travelling—A contrast—Reach Moscow—Portable gas—Foundling hospital—The Moscow and Petersburg railway—Grandeur of Petersburg—Late season—Current topics—Iron-clads—The currency—Effects of Crimean war—Russian loyalty—Alexander II. as a reformer—Leave Petersburg. 343

CHAPTER XXIII.

RUSSIA AND CHINA.

EARLIER intercourse—Analogies and contrasts—Progress of Russia and decadence of China—Permanence of Chinese institutions—Arrogance justified—Not really bigoted—Changes enforced by recent events—The rebellion—Fallacious views in parliament—British interest in China—A bright future—Railways—Telegraphs—Machinery and other improvements—Resources to be developed—Free cities . 357

POSTSCRIPT . 401

LIST OF ILLUSTRATIONS.

	PAGE
PAGODA AND GARDENS OF THE EMPEROR'S SUMMER PALACE, YUEN-MIN-YUEN. (From a Photograph by Beato)	*Frontispiece.*
TOMB AT THE DEPOT. PEKING. (From a Photograph by Beato)	*Vignette.*
TUNG CHOW PAGODA. (From a Photograph by Beato)	27
WALLS OF PEKING. (From a Photograph by Beato)	32
PAVILION OF THE SUMMER PALACE OF YUEN-MIN-YUEN. (From a Photograph by Beato)	37
THIBETIAN MONUMENT IN LAMA TEMPLE. PEKING. (From a Photograph by Beato)	42
GREAT TEMPLE OF HEAVEN. PEKING. (From a Photograph by Beato)	48
PART OF THE EMPEROR'S PALACE, YUEN-MIN-YUEN. DESTROYED 1860. (From a Photograph by Beato)	55
THE NANKOW PASS	63
HALT IN THE DESERT OF GOBI	104
FORDING THE TOLLA NEAR URGA	147
VIEW OF EKATERINBURG. SIBERIA. (From a Russian Photograph)	307

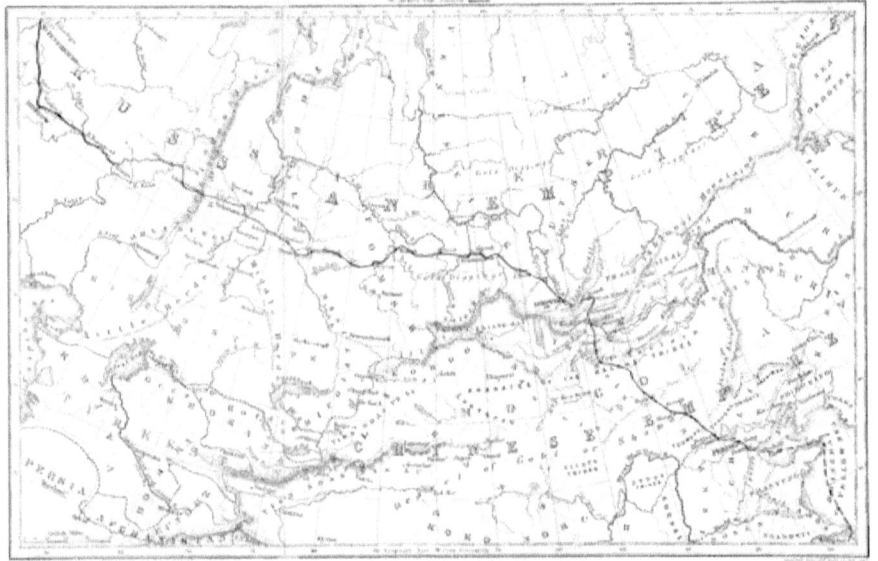

THE
SIBERIAN OVERLAND ROUTE FROM PEKING TO PETERSBURG.

CHAPTER I.

SHANGHAE TO TIENTSIN.

THE charming narrative of John Bell, of Antermony, who, in the reign of Peter the Great, travelled from Petersburg to Peking in the suite of a Russian ambassador, inspired me with a longing desire to visit Siberia and other little-known regions through which he passed. Having occasion to return to England, after a somewhat protracted residence on the coast of China, an opportunity presented itself of travelling through the north of China, Mongolia, and Siberia, on my homeward journey. This is, indeed, the real "overland route" from China, and it may as properly be styled "maritime," as the mail route per P. & O. steamers "overland." The so-called overland route has, however, strong temptations for a person eager to get home. There is a pleasing simplicity about the manner of it which is a powerful attraction to one who is worn out with sleepless nights in a hot climate. It is but to embark on a steamer; attend as regularly at meal times as your constitution will permit; sleep, or what is the same thing, read, during the intervals; and fill up the blanks by counting the passing hours and surveying your fellow passengers steeped in apoplectic slumbers under the enervating influence of the tropics. The sea route has, moreover, a decided advantage in point of time. In forty-five or fifty days I could have reached England from Shanghae by steamer : the land journey *viâ* Siberia I could not hope to accomplish in less than ninety days.

But the northern route had strong attractions for me in the kind of vague mystery that invests the geography of strange countries, and the character, manners, and customs of their inhabitants. Ever-recurring novelties might be expected to keep the mind alive; and active travelling would in a great measure relieve the tedium of a long and arduous journey. Of the two, therefore, I preferred the prospect of being frozen in Siberia to being stewed in the Red Sea. The heat of Shanghae in the summer was intense and almost unprecedented, the supply of ice was fast undergoing dissolution, and an escape into colder regions at such a time was more than usually desirable.

A few years ago it would have been about as feasible to travel from China to England by way of the moon as through Peking and Mongolia. Peking was a sealed book, jealously guarded by an arrogant, because an ignorant, government. Little was known of the city of the khans except what the Jesuits had communicated in the last century, and what that prince of travellers, Marco Polo, had handed down from the middle ages. No foreigner dared show his face there, except in the guise of a native, and even then at the risk of being detected and subjected to the greatest indignities. The Jesuits, it is true, in the face of the prohibition, continued to smuggle themselves into China, and even into Peking itself, and their perseverance and tenacity of purpose are entitled to all praise. But they occasionally paid dearly for their temerity, and not unfrequently got themselves and their "Christians" into hot water with the authorities. This received the high-sounding name of "persecution;" and if any one lost his life for meddling in other people's affairs, or interfering with the prerogative of the government, he was honoured with the name of a "martyr." The Jesuits had their day of power in China, and if they had but used it modestly they might still have stood at the elbow of the Emperor. They were tried and found wanting, expelled from Peking, and China was closed against foreigners, not, it must be confessed, without some reason.

All that has been changed again. The curtain has risen once more; foreigners are free to traverse the length and breadth of China, and to spy out the nakedness of the land. The treaty of Tientsin and convention of Peking, ratified in November, 1860, which opened up China to travellers for "business or pleasure," was largely taken advantage of in the following year. In 1861, foreign steamers penetrated by the great river Yang-tsze into the heart of China. Four enterprising foreigners explored the river to a distance of 1800 miles from the sea, and many other excursions were set on foot by foreigners, in regions previously known only through the accounts of Chinese geographers or the partial, imperfect, and in some instances obsolete, descriptions of the older Jesuits.

Mongolia, being within the dominions of the Emperor of China, was included in the passport system; and although the Chinese government has made a feeble attempt to impose restrictions on foreign travellers in that region on the ground that, although Chinese, it is not China, up to the present time no serious obstacles have been placed in the way of free intercourse in Mongolia; nor can the plain language of the treaty be limited in its interpretation, unless the ministers of the treaty powers should voluntarily abandon the privilege now enjoyed. It is devoutly to be hoped that no envoy of Great Britain will again commit the error of waiving rights once granted by the Chinese. However unimportant such abandoned rights may appear, experience has shown that the results are not so. Sir Michael Seymour's war at Canton in 1856-7 could never have occurred if our undoubted right to reside in that city had been insisted on some years previously. Our disaster at the Taku forts in 1859 would have been prevented if the right of our minister to reside in Peking had not, in a weak moment, been waived. What complications have not arisen in Japan, from our consenting to undo half Lord Elgin's treaty and allowing the port of Osaca to remain closed to our merchantmen! We cannot afford to make concessions to Asiatic powers. Give them an inch and they will take an ell: then fleets and armies must be brought into play to recover ground we have lost through sheer wantonness.

Too late to join a party who preceded me, I had some difficulty in finding a companion for the journey, but had the good fortune to make the acquaintance of a young gentleman from Lyons, who purposed going to France by the Siberian route with or without a companion. We at once arranged matters to our mutual satisfaction, and proceeded with the preparations necessary for the journey. Having the advantage of excellent practical advice on this head from gentlemen who had already gone over the ground, we had little difficulty in getting up our outfit. A tent was indispensable for Mongolia, and we got a very commodious one from a French officer. A military cork mattress, with waterproof sheets, proved invaluable in the desert. Our clothing department was inconveniently bulky, because we had to provide both for very hot and very cold weather. The commissariat was liberally supplied, rather overdone, as it turned out, but that was a fault on the safe side. The accounts we heard of the "hungry desert," where nothing grows but mutton, induced us to lay in supplies not only for an ordinary journey across, but for any unforeseen delay we might encounter on the way.

We had first to get to Tientsin, six hundred miles from Shanghae, and two steamers were under despatch for that port. I embarked on board the *Nanzing*, Captain Morrison, about midnight on the 28th July, 1863. Taking advantage of the bright moon, we steamed cautiously down the river Wong-poo for fourteen miles, past the village of Woosung, "outside the marks," and into the great river Yang-tsze, where we cast anchor for the night. It would be hazardous to attempt the navigation of the estuary of the Yang-tsze, even in bright moonlight. Its banks are so flat as to afford no marks to steer by. The estuary is very wide, but the deep water channel is narrow, with extensive shallows on either side. The upper parts of the Yang-tsze-kiang, where the river narrows to a mile or two in breadth, and flows through a bolder country, are more easy of navigation. In the broad part of the river, near its mouth, the deep water channels have a tendency to shift their positions. The surveys of the river from its mouth to Nanking, made in 1842, were found inapplicable in 1861. Where shallows were marked in 1842, deep water was found in 1861, and dry patches were found where the navigable channels were before. The delta of this noble river is rapidly growing into dry land; the "banks" are fast rising into islands, and the channels of the river becoming more circumscribed. The rapidity with which this process is going on is most remarkable. From a point nearly fifty miles from the mouth of the river it is divided into two great branches, called by hydrographers the north and the south entrances. Twenty years ago extensive shallows lay between, and many a good ship found a final resting-place on these treacherous banks. The most dangerous of these are now above water, and are visible from a distance sufficient to enable the pilot to keep clear of them. In the small river Wang-poo also, at and below the town of Shanghae, the land is gaining considerably on the water. An island has formed and is still growing near the mouth of the Wang-poo, known to pilots as the "middle-ground." Until a very few years ago it was entirely under water. In the year 1855 I was aground on the top of it in a schooner near low water, and the rising tide floated us off easily. The island is now so high as to remain uncovered in the highest spring tides. Thus, in the space of eight years, this island has risen more than twelve, and probably not less than eighteen feet. The formation is extending itself downwards; the tail of the island stretching away under water brought up many vessels in 1862 and 1863, where there was plenty of water a year or two before. On the south shore of the Yang-tsze-kiang the lines of embankment mark the different stages of the aggression of the land on the water. When a dry flat was formed liable to inundations in high tides, an embankment of mud was built for the protection of the inhabitants who settled on the reclaimed land. In process of time more land was made, and another embankment formed. Thus three distinct lines of embankment, several miles inland from the present water line, are to be traced from below Woosung towards Hang-chow Bay, and a very large tract of good arable land has been reclaimed from the river, or, as the Chinese call it, the sea, within comparatively modern times. From the causes we see now in active operation, it is easy to trace the formation of the vast alluvial plain which now supports so many millions of inhabitants.

There are, indeed, intimations in the Chinese records of some of these changes. Islands in the sea are mentioned but a few centuries back, which are now hills in inhabited districts. In the dawn of Chinese history allusions are made to a great flood which desolated the land, and the Emperor Yaou has been immortalised for his achievements in subduing and regulating the waters. Yaou reigned about 2200 B.C., and the rising of the waters in his time has been referred by some to the Noachian deluge. But the Chinese empire at that time extended as far south as the Great River, and included three great valleys. It is not an improbable conjecture therefore that there was a large circumference of debateable land barely reclaimed from the sea. With the imperfect means then at command for keeping out the water it is easy to suppose that an unusually high tide would break down the defences and overflow the flat country. It may also be, of course, that then, as now, the Yellow River caused trouble by arbitrarily changing its course, and the patriotic labours of Yaou may have been limited to damming up that wayward stream, which has been called "China's sorrow." But the chronicles of the great inundation do not appear to have been satisfactorily explained, and it may be said of the annals of the reigns of Yaou and Shun, that the interest which attaches to them is in direct proportion to their obscurity.

A few hours' steaming on the 29th took us out of the turbid waters of the Yang-tsze-kiang, but during the whole of that day we continued in shallow water of a very light sea-green colour. The weather was fine, and though still extremely hot, the fresh sea air soon produced a magical effect on our enfeebled digestion. The voyage was as pleasant as a good ship, a good table, and a courteous commander could make it. On the 30th a thick fog settled down on the water, and on the following morning all eyes were anxiously straining after the Shantung promontory, which was the turning-point of our voyage. By dead reckoning we were close to it, but there is no accounting for the effect of the currents that sweep round this bold headland. The tide rushes into the

Gulf of Pecheli by one side of the entrance, and out at the other. But from the conformation of the gulf the tidal currents are subject to disturbances from various causes, of which the direction of the wind is the most potent. A northwesterly wind keeps the tide wave at bay, and drives the water out of the gulf, until its level has been lowered several feet below that of the ocean. Great irregularities in the ebb and flow are occasioned by this; and when the cause ceases to act, the reaction is proportionate to the amount of disturbance; the pent-up waters from without flow in with impetuosity, and the equilibrium is restored.

In the dense fog, our commander could only crawl along cautiously, stopping now and again to listen for the sound of men's voices, or the barking of dogs, take soundings, and watch for any indications of the near vicinity of land. At length, to our great joy, the fog lifted over a recognisable point of the promontory, and immediately settled down again. The glimpse was sufficient however, and the good steamer was at once headed westward, for the mouth of the Peiho river, and bowled along fearlessly on her way. As the sun rose higher the mist was dispersed, and the bold rugged outline of the Shantung coast was unveiled before us. The clear blue water was alive with Chinese coasting craft, small and large, of most picturesque appearance. The heavy, unwieldy junks of northern China lay almost motionless, their widespread sails hanging idly to the mast, for there was just wind enough to ripple the surface of the water in long patches, leaving large spaces of glassy smoothness untouched by the breeze.

The crews of the northern junks are hardy stalwart fellows, inured to labour, and zealous in their work. Their vessels are built very low-sided, to enable them to be propelled by oars when the wind fails them. The crews work cheerily at their oars, both night and day, when necessary, keeping time to the tune of their half-joyous, half-melancholy boat-songs. With all their exertions, however, they drive the shapeless lump but slowly through the water, and one cannot help feeling pity for the poor men, and regret for the waste of so much manual labour. It is to be hoped that this hardy race of seamen will find more fruitful fields wherein to turn their strength to account when foreign vessels and steamers have superseded the time-honoured but extravagant system of navigation in China. This end has, indeed, been already reached to a certain extent. China has been imbued with the progressive spirit of the world, to the great advantage both of themselves and foreigners. The southern coasts swarm with steamers, and the Gulf of Pecheli, in this the third year from the opening of foreign trade in the north, was regularly visited by trading steamers. In all discussions in England on the subject of the development of trade in China, the vast coasting trade is generally overlooked, as a matter in which we have no interest. This is a mistake, however, for foreigners have a considerable share in that trade directly, and their steamers and sailing vessels are employed to a very large extent by the Chinese merchants. All produce is very materially reduced in price to the consumer by the facilities for competition among merchants which improved communication affords, and by the diminution in expenses of carriage, which is the necessary result. The rapidity with which foreign vessels can accomplish their voyages as compared with Chinese junks enables the native trader to make so many more ventures in a given time, that he can afford to take smaller profits than formerly, and yet on the average be no loser. Or even if the average results of the year's trade be less profitable to individuals than before, its benefits are spread over a greater number, and, in the aggregate, suffer no diminution. The general interests of the country have been subserved in an important degree by the extension of the coasting trade, where no disturbing influences have been at work; and the prosperity of the general population cannot fail to react favourably on the mercantile class, through whom the prosperity primarily comes.

Chefoo, the new settlement on the Shantung coast, is frequently a port of call for steamers trading between Shanghae and Tientsin. We did not touch there in the *Nanzing*, but passed at a distance of twelve miles from the bluff rocky headland from which the settlement takes its name. Before darkness had closed in the view we had reached the Mia-tau group of islands which connect the mountain ranges of Shantung, by a continuous chain, with the Liau-tung promontory at the north of the entrance of the Gulf of Pecheli. There is not much difficulty or danger in getting through these islands even at night, but it is always an object to a navigator to reach them before dark. The course is then clear for the Peiho, and he has a whole night's straight run before him with nothing to look out for.

The Peiho river must be an awkward place to "make," except in clear weather. The land is lower even than that of the valley of the Yang-tsze-kiang; the shoal water runs out a long distance into the gulf; and a dangerous sand spit, partly above, and partly under water, stretches fifty miles out to sea on the north of the approach to the river. On reaching the outer anchorage, where vessels of heavy draught lie, the celebrated Taku forts are dimly visible in the haze of the horizon, and masts may be seen inside the river, but the low land on either side is still invisible. A shoal bar, with a very hard bottom, lies between the outer anchorage and the river, and the *Nanzing*, drawing less than ten feet, was obliged to anchor outside until the rising tide enabled her to get in.

Our Chinese fellow passengers, who had kept remarkably quiet during the voyage, as is their invariable custom, became animated as we ran in between the Taku forts. They were a motley crowd of all classes of people—mercantile, literary, and military. The students who go to Peking to undergo examinations for literary degrees travel now in great numbers by steamer, and doubtless many who, from want of means, want of time, or from any other cause, might hesitate before undertaking such a long journey by the old land route, are now enabled, by means of the coasting steamers, to accomplish the object so deeply cherished by all Chinese literati. The "plucked" ones, and there are many such in China, can now more easily renew their efforts. Men have been known to repair year after year to the examination-hall from their youth upwards, and get plucked every time,—yet, undaunted by constant failure, they persevere in their vain exertions to the winter of their days. The country that can produce such models of perseverance in a hopeless cause may claim to possess elements of vitality, and the usual proportion of fools.

Among our Chinese passengers was an athlete from Fokien, who was bound to Peking to try his prowess in archery. He was a man of great muscular power, fat, and even corpulent. It is remarkable that the training system adopted for the development of the muscles should produce so much fat. I had not observed this before in the Chinese; indeed, the few feats of strength I have seen performed by them have been by men well proportioned and free from fat. But the Japanese wrestlers, who are carefully trained, are generally fat.

The entrance to the Peiho was, as usual, crowded with native and foreign craft, and so narrow and tortuous is the river that great care is necessary to work a long steamer through without accident. Tientsin is distant from Taku, by the windings of the river, between sixty and seventy miles.

By the cart road it is only thirty-six. The *Nanzing* made good way up the river until darkness compelled her to anchor. In the morning the difficulties of the inland navigation began. The river was actually too small for a steamer over two hundred feet long, the turns were too sharp, the ordinary means of handling a steamer were no longer of any avail,— we hauled round several bad turns by means of anchors passed on shore in the boats, but were at length baffled after running the steamer's nose into cabbage-gardens, breaking down fences, and alarming the villagers, who turned out *en masse* to watch the iron monster as she struggled to force a passage out of her natural element. Partly out of compassion for the men, who were worn out with the uncongenial toil of trudging knee-deep through heavy mud, planting anchors and picking them up again, and partly from some vague hope of a change of tide in the afternoon, the steamer was brought to anchor and hands piped to dinner.

The crews of steamers on the coast of China are usually of a cosmopolite character, chiefly Malays, with a boat's crew of Chinese, the foreign element being reduced to a minimum comprising the officers and engineers. Asiatic sailors do very well when there are plenty of them, the estimate of their value being two of them to one European. They sail for lower wages, but not low enough to compensate the shipowner for the additional numbers that are necessary. But the Asiatics are more easily handled than Europeans; their regular "watches" may be broken in upon with impunity; they are easier fed, and less addicted to quarrelling with their bread and butter than Europeans, and more especially Englishmen. But any doubt on the part of a shipmaster as to what crew he will employ, will generally be solved by the sailors themselves, who, if English or American, will desert at every port the vessel touches at.

Having my saddle and bridle handy I landed at a village,

and borrowing a horse from the farmers, rode to Tientsin, which was only some eight miles distant by the road. The heat was scorching, but greatly mitigated by the mass of bright green foliage that covered the whole country. The soil though dry and dusty is rich to exuberance, fruit grows in great abundance, and, for China, in great perfection. Apples, pears, peaches, apricots, loquats, grapes, are common everywhere in the north, which may be considered the orchard of China. The waving crops of millet, interspersed with patches of beans, and here and there strips of hemp, fill up a vast green ground dotted thickly with villages and pretty clumps of trees. The houses form a dull contrast to the cheerful aspect of the country. In most of the villages they are constructed of mud and straw, which becomes hard enough to be impervious to rain, but the dull parched colour, the small apertures for doors and windows, and general cheerlessness of exterior painfully oppress the sight. The dust of the roads is also an unfavourable medium through which to view the tame though rich beauties of the country. The north of China is cursed with dust, the roads generally are as bad as the road to Epsom on a "Derby day," when that happy event happens to come off in dry weather.

I got back to the *Nanzing* in time for the final effort to double the difficult corner. The first attempt was successful, and we steamed on gaily through fields and gardens, washing the banks with the wave formed in our wake, which sometimes broke over the legs of unwary celestials who stood gazing after the steamer in stupid wonder like a cow at a railway train. The Chinese take such mishaps good-naturedly—the spectators are always amused, and the victims themselves when the shock of surprise passes off laugh at the joke. The most serious obstacle to our progress had yet to come, however, the "double," a point where the river bends abruptly like the figure S compressed vertically.

Extra caution being used there, the appliances of anchors and warps were efficacious, and we passed the double successfully. The smoke of the *Waratah*, a steamer that left Shanghae the day before us, and which we had passed at sea, now appeared over the trees close to us. There were several reaches of the river between us, however, and we traced the black column of smoke passing easily round the bends that had caused us such difficulty. The *Waratah* was gaining on us fast, and late in the evening her black hull appeared under our stern, while the *Nanzing* was jammed at the last bend of the river, unable either to get round herself or to make room for the smaller vessel. Hours were spent in ineffectual endeavours to proceed—the tantalised *Waratah* could stand it no longer—the captain thought he saw room to pass us, and came up at full speed between us and the bank. But as the sailors say "night has no eyes" even when the moon is shining, and our friend paid for his temerity by crashing his paddle box against our bow. Time and patience enabled us to reach Tientsin at midnight on the 1st August, after spending half as much time in the Peiho river as the whole sea voyage had occupied. I have said enough, and probably much more than enough, to demonstrate the difficulty of navigating the Peiho river with vessels not adapted to it. No vessel should attempt it that is over one hundred and fifty feet in length, for though the risk of loss from stranding is extremely small, the loss of time to large vessels must be serious.

A marvellous transformation had taken place in Tientsin since my previous visit to it in 1861. At that time the few European merchants who had settled there were confined to the Chinese town, the filthiest and most offensive of all the filthy places wherein celestials love to congregate. Now in 1863, the "settlement," that necessary adjunct of every treaty port in China, had been made over to foreigners, laid out in streets, and a spacious quay and promenade on the river bank formed, faced riverwards with solid masonry, the finest thing of the kind in China, throwing into the shade altogether the famous "bund" at Shanghae. The affairs of the settlement are administered by a thoroughly organised "municipal council" after the example of Shanghae, the "model settlement." The newly opened ports have an immense advantage over the original five in having the experience of nearly twenty years to guide them in all preliminary arrangements. That experience shows first—although the soundness of the deduction has been questioned by some able men—the desirability of securing foreign settlements where merchants, consuls, and missionaries may live in a community of their own entirely distinct from the native towns, within which they may put in operation their own police regulations, lay out streets to their own liking, drain, light, and otherwise improve the settlement, levy and disburse their own municipal taxes, and, in short, conduct their affairs as independent communities. These settlements have the further advantage of being susceptible of defence in times of disturbance with the minimum risk of complication between the treaty powers and the Chinese government. Much of the importance Shanghae has achieved of late years is due to the foreign settlement which, being neutral ground and defensible, has become a city of refuge for swarms of Chinese who had been ousted from their homesteads by the rebels. The cosmopolite character of the Shanghae settlement has entailed various inconveniences, which it is thought might be obviated in the new settlements by keeping the different foreign nationalities distinct. Time has not yet pronounced on the success of this experiment. There will probably be a difficulty in putting it thoroughly in practice; no arbitrary regulations will be able to prevent nationalities from fusing into each other to such an extent as the higher laws of interest and policy may dictate. And it will be impossible in practice to subject a mixed community to the laws of any one power. In the meantime concessions are claimed from the Chinese government by each of the treaty powers separately, and so far they have been granted. Whether the isolation of the various concessions be permanent or not, it secures for them at the outset more unanimity in laying out streets and framing preliminary regulations for their good government hereafter. This is of great importance, and the experience of Shanghae is most valuable in this respect. The narrowness of the streets in the settlement there—twenty-two feet—is a standing reproach on the earlier settlers who, with short-sighted cupidity, clung with tenacity to every inch of land at a time when land was cheap and abundant. This fatal error has been avoided in the recent settlements.

The municipality of Shanghae established under the auspices of Sir Rutherford (then Mr.) Alcock, at that time British consul, has on the whole proved such a success that the same system has been adopted in the new settlements. The legality of the institution has often been questioned, but the creation of some such authority was a necessity at the time, and it has worked so well for ten years that it has not only subsisted, but gathered strength and influence by the unanimous will of the community.

Several fine European houses were already built and inhabited on the Tientsin settlement. The ground had been well raised, so as to keep the new town dry, and ensure it a commanding position. It is about two miles lower down the river than the native town, has a fine open country round it, and plenty of fresh air. It is several degrees cooler in the British settlement than in the Chinese town, and altogether the very best site for the purpose has been selected. The merchants retain their offices in the Chinese town, riding or sailing to and fro every day. This system will probably continue to be practised for some time longer, or perhaps altogether, for the convenience of the Chinese dealers. A small minority of the foreign merchants would compel all to retain their business premises in Tientsin, and nothing less than an almost entire unanimity among them would effect the transfer to the new town.

As a dépôt of trade, Tientsin labours under certain disadvantages; the shallow bar outside, and intricate navigation of the river, prevent any but small craft from trading there. Larger vessels do sometimes, or rather did,—for I fancy the practice is discontinued,—repair to the outer anchorage. But the expense of lighterage, and the detention incurred in loading or discharging at such a distance from the port, are so great as to drive such competitors out of the field. The other drawback to Tientsin is the severe winter, and the early closing of the river by ice. This generally happens before the end of November, and the ice does not break up before February or March.

However, Tientsin is the feeder of a large tract of country containing a large consuming population, and the trade is no doubt destined to increase. Much disappointment has, indeed, been felt that the extraordinary start made, chiefly in the sale of foreign manufactures, in the first year of its existence as a port of foreign trade, has not been followed up. This may be explained, however, by the circumstance that in 1860-61 manufactured goods were extremely depressed by over-supply in the south of China. These goods were introduced into Tientsin, and sold direct to the Chinese there, untaxed by the intermediate profits and charges they formerly had to bear when sold in Shanghae, and thence forwarded by Chinese merchants, in Chinese junks, to Tientsin and the north. Prices in Tientsin soon fell so low that the merchants were tempted into large investments during 1861. The markets of the interior became overstocked, and, before the equilibrium was restored, the cotton famine began to be felt, and prices of goods (the Tientsin trade is chiefly opium and cotton goods) rose so high as to deter purchasers, and in a material degree to reduce the consumption of foreign cottons. Another circumstance also operated adversely to a maintenance of the lively trade that grew up in 1861. There were no exports in Tientsin suitable to any foreign market. The foreign trade was therefore limited to the sale of imports, which were paid for in specie. A heavy drain of bullion was the result, more than the resources of the country could bear for any length of time. This of itself was enough to check the further development of trade; for though the precious metals were merely transferred from one part of the country to another, no counter-balancing power then existed by which they could be circulated back to the districts whence they came. There is no good reason why produce suitable to foreign markets should not be found in Tientsin. Wool and tallow will no doubt be obtainable in considerable quantities in process of time, for the country is full of sheep and cattle, and Tientsin is only six days' journey from the frontier of Mongolia, where flocks and herds monopolise the soil.

I must mention a circumstance connected with the Tientsin trade, which is remarkable among an eminently commercial people like the Chinese. At the opening of the trade, in the end of 1860, the relative values of gold and silver varied fifteen per cent. between Tientsin and Shanghae. Gold was purchased for silver in the north, and shipped to Shanghae, at a large profit, and a good many months elapsed before an equilibrium was established.

In and about Tientsin, as almost everywhere else in China, the population is well affected towards foreigners. The British troops that garrisoned Tientsin from 1860 till 1862 left behind them the very best impressions on the inhabitants. Not that these troops were any better than any other well-disciplined troops would have been, but the Chinese had been taught to regard foreigners as a kind of aquatic monsters, cruel and ferocious; so when the horrible picture resolved itself into human beings, civil and courteous in their disposition, honestly paying for all they wanted, of vast consumptive powers in the matter of beef and mutton, fruit and vegetables, and, on the whole, excellent customers, the Chinese took kindly to the estimable invaders, and had cause to regret their departure. Foreign merchants were held in high estimation from the first. The free hospitals for Chinese, set on foot by the army surgeons, not only did a great deal of good in alleviating suffering, but prepared the way for mutual good feeling in the after intercourse between natives and foreigners. It has been questioned whether the Chinese, as a race, are susceptible of gratitude. But, at any rate, the respectable classes are sufficiently charitable themselves to appreciate philanthropy in others; and, in the self-imposed and gratuitous labours of the surgeons for the benefit of the sick poor, they saw an example of pure benevolence, which could not but excite their admiration.

The population of Tientsin is supposed to be about 400,000, residing chiefly in the suburbs, for trade is generally carried on without the walls, not only here, but in all Chinese cities. There is an unusually large proportion of beggars about Tientsin, and loathsome objects they are, as they whine about the streets, half clad, in tatters, starved, and often covered with sores. They never sleep but on the ground. At night, when the streets are quiet, the beggars may be discovered huddled together at every corner and on every door-step. Begging is an institution in China, and to qualify for the craft, men have been said to burn out their own eyes, in order to excite compassion for their blindness. A Chinese

householder seldom allows a beggar to go away empty.
Charity is cheap; a handful of rice, one copper cash, value
the fourth part of a farthing, suffices to induce the disgusting
object to move on to the next shop. The beggars have seldom any cause to starve in China, but they do very often,
and it is probable they bring diseases on themselves in
their efforts to excite pity, which carry them off very rapidly.
In winter, especially in the north, they seem to die off like
mosquitoes, and no one takes any notice of them except to
bury them—for the Chinese don't like to leave dead bodies
about the streets. In spring they reappear—not the identical beggars, certainly—but very similar ones, and the ranks
of the profession are kept filled.

The wealthier natives of Tientsin, traders and shopkeepers,
are fond of good living and gambling. They are robust
people, and bear up well against the effects of late hours and
gross dissipation. The close, filthy atmosphere in which they
live and breathe does not seem to injure their health. Epidemics do make great havoc among them occasionally; one
year it is cholera, another year it is small-pox; but the
general healthiness of the people does not seem to suffer.
The climate is exceedingly dry. Little rain or snow falls;
but when it does rain, the whole heavens seem to fall at once,
not in torrents, but in sheets of water. The peculiar sandstorms, so common in the north of China, have not as yet
been satisfactorily investigated. They often come on after a
sultry day. A yellow haze appears in the sky, darkening the
sun; then columns of fine dust are seen spinning round in
whirlwinds. At that stage every living thing seeks shelter,
and those who are afield are lucky if they are not caught in
the blinding storm before they reach their houses. But even
a closely shut-up house affords but half protection, for the
fine powdery dust insinuates itself through the crevices of
doors and windows, and is palpably present in your soup and

your bread for some time after. The most obvious source whence these sand-storms come, is the great sandy desert of Mongolia, but such an hypothesis is hardly sufficient to account for all the phenomena which accompany the sand-storms. It has been supposed that they are due to some peculiar electrical condition of the atmosphere.

The Chinese are passionately addicted to gambling, and the endless variety of games of chance in common use among them does credit to their ingenuity and invention, for it is not likely that they have learned anything from their neighbours. The respectable merchant, who devotes the hours of daylight assiduously to his business, sparing no labour in adjusting the most trifling items of account, will win or lose thousands of dollars overnight with imperturbable complacency. Every grade of society is imbued with the passion. I have amused myself watching the coolies in the streets of Tientsin gambling for their dinner. The itinerant cooks carry with them, as part of the wonderful epitome of a culinary establishment with which they perambulate the streets, a cylinder of bamboo, containing a number of sticks on which are inscribed certain characters. These mystic symbols are shaken up in the tube, the candidate for hot dumpling draws one, and according to the writing found on it, so does he pay for his repast. So attractive is gambling in any form to the Chinese, that a Tientsin coolie will generally prefer to risk paying double for the remote chance of getting a meal for nothing. On one occasion I volunteered to act as proxy for a hungry coolie who was about to try his luck. The offer was accepted with eagerness, and I was fortunate enough to draw my constituent a dinner for nothing. I was at once put down as a professor of the black art, and literally besieged by a crowd of others, all begging me to do them a similar favour, which, of course, I prudently declined. Had I indeed been successful a second time, the dispenser of the tempting morsels would certainly have protested against my interference as an invasion of his prerogative, which is to win, and not to lose.

The Chinese gamblers are, of course, frequently ruined by the practice. They become desperate after a run of ill luck; every consideration of duty and interest is sunk, and they play for stakes which might have startled even the Russian nobles, who used to gamble for serfs. In the last crisis of all, a dose of opium settles all accounts pertaining to this world.

In games of skill the Chinese are no less accomplished. Dominoes, draughts, chess, and such like, are to be seen in full swing at every tea-house, where the people repair to gossip and while away the evening. The little groups one sees in these places exhibit intense interest in their occupation; the victory is celebrated by the child-like exultation of the winner, and any pair of Chinese draught-players may have sat for Wilkie's celebrated picture.

CHAPTER II.

TIENTSIN TO PEKING.

THERE are several modes of going from Tientsin to Peking. The most common is in a mule cart, which is not exactly a box, but a board laid on wheels with a blue cotton covering arched over it. The cart is not long enough to enable one to lie down full length, nor is it high enough to enable him to sit upright in the European fashion. It has no springs; the roads are generally as rough as negligence can leave them; it is utterly impossible to keep out the dust; and the covering gives but slight protection from the sun. A ride in a Chinese cart is exquisite torture to a European. It is true that experience teaches those who are so unfortunate as to need it several "dodges" by which to mitigate their sufferings, such as filling the cart entirely with straw, and then squeezing into the middle of it. But then the traveller must have some means of securing the feet to prevent being pitched out bodily, and he must hold on to the frame-work of the side by both hands to break the shock of sudden jerks. With all that he will come off his journey feeling in every bone of his body as if he had been passed through a mangle. That the Chinese do not suffer from such treatment I can only attribute to a deficiency in their nervous system. If they suffered in anything like the same degree that a European does, they would have invented a more comfortable conveyance before the Christian era. But the only improvement in comfort I ever heard of is in the carts made for the great mandarins, which have the wheels placed far back, so that between the axle-tree and the saddle the shafts may have an infinitesimal amount of spring in them.

The next mode of travelling is on horseback, which, if you happen to have your own saddle and bridle, is very pleasant, provided the weather is not too hot or too cold. There are plenty of inns on the road-side where you can rest and refresh yourself; but woe betide the luckless traveller who, like myself, nauseates the Chinese *cuisine*, should he have neglected to provide himself with a few creature comforts to his own liking.

The weather was excessively hot, and judging that there would be many calls on our stamina before our long journey was done, we prudently husbanded our strength at the outset. We therefore chose the slower but more luxurious (!) means of conveyance by boat up the Peiho river to Tungchow, a walled city twelve miles from Peking. Boat travelling in the north has not been brought to such a state of perfection as in the creek and canal country in Chekiang and Keangsoo. In the latter provinces it is practically the only means of travelling, and though slow, is most comfortable. In the north the boats are a smaller edition of those used for transporting merchandise, the only convenience they have being a moveable roof. In two such craft our party embarked on the night of 5th August, 1861, and at 11 p.m., by moonlight, we languidly shoved off from the filthy banks of the Peiho river, the few friends who were kind enough to see us off, with a refinement of politeness worthy of a Chinaman, refusing a parting glass, knowing that we had none to spare. Our sails were of little assistance, so after threading our way through the fleet of boats that lay anyhow in the first two reaches, our stout crews landed with their towing line, by which means we slowly and painfully ascended the stream. Tientsin, as I have said, is the filthiest of all filthy cities; and the essence of its filth is accumulated on the banks of the river, forming an excellent breakwater, which grows faster than the water can wash it away. The putrid mass is enough, one would think, to breed a plague, and yet the water used by the inhabitants is drawn from this river! It was pleasant, indeed, to escape from this pestilential atmosphere, and to inhale the cool fresh air of the country for an hour or two before turning in, as we reflected on the long and tedious journey we had before us, embracing the whole breadth of the continents of Asia and Europe.

The voyage to Tungchow was monotonous in the extreme. Nothing of the country could be seen; for though the water was high enough at the time to have enabled us to look over the low flat banks, the standing crops effectually shut in our view. Four days were occupied in travelling 400 li. We had engaged double crews, in order that we might proceed night and day without stopping, but it was really hard work for them, and we did not like to press them too much. There is no regular towing path on the banks of the Peiho, and at night the men floundered in the wet mud amongst reeds. A youngster of the crew gave us a great deal of trouble—always shirking his work and complaining of hunger. He was a wag, however, and kept both us and the crew in amusement. I have noticed in nearly all Chinese boat-crews there is a character of this sort, whose business seems to be to work as little as possible himself, and keep up a running fire of wit to beguile the toil of the others. A good story-teller is much valued among them. We had also an old man, whose chief business was to boil rice and vegetables for the others, and to steer the boat. His kitchen duties were no sinecure, for the men did get through an incredible quantity of rice in the course of the day. Rice is a poor thing to work on; it is a fuel quickly consumed, and requires constant renewal.

It is the nature of Chinese boatmen to be constantly asking for money. The custom is to pay about half the fare in advance before starting, and the other half when the journey is completed. But no sooner are you fairly under way, than a polite request is made for money to buy rice. It is in vain you remind them of the dollars you have just paid as a first instalment. That has gone to the owner of the boat, of course, but as for them, the boatmen, they have nothing to eat, and cannot go on. Defeated in your arguments you nevertheless remain firm in your purpose ; the morning, noon, and evening meals succeed each other in due course. Every one is to be the last, and is followed by the most touching appeals to your benevolence—they will go down on their knees, they will whine and cry, they will beat frantically on their empty stomachs, and tell you " they are starving " in tones and gestures that ought properly to melt the heart of a stone. It is in vain that you deride their importunity ; it is in vain that you reproach them with their improvidence. You sternly order them to their work, but are met by the unanswerable question, how can they work without food ? You—if you have gone through the ordeal before—know well that you will have no trouble on this score on the second day out.

Has any one ever tried to arrive at the exact value of a Chinese measure of distance ? Their li has no doubt been reduced to so many yards, feet, and inches, equal to about one-third of an English mile, on paper ; but on the road it is the vaguest term possible. Ask a countryman how far it is to Chung-dsz, and he will answer after a great deal of prevarication ten li. Walk about that distance and inquire again, and you are told it is fifteen li. This will puzzle you if you are a stranger, but go on another half mile, and you find you are at your destination. In the common acceptation of the word, I am convinced it is more a measure of time

TUNG CHOW PAGODA. (Page 27.)

than distance, and 100 li is an average day's journey. Our Tientsin boatmen put this very prominently when questioned, as they were nearly every hour of the day, as to how far we still were from Tungchow, one of them answered, "If you travel quick it is about 100 li, but if slow it is well on to 200!"

In the first part of our journey we met with no traffic on the river, but towards Tungchow we passed large fleets of junks bound upwards and a few bound down. John Bell says of this river, "I saw many vessels sailing down the stream towards the south-east. And I was informed there are nine thousand nine hundred and ninety-nine vessels constantly employed on this river; but why confined to such an odd number I could neither learn nor comprehend." I should say that during the 140 years that have elapsed since that was written the fleet is more likely to have been shorn of a few odd thousands than increased by the odd unit.

On the fourth day, as we were panting for breath, with the thermometer standing at 97° Fahr., and with anxious eyes contemplating our almost empty ice-box, the pagoda of Tungchow was descried over the tall reeds on the river bank, and we soon were made fast in front of a temple called Fang-wang-meaou.

At this point the Peiho dwindles away into a very small and shallow stream, and practically Tungchow is the head of the navigation, the shipping port of Peking, and the beginning of the land carriage to the north-west provinces of China.

The Fang-wang-meaou is much used by Russians as a dépôt for their goods in transit from Tientsin and Shanghae to Siberia. We found a considerable quantity of tea stored in the temple waiting for transport. In this temple, therefore, by the favour of the reverend personages who preside over it, we bestowed our *impedimenta*, and took up our quarters for the night in a wing of the building.

The Bhuddist priests are in the habit of transacting business for strangers, and we therefore entered into negotiation with them to provide us carriage either by mules or camels, from Tungchow to Chan-kia-kow, the frontier town between China and Mongolia. We thought by this arrangement we could ride to Peking, do what we wanted there in the way of getting passports, &c., and return to Tungchow and take our departure thence. This proved a delusion, and lost us some valuable time.

There is nothing remarkable about the city of Tungchow. It is situated on a dead level. From a tower on the wall a view of the country is obtained, including the mountains north of Peking. There is a tall pagoda in the city, but as it has no windows in it, it is useless as a look-out.

I found here two ponies that I had sent from Tientsin, in charge of a Chinese " ma-foo " or groom, who agreed to accompany me as far as Chan-kia-kow. My object was to be independent of the Chinese carts at Peking and on the road, and I looked forward to taking one, if not both, of my ponies a considerable distance into the desert of Mongolia. I strongly recommend this plan to any one travelling in that quarter.

On the 10th of August I rode to Peking, the rest of the party following in carts. This would no doubt be a very pretty ride at another season of the year, but in the month of August the millet crops stand as high as twelve and fifteen feet, completely shutting in the road for nearly the whole distance. At eight li from Tung-chow we passed the village and handsome stone bridge of *Pa-li-keaou* or "eight-mile-bridge," which euphonious name gives a title to a distinguished French general. There are no " high " roads, but many bye-roads, and it is not difficult to lose one's way amongst the standing millet. Many parts of the country are very prettily wooded, and there is a half-way house at a well-shaded part of the road, where you naturally dismount to rest yourself under a mat shed, and indulge yourself with hot tea, than which nothing is more refreshing on a hot day, provided the decoction be not too strong, and is unadulterated by the civilised addition of sugar or milk. You may eat fruit here also if you are not afraid of the consequences (but take care that it is ripe), and some naked urchins will cut fresh grass for your beasts. This little place, like many others of its kind, is a "howf" for many loafers, who seek the cool shade, and sit sipping their boiling tea, and languidly fanning themselves while they listen abstractedly to the conversation of the wayfarers.

As we near Peking we come to some slight undulations, and notice some very pretty places with clumps of old trees about them. These are principally graves of great men, and it is remarkable to observe how much attention is paid by the Chinese to the abodes of their dead. Wealthy people will pass their lives in a dismal hovel, something between a pig-stye and a rabbit-warren, into which the light of day can scarcely penetrate; the floors of earth or brick-paved, or if the party is luxurious, he may have a floor of wood, encrusted with the dirt of a generation. But these same people look forward to being buried under a pretty grove of trees, in a nicely kept enclosure, with carefully cultivated shrubs and flowers growing round. Some of the loveliest spots I have seen in China are tombs, the finest I remember being at the foot of the hill behind the city of Chung-zu, near Foo-shan, on the Yang-tsze-kiang. These tombs, adorned with so much taste and care, were in strange contrast with the general rottenness around. But armies have since been there, and it is probable that the angel of destruction has swept it all away.

I am unable to say from what feeling springs this tender regard for tombs among the Chinese. It may be that they consider the length of time they have to lie in the last resting-place, reasonably demands that more care be bestowed on it than on the earthly tenement of which they have so short a lease. Or it may arise simply out of that strong principle of filial piety so deeply engraven in the Chinese mind, and which leads them to make great sacrifices when required to do honour to the manes of their ancestors. From whatever motive it comes, however, this filial piety, which even death does not destroy, is an admirable trait in the Chinese character; and I have even heard divines point to the Chinese nation—the most long-lived community the world has seen—as an illustration of the promise attached to the keeping of the fifth commandment. The greatest consolation a Chinaman can have in the "hour of death" is that he will be buried in a coffin of his own selection, and that he has children or grandchildren to take care of his bones. It is to this end that parents betroth their children when young, and hasten the marriages as soon as the parties are marriageable. To this end also I believe polygamy is allowed by law, or at all events not interdicted. If a Chinaman could have the promise made to him, "Thou shalt never want a man to stand before me," he would live at ease for the rest of his days.

There are no cemeteries in China, that I know of, except where strangers congregate—when they of a family, a district, or even a province, combine to buy a piece of ground to bury their dead in. In hilly countries pretty sites are always selected for tombs. In the thickly settled parts of the country every family buries its own dead in its own bit of ground. Thus, when they sell land for building purposes, negotiations have to be entered into for removing the coffins of many forgotten generations. The bones are carefully gathered up and put into earthenware jars, and labelled. This operation is profanely called "potting ancestors." These jars are then buried somewhere else — of course with great economy of space. A house built on the site of an old grave that is suspected of having been only partially emptied, would remain tenantless for ever, and if the ghosts of the departed did not destroy the house, the owner would be compelled to do so.

But I am getting away from the Peking road. Amongst the tombs of great families, outside the walls of the city, are many old marble colossal sculptures of men and animals. The same figures, in limestone, are common in other parts of the country. These sculptures are all more or less dilapidated; some of the figures are still erect; many have fallen down and got broken; and many have been ploughed in. There is nothing remarkable about the workmanship of these, although the colossal size of some of them is striking. They are interesting as memorials of departed greatness, and record their silent protest against the corruption, decay, and degeneracy that has brought the Chinese empire so low.

Water communicating with the Peiho river goes up to the walls of Peking, but is not navigable. It forms a quiet lagoon, the delight of great flocks of the most beautiful ducks and geese. The streams that run through the city can also be connected with the water outside through the arches in the wall; and I am told the intention of those truly great men, who conceived and executed the grand canal, was to bring the water through the city and into the imperial quarters by navigable canals, so that the grain-junks from Keangsoo, which were to supply the capital with food, might be brought in to the gate of the Emperor's palace. It is not to be wondered at that this scheme should have broken down, considering the engineering difficulties attending it.

CHAPTER III.

PEKING.

NOTHING of the city of Peking is visible until you are close under the walls, and then the effect is really imposing. The walls are high, massive, and in good repair. The double gates, with their lofty and large three-storied towers over them, and the general solid appearance, inspire one with some of the admiration which poor old Marco Polo used to evince when speaking of the glories of Kambalic, or the city of the Grand Khan.

Once inside the walls you instinctively exclaim, What a hot, dusty place this is! and you call to mind that that is exactly what everybody told you long before its threshold was polluted by barbarian footsteps. Peking is celebrated for its carts, its heat, and its dust. If it rained much the streets would be a sea of mud.

We pursue our way along the sandy tracks between the city wall and the buildings of the town for a mile or two, then plunge into the labyrinth of streets, crowded, dirty and odoriferous. We are being conducted to an inn which is to be better than any that foreigners have been admitted to before.

In our way we crossed the main street which leads from the imperial city straight to the Temples of Heaven and Earth. This street is very wide, and has been very fine, but now more than half its width is occupied by fruit, toy, and fish stalls. The centre of the street has been cut up by cart-

WALLS OF PEKING. (Page 32.)

From a photograph.

wheels for many centuries, and is full of holes and quagmires, so that the practicable portion of this wide thoroughfare is narrowed down to nothing. So it is with all the wide streets of Peking. They are never made. Filth accumulates incredibly fast; and the wider the street the dirtier it is, because it can hold the more.

At last we arrived at this paragon of inns, and passing through the courtyard, where the horses and mules of travellers were tied up, we threaded our way as far into the interior of the establishment as we could get, and then called the landlord. He pretended to make a great to-do about receiving us, and strongly urged that we would find much better accommodation at the West-end. This was not to be thought of, and we soon installed ourselves in a room—but such a room! and such an inn! and such attendance! and such filth everywhere! I have slept in a good many Chinese inns of all sorts, but the meanest road-side hostelry I have ever seen is a degree better than this swell inn in this fashionable city of Kanbalu. Our room was at the far end of the labyrinthine passages, and was evidently constructed to exclude light and air. It was almost devoid of furniture. We certainly could make shift for sleeping accommodation, for travellers can manage with wonderfully little in that way; but we were miserably off for chairs, the only thing we had to sit upon being small wooden stools on four legs, the seat being about five inches wide.

There was no getting anything to eat in this establishment, so we fell in with the Peking custom of dining at a restaurant, and we found a very good one on the opposite side of the street. This was a nice cheerful place, with good airy rooms, and comfortable cushioned seats—much frequented by the Pekingese. Here we always got a good dinner, and met good society. We could not stomach the pure native messes, but as they had always abundance of

D

good mutton and fish (kept alive on the premises till wanted), also rice, clean and white, with a little preliminary instruction in our manner of living, the *cuisinière* hit off our taste to a nicety. We had our own knives and forks to eat with, and our own good liquor to season the repast, so in Peking we may be said to have lived well.

We used to meet a strange mixture of people in this restaurant—natives of Canton, Yunnan, Szechune, Shansi—in short, of every part of China ; men whose lawful occasions brought them to the capital. Most of them were merchants, and I presume the students who flock to Peking in such number form little cliques of their own. These fellows lead a very jovial life. About seven o'clock, or a little later, they assemble in parties already made up, and dinner is laid, each party having a separate room. They eat heartily, and seem thoroughly to enjoy each other's society. They don't hurry over their dinner, and they have such an infinity of small dishes, that their repast spreads itself over several hours. They are very quiet at the first onset, but as they warm up with their wine, they get very noisy, and make the whole place ring with the sounds of merriment. They drink their wine hot, out of small porcelain cups, and instead of a decanter, a tea-kettle is put on the table. We used to amuse ourselves by going from one party to another, and joining for a few minutes in their conviviality. They were always pleased to see us, and made us sit down and drink with them. We reciprocated their hospitality, and when we had administered a glass of wine to one of them, he would sip it with an air of grave meditation, then slap his paunch vigorously, and, holding up his right thumb, would exclaim with emphasis " Haou !" " super-excellent."

They have a methodical manner of drinking, which is no less entertaining to spectators, than agreeable to themselves. The libations are regulated by a game of forfeits, engaged in

by two at a time. The challenger holds out one or more
fingers, accompanying the action by certain set phrases. The
other has to reply promptly to the word and the pantomime,
the penalty for a mistake being to drink a cup of wine.
They begin this process quietly and soberly, but when an
obstinate antagonist is found, who replies to the challenge
five or six times running without a break-down, the contest
becomes exciting. They gradually rise from their seats, and
approach each other across the table, their faces grow red, as
their shouting gets louder, and the repartee more spirited,
until they reach a climax of passion which flesh and blood
could not long sustain, and then explode like a bomb-shell
amid tremendous bursts of unearthly yells from the full company. The loser sips his liquor with resignation; and the
victor generally joins him, by way of showing himself a
generous adversary. I have heard of drinking "by rule of
thumb," in our own country, but this has probably nowhere
been reduced to a science so much as in China.

About nine or ten, a long string of carts (the cabs of
Peking), would be collected at the door, the parties would
begin to break up, and go their several ways to the theatres,
or other evening amusements. They generally make a night
of it, and that class of the Chinese are everywhere late in
their habits. I never met a more robust-looking, or more
jovial, hearty set of men, than these, our boon companions of
Peking.

On arriving in Peking, I lost no time in calling on Sir F.
Bruce, our minister there, to get passports put in train. I
was fortunate enough to meet Sir Frederick, as he had just
come in for a day from his retreat in the hills. He has
occupied a temple situated on the hills, some twenty miles
from Peking, which forms an admirable summer residence,
free from the putrid smells of the city, and with a temperature many degrees cooler,—no mean advantage when the

thermometer stands about 90°. The building set apart for the English legation in Peking is, from an eastern point of view, magnificent. It was a "foo," or ducal palace, has large space for garden ground round the principal building, while the smaller buildings would easily accommodate a full regiment of soldiers.

We found that it would take several days to get our papers in order; for not only was my passport to be got, but my companion had to get his through the French legation. There was nothing for it but to make ourselves easy, having done all that we could do to accelerate our business. Now, at another season of the year, I could have spent a week in Peking with pleasure, but in the month of August one cannot go out with any degree of comfort or safety, except in the morning or evening, and then the streets are full either of blinding dust, or black mire, in which your horse is always splashing up to his hocks. However, we tried to make the best of it, and I was fortunate enough to meet my old friend, Dr. Lockhart, who had lived long enough in Peking to know the ropes, and who was good-natured enough to show me round the principal objects of interest in the city. Another difficulty besets the sight-seer in Peking, and that is the "magnificent distances" between the various places one wants to see. However, by sallying forth betimes, we did manage to visit a few of the many interesting objects in this old city; for there is nothing really worthy of note in China, except what bears the stamp of antiquity.

The Confucian temple was the first object of our curiosity. Here the great sage is worshipped by the Emperor once a year, without the medium of paintings or images. In the central shrine there is merely a small piece of wood, a few inches long, standing upright, with a few characters inscribed on it, the name of the sage, I believe. On the sides are a number of still smaller wooden labels, representing the dis-

PAVILION OF THE SUMMER PALACE OF
YUEN-MIN-YUEN.

ciples and commentators who have elucidated the writings of Confucius. The temple contains a number of stone tablets, on which are engraved the record of honours conferred on literary men, and to obtain a place here is the acme of the ambition of Chinese scholars. In the courtyard there are a number of pine trees, said to have been planted during the reign of the Mongol dynasty, more than 500 years ago. These trees have been stunted in their growth, however, from want of room, and considering their age, their size is disappointing. The courtyard is adorned by a variety of stone sculptures, the gifts of successive emperors and dynasties. The present dynasty has been rather jealous of its predecessors in this respect, especially of the Ming, and has replaced many fine relics of their time by new ones of its own. There are, however, several Mongol tablets to the fore in the Confucian temple. A connoisseur can at once, from the style, fix the date of any of these works of art, and when in doubt, the inscriptions are for the most part sufficiently legible to tell their own tale. In another part of the building there are some very curious old stones, drum-shaped, dating from 800 years B.C. These have been carefully preserved, but the iron tooth of time has obliterated most of the writing on them. The curious old characters are still to some extent legible, however. The building itself is, from a Chinese point of view, a noble one, and singularly enough, it is kept in perfect order, in strange contrast to Chinese temples and public buildings generally. It has a magnificent ceiling, very high, and the top of the interior walls are ornamented by wooden boards, richly painted, bearing the names of the successive emperors in raised gilt characters. On the accession of an emperor he at once adds his name to the long list.

The hall erected by the learned Emperor Kienloong, although modern (he reigned from 1736 to 1796), is a magnificent pavilion, not very large, but beautifully finished, and in perfect good taste. The pavilion is roofed with the imperial yellow tiles. Round it is a promenade paved with white marble, with balustrades of the same. At a little distance from the pavilion stands a triumphal arch, massive and elegant. The pavilion is intended to be viewed through the arch, from a stand-point a few yards behind it, so that the arch forms a frame for the main building. The effect produced is peculiar and striking, and does infinite credit to the taste of old Kienloong, who, by the bye, seems to have done everything that has been done in modern times to beautify the capital. The pavilion stands in the middle of a large open square, on two sides of which, under a shed, stand double rows of stone tablets, six or seven feet high. On these tablets are engraved, in clear and distinct characters, the whole of the Chinese classics, in such a manner that they can be printed from. Many copies have actually been struck off from these tablets, and are held in very high esteem.

The great lamasery is outside the city, but the lama temple or monastery inside is also well worthy of notice, whether from the vast quantity of bricks and mortar that go to make the range of buildings, the extent of the grounds attached to it, including a fine wooded park, or from the internal economy of the establishment itself. Two thousand Mongol lamas are maintained here by the bounty of the Emperor.* The other lamaseries are in the same manner liberally endowed by the government. The Chinese emperors feel that they have but a slight hold on their Mongol subjects, scattered as they are over a vast desert, where no Chinese troops could penetrate, even were the Chinese a match for the Mongols in a military point of view, which they never were. The independence of the Mongols would

---

* The first Emperor of the Manchu line originated the scheme, but it has been greatly extended by his successors.

be rather a gain than a loss to China in its immediate results, but it would establish a warlike race on their borders, which has been the terror of China from the earliest times. No doubt, ages of peace have done much to subdue the warlike spirit of the Mongols, but they retain their ancient habits and lead a life of privation and hardship from the cradle to the grave. They are susceptible of the greatest enthusiasm, and at a word from their chiefs they would be ready to follow them to death or glory. A few years of fighting would render the Mongol hordes as formidable to a non-military nation like the Chinese, as they were in the days of the terrible Genghis Khan. In the present enfeebled condition of China an irruption of Mongols would be irresistible, and would sweep everything before it like a flood. The Chinese government are quite alive to such a possible contingency, and hence the care they take to conciliate the Mongols. Their forty-eight kings (of whom San-go-lin-sin is one), nominally tributary to China, are really pensioned by the Emperor, and every inducement is held out to the Mongol lamas to settle in the monasteries in Peking. Here they live in comfort and luxury unknown in their deserts. Their friends have every facility for visiting them, and carrying back to the "land of grass" their reports of the goodness of the Chinese Emperor. The lamas are taken from all parts of Mongolia—we conversed with several from Dolonor and Kuren (Urga), and many others from the north and south, the names of whose districts were not included in my geographical vocabulary. These large Mongol communities, under the eye and hand of the Emperor, answer the double purpose of conciliators on the one hand, and of hostages for the loyalty of distant tribes on the other. The Mongols are as little a match for the Chinese in craft, as they are superior to them in martial energy. It is supposed that the Chinese government have a deep design in supporting and encouraging lamaism, an institution which makes nearly one-third of the Mongol race celibats—for there are female as well as male lamas—the object being to keep down the population of the tribes.

However, the simple-minded Mongols lead a comfortable, easy life in Peking, free from care, and with no occupation except chanting their prayers. I was fortunate enough to witness one of their religious services in the great temple. The building is raised some ten feet from the ground, a fine flight of steps running round the four sides of it. The roof is very high, and the sides are open all round. The lamas muster leisurely out of their cells, dressed in dirty red cotton garments, and armed with an enormous yellow cap, with something of a helmet shape, and crested with a long fringe made, I think, of camel's hair. They carry the cap for the most part under their arm, seldom wearing it on the head. About 200 of them assembled in the temple, and sung a chant which lasted about half an hour. The effect was very striking and solemn, for the music was good, and one or two of the lamas had the finest bass voices I ever heard. The apparent earnestness with which the whole congregation joined in the service, and the deep, devotional character of the music, riveted our attention with an irresistible power. So different was it from the ludicrous mockery of sacred things perpetrated by the Chinese Bhuddists, during whose most solemn services I have seen a dirty fellow push his way through the devotees and coolly light his pipe at the candles burning on the altar.

The analogies between the Bhuddist and Roman Catholic forms of worship have been so hackneyed by writers that it may seem impertinent in me to allude to them. But I cannot help drawing attention to the manner in which M. Huc endeavours to explain them. The analogies are most complete in the Yellow Cap Lama sect, the origin of which is described at length by Huc. In the thirteenth century, in the country of Amdo, bordering on Thibet, a child miraculously conceived was born with a white beard, and from his birth gave utterance to profound sayings concerning the destiny of man. His name was Tsong-Kamba. This prodigy of a child became an ascetic, devoting himself to meditation and prayer. A holy stranger from the west visited him, and amazed him by his sanctity and learning. The stranger was remarkable for his long nose. After instructing Tsong-Kamba for a few years in the mysteries of religion the holy man died; but Tsong-Kamba became a great reformer, and originated the new sect of the Yellow Cap Lamas. Huc clutches at this tradition, and thinks he sees in the mysterious visitor of Tsong-Kamba a Christian missionary, many of whom had penetrated about that period into Tartary. The premature death of the master left incomplete the instruction of the disciple, who, failing to attain Christianity, stopped short as a reformer of Bhuddism.

After the service we had some talk with the lamas, who were pleased to see us, and treated us with every civility. They all speak, and many of them write, Chinese; and in that language we communicated with them. The ethnical difference between two races supposed to be of the same origin could not be more apparent than in the case of these Mongols and the Chinese by whom they were surrounded. The Mongols have all an unintellectual cast of countenance, low narrow foreheads, and a simple and open expression. Their features are not very different from the Chinese. They have the high cheek-bones, small eyes, and some other characteristics of their neighbours; but their noses are on the whole not so short and flat, nor their faces so rounded. It is not so easy to tell in what the difference between them and the Chinese consists, but the distinction is so marked that I hardly believe it possible for any one to mistake a Mongol for a Chinese. The Mongols have unsuspecting honesty written on their faces. The Chinese, from north to south, bear the stamp of craft and cunning, and are much superior in intellect to the Mongols. It is only necessary to remark the physiognomies of the two races to understand how the Chinese outwit the Mongols in their dealings with them, and how the Chinese name has in consequence become a bye-word among the Mongols for everything that is detestable. It should not be forgotten of course that it is probably the worst class of Chinese with whom the Mongols come in contact. They are mostly adventurers who seek their fortunes among the Tartars, for the hard life they are compelled to live in these outlying countries is not at all suitable to the Chinese taste. The better sort of merchants are therefore not likely to wander so far; and those that do go are in the first instance below the average moral standard of the Chinese, and, when liberated from the restraint of public opinion in their own country, they are likely to deteriorate still more. It would also appear to be true that demoralisation naturally grows out of the intercourse between two races, one of whom is in a marked degree inferior to the other in intellectual capacity. In commercial dealings the Chinese find it so easy to overreach the simple Mongols, and the temptation to do so is so strong, that the habit is engendered, which soon becomes part of the character of the Chinese in Tartary. The Mongols, on their part, learn to form a low estimate of the honour of human nature. They know they are victimised by the Chinese, but they are powerless to escape from it; hence they, by a very natural process, acquire a settled hatred to the whole race.

But we have not yet seen the great gilt image of Bhudda, which stands in a separate building erected for the purpose. We failed in getting in on the first visit, but afterwards

THIBETIAN MONUMENT IN LAMA TEMPLE, PEKING. (Page 12.)

succeeded. The image is seventy-two feet high, well formed, and symmetrically proportioned. By a series of narrow and steep staircases we ascend several stories, at each getting a view of a part of the image. At the top of all we get out on a balcony, from which a good view of the city and environs is obtained.

The Grand Lama of this monastery is a Chaberon or living Bhudda, of whom there are several in Mongolia; and as such he is a sacred person, and a man of great authority among Mongols, whether lamas or laymen. We had business to transact with this incarnation of Bhudda, but, on inquiring for him, we learned that he had left on some holy mission to the great lamasery at Dolonor, a Mongol town a few days' journey north-west of Peking. We had a letter from the head priest of the Fang-wang temple at Tungchow, who, though not belonging to the Lama sect, which so far as I am aware consists exclusively of Tartars, was nevertheless on easy terms with the Grand Lama. The purport of the letter was to recommend us to the attentions of the Grand Lama, and to request him to give us another letter to the lamas of a monastery in Mongolia, a short distance beyond the Great Wall at Chan-kia-kow, to enlist their services in procuring camels for our journey across the desert of Gobi. We anticipated some difficulty about this, and wished to have as many strings to our bow as possible. The letter was written in Mongol, and put in an envelope addressed in Manchu, for the priest at Tung-chow was a learned man. No one in the monastic brotherhood could be found who could read the Manchu address, and they had great difficulty in finding one who could master the Mongol characters in which the letter itself was written. We were surprised that they should not be able to read their own language, and on inquiry found that lamas are not taught to read Mongol as a necessary branch of study. They all learn the Lama writing, which they call "Tangut," but which must be Thibetian, as all their books and prayers are written in that character, and those lamas who live in Peking generally learn to read a little Chinese for their own convenience. While the letter was being deciphered we were introduced to the lay brother of the monastery, the confidant of the Grand Lama, and factotum in all secular affairs. A fine, hard-headed, swarthy complexioned, rough-and-ready burly fellow he was, and he received us with his rude native hospitality, showing us into the room, and making us sit on the very *kang* used by the absent Bhudda. Being naturally slow of comprehension, and his secretary being equally slow and uncertain in deciphering the missive, the old fellow had many questions and cross-questions to ask, with many repetitions, which all being carried on in a very loud tone of voice, as if he had been bawling to a man on the main-top, began to get rather tiresome. Having satisfied himself about the contents of the letter, he entered into conversation with Noetzli, who, having been in Mongolia before, and in the very monastery of Bain-tolochoi to which we sought to be accredited, very adroitly led the conversation to that subject, and soon showed our Mongol friend that he knew all about the locality and the personal appearance of the head Lama there, whose chief characteristic seemed to be that he was inordinately fat. No sooner had our friend convinced himself that Noetzli had actually been the guest of the fat Lama, than he took us yet closer into his confidence, ordered the letter to be written, and at the same time despatched a boy into the street with some money in his hand. When the letter was finished, and we rose to leave, the old fellow, on hospitable thoughts intent, protested, seized our hats, and by main force pushed us back to the seat of the Grand Lama. To keep us in play he put fruit before us, but we did not know what it was all about until our breakfast was brought in in a large basin. It consisted of about twenty pounds of plain boiled mutton, without bread, rice, potatoes, or vegetables of any kind. All we had to eat with it was a solution of salt, soy, vinegar, and sugar. Eat we must, there was no help for it, and we honestly set ourselves to do as full justice to the unsavoury meal as we were capable of, although we had a good breakfast waiting us at home, that is, at our restaurant, our host all the while standing over us like a taskmaster to keep us up to our work. When no entreaties would make us eat more, with looks and expressions of pitying regret, our uncouth friend showed us how Mongols eat mutton by taking out a good-sized piece with his fingers, and dropping it down his throat. Then turning to the youngsters who crowded the room he pitched lumps of mutton to each of them, who, in like manner, gobbled it like hungry eagles. Our reception at the Lama temple gave us a fair idea of Mongol hospitality and habits, and impressed us favourably with the former. A long ride through the dirty streets of Peking, in a hot sun, was the least agreeable part of our morning's work.

The old Observatory on the Wall is interesting as a monument of the early astronomical tastes of the Chinese emperors, and of the ingenuity of the Jesuits. It was first erected by the Ming before the Jesuits came to China, or, at all events, before they began to be influential, and afterwards greatly enlarged and improved under the auspices of the Jesuits. There is even an old instrument cast out and lying dishonoured in the grass—an orrery, if I rightly remember, dating from the Mongol dynasty, 600 years old. It is probable that the Chinese or Mongols were then in advance of European nations in their knowledge of celestial phenomena. The great celestial globe made under the direction of Verbiest, is a superb casting in bronze, and although the instrument sent from Paris is the finest in the Observatory, Father

Verbiest's celestial globe was the most interesting to me as a specimen of what a clever man can do under almost insuperable difficulties. Since the fall of the Jesuits little attention seems to have been paid to, or use made of, the Observatory, and the teaching of those talented men is well nigh lost.

The Temple of Heaven, or, as some people call it, the Altar of Heaven, is situated near the south wall of the city. We had several miles to go to it from our residence, in a direct line south, along the main street from the centre gate between the Tartar and Chinese cities. The street is wide and straight, but very dirty, and blocked up with trumpery stalls of all sorts, and kept alive by the incessant shouts of boys and old women. "Apples! fine apples, to be sold cheap, —those who have no money can't have any," reminded us of the pathetic story of "Simple Simon." Jugglers also disported themselves in the street and attracted good audiences to witness the swallowing and disgorging of huge stones, feats of strength, and other miracles. The poor juggler does not seem to take much by his motions, however, for, after swallowing an intolerable quantity of stone, and throwing up large bricks, and allowing them to break themselves on his head, thereby creating baldness on the crown, and otherwise amusing a distinguished circle of spectators for twenty minutes, he mildly solicits "cash," and has a wretched pittance thrown into the ring, much as one would throw a bone to a dog. I could not help wishing him some more useful outlet for his talents. Another man would stand with a white painted board in his hand, slightly covered with ink in a half-liquid state, and, while conversing with the crowd, he would, by means of his thumb and fingers, throw off such excellent representations of fishes, birds, &c., with every fin, scale, and feather done to the life, as one never sees in the most highly finished Chinese paintings. The talent displayed by these peripatetic artists proves conclusively that the Chinese do possess the skill to draw after nature. Then why don't they do it? A question more easily asked than answered. But we are supposed to be on the road to the Temple of Heaven. After walking two miles or so down this great street, we suddenly come to a break in the houses. There is no more street, but a large open space before us, lying very low, the road being continued on a raised causeway, on the same level as the street we have left. This space was originally a parade-ground. It is now a mud-puddle, cut up in all directions by innumerable cart-ruts, and most unsightly to behold. But the Temple of Heaven itself is now in sight, the outer wall stretching from a point abreast of us on the left to the south gate of the city, which is dimly visible in the distance over the miscalled parade-ground. The great centre pavilion, with its blue roof and large gilt top, resplendent in the afternoon sun, shoots up into the air, the most conspicuous object to be seen in all Peking. The outer wall alluded to encloses a square mile of ground. Opposite to the Temple of Heaven, and on our right, is the Temple or Altar of the Earth, where the emperors of China repair according to traditional custom on the first day of spring to inaugurate the happy season by ploughing the first furrow. The little boy who now wields the sceptres of the khans must be too young to hold a plough, and I suppose he does it by commission, if indeed he is not too degenerate to do it at all.

Entering the outer gate of the Temple of Heaven, we are ushered into a large park, beautifully laid out with avenues of trees, and with regular well-paved walks. The whole place is terribly overgrown with long grass, and the neatly paved walks are all but obliterated by the same. As we proceed we come to a number of rather fine buildings for the accommodation of the priests. We saw none of these gentry, however, and the outer gate is kept by a dirty coolie, who takes a fee for opening it. The great pavilion stands on the top of a high causeway, the best part of a mile long, with flights of steps leading up to it at various parts. The causeway is beautifully paved with square stones, so regular and well fitted that the joinings can be traced in straight parallel lines along the whole length, except where the line of sight is intercepted by rank grass shooting up through them. The altar is in the great pavilion, which is a circular building of three storys, each story having wide eaves projecting over it, all covered with bright blue enamelled tiles. The roof of the building is of the same material, and is rather a sharply-pitched cone surmounted by a large round gilt ball. The whole effect is bright and beautiful. The pavilion is ascended from the causeway by flights of white marble steps, and a promenade of the same material runs all round it. On the causeway, and at some distance from the altar, are large massive arches with gates in them, and beyond the arches, at a great distance, there is another pavilion of similar construction to the principal one, but much smaller, being only one story high, where the Emperor comes once a-year to worship the true God, or, as some call it, the Dragon. Be that as it may, however, this is doubtless the purest form of worship known to the Chinese. When the Emperor takes his place in the small pavilion the gates of the arches are thrown open, and through them he can see afar off the altar of Heaven, or the Dragon throne, as you may please to call it. Sacrifices are made on those occasions; a large house or temple is set apart for the slaughter of the animals, and another circular tower of green bricks stands near it, where the remains of the sacrifices are buried. The whole plan of this splendid monument is nobly conceived, and would do credit to the most advanced nation in the world. Unhappily, it seems now to be utterly uncared for. The pavements on

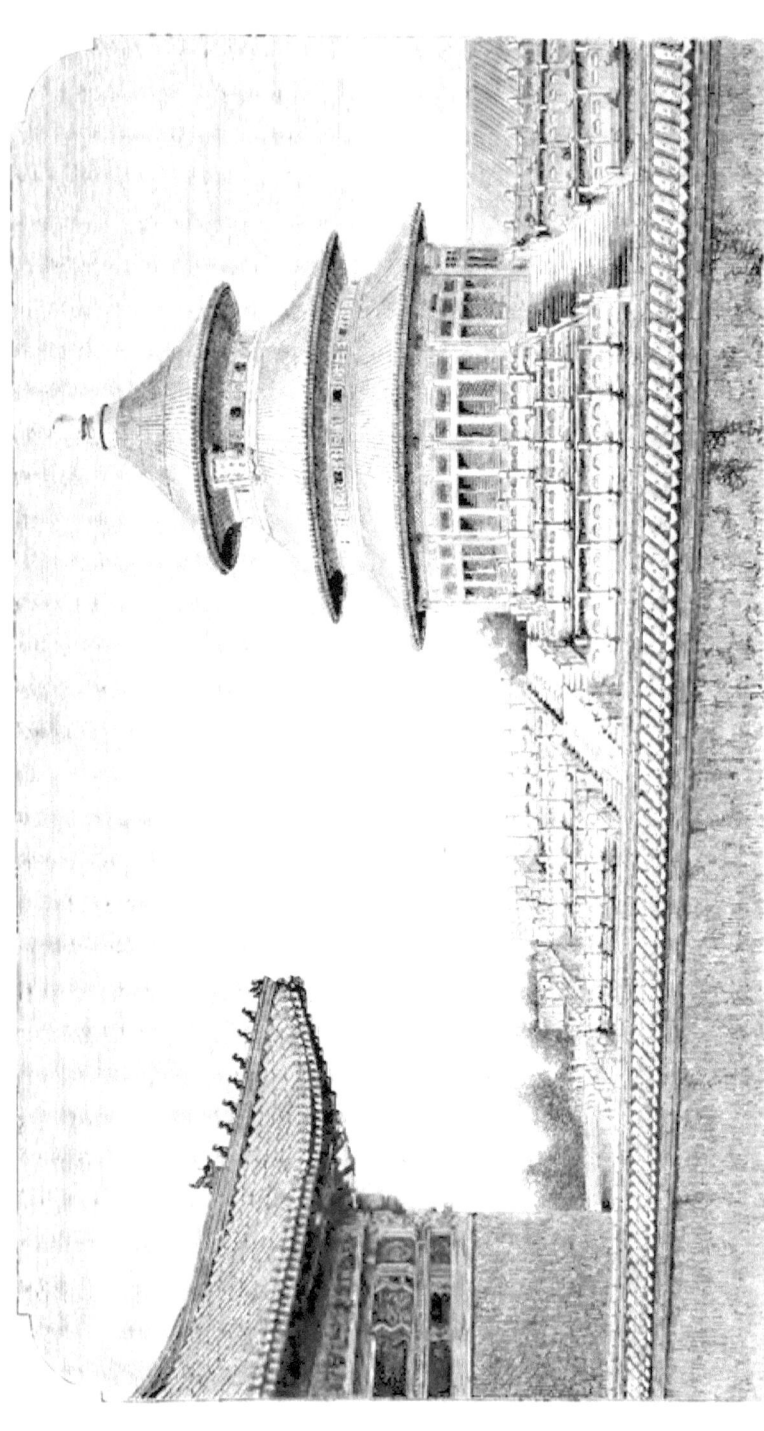

From a photograph by Beato.

GREAT TEMPLE OF HEAVEN, PEKING.

(Page 45.)

which so much care, labour, and money have been expended, are being rapidly covered up with grass. The avenues are like a wilderness, and weeds are even taking root in the beautiful blue-tiled roofs, which, if not soon ruined by it, will at all events be twisted out of their symmetrical proportions. It is melancholy to see that what men of large and enlightened ideas have been at such pains to build, the present degenerate race do not consider it worth while to hire half-a-dozen coolies to keep in order. No further proof is necessary of the state of imbecility into which the Chinese rulers have fallen than this, that in their own city they should allow such a monument of the active energy of their ancestors to go to wreck and ruin for want of a little looking after. I do not see how good government can be looked for in the distant provinces when the body politic is so rotten at the core.

My opportunities did not allow of my seeing more of the great sights of Peking, but we have not yet done the theatres. It was, of course, necessary to patronise some of these establishments, and they afford great facilities for admitting people whose time is not all their own. Ours certainly was our own, but we had let it out for other purposes, and could only steal an hour now and then to give up to this enjoyment. The theatres are open all day long, and all night, too, for anything I know. The acting goes on incessantly—one piece following another without interruption. The favourite pieces with the actors, and by a natural inference with the audience, are old historical heroic pieces, which are performed in a wretched falsetto sing-song voice, and accompanied by the most die-away pantomimic gestures, even in the chief male characters, painfully monotonous to European ears and eyes. They are heavy and slow, but afford great scope for the display of *outré* costumes, overlaid with fiery dragons and hideous forms, which delight the eye of the Chinese. The theatres at Peking are certainly superior, both in the get-up and acting, to anything else of the kind I have seen in China, and some comic pieces we saw were so admirably acted that we, knowing scarcely a word, could follow the story throughout. The houses were always crowded, and the audience seemed to take more interest in the performance than is usual in the south of China, no doubt owing to the language used being the Peking dialect, which is but indifferently understood by provincial audiences. On our entrance to a theatre we were always civilly greeted by the officers, and shown up to the most eligible places in the galleries, where we met people from all parts of the country, not excepting swell Cantonese, all dressed in spotless white muslin, as light and airy as if made from the gossamer's web. We were at once beset by half-naked peripatetic vendors of fruits, cakes, and comfits, and even cups of hot tea. The tea was very refreshing in such a hot place, but our neighbours insisted on giving us little dumplings and other Chinese delicacies, whose component parts we could not even guess. It was useless refusing—that was regarded as mock-modesty. We could only take a quiet opportunity of depositing the suspicious viands in our pockets, and give them to the first dirty urchin we met in the street. The Chinese themselves go on crunching ground nuts, melon-seeds, and rubbish of that sort, the whole time.

Women do not act in China except under very exceptional circumstances. The female part is acted by men, who, thanks to their naturally effeminate appearance, make up very well as women, and the squeaky voice which they practise helps them out. Actors are by no means held in high repute in China, and they are in general very ill paid. One of the best actors, who was also highly esteemed as a singer, that is a squeaker, lodged at our hotel, and he informed us that he earned on an average about half a dollar a day.

Our lodging being in the Chinese city, was far removed from the European residents, who all live in the Tartar quarter, and the gate between the two is closed at sunset. We therefore saw less of our respective countrymen than we might otherwise have done. The foreign community in Peking is but small, and foreign trade being interdicted in the capital, is not likely to be very much increased. There are the Russian, English, French, American, and I suppose now the Prussian legations, all well quartered in commodious official buildings. The Russian is the smallest, because the oldest. At the time of its establishment it was a great thing to have a place at all, without quarrelling about the size of it. The head of the foreign custom-house lives in Peking, and there are a few student interpreters attached to him, who are in training for the custom-house service. Two Church missionaries also reside in Peking, and last, not least, Dr. Lockhart, who has established a medical mission under the auspices of the London Missionary Society, on the plan of the one he for many years successfully conducted in Shanghae. Whatever may have been the past success of medical missions as an indirect means of introducing Christianity into China, there can hardly be a doubt that they are of all methods the best calculated to attain the objects for which they have been organised. The Chinese are pre-eminently irreligious, I mean with reference to their own nominal creed—Bhuddism. They are too keenly intent on minding their worldly affairs to have any thought to spare for higher considerations. They are entirely free from the fanaticism which animates other pagan races. Their temples and priesthood are universally despised and neglected. The only semblance of religious observances practised by the bulk of the people, is a very low kind of superstition, and that sits lightly on them as a rule wherever dollars stand in the way. It is not unfair to say that they are devoid of the religious faculty, and are "sunk in material interests." Hence, the didactic inculcation of strange doctrines is foolishness to them who are indifferent to any doctrine whatever. Of course I only speak from a secular point of view, without forgetting that the most impossible things are easy to the Omnipotent; and he would be a bold man who would venture to circumscribe the possible results that the future may develop from the dissemination of the Bible among a reading, and on the whole not an unthinking people. But the medical missionary presents Christianity in its most attractive phase, that is, associated with a noble philanthropy, after the example of the Founder of our religion, who always accompanied his teaching with healing the sick. And there is perhaps no form of mere philanthropy so powerful to exact gratitude from the most unlikely objects, as that of alleviating pain. The Chinese are probably more open to this mode of reaching their hearts than to any other. In my rambles in out-of-the-way places in China, I have frequently been appealed to for medical aid by poor people who had heard of the repute of foreign doctors, both for skill and benevolence. And although the Chinese character is the most hopeless one to expect gratitude from, still I affirm that if anything can touch them with the sense of an obligation, it is the ministering to their fleshly infirmities; and in the case of medical missions, they cannot escape the connection between them and the religion that prompts them. But I fear I am getting into too deep waters.

No difficulty was experienced in getting our passports, although it was intimated to Sir F. Bruce that the passport for Mongolia was not exactly a thing which could be demanded under the treaty, and therefore that the issue of such a document might at any time be refused by the Chinese authorities without infringing any of the treaty stipulations, the argument being, that Mongolia, though tributary to China, is not a part of the Chinese empire, in the treaty interpretation of the word. This is fudge, of course, but as long as they grant the passports, all right. When they refuse, it will be time to argue about it. They are no doubt a little jealous about foreigners poking about in Mongolia : their own hold on it is so uncertain, and the encroachments of the Russians so gigantic of late years in other quarters, that is, in Manchuria, that the Chinese government, who now, if never before, feels its own decrepitude, does not know which way to turn for security against aggression. As usual with them, they, in their blindness to their own best interests, do just the wrong thing. Two schemes for telegraphic communication from Europe through Mongolia have been proposed to them, both from English sources : both have been rejected, from the general and ignorant dread they have of foreigners establishing stations in Mongolia. Now were their eyes opened they must see that it is not from England or France they have anything to fear of aggression in that part of their dominions ; but from Russia alone. But were English or French subjects to settle, for any purpose whatever, in the Mongolian steppes, under authority from the Chinese government, no better guarantee could be secured against Russian aggression. As it now stands, the Russians are left alone in the field. When *they* really want to have telegraphic stations in Mongolia they *will not* be refused, and before many years are over a large slice of Mongolia will be Russian. The Russians have certain winning ways of their own, altogether foreign to our system of diplomatic procedure, of getting what they want from the Chinese. While we are spending millions in sending armies to fight the Chinese, for questions which are as much or more for their own interests as for ours, and then as conquerors astonishing the Chinese by the moderation of our demands,

PART OF THE EMPEROR'S PALACE, YUEN MIN YUEN
DESTROYED 1860

(Page 56.)

but to pay through the nose for a corner to sleep in, which no gentleman would think fit for his hounds, did go sorely against the grain. I cannot imagine what makes things so dear in Peking, nor do I believe they are so dear to the initiated. One thing is cheap, and that is *ice*, and the most refreshing sight we saw during our stay in the capital, was the cartloads of the precious commodity being carried about in large square blocks; and how did we pity our friends whom we had left in Shanghae, sweltering through the worst part of the summer without this luxury—I ought to say necessary—in such a climate. No care is taken of ice in Peking. It is collected and thrown into large pits, and may melt as much as it likes. If there was any chance of its falling short, it would simply be a question of a few thousand tons more to be thrown into the heap in the winter.

The local bank-notes in Peking are a great convenience. They are issued in amounts from 1000 cash (about a dollar) and upwards, and are in universal use in the city. The use of them saves the natives from lugging about huge strings of copper cash, the only coinage of China, 50 lbs. weight of which are worth about sixty shillings. These notes are not current outside the city walls, however, and here is an inconvenience; for whatever cash balance you may have in that medium must be paid away for something or other before you leave. It would be possible to change them for copper cash or Sycee silver, but that would involve delay and perhaps trouble.

CHAPTER IV.

PEKING TO CHAN-KIA-KOW.

On the 14th of August, having arranged all our affairs in Peking, we set out for Tung-chow, where we had left the priests to provide us transport to Chan-kia-kow. Disappointment awaited us—nothing was done. We were very angry, and a hot discussion ensued between us and the head priest, but we could make neither rhyme nor reason out of him. Here was a dilemma. Ought we to wait till the morrow, and try ourselves to hire beasts of burden at Tung-chow, with this shaven head probably plotting against us? Or ought we to start by break of day with our whole baggage to Peking, and trust to arranging matters there? To do that even, we were helpless, unless the priests were on our side. We resolved, therefore, to conciliate the monk. At this juncture M. Noetzli, who had kindly volunteered to accompany us so far, being acquainted with the ways of the road, addressed the priest in Russian. The effect was marked and instantaneous—the priest's countenance changed—he opened himself out—explained the true causes why he had not been able to get the mules, and suggested that we should get carts to take our baggage to Peking the next day. He would accompany us himself, and help us to negotiate for transport in Peking. That settled, we felt relieved, and ate our frugal dinner in peace and comfort.

I must explain the wonderful effect produced by the use of the Russian language. I have already intimated that this

Fang-wang temple has been constantly used by the Russians as a dépôt. Intimate relations have grown up between the Russians and the priests, and mutual confidence and kindliness has been the result. Several of the priests have learnt the Russian language in their frequent intercourse with the Russians. The priests know no other foreigners. On our own merits we could do nothing with them; but the moment a connecting link seemed to be shown between us and the Russians, we were regarded as belonging to a privileged class.

Next morning, we were again on the road to Peking, bag and baggage. We rode, Noetzli on a mule, which was quiet and tractable enough till a straw touched his tail, when he bounded off, kicking and jumping, floundered in a rut, pitched Noetzli over his head, then tenderly kicked him. *Mem.*—Never ride a mule if you can help it, they are uncouth, unmanageable brutes.

Our late landlord in Peking greeted us obsequiously on our return, and our old friends at the restaurant were no less delighted that their newly acquired art of cooking mutton chops was again in requisition.

Our clerical friend soon appeared with a large, old-fashioned, blue cotton umbrella. We at once went with him to a shop where mules and litters were to be hired, and after the preliminary salutations and cups of tea, we asked for mules, and were told off-hand that they had none. This we knew to be untrue, because we had seen them. We tried several others, but met with the same reply. This looked hopeful, indeed, and it seemed there was nothing left for us that day, but to go to the theatre, where we saw some good acting and an audience thoroughly enjoying it; and so we drowned our own troubles for a time. The next expedient was to order as good a dinner as our ingenuity could devise, out of the materials at hand. A good dinner is a wonderful soother, and has been, perhaps, too much overlooked by philosophers.

The next day, 16th of August, our priest, worn out in our service, came and reported himself sick. He had feverish symptoms, for which we administered quinine.

This break-down of our mainstay was unfortunate, for as we could not get on with his assistance, how could we manage without it? The mule-proprietors still maintained in the morning that there were no mules to be had; but at mid-day they sent to say we could have as many as we liked, at slightly exorbitant prices. We thereupon engaged eight pack-mules at four taels * each, and three mule-litters at eight taels each, to convey us and our belongings to Chan-kia-kow, distant about 400 li, or a four days' journey. It is difficult to divine why it was that these crafty dealers so obstinately maintained the non-existence of the mules. They refused even to listen to an offer on the first day. They were prepared to demand an extortionate price, and we were equally prepared to pay it, but they determined to play with us a little, in order to work our feelings up to the requisite pitch. And when they had reduced us to despair, they thought we would be in a proper frame of mind to accede to their demands, however extravagant they might be. But now everything was satisfactorily arranged, and the mules were to be sent to us early in the morning. The fare amounted to sixty taels in all, of which we paid one-third on the signing of the contract, one-third when the mules were loaded, and the balance on arrival at Chan-kia-kow.

My ma-foo now made himself very busy. Up to this time he had done little but entertain me with cock-and-bull stories about his late master, and his reasons for leaving his service, at every favourable opportunity appealing to me for

* 1 tael equal to 6s. 6d.

my opinion, as to whether he was a "good man." I always answered in the negative, but he solaced himself with the reflection that I would find him out and do him justice when we got to Chan-kia-kow. Now that we were about starting, we thought of many little things we wanted for our comfort on the journey, and who so eligible to make the purchases as "ma-foo." His eagle eye discerned in this a fine scope for his energies, for nothing tickles a Chinaman so much as to have money passing through his hands. "Ma-foo" set to work manfully, and was proceeding very satisfactorily to all parties, bringing the articles we wanted, and rendering an account of the prices paid, until he brought me a coarse cotton bag, which he put in at two dollars. "No," I said, "I won't have it at that price. Take it back to the shop." By and by, he re-appeared with the bag, and offered it for a dollar and a-half. I refused it; and sent him back to the shop. After a while, he returned to the charge with the wretched bag: told me he could not take it back, but reduced his demand to one dollar. I asked him how he could afford to sell it for one dollar, seeing he had paid two for it. "Maskee—you take it." I saw he was "stuck" with it, and that if he failed to realise, he would be under the necessity of stealing something from me to make up for his loss. I therefore accepted it—not without making him confess that he had paid only one dollar for the bag. It was now my turn to ask him where his vaunted goodness was, seeing he tried to cheat me of a dollar. He only grinned, and said, in this instance he was a "little" bad. He was but an inexperienced knave. A clever Chinaman, that is, an ordinary average Chinaman, would have managed an affair of that kind so adroitly as to defy suspicion, except the general feeling one always experiences that all Chinamen are rogues. But small peculations are considered by the Chinese as their legitimate game. When they are intrusted with commissions, they look on it as a sacred duty to scrape as much as they can out of the affair for themselves. This runs through the whole race, and every grade of society, from the highest official in the empire to the meanest beggar.

In case these remarks should be taken to contain a general sweeping charge of dishonesty against the whole Chinese race, I must explain myself a little more fully. The system of peculation is recognised in China, as a legitimate source of emolument; and within certain limits, arbitrarily fixed by custom, it is not held to be inconsistent with honesty. The government connive at it to an alarming extent, by paying responsible officers mere nominal salaries, leaving it to their own ingenuity to improve their fortunes. But with all that, it is a rare thing for a Chinaman to betray a trust; the best proof of which is that they are trusted, under the slenderest of guarantees, with large sums of money. Among the respectable class of merchants, their word is as good as their bond. A bargain once concluded is unflinchingly adhered to. Their slipperiness is exhausted in the preliminary negotiations. Their "cheating" is conducted on certain broad and well understood principles. But for practical honesty, the Chinese may well excite the admiration of many who think themselves vastly superior. When we were at war with the Viceroy of Canton, the European factories were burnt, and foreigners compelled to abandon the place, leaving a great deal of property in the hands of Chinese merchants. Repudiation never occurred to these Chinamen's minds. On the contrary, they found their way to Hong-kong, during the blockade of the Canton river, for the purpose of settling accounts with the foreigners. China contains good and bad in about the same proportion as other countries. Old John Bell says of them:—"They are honest, and observe the strictest honour and justice in their dealings. It must, however, be acknowledged, that not a few of them are much addicted to knavery, and well skilled in the art of cheating. They have, indeed, found many Europeans as great proficients in that art as themselves." A very fair summary of Chinese character.

Bright and early in the morning the mules and litters came, and we were three hours at work, loading and arranging everything. It required a good deal of management, as the loads are not lashed on the mules' backs, but balanced, so that they must be pretty equally divided on each side of the pack-saddle.

We had somehow nine mules instead of eight. We had under 3000 lbs. weight of baggage to carry. That did not give a full load to each mule, for they are reputed to carry 300 catties, or 400 lbs. each. The loads of our team averaged 325 lbs.

The mule litter, used in the north of China, is a large palanquin suspended on the backs of two mules, length-wise. Strong leather bands connect the points of the shafts, resting on the saddles of the respective mules. An iron pin, fixed in the top of the saddle, passes through a hole in the leather, and so keeps it in its place. The shafts are, of course, a good length, to reach from one mule to the other, and to leave the animals plenty of room to walk. There is, consequently, a good deal of spring in the machine. The motion is not at all disagreeable; compared with a cart, it is luxurious. There is hardly room in the palanquin to stretch out full length, but in other respects it is very commodious, having room in the bottom for a good quantity of baggage.

About 10 o'oclock on the 17th August our caravan moved slowly out of the courtyard of the inn, which we left with no regret, and we slowly felt our way through the dusty, crowded streets of Peking towards the North Gate, which was our exit from the city. I was on horseback, intending to get into my litter should the sun prove too powerful, which it did when we got to the sandy plain a little way outside the city. The slow pace of the mules was most disheartening, but I had yet to learn much patience in travelling.

Our first resting-place was at Sha-ho, a village sixty li or twenty miles from Peking. Here we made ourselves a dinner, and fed the cattle. There are two very fine old stone bridges at Sha-ho, but the river that runs under them is only a ditch now. It was drawing late in the afternoon before we were on the road again, and we had not gone many miles before darkness came. The country is well cultivated with cereals, the chief crop being Barbadoes millet, standing from ten to fifteen feet high. Strips of cotton plants appear here and there. It is a delicate-looking plant in this part of the country. The last five miles of the road to Nankow is very rough and stony, and as the night was dark when we passed it, our animals had great difficulty in keeping their legs. About 11 p.m. we arrived at the inn at Nankow, and created a scene of no small confusion by our entry into the courtyard. It was already filled with travellers' gear of all sorts, and it was long before we could pick out a clear space to unload our mules. The fitful glimmer of the dimmest of all lanterns helped to make the darkness visible, but did not assist us in clearing the heels of horses, mules, and donkeys that were straggling all over the place. In the midst of the Babel of tongues, and the senseless yells of our fellow-travellers, as they one after another awoke in a nightmare, we were fain to retreat to our dormitory, and with a scant supper, lay down to rest hoping to find everything in its place in the morning.

The village of Nankow is at the entrance of the mountain pass of that name. It is for this pass alone that the mule-litters are necessary, for it would be impossible to take any wheeled carriage through. In a Russian sketch of the route from Peking to Kiachta, it is stated that the

THE NARROW PASS. (Page 63.)

road is passable for carriages throughout. There are several very difficult rocky passes on the road, but this one at Nankow is, I am certain, impracticable for carriages.

On the 18th August, early in the morning, we entered the defile. It is indeed a terrible road, over huge boulders of rock. The pass is about thirteen miles in length, and for the greater part of that distance nothing breaks the monotony of the precipitous mountain wall on either side. The remains of several old forts are seen in the pass, showing the importance that has been attached to it in former times. It certainly is the key of the position, and the last step of an invader towards Peking. But it is so well defended by nature, that a handful of men could keep an army at bay, if any were so bold as to attempt to force this thirteen miles of defile. The care bestowed on the defences hereabouts shows the terror inspired by the Mongols and other outer tribes in the hearts of the rulers of China.

Our mules struggled gallantly with their loads, slipping and tripping at every step, and landed us at the outside of the pass, without accident of any kind, but not without a good deal of wear and tear of hoof. They even kept up almost their full travelling pace of three miles an hour. At the northern exit from the pass a branch of one of the inner "Great Walls" crosses. It is out of repair, but still the archway over the port is good, and it would puzzle anyone to get in or out of the pass without going through the gate.

At a small walled town, called Cha-tow, just clear of the pass, we halted for our mid-day meal, at a very good inn. The inns hereabouts are nearly all kept by Mahommedans, called in Chinese "Hwuy-Hwuy." The modicum of extraneous civilisation they have acquired, through the religion of the Prophet, is sufficient to mark them as more intelligent and enterprising than their fellows. It is not likely that their tenets are very strictly kept, but they are sufficiently so to enable the Mohammedans to keep together, and form communities and associations of their own. Mine host at Cha-tow asked me for some wine, on which I read him a lecture on the duty of abstinence inculcated by the Prophet. He admitted this was so, but said they were not over straitlaced in those parts. The Mohammedans have their mosques at Tientsin, Peking, and in most large cities in the north and west of China. They are evidently left unmolested in the exercise of their religion, and enjoy every social privilege. The Chinese government is really very tolerant of all religious opinions, and the Chinese as a race are so supremely indifferent to religious matters, that they are the last people in the world who would be likely to work themselves up to fanatical persecution. They are all too busy to attend to such matters. The Chinese government has, no doubt, shown itself jealous of the propagation of the Christian religion, but it is its political tendencies only that frighten them. They have a wholesome recollection of the ambitious projects of the Jesuits in their day of influence,* and they have been constantly kept in hot water by the Propaganda. They have to meet ever-recurrent demands by the self-constituted champion of religion in the East, for the murder of some French or Italian priest in some unheard-of part of the country, where he had no right to be, except at his own proper peril. They see in every native convert a contingent *casus belli* with some powerful state, and very naturally seek to check the spread of such dangerous doctrines by all indirect means. This unfortunate mixing-up of politics with religion has been a deadly blow to the real advancement of Christianity in China. And the abuse of the Christian vocabulary by the Taeping rebels is not calculated to prepossess the Chinese

* Father Gerbillon, a Jesuit, was the Chinese plenipotentiary who concluded the treaty of Nerchinsk with the Russians, in 1689.

authorities in favour of the Western faith. Japan is another country where the government, and I may say also the people, are utterly indifferent to religion, but where the Christian religion has been, and is, tabooed with a vigour unsurpassed in the history of the world. And who that has read the story of the introduction of Christianity into that country by the Jesuits, can blame the government of Japan for its arbitrary exercise of power?

Huc laments the low status of the Chinese Christians, as compared with the Mussulmen, and attributes it to the want of self-assertion. When a Christian gets into trouble his brethren hide themselves. Huc would have driven them to the other extreme. He advocated strong associations by which the Christians might "awe" the Mandarins, as if there must necessarily be antagonism between the two. The inference from which must be either that the Christians are systematically persecuted, as such, or that they are in the habit of committing offences against society. The Chinese government and people have a horror of secret societies and of any political associations whatever. But if Huc's converts had been content to live like ordinary good citizens, neither shrinking from nor courting publicity, they would probably have disarmed suspicion and escaped molestation. Above all, if Huc and his clerical brethren could have divested themselves of the character of spies who had crept into China in defiance of the law of the land, for purposes which the government could not understand, and therefore assumed to be pernicious, they might have saved their disciples from some annoyance, or, as they love to call it, persecution.

In the inn at Chatow, and in all the other inns north of Peking, we found a large cauldron of boiling mutton in a central position in the kitchen. This is kept boiling from morning till night; and the broth, which, by itself, is by no means unpalatable, is always handy as a stock for any messes the wayfarers may fancy. A youth spends his time in kneading chow-patties, which he does very skilfully and rapidly. These are torn and thrown in pieces into the boiling mass, and, when sufficiently done, are served out with a due proportion of broth, as a savoury dish for a hungry man. The "steward of the cauldron," as Huc would probably have called him, has acquired great expertness in serving out his stuff. With a variety of ladles, all sieves, more or less fine, he will serve up either the plain broth, or nimbly seize any of the morsels that are tumbling about in confusion in the pot.

Mutton is cheap and abundant here, and is the staple article of food. The sheep are pastured on many hill-sides that are not fit for anything else, and the constant droves of sheep that come in from Mongolia, for the supply of Peking, pass along this road, and are no doubt to be had cheap.

We now enter a plain about ten miles broad, bounded on either side by bold mountain ranges running east and west. We cross the plain obliquely towards the northern mountain chain. This plain must be elevated more than 1000 feet. The air was fresher than about Peking, and a very marked difference was apparent in the fertility of the soil. The millet and other crops were stunted, the soil was arid and rather stony. The hills are quite bare, but a few trees are dotted over the plain.

At Hwai-lai-hien, a good-sized walled town, we halted for the night. Outside the city is a very large stone bridge, evidently of the same period as those at Sha-ho. Five gothic-shaped arches are still standing, and another is detached at a distance of some 200 feet, the intermediate part of the bridge having no doubt been destroyed. There is no water now in the river, but the bed is still well marked, and the old embankments remain, about 500 or 600 yards apart. The old bed of the river is in a high state of cultivation now.

I find the following notice of this bridge and this river in Bell's Travels. He does not, indeed, give the name of the town, but, tracing up his march from stage to stage, between the Great Wall and Peking, it is evident that Hwai-lai is the station referred to. He says: "About noon, next day, we came to a large, populous, and well-built city, with broad streets, as straight as a line. Near this place runs a fine river, which appears navigable, having across it a noble stone bridge, of several arches, and paved with large square stones."

Bell also makes frequent allusion to an earthquake, which did great damage to this part of the country in July, 1719. Many towns and villages were half destroyed, and some were wholly laid in ruins, and "vast numbers of people" were engulfed. "I must confess," says Bell, "it was a dismal scene to see everywhere such heaps of rubbish." The district being subject to earthquakes, makes it probable that the fine bridge has been destroyed by that agency. But what has become of the fine navigable river that existed in 1720, and has now disappeared? Has it also been upset by an earthquake? The river was probably the Kwei-ho, which now runs in another direction, but some of the gentlemen of Peking or Tientsin, who have explored the country, will no doubt elucidate this interesting question.

On the 19th we made an early start, and went at a very steady pace towards the northern chain of mountains. On approaching them we turned slightly to the left, and skirted the base of the hills. We met a good deal of traffic on the road here, all goods being carried on the backs of mules and donkeys. Coal formed a conspicuous object, on its way to Peking, where it is used to a considerable extent.

Immense flocks of sheep are continually passing in the

direction of Peking, and we also met a good many herds of horses bound the same way. Our mid-day halt was at Sha-cheng, a walled town.

All over this country are the ruins of old forts; and a line of square towers, with a good many blanks, runs nearly in the direction of the road. If these forts could speak they could tell a tale of many a hard-fought battle before and after the Mongol conquest of China.

This part of the country was hotly contested by Genghis Khan; and, in the years 1212 and 1213, the town of Suen-wha-foo, and other places in the neighbourhood, were several times taken and re-taken. "A bloody battle" was fought near Hway-lai, wherein Genghis defeated the Kin, a Manchu dynasty who then ruled Kitay or Northern China. The pass at Nankow, and its fortresses, were taken by Chepe, one of Genghis's generals.

A story is somewhere told that, in olden times, when intelligence was transmitted through the country by beacon fires lighted on these towers, an emperor was cajoled by one of his ladies to give the signal of alarm and summon his generals and officers from all quarters. The word was given, and the signal flashed through the Chinese dominions. The Mandarins assembled in the capital to repel the invader, but, finding they had merely been used as playthings to amuse a woman, they returned in wrath to the provinces. By and by the Tartars did come; the alarm was again given; but this time no one responded to the emperor's call for aid.

At Chi-ming-i, another walled town, we had done our day's work, but it was too early to halt, so we pushed on to a small village called Shan-shui-pu. At Chi-ming-i we met the Yang-ho, a small river that seems to lose itself in the sand. Turning northwards we followed the course of the Yang-ho, and entered another defile. The scenery at the entrance of the pass, where the opening is wide, with a number of valleys running into the hills, and snug-looking villages nestling in cosy nooks, is a relief from the dull monotony of the plain on the one side, and from the wild rocky barriers on the other. It is a romantic little spot, full of verdure, and completely sheltered from the north winds. It has therefore been a favourite resort for ecclesiastics; for, with all their dullness, the Chinese priests have everywhere displayed excellent taste in the selection of sites for their temples and monasteries.

The following pretty legend of the place is given by Bell, and, as he says, it is a fair specimen of the numerous fabulous stories which the Chinese imagination delights to feed upon: —" Near this place is a steep rock, standing on a plain, inaccessible on all sides, except to the west, where a narrow winding path is cut in the rock, which leads to a Pagan temple and nunnery built upon the top of it. These edifices make a pretty appearance from the plain, and, as the story goes, were built from the foundation, in one night, by a lady, on the following occasion. This lady was very beautiful, virtuous, and rich, and had many powerful princes for her suitors. She told them she intended to build a temple and a monastery of certain dimensions, with her own hands, in one night, on the top of this rock; and whoever would undertake to build a stone bridge over a river in the neighbourhood, in the same space of time, him she promised to accept for a husband. All the lovers having heard the difficult task imposed on them, returned to their respective dominions, except one stranger, who undertook to perform the hard condition. The lover and the lady began their labour at the same time, and the lady completed her part before the light appeared; but as soon as the sun was risen, she saw, from the top of the rock, that her lover had not half finished his bridge, having raised only the pillars for the arches. Failing, therefore, in his part of the performance, he also was obliged to depart to his own country, and the lady (poor lady!) passed the remainder of her days in her own monastery."

The Yang-ho had been flooded a few weeks before. It had now subsided, but still it came down from the hills roaring like a cataract. It runs through the pass, and falls not less than 200 feet in a distance of five miles. We followed its course through the mountains, sometimes close to the river. The noise of it at times was deafening, and one of my ponies could with difficulty be kept on the path from fright at the noise. The road became very difficult as we ascended the pass, and it grew dark long before we reached our halting-place, Shan-shui-pu. When we got there we found but poor accommodation. We managed to eat some rice and eggs, and surveyed the premises to find a decent place to sleep, but without success. Six Mongol travellers were lying on the ground in the outer yard, side by side, their sleep undisturbed by the noise our party made in coming into the hostelry. We slept in our litters.

Coal is worked in this neighbourhood, but in a very imperfect way. As far as I could detect, it is merely scooped out of the hill-sides where the seam happens to crop out.

At half-past five next morning we left Shan-shui-pu. The road continued very rocky for a mile or two, and led through an undulating country. We then got on to another terrace very much like the one we crossed yesterday, and bounded by two parallel ranges of hills.

At Suen-wha-fu, a large walled city, we halted to breakfast in a very comfortable inn, much frequented by Russian travellers, who had inscribed their names on the walls as far back as 1858.

Mr. Noetzli and I rode ahead of the caravan in order to reach Chan-kia-kow early, and see how the land lay. Chan-kia-kow was the critical point in our journey, and we were naturally anxious to manage matters there with proper address. If we could but get camels to carry us across the desert to Kiachta, we were safe from all annoyance and delay for the rest of our journey. So we innocently thought ; but the sequel will show how short-sighted we were.

CHAPTER V.

CHAN-KIA-KOW.

WE reached Chan-kia-kow at 1 o'clock, after a hard ride. It is a large, straggling town, lying in a valley surrounded on three sides by mountains, and is bounded on the north by the Great Wall, which descends precipitously from the brow of the hill, crosses the valley, and up the other side. The town of Chan-kia-kow has a character peculiarly its own. It derives its importance from its being the focus of the trade between Russia and China. All goods to and from Kiachta must pass this way, whether on the direct route for the Hu-quang provinces or *via* Tientsin. The result is a large "foreign" population—that is, of Chinese from other provinces. Many of these men have passed most of their lives in Kiachta, and speak Russian. Most of them are wealthy; indeed, the Kiachta trade has been the means of enriching both Chinese and Russians, and many of both nations who have been engaged in it have amassed large fortunes. There is an outward appearance of wealth in Chan-kia-kow, and more show of newness than one meets with in other of their fusty old towns. Some new temples have lately been built by the merchants, and new archways, of which the paint is fresh and good, a thing rarely seen in China. This being the frontier town between China and Mongolia, attracts considerable numbers of Mongols, who bring in their camels to hire for the transport of goods across the desert, and drive in their sheep, cattle, and horses for sale, taking back with them in exchange store of brick-tea and small articles of various sorts, such as pipes, tobacco, &c. The Russians, also, have had a factory here for a few years, and altogether a rare motley crowd is the population of Chan-kia-kow. The Russians call it Kalgan, a name of Mongol origin, meaning, according to Bell, "the everlasting wall." But it is more probably a corrupt form of Halgan, or Khalgan, signifying a gate. The name is quite out of use among the modern Mongols, who invariably employ the Chinese name.

Mr. Noetzli first endeavoured to hunt up some of his Chinese acquaintance, and a tedious business it was, in the interminably long streets, and in a rather hot sun, fatigued as we were with a long ride. After several false scents, we hit on the establishment of a Shanse man who had been thirty years in Kiachta. He and his household spoke good Russian, and he was proud to serve up tea, European fashion, with cups and saucers, sugar and teaspoons. This was very acceptable to us; and we rested as long as we could under his roof, while he entertained us with much interesting conversation, and many cups of the cheering beverage. Having got directions by which to find out the Russians, who had lately gone into new quarters, we soon traced them out in a neat little house built on the hill-side, out of town, that is, beyond the Great Wall, in the narrow pass leading into Mongolia. Mr. Noetzli, being already acquainted with some of them, and speaking a little Russian, we soon made friends with them, and induced them to invite us to take up our quarters with them. So, tying up our beasts, we abandoned ourselves to tea-drinking for an hour or two. The Russians were exceedingly kind and hospitable to us. We were much more comfortable with them than we could hope to be in a Chinese inn; but we derived other advantages from living with the Russians which were of more importance to us. We were not friendless; the cunning Chinese could not look on us merely in the light of victims who had come there to be choused and swindled. Our negotiations for transport would pass through the hands of our Russian friends, who were accustomed to deal in such matters. So far all was well. But Mr. Noetzli had sent an express on some time before to ask the Russians to prepare us camels. Had they done it? No. This looked black rather, but we resigned ourselves to circumstances, confidently believing that things would mend when they came to the worst. We now prepared to play our last card, which was that Mr. Noetzli should go, accompanied by Chebekin, the Russian factotum, a most indefatigable fellow, who speaks Mongol like a native, to a Lama convent, called Bain-tolochoi, two days' journey into Mongolia. There they were to discover a certain priest, to whom Noetzli was accredited by the lamas at Peking, and endeavour to get him to advise some of his Mongol brethren to give us camels. The simple Mongols reverence their lamas, and will readily execute their behests, even at great personal inconvenience. This lama was a man of great influence in his own circle, and we were a little sanguine about the result, if only a favourable reception could be had. It was arranged, therefore, that our two friends should set out on horseback on the morrow, while we kicked our heels about in idleness and suspense at Chan-kia-kow.

The next morning, 21st of August, while we were at breakfast, two Mongols came lounging into the place. One of them was the courier who carries the post-bag to Kiachta, who was hanging about waiting for post-day; the other was a friend of his, but apparently a stranger to our hosts. We took the opportunity of asking about camels, and Chebekin set to work palavering. In a quarter of an hour the whole thing was settled, we were to have camels in four days, and we should be ready to start on the fifth day. The price we paid for eight camels (we really had twelve) for 800 miles, was 150 taels (£50), and two bricks of tea to the ferryman of a certain river. Thus we were once more at ease in our minds; the two scouts were well pleased to see their horses unsaddled again, and we were all happy together.

The next day Mr. Noetzli left us to return to Tientsin, and we were rather in a bad plight, not being able to communicate with our Russian friends, except in Chinese, a language of which we were almost wholly ignorant. One of them vigorously rubbed up some English he had once learned, and in a few days made great progress.

While we are waiting for our camels we have plenty of time to see Chan-kia-kow, but after all there is not much to see. The view from the house where we lived was across the pass, and looked straight on the mountain wall on the other side. So close were we to the mountain that the sun was several hours up before he was seen topping the hill. The Great Wall runs over the ridges of these hills, nearly east and west. This structure is entirely in ruins here. The rubbish that once composed it remains and marks the line. Many of the towers are still standing. I doubt if the wall ever has been so massive in this quarter as near its eastern terminus, where I crossed it a few years ago. Where the Great Wall crosses the town of Chan-kia-kow it is kept in good repair, and has a good solid arch with a gate which is closed nominally at sunset. There is no traffic from the town except through this port, and all Mongols and Chinese dismount in passing.

One of our amusements in Chan-kia-kow was to attend the horse-fair which is held every morning on an esplanade just outside the city on the Mongol side of the Great Wall. It is a most exciting scene, and attracts a great concourse of people. Several hundred ponies, chiefly Mongol, are here exposed for sale every morning. They are tied up in line on either side, leaving the middle space clear, and are taken out in turns and ridden up and down the open space by wild-looking jockeys, who show off their paces to the highest advantage. The fast ones are galloped as hard as their legs can carry them from end to end of the course, pulling up dead short, about ship and back again, the riders all the while holding out their whip hand at full length, and yelling like infuriated demons. There are generally half a dozen on the course at a time, all going full tilt, and brushing past each other most dexterously. They go tearing through the crowd of spectators without checking their pace, and yet it is rare for any one to get ridden over. Amongst these ponies are many extraordinary trotters, and many trained to artificial paces. These are generally more sought after by purchasers than the gallopers.

A number of men hang about the horse-fair who act as brokers between buyers and sellers. These men are invariably Chinese. They soon attached themselves to us, offering their services, and descanting on the merits of the various steeds that were constantly scouring past us. Their mode of making and receiving offers is to pull their long sleeves down and communicate with each other by the touch of the fingers. This seems to be more of a traditional ceremony than anything else, for when they have made a bid with so much show of secrecy, they frequently continue the bargaining *vivâ voce* in the hearing of the whole multitude. The prices of the ponies sold varied from five taels to twenty, or say from thirty shillings to six guineas. We had occasion to make some purchases, and paid about ten taels each for very good useful ponies. One of mine that I had brought from Tientsin had got a very bad sore back from the last day's ride with a badly fitting saddle. He was useless to me in that condition, and I sold him to a horsedealer for five taels.

Large droves of cattle and sheep came in from Mongolia, but the sale of these is not carried on with so much ostentation as that of the horses.

We daily, almost hourly, observed long strings of ox-carts coming down through the pass loaded with short square logs of soft wood. The carts are of the roughest description, and have not, I think, a bit of iron in their construction. This wood is brought from the mountains near Urga, across the desert of Gobi, a distance of 600 miles, and is chiefly used in the manufacture of coffins by the Chinese. These ox caravans travel very slowly, a journey of 600 miles occupying forty days or more; but it is a cheap and convenient mode of conveyance. The animals feed themselves on the way, and cost very little to start with. Camels could do the work, but a camel is a wretched object in harness, and is quite unable to drag even a light cart through a steep pass. Horses or oxen have to do this work for them. The pass at Chan-kia-kow is very stony for some fifteen miles, and the oxen have to be shod with thin iron plates. The Chinese farriers at Chan-kia-kow are very expert at shoeing cattle and horses. They don't attempt to make a shoe to fit any particular hoof, but keep a stock on hand, and selecting the nearest size, they hammer the shoe approximately to the shape of the hoof. They don't trouble themselves to cut the hoof down much, and you can have your beast shod on all four feet in a remarkably short time.

The head of the Russian establishment had been absent on a journey to Peking. He returned while we were in his house, travelling, as we had done, in a mule-litter. Amongst his travelling gear that we saw turned out of the palanquin was a small sized "*samovar*," or tea-urn, which is the greatest institution in Russia, and as we were first introduced to it in Chan-kia-kow I must give some account of it here. *Samovar* is composed of two Russian words, meaning, I believe, "self-boiling." It is a very simple and admirable contrivance for boiling water quickly, and keeping it boiling, without which it is impossible to make tea fit to drink. The samovar is an elegantly shaped vase, made of brass, with a tube about two and a half inches in diameter going down the centre from top to bottom. A charcoal fire burns in this tube, and, as the water is all round it, a large "heating-surface" is obtained, and the water is acted on very rapidly. Samovars are made of all sizes, the capacity being estimated in tea cups. An average sized one contains twenty to twenty-five cups, or rather glasses, for it is customary among the Russians to drink tea out of tumblers. Those who can afford it drink very good tea, and they are probably the most accomplished tea-drinkers in the world; our countrywomen might even learn a lesson from them in the art of tea-making. They use small earthenware tea-pots, and their first principle seems to be to supply the pot bountifully with the raw material. The infusion comes off very strong, and they judge of its strength by the colour in the glass. They put but a little tea in the glass, and then dilute it with boiling water from the samovar, in about the proportions of the whiskey and water in toddy. As a rule, they use sugar and milk, or cream, when procurable. At Chan-kia-kow it was not to be had, for the Chinese do not use milk, or any preparation from it; and it probably never occurred to the Russians that they might keep their own cow for a mere song. The Russian gets through an amazing quantity of tea in the course of a day, and I verily believe they consume more per head than the Chinese themselves. The samovar is almost constantly blowing off steam—morning, noon, and night it is to be seen on the table, and they never stop sipping tea while there is any water left. It is as much a necessary of life with them as their daily bread, or tobacco to an inveterate smoker, and their attachment to their own way of making it, is strikingly exhibited by the fact, that a Russian, travelling among the Chinese, where every possible facility for tea-making is at hand, should consider it essential to his comfort to carry his own samovar about with him.

During our stay at Chan-kia-kow, we experienced a considerable change in the weather. The first two days it was hot, but with a fresher and more elastic atmosphere than about Peking. This is probably due to the elevation, and the vicinity of mountains. We had ascended by successive passes and terraces from Peking about 2500 feet, which is approximately the elevation of Chan-kia-kow. A thunder-squall on the 21st of August cooled the air so much that we had to sleep under a blanket that night. Next morning was quite chilly with the thermometer at 71°. At mid-day on the 23rd it stood at 72°, and on the morning of the 24th it was 65°. It got warmer again afterwards, but we began to think there was something in the Russian warnings of great cold in Mongolia, and we did not regret being well provided with blankets and furs.

As the time drew near for our departure we seriously set to work to supply ourselves with necessaries for the journey across the desert. Our Mongol friends had contracted to carry us to Kiachta in thirty days, but to provide against accidents we allowed a good deal more. Although we were well supplied for the desert journey with preserved provisions, wine, and bottled porter, the opportunity of procuring fresh vegetables was too tempting to be overlooked. At Chan-kia-kow we found some of the finest cabbages * in the world, carrots, &c. Potatoes are also to be had in the season, but we were too early. These and some fresh beef equipped us fully in that department.

Then we had to purchase two carts to travel in. The

---

* These cabbages are said to have been originally introduced from Russia.

Russians and Chinese always travel so, for it would be too fatiguing to ride on a camel all the way, they go so long at a stretch—sixteen to eighteen hours without stopping. The carts are built on the same principle as those in use about Peking and Tientsin, but larger. They are drawn by camels. We essayed to make these purchases, and soon found one cart in good order, barring the wheels. We then asked a wheelwright to make a pair of wheels for it, but he would have charged more for the wheels than the cost of a new cart, completely furnished.

It was evident that we could not manage these matters without being shamelessly imposed upon, and we therefore begged our good friends, the Russians, to take our business in hand. Everything now went smoothly. Two carts were quickly found, second-hand, and at moderate prices. When we had got them we found they wanted harness, that is, sundry strips of leather thongs, attached to the points of the shafts, and which are secured in a very primitive, but effective, way to the saddle gear of the camels. Then the covers of our carts looked rather weather-beaten, and it would be cold in Mongolia. New felt covers had therefore to be obtained, and for extra warmth, nailed on over the old ones. Our wheels would want oiling. We must therefore have five catties of oil, cost 500 cash. But how to carry it? A pot was requisite—cost 150 cash more. There was really no end to the small things that suggested themselves. We had ponies—extra felt saddle cloths were wanted to protect their backs. And how were we to catch them when turned out to graze during our halts? Hobbles must be got for this. We also took some dry food for our ponies to eat when the grass was very thin, but they would not look at it, and we had eventually to throw it away to lighten our camels. What with extra rope, a bag of charcoal, covers for our baggage in case of rain, lanterns, and a variety of other things, we made up a formidable list of odds and ends. The account rendered filled a sheet of foolscap, but the whole amount of our purchases at Chan-kia-kow, exclusive of the first cost of two carts, came to less than six pounds, and this included several pairs of felt boots and a couple of goat-skin jackets. No one travelling that way (unless it be in the early summer), should omit to procure a couple of pairs of these felt boots. There is nothing like them for warmth, and they can be got large enough to pull over your other boots. I used mine nearly all the way to Moscow, and rarely experienced the sensation of cold feet, though exposed in all sorts of carriages, and in severe weather.

On the 25th of August, the Mongol gave notice that the camels were at hand, and on the 26th they came into the courtyard, uttering that disagreeably plaintive cry that is peculiar to the camel, and more particularly to the juveniles. The camels looked very large and ungainly in the small enclosure, but the Mongols soon made room by making them kneel down close together, when they immediately commenced chewing the cud. The Mongols manage their camels by means of a tweak passed through the nose, with a thin string attached. They pull the string with a slight jerk, saying "Soh, Soh," and the animal, screaming the while, falls on his knees, and with three oscillating movements he is flat down with his belly on the ground.

The Mongols had already tackled our baggage and arranged it to their own satisfaction, so as to suit not only the weight each camel was to carry, but to balance one side equally with the other. Each package is well lashed up with stout rope, leaving a short loop. In loading, a package is lifted up on each side simultaneously, the loops crossed over the camel's back between the humps, one loop passed through the other, and secured by a wooden pin. The load is then allowed to fall, the weight comes on the wooden pin, and so keeps it in its place. The back of the camel is protected by a series of pieces of thick felt, ingeniously laid round the humps, on the sides, and very thickly over the hollow between the humps. This mass of felt is kept in its place by means of a framework of wood on each side, lashed together across the camel's back.

Some hours were occupied in adjusting the camel loads and getting all ready for the start. We did not hurry, as we could not afford to forget anything now, as we were about to plunge into the desert, where we would be as entirely thrown on our own resources as if we were in a ship at sea.

Horses had to be hired to take our carts through the pass, a distance of fifteen miles, the camels being unequal to the task. The camel has little strength in proportion to his size. His formation peculiarly adapts him to carry weight, his whole strength being concentrated in the arch of his back; and yet in proportion he carries much less than a mule, that is, considerably less than double. For draught purposes, as I have already mentioned, the camel is ill adapted. His pace is remarkably slow, and in short he is only fit to work in deserts where, comparatively speaking, no other animal can live. His faculty of going for many days without food or water, and of nourishing himself on any sort of vegetable growth that comes in his way, is invaluable to his nomad masters.

CHAPTER VI.

MONGOLIA.

WE left Chan-kia-kow on horseback, escorted by three of our kind Russian friends, Messieurs Weretenikoff, Iguminoff, and Beloselutsoff, who accompanied us a few miles up the pass, and bid us God speed. It took a long time for our camel-drivers to form the order of march, and we had got far ahead of them. So, coming to a spot where there was a little grass, we dismounted to give our beasts a feed, thus putting in practice a maxim which travellers in strange countries learn by daily experience to adopt for themselves and their beasts,—to eat when they can.

My pony, being rather sharp in the back, I had over-done him with thick saddle-cloths in my anxiety to preserve him in ridable condition; for though very old he was a rare good one, but viciously inclined, having once before had his paws on my shoulders. As the camels hove in sight, I essayed to mount, but had not got into my seat when, what with the pony's capers and bad saddling, I came to grief, and was left sprawling on my face on the stones, which spoiled my physiognomy and my temper at the same time, and nearly obliterated one optic. It was painful to contemplate my brave steed careering about with my good saddle under his belly, and reins going all to pieces amongst his legs. The vision of a month's riding vanished away in a moment. A ray of hope dawned on me as I saw my favourite settle down in a small enclosure, bearing a poor crop of under-grown millet, but there was no one near to catch him. After a little, the husbandman appeared, and stoutly remonstrated with me for turning my cattle into his field. I was in no mood to tolerate abuse, for my abraded skin was smarting considerably. I offered the aggrieved agriculturist the alternative of catching my pony, or leaving him where he was. The Mongols, and also the Chinese borderers, are very expert in catching horses—their favourite dodge is to crawl up to his head on all-fours. My friend tried this, but he was unfortunately too fat, and when he got his hand within an inch and a-half of the remnant of my poor bridle, the pony started off and went straight back at full gallop in the direction of Chan-kia-kow. My heart died within me at the sight. The camels having now come up, one of the men went in pursuit, and with the assistance of the country people brought back the renegade, with the loss of my bridle and one stirrup—not so bad as I expected.

The pass is a narrow gorge between steep hills, with little cultivated corners here and there. A small stream trickles down the side, and the road is strewn with round pebbles, which gives it the appearance of the bed of a river. The ascent is very steady and regular, gaining considerably more than 2000 feet in fifteen miles. The road is tolerable all the way, until about the top of the ascent, which is very rough and rocky. Rather late in the evening we got to our halting-place well on to the table land, which is at an elevation of 5300 feet above the sea.

The Chinese are the most patient and persevering agriculturists in the world. They have pushed their aggressions through the pass at Chan-kia-kow—on the hill-sides, wherever they can find soil enough to hold together—and into the skirts of the desert itself. They get but a poor return for their labour, however; their crops seem to struggle for bare existence, and the farmers must depend more on their live stock than their crops.

In other parts of Mongolia the Chinese have been more successful in extending their civilising influence into the prairie. In the kingdom of the Ouniots, further to the north, Huc tells us that since the Chinese, following their invariable custom, began to penetrate into the country of the Mongols, about the middle of the seventeenth century, the forests have disappeared from the hills, the prairies have been cleared by fire, and the new cultivators have exhausted the fecundity of the soil. "It is probably to *their system of devastation* that we must attribute the extreme irregularity of the seasons which now desolate this unhappy land." A curse seems to have rested on the industrious invaders. The seasons are out of joint. Droughts are frequent, then sand-storms and hurricanes, then torrents of rain which wash away fields and crops together in a general deluge, and the land is thenceforth incapable of being ploughed. Famines follow, and the people torment themselves with presentiments of calamity.

That all this is due to the Chinese agriculturists is hard to comprehend. It is not their practice elsewhere to "exhaust the fecundity of the soil." Huc propounds the new and strange doctrine that cultivation of deserts is a system of devastation. The truth seems to be that Huc, with the strong partiality he always evinces to the Mongols, was over-credulous of their stories. The Mongols, very naturally, consider themselves aggrieved by the Chinese. The latter first bought the right of cultivating the prairie, and, as their numbers increased, the weaker race necessarily gave way, moving their tents and their sheep further and further into the desert. The poor Mongols now see, with feelings of sorrow, the plough desecrating the ground where their fathers fed their flocks; they look with hopeless regret on the past as a kind of golden age, which their fancy dresses in a halo of peace, happiness, and prosperity. The hated Kitat at once suggests himself as the cause of these changes, and the Mongols delight to feed their hatred out of the copious store of their imagination.

A process exactly analogous has been going on in the country of the Manchus, where the arable soil has been occupied by Chinese colonists, almost to the entire exclusion of the natives. Hatred is strongly developed there also; but I can answer for it that there, at least, cultivation has not exhausted the fecundity of the soil, nor devastated the country.

The Chinese also with whom Huc conversed would readily admit the superiority of the past. They have a reverence for antiquity, and whenever they could spare a thought from the stern realities of the present, they would mourn their hard fate, and exalt the glories of the past.

The sun had been very hot all day, but when we came to pitch our tent at night we were shivering with cold, and could with difficulty hold the hammer to drive the pins into the ground. It is always chilly at night in Mongolia, even in the hot weather, but we were not prepared for such a degree of cold on the 26th August, in latitude 41°. All our blankets were brought into requisition, and we passed a comfortable night. Next morning the thermometer, which was under a blanket, showed 35° Fahrenheit.

The morning of the 27th of August was as bright and cheery as the most lively fancy could paint. The air resounded with the notes of hosts of skylarks, which one does not often hear in these far-off regions. The sun warmed up fast, and in a few hours dried up the heavy dew that lay on the grass in the early morning. The pasture was exceedingly rich, and sprinkled with "gowans" and other wild flowers, which imparted a delicious fragrance to the fresh morning air. Many herds of cattle and horses were scattered over the plain, the Mongol herdsmen incessantly galloping round their flocks to keep them together, their shouts audible from great distances in the still air, and the perpetual movement of vast numbers of parti-coloured beasts gave an animation to the scene which was quite exhilarating to the spirits. A small brook trickled tortuously through the plain, where we managed to kill a few snipe, greatly to the delight of the straggling Mongols, who rode up to us from various quarters. The only building in sight was a temple which we had passed in the night, and which was the last brick-and-mortar structure we were to see for many days. We were now fairly among the dwellers in tents, and began to realise what it was to be cut off from civilised life ; for, whatever may be the various opinions of Chinese civilisation in its higher developments, you can at all events obtain in China every necessary and many luxuries for money. In the "Land of Grass" we had to depend on our own resources, but with the comfortable assurance that these were amply sufficient for us. Our introduction to nomad life was under happy auspices, and we were at the outset favourably impressed with the Mongols and their country, an impression which never entirely wore out, even under very adverse circumstances. I never till that morning experienced the consciousness of absolute *freedom*. Many Mongol visitors rode up to our encampment, bringing plentiful supplies of new milk, cheese, and other preparations from milk very like Devonshire cream.

About 8 o'clock the camels were got in, and we made a start, halting again at noon near the "yourts" of some Lama friends of our camel-drivers. This was a short stage, and we endeavoured to remonstrate with our conductor, but as at that time we could not understand a word of each other's language, the broad Saxon merely provoking a volley of guttural Mongol, we made no progress towards a mutual understanding. We were again favoured with numerous visitors, and our conductor had evidently serious business to negotiate, which occupied the whole afternoon. It ended in his exchanging his pony for another, and getting a fresh camel. It was close on sunset before the camels were loaded, and a fresh start effected. During our halt we had time to make the acquaintance of our camel-drivers. The chief was a Lama named Tup-tchun, a good, easy man, with all the native simplicity of his race. He was the responsible man to us, and I believe owned the camels. He had two assistants; the first a clansman of his own, Tellig by name, a fine, good-natured, bullet-headed, swarthy-complexioned, indefatigable fellow, the equanimity of whose temper nothing could ever disturb. The Lama placed his whole confidence in Tellig, and we naturally did the same as we became better acquainted with the excellence of his character. The other had a name I never could pronounce, so I will not attempt to spell it. He had some taint of wickedness in his eye, and showed more craft and cunning than the average Mongol. He could likewise speak a few words of Chinese, hence we gave him the nickname of *Kitat*, the Mongol name for Chinese, a word abominated by all true Mongols. He stoutly rebelled for a long time against his new name, but it greatly amused his companions, and, as he was never called by any other appellative, he was compelled at last to answer to Kitat.

The order of our march was this. One of the Mongols on a camel rode ahead, leading the next camel by a string from his nose. Half the caravan followed him in single file, each camel being slightly attached to the preceding by his nose-string. The other driver, also on a camel, brought up the rear-guard in the same way. The Lama was more privileged, for he never took any active part in leading the caravan, but rode about on a pony, talking now to

Tellig, now to the Kitat, and now to us, then suddenly breaking out into some of his wild native chants. He had a fine sonorous voice, and his singing was a pleasant relief from the monotony of the way, and when Tellig joined in chorus they made the welkin ring. The Mongols sing with their natural voice, and have far more music in their souls than the squeaking Chinese. The Lama indulged himself in a gossip with every traveller he met, and would often be left out of sight, but with his active pony he could easily overtake the slow-moving camels. When he descried a Mongol yourt in the distance he seldom missed a chance of riding up to it, to bestow his benediction on the inmates, and drink tea with them. Nor was the Lama entirely useless on the march, for the rearward camels were frequently getting loose, and dropping into the rear, as Tellig and the Kitat seldom thought of looking behind them. The moment a camel feels himself at liberty he stops to graze. I have never seen one voluntarily follow his leader. Great delay occurred sometimes from this cause, and the Lama saved us much time by riding after a stray camel, dexterously catching up the nose-string with his whip-handle, and leading the straggler up to the caravan. The leading-string of the camel is fastened to the gear of his leader in such a loose manner that a very slight resistance is enough to undo it. The reason for this is that if the string were secured firmly, any check in the rear camel, or the leading one advancing from a halt before the rear one was ready, would tear the camel's nose. A nose once broken in this way, it is difficult to find good holding ground for the tweak, and the Mongols are therefore very economical of camels' noses.

As for ourselves, we each had two ponies to ride, and we varied our manner of travelling by alternately sitting in our carts and riding our ponies. We also walked a good deal with our guns, for the pace of the camels was so slow that we could range at will over the country, and still keep up with the caravan. The camel's pace is slow and sure, the average of a day's march being two miles an hour. The actual pace is of course quicker, but the frequent stoppages to adjust loads, and from camels breaking loose, reduce it to two miles per hour. Sitting in the cart is never very agreeable. The track is not cut up with ruts like a road in China, and the jolting is considerably less; but it is difficult to get a comfortable posture without lying down, and sitting in the front of the vehicle you are unpleasantly near the odour that exudes from the pores of the camel's hide, to which it requires a long apprenticeship to get accustomed. It is most uninteresting, besides, to sit for an hour or two contemplating the ungainly form of the ugliest of all created things, and to watch his soft spongy foot spreading itself out on the sand, while you reckon that each of these four feet must move 700,000 times before your journey is accomplished.

Our ponies were tied behind the carts, and all went quietly except my old one "Dolonor," who was sagacious enough to break his halter regularly, and follow the caravan in his own way, which was to trot a few hundred yards ahead and apply himself vigorously to the grass until the caravan had passed some distance, when he would trot up and repeat the operation. With all that he fell off in condition more than any of the others.

Starting at sunset, as I have said, we proceeded all night without stopping. It was a fine moonlight night, but an uncomfortable one for us. Not knowing we were to travel all night, we were unprepared for sleeping in our carts, and suffered a good deal from cold and disturbed rest. With every precaution to close them in, the carts are thoroughly well ventilated; but subsequent experience taught us to roll up warmly, for most of our nights in the desert were spent in our carts on the road.

At sunrise on the 28th my thermometer beside my bed stood at 43°. At 8 o'clock we halted and pitched our tents. Our Mongols had a tent for themselves, made of thin blue cotton stuff, and black inside with the smoke of years. Their contract with us included tent accommodation, as also fuel and water; but we congratulated ourselves daily on being provided with our own commodious and substantial bit of canvas. The Mongols make their fire in the tent and lounge round it while the pot is boiling. Some of the smoke manages to escape through the opening that answers the purpose of a door, running from the apex of the tent to the ground in the shape of a triangle. For the rest they don't seem to mind it, although it is almost suffocating to those who are unaccustomed to it. I noticed the eyes of the Mongols have mostly a bloodshot hard appearance, often showing no white at all, attributable no doubt to the argol smoke in which they pass so much of their time. The tents being pitched, the next operation is to procure a supply of *argols*, or more correctly *ar'ch'l*, which is dried cow or horse dung, and is to be found all over the desert. So long as we were in a populous part of the country, that is, if there were three Mongol yourts within as many miles of us, we were saved the trouble of going out to gather them, for our tents were seldom up for many minutes before a woman would appear bearing a large basket of the precious material. This seems to be the ordinary custom of the Mongols, and is a part of the genuine hospitality they show to strangers. Our halting-places were selected with a view to water. There is no scarcity of water in the desert, but a stranger would be sorely puzzled to find it, for there is nothing to mark the position of the wells. The Mongols have an instinctive knowledge of the country, and in order to encamp near good water they make their march an hour or two longer or shorter as the case may be. When the caravan halts, one of the Mongols is despatched on a camel with two water-buckets to fetch water from the well, generally some distance from the line of march. The buckets have a head to them with two holes in it stopped with wooden plugs. The water is poured out of the larger hole at the side, while the smaller one in the centre is opened to admit the air, to enable the water to pass out freely. In selecting a halting-place, the Mongols generally contrive to combine a good bit of pasture with the vicinity of water, for this is naturally of much importance to them, as the only feeding the animals get is a few hours' grazing during the halt, and that only once in twenty-four hours. Before the tent is set up the camels are unloaded and set free to graze, the horses are taken to water, and then hobbled and let loose. The camels are not supposed to want water, and they very rarely get it. Their lips and mouth are peculiarly adapted to quick feeding, the lips being long and very pliable, and the incisor teeth projecting outwards. They gather up a good mouthful of grass in a very short time, even where it is exceedingly scant, and as their food requires little or no mastication, they are enabled to take in a full daily supply of food in a few hours.

So far, Mongolia is a succession of plains and gentle undulations, much resembling the long swell of the ocean, and here and there the country is a little rough and hilly. The undulations stretch across our track from east to west. The whole face of the country looks like the sea. There is not a tree or any object to break the monotony of the vast expanse, but occasionally the yourt or tent of a Mongol family. The sunrise and sunset encourage the illusion, and the camel has been aptly called the ship of the desert.

The sun was hot during the day, but the thermometer in the shade only showed 73° at noon. Yesterday it was 71°.

After dinner we went out with our guns and bagged a few small birds of the curlew kind. We also came across a flock of wild geese, but, as usual, they were very wild. We had a chase after a herd of animals which have been called wild goats. The Chinese call them *whang-yang*, or yellow sheep: other tribes call them *dzeren*. The Mongols give them a name of their own, *gurush*, and do not associate them with either sheep or goats. They are really a kind of antelope (*Procapra gutturosa*), the size of a fallow deer, and of a yellowish brown colour, approaching to white about the legs. They are exceedingly swift and very shy, and as the country is so flat it is almost impossible to get within shot of them. They are usually found in large herds of several hundreds. We subsequently tried to stalk them on horseback, and did get some long random shots at them with a rifle, but to manage this properly there ought to be three or four people well mounted and with plenty of time. Our poor tired ponies were not fit for such work, and we never stopped the caravan for the sake of sport. Some of the Mongols do hunt the gurush, both on horseback and on foot. I never witnessed any successes, but they must shoot them sometimes, to pay for their powder and shot. They use a small-bored rifle, which has a rest placed about six inches from the muzzle, by which means they can lie on their face and take their aim, the muzzle being raised well clear of the ground by means of the rest.

We had a long halt to-day, partly in consequence of a crack being discovered in one of the camels' feet. This is an infirmity they are subject to, and if sand and grit were allowed to get in, the animal would become lame and useless. The remedy, which is always at hand, is to sew a square patch of stout leather over the part affected, which they do in the roughest cobbler fashion. With a flat needle slightly curved they pierce the horny part of the sole, and fasten the patch by means of leather thongs at each corner. This is only a temporary measure, and when a camel is taken that way, he must soon be turned out to grass. The Mongols have no trouble in getting at a camel's feet. They first make him squat down, and then two of them go at him with a sudden push and roll him over on his broadside, one of them keeping his head down while the other operates on the foot. The animal screams a good deal while he is being turned over, but once down he resigns himself helplessly to his fate.

We did not get off till five o'clock in the afternoon. The night was cloudy and no dew fell, and consequently it was not nearly so cold as the night before. The difference in temperature between a cloudy and a clear night is very marked in Mongolia.

We were now leaving the good pastures and the numerous herds of cattle behind, and on the morning of the 29th August we found ourselves getting into a very desert country with only a little scrub grass, of which our poor ponies found it hard work to make a meal. No horses or cattle were seen in this part, and the country seemed only capable of supporting sheep and camels. About eleven o'clock we halted, and encamped on almost bare sand. Not a single "yourt" was in sight, and, for the first time, we had no visitors. This must have been a relief to our Mongols, for they were compelled by custom and their natural hospitality to receive and be civil to all comers, and it was not easy for them to snatch even an hour's sleep. This must have been a great privation, for their mode of travelling all night precluded their getting any sleep at all, except on the backs of their camels while on the march, and in their tent during the six hours' halt in the day; and as that was broken up by cooking and eating, pitching and striking tents, loading and unloading camels, and other necessary matters, and the frequent and protracted visits from neighbouring yourts, or travellers on the road, our poor Tartars had often to go for days together with hardly any sleep at all. But they never complained, and certainly were never betrayed into any rudeness to their inconsiderate countrymen.

We started again at 4·30 in the afternoon, and continued through gentle undulations, proceeding, as before, all through the night. Before morning we passed some rocky places over low hills, which sadly disturbed our sleep in the carts—in fact, our usual night's rest, while on the move, was far from being uninterrupted or comfortable, and it was only our fatigue and exposure to the air all day that enabled us to sleep at all under such circumstances. The rough hilly part was again succeeded by low undulations continually unfolding before us, and which became painfully monotonous to the eye. Distances are altogether deceptive, partly owing to the smooth, unbroken surface of the country, and partly to the mirage which is always dancing on the horizon, making small objects look large, and sometimes lifting them up into the air and giving them a variety of fantastic shapes.

About 11 o'clock on the 30th of August we halted, and went through our usual process of cooking and eating. We began to find that one meal a day did not suit our habits, and we soon learned to keep out a certain quantity of biscuit and cold meat when we had it, so that we could make a breakfast or a supper without stopping to unload the camels. To these materials we added a handful of tea or some chocolate-paste, and in the morning rode up on our ponies to any yourt we happened to see that was smoking, and there made our breakfast. In the evening we often managed to do the same, but it frequently happened that we had no opportunity of doing this.

But I have not explained what a " yourt " is. It is simply the habitation of a Mongol family—a tent, but of a more permanent construction than the ordinary travelling tent. It consists of a frame of light trellis work covered with thick felt, is circular in form, with a conical shaped roof, but nearly flat. A hole in the apex of the roof lets out the smoke from the argol fire which burns all day in the middle of the tent. At night, when the fire is out, and before the inmates retire to rest, the hole in the roof is covered up. I did not measure the upright part of the wall of the tent, but it is under five feet, and you cannot enter without stooping. The tent is about fifteen feet in diameter. A piece of felt hanging from the top forms a door. The Mongols sleep on mats laid on the ground, and pack very close. They have no bedding, but sleep generally in their clothes, merely loosing their girdles. In addition to the family, I have frequently observed a number of young kids brought into the tent for shelter on cold nights. When the owner decides on moving to better pastures, his yourt is packed up in a few hours and laid on the back of a camel, or, failing that, two oxen answer the purpose. Although yourt is the name always used by foreigners, I never heard it from a Mongol. They call it "gi-rai," as distinguished from a travelling tent, which they call "mai-chung."

Such are the dwellings of the Mongols, and so much are they attached to them, that even where they live in settled communities, as in Urga, where they have every facility for building wooden houses, they still stick to their yourts, merely enclosing them with a rough wooden paling. In the whole journey I did not meet with a single instance of a Mongol living in a house, or in anything else than a yourt or girai. The Mongols are very superstitious, and certain rules of etiquette have to be observed in riding up to and entering a yourt. One of these is that all whips must be left outside the door, for to enter a yourt with a whip in the hand would be very disrespectful to the residents. Huc explains this almost in the words—"Am I a dog that you should cross my threshold with whips to chastise me?" There is a right and a wrong way of approaching a yourt also. Outside the door there are generally ropes lying on the ground, held down by stakes for the purpose of tying up their animals when they want to keep them together. There is a way of getting over or round these ropes that I never learned, but, on one occasion, the ignorant breach of the rule on our part excluded us from the hospitality of the family. The head of the house was outside his yourt when we rode up; we saluted him with the customary *Mendo! Mendo!* &c.; but the only response we got was a volley of quiet abuse, in which our salutation was frequently repeated in ironical tones, as much as to say, "Mendo! Mendo! you come to my tent with sugared words on your lips, and disregard the rules of civility, which a child would be ashamed of doing. Mendo! Mendo! If you do not know how to conduct yourselves like gentlemen, you had better go about your business." So we turned and went away, not in a rage, for we knew we had committed some grave offence against propriety.

The furniture of a Mongol yourt is very simple. A built-up fireplace in the middle of the floor is the only fixture. A large flat iron pan for cooking, or, if the parties are luxurious, they may possess two such utensils, and sport two fireplaces, by which means they can boil their mutton and water for their tea at the same time. A basin to hold milk, and a good large jug with a spout for the same purpose, and for the convenience of boiling it at the fire while the big pan is on, comprise all their kitchen and table service. Each person carries his own wooden *ei-iga,* or cup, in his bosom, and, so armed, is ready to partake of whatever is going anywhere; and his small pocket-knife, by which he can cut up his quota of mutton. A wooden box serves as a wardrobe for the whole family. No tables or chairs are necessary, and I found no trace of a toilet service. These, with a few mats on the ground for squatting on by day, and sleeping on by night, comprise all the actual furniture of a yourt.

To-day, 30th August, we killed some sand-grouse. They were of the same species as those found about Peking and Tientsin (the *Pallas* sand-grouse), but were in much finer condition. They were fat, and of such excellent flavour that they would be considered a delicacy anywhere. All their crops which we dissected were full of small black beetles, and the same was the case with the curlew we killed. We fell in with a herd of gurush, and had some long shots; but we were never fortunate enough to bag any of these animals.

In leaving the caravan there is always more or less danger of getting lost. It has happened more than once to travellers. But still there is a beaten track all the way through the desert, which is distinctly marked in the grassy parts, and even in the sand it is traceable. In winter it may be obliterated, but still I think, with ordinary care, one ought not to lose himself in the desert.

At 6 p.m. we had returned to our caravan and again took the road. It came on very windy at night, with some rain, and as the winds were always from the north, and consequently in our teeth, we were miserably cold and uncomfortable in the carts, so much so that we ardently hoped that the Mongols, who were more exposed than we, would propose a halt. We could not do so ourselves, for that would have given the Mongols an excuse for all manner of delays in our journey, but we would have been glad to consent had we been asked. There was nothing for it, however, but to bear our burden patiently. The few bottles of water and milk we invariably carried with us in the carts were exhausted, and being much in want of something, we knew not what, we ordered the Mongols to stop at the first yourt they saw.

This they did at 11 o'clock, and having turned out an old woman we asked for water. They had none of that precious beverage (and if they had it might have been bad), but we got some boiled milk. I did not really want anything, but during the time the Mongols were negotiating with the lady, our carts were turned with the backs to the wind, and it seemed that I had never known what enjoyment was till then. It lasted but a quarter of an hour. The inexorable camels turned their noses to the wind again, and I spent the night in manipulating blankets and contorting limbs, but all to no purpose, for the merciless gale swept under and over and through me. In the morning as soon as daylight came we got out of our cold quarters and on to our ponies, stopped at a yourt where we indulged in a cup of hot chocolate, and warmed ourselves at the hospitable fire. In this yourt we found a record of the party who had preceded us on the journey, dated 11th June. Our poor Mongols and their camels were fatigued, and we did not object to an early halt on the 31st August. We camped in a very desert place, scarcely any grass at all; shot grouse for breakfast, and tried to believe that we were comfortable. But we were not, for if we had no other annoyance, the impossibility of keeping the blowing sand out of our food was an evil hard to bear patiently. Everything, even the inside of our boxes, was filled with sand. Every means was tried in vain to prevent it from blowing under our tent. We walked about most of the day and tried to shoot, but the guns were nearly blown out of our hands, and that resource for the destitute had to be abandoned in despair.

About 4 in the afternoon we started again, wind still blowing a gale. The road became very rough, which was an additional reason for a restless night. We had many stoppages besides, and much shouting all through the night, which seriously disturbed our fitful naps, and in the morning it was painfully evident that our poor camels were breaking down. One of them had several times refused to go on, and had eventually lain down with his load, and resisted all persuasion to rise. He had to be unloaded and the extra weight distributed among the stronger ones, at the risk of breaking them down also. The truth is the camels were not in condition when we started. We were too early for them. The practice of the Mongols is to work their camels hard from the autumn to the spring. Before the summer comes everything is taken out of them; their humps get empty and lie flat on their backs; their feet get out of order, and they have mostly bad sore backs. They are then taken off the road and turned out to grass. About this time they shed their long hair and become naked, and all through the hot weather the Mongol camel is the most miserable object that can be imagined. In the early autumn they have recruited their strength, their humps are firm and stand erect, their backs are healed, and they begin the campaign fresh and strong.

Our progress during the night was very slow, and towards morning the road became sandy—in some places very heavy. The cart-camels now suffered most, sweating and struggling with their work in a way that was far from reassuring to us who had the greater part of the journey still before us.

The whitened bones of camels are scattered all over the desert, but in this place they were more numerous than ever. I believe the camels always die on the road. They are worked till they drop, and when one of a caravan fairly breaks down, there is no alternative but to leave it to die on the sand.

Yourts are few and far between, and few cattle are to be seen; there is barely grass enough to support sheep and camels. We pushed on till 11 o'clock, and encamped at Mingan, where there were no yourts actually in sight, but several within a few miles. There was really little or nothing to eat, and our trusty steeds were palpably suffering from their long stages and short commons. Serious misgivings crossed our minds as to the probability of our ponies carrying us much further, and we were concerned for them as well as for ourselves, for they had done our work well so far, and we felt kindly to them as the patient companions of our journey.

CHAPTER VII.

MONGOLIA—*continued*.

Our lama received sundry visitors at Mingan, and had evidently some business to transact with them, for we soon saw him in earnest converse with some of the strangers in his tent, passing their hands into each others' sleeves as if bargaining with the fingers. This resulted in the sale of one of our camels—the one that had broken down.* Our conductor had more matters to settle than that, however, but he was prevented by circumstances beyond his control. The fact is that on such occasions the Mongols consider it indispensable to imbibe freely of spirits, and our lama had to stand a bottle of *samshu*, a very ardent spirit made from rice. The Mongols drink liberally when they have a chance, and the Mingan lama was no exception to the rule, for in a short time he got so drunk as to become unmanageable. He began by breaking the tent-poles, no slight calamity in a country without wood; he soon became helpless, and lay down on his back, refusing absolutely to move. All idea of further business was abandoned, and the drunken Mongol's friends were ashamed, not so much at the exhibition he was making, but at the mischief he had perpetrated. He could hardly lie on his back, but they deemed that no valid objection to his riding on horseback. They therefore caught his pony, by main force lifted him on, and put the reins in his hands. The pony started off across the plain in the direction of his home, quietly enough at first; but the drunken rider began to swing about and stretch out his right hand, as the Mongols do when they want to excite their ponies to unusual exertion. The pony went off at full gallop, throwing up clouds of sand behind him as he went; the rider's motions became more and more centrifugal until at last he rolled over and sprawled full length on the sand, apparently with no intention of moving. His friends rode after his pony, caught it, and hobbled it beside its master, and as evening was drawing on they left them both to their fate. Another of the party, not so far gone, was merrily drunk. He tried to work up a dispute with our Mongols, and promised us some amusement, but he also was got on his pony by the persuasion of his son, who was with him. The boy was ashamed of his papa, and did his best to take him off the field. They made several false starts together, but the old fellow grew warmer and more excited, again and again turning his horse's head and returning to our tent to "have it out." At last the young one prevailed, and they rode off together and disappeared in the distance. We were now left alone, at sunset, and our poor lama was left lamenting on his bad day's work, his waste of much good liquor to no purpose, and his broken tent-poles.

The Mongols are a pitiable set on foot, with their loose clumsy leather boots, but they are at home on horseback. From their earliest years they may be said to live on horseback, and the women are almost as expert as the men, mounting any animal that comes handiest, whether horse, cow, or camel, with or without saddle. Huc says he never saw a Mongol unhorsed; but probably he never saw a dead-drunk lama forcibly put on a fiery steed.

Our lama received Sycee silver for the camel he sold. Silver is not much in use among the Mongols, their only real currency being very coarse brick tea. But it is a mistake to suppose, as has been stated, that they are ignorant of the value of money.

We got away about 7 in the evening. The wind had fortunately lulled, and we passed a pretty comfortable night on the road, which was alternately hard and sandy. My "Dolonor" pony, that had been voluntarily following the caravan, began to find the pastures getting too poor even for him, who had the privilege of grazing day and night. The last two days he remained faithful, but on the morning of the 2nd September, finding matters getting from bad to worse, he pricked up his ears, about ship, and galloped straight back by the way we had come. This was not much to be surprised at, all things considered, and I could not help commending him for his sagacity. The "Kitat" was despatched on his camel in quest of the fugitive before I was awake. Had I been consulted I certainly should not have consented to such a wild-goose chase, but the Mongols thought themselves bound in honour not to lose anything, although it was not in the contract that they were to look after ponies on the journey.

It was a very dry morning, but we got water for ourselves and our horses passing Borolji. The well there was very deep, and we were indebted to the friendly aid of some Mongols, who happened to have driven their cattle in to water, for obtaining a supply for our beasts. The head shepherd had brought with him a small bucket made of sheepskin, attached to the end of a long pole to enable him to reach the water. His own beasts were very thirsty and impatient to drink; the horses especially crowded eagerly round the well, neighing, biting, and kicking each other in their efforts to gain the best places. Nevertheless, the polite Mongol drew water for us first, and allowed us to continue our march. We kept on till 1.30, when we pitched our tents on the steppe, called "Gunshandak." No grass at all grows here, but the sand is slightly shaded with green by a small wild leek, that

HALT IN THE DESERT OF GOBI

grows in form much like the Mongolian grass. We had frequently observed this plant already sprinkled amongst the grass, but in Gunshandak it flourishes to the exclusion of everything else. The sheep and camels thrive on it. Our ponies also ate it freely, perhaps because they could get nothing else, and when our cattle were brought in from feeding they had a strong smell of onions about them.

The Kitat not having come up with my pony, we did not hurry away, and our Mongols availed themselves of the delay to buy and kill a goat from a neighbouring flock. We also bought a sheep for two rubles, or about six shillings. The seller, on being asked to kill it, told us we might do it ourselves. This was not to be thought of, and our own Mongols were too much occupied with their goat. We had, therefore, to resort to a little craft, for the sheep must certainly be put to death before we could eat it. Addressing the man, we said, how can we lamas kill an animal? This was sufficient. "Oh, you are lamas!" and he proceeded at once to business. The dexterity with which these Mongols kill and cut up a sheep is truly marvellous. They kill with a small knife which they insert into the belly, just below the breast-bone. Death is almost instantaneous. The object of this mode of slaughter is to save the blood inside the animal. Skinning is an easy process and soon done. The sheep is laid on his back on the sand, the skin is spread out on either side, a strip down the back being left attached while the cutting up is going on. The skin thus serves as a table, and so well does it answer the purpose that they will cut up a sheep into small pieces, and put everything, including lights and liver, on the skin, without ever touching the sand. The Mongols have a perfect practical knowledge of the anatomy of the sheep, and sever every joint with perfect ease, with only a small pocket-knife, no other instrument being used in any part of the process. The rapidity with which the whole thing is done, is astonishing. Our butcher was unluckily called away during the operation to retrieve a young camel that had been crying for its dam all the morning, and had now broken its tether, so that I could not time him accurately. I shall not state the number of minutes usually occupied from the time a sheep is purchased till the mutton is ready for the pot, for I could hardly expect to be believed. On removing the intestines, &c., the blood is found all together in a pool. It is then carefully baled out and put into the cooking pan, or *taga*, for nothing is thrown away here. We gave ours to the butcher, as also the skin and the whole of the inside, except liver and kidneys. The wandering Mongols scent a sheep-killing like vultures, and there are never wanting some old women to lend a hand in making black-puddings, and such like, who are rewarded for their trouble by a share of the feast; for among the Mongols the first instalment of their sheep is eaten in less than half an hour from the time it is killed. The Mongol sheep are generally in good condition, but there is no fat about them at all, except in the tail, which is a heavy lump of pure suet, said to weigh sometimes ten pounds. The condition of the animal is judged by the weight of the tail. The Mongols use but little water in cleaning their mutton. The ubiquitous old woman, who instals herself as pudding-maker, handles the intestines in a delicate and artistic manner. She first of all turns them all inside out, and then coils them up into hard, sausage-shaped knots, without stuffing, which take up very little space in the pot. These and all the other loose things are first put into the pot, with the addition of as much of the meat as it will hold. The pot is filled so full that the water does not cover the meat, but that is of no consequence to the Mongols. It is soon cooked, and quickly eaten. When sufficiently boiled, one of the company adroitly snatches the meat, piece by piece, from the boiling cauldron, with his fingers, and distributes it in fair proportions to the anxious expectants seated round. They never burn their fingers by this snap-dragon process. Their manner of eating mutton is most primitive, and I will also say disgusting. Each person gets a large lump or two, either in his lap, or on the mat on which he sits. He then takes a piece in his left hand as big as he can grasp; and, with the inevitable small knife in his right, he cuts off nuggets of mutton, using his thumb as a block, in the manner of cutting Cavendish tobacco. They literally bolt their mutton, and use no salt, bread, or sauce of any kind in eating it. When they have got all the meat off, they pare and scrape the bones very carefully, and when that is done, they break the bones up, and eat the marrow. Nothing is thrown away, except part of the eye, and the trotters. The tail is considered a delicacy, and is reserved for the head lama, or the honoured guest, who generously shares it with the others. I need only say that this mass of rich suet is eaten as I have described above.

When the solid part of the entertainment has been despatched, they put up their knives after wiping them on their clothes, and then proceed to drink the broth in their wooden cups. If they have any millet, they like to throw a little into the broth as they drink it. The millet gets softened a little as the cup is rapidly replenished, but no further cooking is necessary. When the broth is finished, they put clean water into the taga with a handful or two of brick tea, and go to sleep while it is boiling. The tea so made has of course a greasy appearance, and this practice of cooking everything in the same pot has probably given rise to the belief that they boil mutton and tea together, eating the leaves of the tea with the mutton. There may be Tartar tribes who do this, but the Khalkas Mongols certainly do not. The tea leaves, or rather stalks,—for their bricks are made up of tea dust and timber,—are always thrown away. It is necessary to boil the tea to get anything out of it at all, and it is of course bitter and ill flavoured. I have drunk it when hard up; and when it is well diluted with milk it is not unpalatable, when you can get nothing else.

The Mongol tastes no doubt seem to us very unrefined, but they are natural. The great esteem in which they hold the fat as compared with the lean of mutton, is a plain expression of the direction in which their ordinary regimen is defective. It is well known that fat and farinaceous foods ultimately fulfil the same purposes in the human economy; they mutually compensate, and one or other is absolutely necessary. We thus find fat and oils eagerly sought after, wherever, as among the Mongols and Esquimaux, the cultivation of cereals is forbidden by soil and climate.

The value of a scale of diet does not, as might at first sight be supposed, consist in the prominence of any one article, but depends on the different ingredients which are necessary to sustain health, being duly proportioned; and wherever the food of a people is necessarily composed of one substance almost exclusively, the natural appetite will always mark out as delicacies those which are deficient. It is to this want of due proportion in the elements of diet that we must attribute the comparative muscular weakness of the Mongols, in spite of the abundant supply of mutton and the bracing air of the desert. The coolies of China and Japan greatly excel them in feats of strength, and in power of endurance, because the rice on which they feed contains a more varied proportion of the elements that nourish life, the poor quality of the fare being compensated by the incredible quantities which they consume.

Our Mongols having slept off their first meal and drunk their tea, put the pot on the fire again, and cooked the remainder of the goat, on which they had another heavy blow-out late in the afternoon. The rapacity and capacity of a Mongol stomach is like that of a wild beast. They are brought up to eat when they can, and fast when they must, and their digestion is never deranged by either of these conditions. They very much resemble their own camels in those useful qualities so necessary to the inhabitants of a desert. Our Mongols had really eaten nothing since leaving Chan-kia-kow. They had fasted for seven days at least, and gone almost entirely without sleep all that time, and yet suffered nothing from the fatigue they must have endured. They had certainly some millet seed and some Chinese dough, a little of which they put into their tea as they drank it, but of actual food they had none. They had now laid in a supply which would last them another week. They seldom carry meat with them, finding it more convenient to take it in their stomachs.

Lest it be thought that we also adopted the Mongol way of living, I must explain that we had a very complete set of cooking utensils, plates, knives and forks, and every other accessory to civilised feeding. We certainly had to a great extent to educate ourselves to live on one meal a day, but that was but a distant approach to the Mongol habit of eating but once a week.

We made a long day of it on the steppe Gunshandak, hoping every hour that the Kitat would return. The country was so desert that there was no population, and only two yourts were near us. Our encampment was some distance off the track, and we had consequently no visits from travellers, so we spent a very quiet day. In the afternoon the camels were brought in, and Tellig and the lama examined them all narrowly. Their condition was really becoming serious, for not only were they tired and worn out, but their backs were getting very bad. They are very subject to this. Nearly all of them had large deep holes in their backs, which penetrated almost through the flesh between the ribs. Maggots breed very fast in these wounds, and every few days the Mongols probe deep into the wound with a bit of stick, and scoop the vermin out. The animals complain a little during this operation, but on the whole they bear their ills with marvellous patience. While the camels are grazing, the crows sit on their backs and feed on the worms. It did seem cruel to put heavy loads on such suffering creatures, but what else could be done?

Our ponies were falling off fast from want of food and rest. It was severe on them to go eighteen hours without eating. But they were, comparatively speaking, a luxury, and could be dispensed with. The camels were essential, and could not be replaced in the desert. The lama betrayed considerable anxiety for his camels, and began to talk of getting fresh ones at a place called *Tsagan-tuguruk*, where there is a *sumé* or temple. We gathered from him that his family lived there, and that he could easily exchange his camels for fresh ones, if only he could reach that rendezvous. But Tsagan-tuguruk was four days' journey from us, and our used-up cattle did not look as if they could hold out so long. But we live in hope, for it is foolish to anticipate misfortunes.

We have hitnerto met no caravans since leaving China, excepting long trains of ox-carts carrying timber from Urga.

The day wore on and no Kitat appeared. The Mongols strained their eyes to descry some sign on the horizon, then looked anxiously at the sun fast sinking in the west, and made up their minds to remain in the steppe all night. The Mongols have no means of judging of time except by guessing from the height of the sun or moon. I speak only of my own experience, for Huc says they can tell the time of day by looking at a cat's eyes. For my part I did not see a cat in the whole of Mongolia. Dogs they have in plenty. They are of the same breed as the common dog of China, but rather larger and with thicker coats. They are useful to the shepherds and are good watch dogs, not so thoroughly domestic as their Chinese congeners, but will run after one a great distance from their yourt barking ferociously. They are great curs, however, and their bark is worse than their bite. It is a singular thing that the Mongols do not feed their dogs; nor do the Chinese, as a rule. They are supposed to forage for themselves, and in Mongolia they must be put to great straits occasionally.

The day had been very warm, and, the air being still, in the evening we slept in the carts. It was always warmer and more comfortable to sleep in the tent, but our bedding had to be moved, and the oftener that was done the more sand got into our blankets.

The nights in Mongolia were beautiful, sky very clear, and stars bright. The "harvest moon," that had been such a boon to us in our night travelling, now rose late. In a few days it would be over, and we should have dark nights to travel in.

After a luxurious night's rest, the first we had had for a week, we awoke to see the sun rise on the steppe, and almost fancied ourselves at sea. So indeed we were in a figurative sense, for there was still no appearance of the missing Mongol. We were now in the humour to take things patiently; and the sheep we had killed yesterday enabled us to prepare a breakfast that for a desert might fairly be called sumptuous. The day was passed in idleness, for not a feather of a bird was to be seen to afford an excuse for taking our guns out. Visits were paid and received between us and the Mongols who lived in the two yourts near us, and our lama fraternised with them, and got the women to bring us argols and water. The women, as a rule, keep the house and do the cooking and darning, only going out after the flocks when the men are out of the way.

The lamas carry their principle of not killing animals to an extremity that is sorely inconvenient to themselves. They are not exempt from parasitical connections; in fact, the person of a lama, considered as a microcosm, is remarkably well inhabited. He cannot, with his own hand, "procure the transmigration" of any animal, in case it should contain the soul of his grandfather, or some past or future Bhudda ; but when the population presses on the means of subsistence, something must be done. In this juncture the services of some benevolent female are called in, the lama strips to the waist, and commits his person and his garment to her delicate and practised manipulation.

We determined to start at sunset, Kitat or no Kitat, and with one long-lingering look over the vast plain we had crossed, at sunset we did start. We soon met a caravan of sixty camels, which was refreshing to our eyes as evidence of the travelling season having fairly commenced, affording us a better hope of finding fresh camels.

We had again to encounter rough stony roads during the night; in fact, we seemed just to come to the bad roads as we were going to sleep. How was it that we did not sometimes by accident stumble on a bit of soft ground at night-time ? The roads were perhaps not so bad as our nocturnal imagination, stimulated by want of proper rest, painted them. But whether or no, we had nothing to complain of on this occasion, having enjoyed a sound unbroken sleep the previous night; and surely one good night out of two is enough for any reasonable being.

In the morning, passing over some rather steeper undulations than usual, and in a very desert country, we came across a herd of gurush. Some ineffectual shots were fired as usual. It was tantalising in the extreme not to be able to bag one of these fine animals when met with in such numbers as would have delighted the heart of Gordon Cumming.

About two o'clock we halted at Kutul-usu, where we were agreeably surprised to find no less than six yourts near our encampment, which was remarkable considering the scarcity of grass. There is no grass at all, in fact, and our beasts return from their grazing redolent of onions. A large ox-cart caravan was also encamped at this place.

Our lama had long and earnest conversations with the Mongols of Kutul-usu, and there was much going to and fro between our tents and the yourts. There was something in the wind—we could not divine what—until the lama again broached the subject of *Tsagan-tuguruk*, the place where he expected new camels. His proposal was that he should ride ahead on a pony, and get the camels ready by the time the caravan came up. There were grave objections to this course, for we were already short-handed from the absence of the Kitat, and were we to be left with only one camel-driver, we should never be able to keep the caravan together. The lama was importunate, and at last we consented to his plan on condition : 1st, that he should find a substitute to assist Tellig with the caravan ; and 2nd, that he should provide us with fresh ponies at Tsagan-tuguruk. The substitute was soon found in an active-looking, wiry old man with very bad eyes. The sun had set some time before the discussions and preparations were concluded, and we were consequently compelled to remain till the moon rose, which was not before eleven o'clock—half the night gone and no progress made.

We had a rough night as usual, but we are getting into a more broken country. In the morning we passed one of the numerous salt plains that are spread over the great desert. Sometimes there is water in them and sometimes not. This one was dry, but had a white scurf of salt on the ground. A dark-green plant grows in tufts over these plains, and is eaten by the animals in the absence of grass ; indeed, I am not sure

I

whether the camels don't prefer it. It was a hot thirsty day, and we were at great trouble to find a yourt in which to rest and make chocolate in the morning. We did discover one eventually after riding many miles, and there we fell in with a sporting lama with two good-looking ponies, riding one and leading the other. This seemed a good opportunity for business, and my companion soon concluded an exchange operation, giving a pony with an incipient sore back and two dollars to boot, for a good old sound one of the lama's. We were in some doubt about finding our caravan, having let it get a long way out of sight; but the wandering lama, having a direct interest in discovering our party to get his two dollars, soon scented them out by the same kind of instinct that directs a bee to his distant hive. We took him some miles back out of his way, but these people seem to care little in which direction they go, or how much time they may lose in going from one place to another.

The facility with which our Mongol friends found their way in the open desert had often excited our admiration. At the end of a night's march, although interrupted by numerous accidental stoppages, they were never at a loss to know where they were. They needed no land-mark to guide them, and in pitching their tent near a well they never made a mistake as to its position. The explanation seems to be that certain instincts are developed in proportion to the want of artificial aids. Thus Chinese sailors cruise about their dangerous coast by a kind of rule of thumb, and are able to judge of their position in darkness and fog where scientific navigators would be at fault. In Australia also it is found that the best bushranger is generally the most ignorant man of the party. The effect of education being to cause men to trust more and more to acquired knowledge, the faculty of perception, which is possessed in a high degree by the lower animals, becomes weakened for want of exercise. Instinct and education mutually compensate each other; and the lower we descend in the scale of humanity,—the nearer man approaches to the condition of the inferior animals,—the more does his mere instinct predominate over his higher mental faculties. The senses are very acute in primitive peoples, because of the constant exercise they get, or rather because of the necessity which compels them to be guided by the senses in their daily lives. For to hear or see abstractedly, or for pleasure or instruction, is a different thing from using these senses with the conviction that the supply of food perhaps depends on the accuracy of their indications.

As we approached our halting-place, *Ulan-Khada*, we witnessed a remarkable phenomenon, which was a few dwarf trees, scorched and scraggy, but still alive, growing in a sheltered nook in a pass over some rocky hills. A little rill filters through the stone and sand, and fresh soft grass is found in modest quantity beside the water. Ulan-Khada is in a hollow surrounded by high ground, and three yourts were seen from our camp. The wild leek still prevails.

The following day we stopped at Ude, and early on the morning of the 7th of September, to our great joy, we reached the land of promise,—the well-watered, grassy plain of Tsagan-tuguruk. There was something cheering in the very name, associated as it had been in our minds with the hoped-for end of our troubles and uncertainties. Vast flocks and herds were seen in all directions, and yourts in good number, though at great distances from each other. Our lama, Tupchun, was not here, but at his family yourt, said to be six miles off. It was clear we must make a day of it, at least, at Tsagan-tuguruk, and we at once proceeded to make acquaintance with the natives of the nearest yourts, who came to visit us. The next move was to buy a sheep, for we had been out of mutton for some days, the hot sun preventing our keeping it long. A Mongol jumped on his pony, and galloped off to his flock, caught a big, fat sheep, swung it across the pommel of his saddle, and rode back with it to our tent. That was soon done, but now came the lama question again. Were we lamas, or Chara-chun? Now, *Chara-chun* means, literally, "black man," and is the name applied to all Mongols who are not lamas. To one or other of the two classes we must belong. But we certainly were not black men, that was clear; and if not black men, we were necessarily lamas. The Mongols worked out the conclusion satisfactorily in their own minds, and lent cheerful aid in killing and dressing our mutton, for that was the great practical issue of the question.

We had heard much from Tellig and others of the *sume*, or temple of Tuguruk, and we took a few Mongols with us and started off to visit it. It is a neat little house built of stone, but the smallest place of worship perhaps in the world, smaller even than some missionary chapels I have seen. A priest came out of a neighbouring yourt, and opened the door for us. The interior was covered all over with dust, but we were already so dusty that we did not scruple to sit down. Half the space was occupied by the materials for making yourts, apparently new; and no doubt left by some wandering Mongol for safe custody. A second priest soon joined us, and the two together took down two old brass trumpets, like the Chinese bagpipes, to give us some music. These instruments were so dusty inside and out, and their joints so loose, that no sound of any kind could be produced from them. The priests puffed and blew as if they would have burst their boilers, but the rusty old brass would yield no sound.

Among our new acquaintances was a youth of fifteen, called *Haltsundoriki*, the most active and intelligent of the Mongols we had met with. He was much interested in us and our belongings, and during our few days' stay at this place, he came regularly every morning, and stayed with us till nightfall. He was a most willing servant to us, collecting argols, lighting our fire, washing our dishes, taking our ponies to water, and making himself universally useful. As our visitors increased in numbers, they crowded our tent inconveniently, especially at meal-times, for they had a nasty habit of fingering everything they saw. *Haltsundoriki* was therefore installed as master of the ceremonies, and vigorously did he exercise his authority over young and old. It was quite understood that he might bore us as much as he liked himself, but he was not to permit any one else to do it. He used the utmost freedom with all his countrymen who came in his way, riding their horses or camels without asking leave, and levying contributions on all and sundry in the shape of tobacco, cheese, or anything they might happen to possess. He furnished us with amusement by chaffing and playing practical jokes on his friends, without regard to age or sex. His wit was in a great measure lost on us, but we made great progress in the Mongol language under his tuition. Although not a lama, he was educated, and could read and write both Mongol and Tangut. He was probably the son of some small chieftain who lived in the neighbourhood, and had had an opportunity of seeing better society than the cowherds.

On intimating that we were prepared to do a little horse-dealing, we at once set in motion several Mongols on their ponies. Armed with a long light pole, with a large loop at the end of it, they ride at the drove, and singling out the one they want, they generally manage to throw the loop over his head without much difficulty. An old hand, that has been hunted for a good many years, will sometimes lead them a chase of an hour or two; for though the pony that is ridden is always the fleetest, the hunted one doubles and dodges his pursuer in every possible way. My Chan-kia-kow pony was so done up as to be useless, and I exchanged him for a big, strong beast, with doubtful feet, but the most likely I could find.

We were much pestered for biscuit, liquor, and empty bottles. It was useless to tell our persecutors that we were on a long journey, and required all our supplies. They have no consideration for travellers, and would eat you up to the last morsel of food you possessed. We found it a good plan to give them porter when they asked for drink. The wry faces it produced were most comical, and they never asked for more. As for the empty bottles, we reserved them to requite any little services that were performed for us, and to pay for milk. One old hag, a she-lama, came begging for drink, and would not be denied. Her arguments were after this sort:—" You are a lama, and I am a lama, and we are brethren, and our hearts are in unison; therefore it is right that you should give me this bottle of wine." The only reply to such an appeal would be :—" True, I am a lama, and you are a lama, &c., but as the bottle is in my possession, it is right it should remain so." The old woman would still go rummaging about the tent, and it would have been rude to turn her out *vi et armis*. At length she came across a bottle uncorked, and pouring a little of its contents into the palm of her hand, she licked it up with her tongue. The effect was remarkable, her features were screwed up in hideous contortions, she went out of the tent spitting, and did not ask for any more drink. The bottle proved to contain spirits of wine which we used for boiling coffee.

The first theft we were conscious of was perpetrated during our stay at Tsagan-tuguruk. Hitherto we had relied implicitly on the honesty of the Mongols, leaving all our small things lying about at the mercy of our numerous visitors. But now a few nick-nacks that our lama had asked me to take charge of for him, were stolen out of my cart during the night. We were very angry at this, and proclaimed aloud that we would allow no Mongol to come near our tent till the thief was discovered, and the property restored. It was impossible, however, to stem the tide; and it seemed hard, moreover, to punish the whole tribe for the misdeed of one who might have no connection with the neighbourhood. We deemed it quite fair, however, to stop their biscuit and brandy. On the return of the lama, we reported the theft, but he received the news with perfect equanimity. In the evening he got two other lamas to perform the prescribed incantation for the purpose of discovering the thief. They performed their task in a Mongol yourt with bell, book, and candle (literally, as regards the bell and the book), reciting many yards of lama prayers, while they told their beads. Our lama had asked us for some wine for the ceremony. This was poured into three small brass cups which stood on the table (the family box, or chest of drawers) during the ceremony. It was too tedious to see it out, but our lama informed us next morning that the incantation had been successful (of course) —that they had discovered who the thief was, but as to catching him and recovering the property, that seemed as far off as ever.

On the second day of our halt the Kitat arrived, in company with a friend, both on camels, and with my pony, "Dolonor." He had managed to lose his own camel in the chase, and had come up to us on one borrowed from his companion. The lama gave him a cold reception, lamenting bitterly over the loss of his camel. As to the pony, he came full of spirits, but being rather poor when he ran away, the six days' hard hunting in the desert had not improved his condition, and I wished they had left him where he was.

We were two days kicking our heels about in the utmost impatience before our lama deigned to make his appearance with the new camels. As soon as he came, Tellig started on an expedition to see his friends, who also lived some six or eight miles off, and did not return till the next day. The lama, instead of preparing for the journey, went dilly-dallying about, drinking tea and gossiping with all the old women in the country, which we considered a wanton waste of *our* time, and we exhibited the feelings natural to us under such circumstances. The lama tried every device to keep us till the 10th, but we were desperate, and forced them to commence packing late at night, which was no easy matter in the dark, with unwilling workmen. Tellig was civil and good-natured. The Kitat showed the cloven foot so disagreeably as to provoke some rough treatment, which led to his leaving our service. I suspect this had already been arranged, for a substitute was found at a moment's notice. The new camels not having been tried in harness, were first put into the empty carts, and carefully led about for some time, before they could be depended on for steadiness. All this occupied a good many hours in a very cold night, and it was midnight before we got away from Tsagan-tuguruk. Two friends of the lama accompanied us on our first stage, which was only a few miles, for we were halted before daylight. The lama's business matters had not been quite settled, and he had a few more last words with his two friends. The packing, so hurriedly done in the dark, had all to be done over again.

While these little matters were being arranged, we had time to take stock of our new establishment. The camels were certainly fat and fresh, humps full and erect, backs whole, with only the marks of old scars. The camel department could not be in a better state than it was. Kitat's substitute turned out to be a lama, a good-natured looking fellow, whom we afterwards discovered to be well-meaning but stupid. He could speak a few words of Chinese, and we therefore christened him, in contradistinction to our chief of the staff, who was *the* lama *par excellence,* the " Kitat lama." We further observed that *the* lama had somehow got rid of his pony, and now rode a camel, which looked ominous for the success or even the preservation of our equestrian stock ; for the lama hated camels, and never rode one himself when he could help it.

CHAPTER VIII.

MONGOLIA—*continued*.

THE grass was still copiously sprinkled with onions. As we advanced we crossed some marshy ground with a good deal of water, enough to make it necessary to pick the way judiciously, for the camel hates water or slippery mud. Their broad soft feet don't sink into the mud sufficiently to enable them to get a good foot-hold like a horse, and their long weedy legs are so loosely knit together, that they run a great risk of splitting up when their feet slip. A caravan of seventeen camels, that had accompanied us since morning, took a wrong road across the marshes and stuck, the camels being unable to proceed. Our lama took a round-about road, for which we abused him at the time ; but when he saw the other caravan brought up all standing on the short cut, he merely pointed it out to us with a triumphant chuckle, and quietly asked, " Who knows the road ? "

A 60-camel caravan was passed encamped near the marsh. It was from Urga, and probably from Kiachta, loaded with merchandise for China, and for account of Chinese. Two celestials were in charge of the goods, jolly roystering fellows, with whom we stopped awhile and held such conversation as to the road, the state of the pastures, time occupied, &c., as will usually occur to travellers in such regions. It was curious to notice how untruthful these travellers' stories generally were. They seemed to say whatever came uppermost in their minds, as a man of a happy disposition will often say, " It is a fine day," when it is raining cats and dogs. But yet if you are to believe *nothing* of what you hear on the road, you will deprive yourself of a great deal of information which might be valuable ; and if you believe *all*, you will keep yourself and your people constantly in hot water. It is difficult to steer a safe course between too much credulity on the one hand, and too little faith on the other.

We halted again at 2 o'clock at *Taryagi*, a region unpeopled ; but we were near a shallow lagoon, with thick chalk-coloured water. It was most unpalatable, but the Mongols seemed to like it. It is easier for them to draw their water from a pool than to fetch it from a distant well ; and to cover their indolence, they invariably assure you that the wells are salt. You are of course obliged to accept their explanations, for if they were to assert that there were no wells at all, you would not be a bit the wiser. Although the pastures were pretty fair at Taryagi, our camels were not allowed to graze, the reason being, that in their condition, they would blow themselves out in a couple of hours to such an extent, that they would not be fit to work.

It was pitch dark before we got ready to start. We had difficulty in collecting the beasts, particularly the ponies, and a young unruly camel. Our two Chan-kia-kow lanterns were sufficient to make the darkness visible, but no more. The Mongols, when looking for cattle in the dark, stoop down to the ground and scan the horizon round. In a steppe, this plan is very useful, for if the animal is not very far off, his outline can be descried against the horizon.

At daylight we were in the steppe *Butyn-tala*, where another large caravan was encamped. This steppe has also a great deal of surface water in it, and in the small valleys round it. The grass is pretty good, and cattle abundant. Game was again met with in Butyn-tala.

Our next halt was near *Sain-kutul*, where there were

good pastures, but shocking water. We really could not drink it, and, as the day was still hot, we had to suffer from thirst. Milk was of no use, and only aggravated our sufferings. At Sain-kutul, a strange Mongol (a lama) rode up on a camel, and after the usual greetings, he undid his camel's load, and took up his quarters in the tent of our people. On inquiry, we found he was going to *Kuren* (Urga of the Russians), and gave us to understand we might have his company if we liked. He had started from his home with his one camel to perform a long journey, without any of the necessaries usually carried on such a journey, trusting that Bhuddha would furnish a table for him in the wilderness, and a covering as well, by directing him to the tent of some travellers who were better provided than himself. He was a man of a mean character. Our first impressions of him were decidedly unfavourable, and subsequent experience confirmed them. Not that the man ever did anything wrong; on the contrary, his conduct was regulated by the strictest rules of propriety. But that merely served to aggravate his offence, for it gave us no excuse for disliking him. On the first day of our acquaintance I lent a hand to lash up his gear, not from any desire to help him, but from the same motive that induces people to twirl their thumbs for want of some more intellectual amusement; or children to pull and haul at anything they can lay hands on, more especially where they have a chance of doing mischief. As I was pulling at his ropes, the fellow looked up in my face, and, with the most abject expression, but with great gravity, said, "*Sain chung! Sain chung!*" Good man! Good man! The Mongols use this expression in two senses, one with a meaning, and one without. Now, in which sense soever this individual used it, it was equally bad, and I much fear I never forgave him for it. Indeed if he had asked forgiveness (which he did not) I could not have believed him sincere. And this man was to stick to us like the old man of the sea all the way to Urga! He affected great learning too—knew all the lama books, according to his own account, and had been to Tangut. Whether by Tangut the Mongols mean the old country of Tangut, or whether it means Thibet, I am unable to say. It is most probably the latter, and the confusion of names is very likely to have occurred from the fact that Tangut was peopled with a Thibetian race.

After leaving Sain-kutul, we were joined by a Russian courier, a lama, mounted on a camel, a very unusual thing, for they generally ride horses, changing them every twenty or thirty miles. The courier, knowing Russ, tried to get up a conversation with us in that language, which we evaded, for we had already discovered the advantage of passing for Russians. It would, indeed, have been useless to explain to the lama that we were not Russians. It would probably have staggered his belief to begin with, for I am persuaded that more than half the Mongol population believe Mongolia to be in the centre of the world, with Russia at one end, and China at the other. The Russian courier or postal service through Mongolia is all done by lamas, whom an idle roaming life seems to suit better than it does the black men. They perform the distance from Chan-kia-kow to Kiachta, 780 miles, in eleven or twelve days easily, by means of their relays of horses. This seems very fast travelling, compared with our weary thirty days' journey; but it is really very slow, and if the courier were pushed, he could do the distance in six days even, with the same facilities as they have at present, excepting, perhaps, that the rider should be relieved once. We met several of them on the road, and they travel as if time were no object to them; for example, the courier now alluded to kept company with us at our two mile an hour pace from 6 o'clock in the evening till 10 next day. Others of them on ponies have done the same thing, and I know they spend their time in yourts, gossiping and drinking tea for hours together. In short, the couriers to and from Kiachta take matters exceedingly easy. There are three couriers monthly; one for the Russian government, starting from Peking, and two for the Kiachta merchants; the latter go to and from Tientsin. The Russian government courier is entirely under the control of the Chinese government, and is also, I believe, at its expense. The merchants' posts are managed by themselves.

Near *Ichi Khapstil* we encamped in rather good pastures, and near a large pond of very dirty water, with wild fowl on it. A large kind of duck, nearly all white, and dab-chicks, were the tenants of this pond, but we elsewhere saw many species of wild fowl.

Six of our camels were now allowed to eat and drink, after fasting for four days, to our knowledge, and perhaps a couple of days before they were brought to us.

The water from the pond was nauseous. I could not touch it, and suffered severely from thirst in consequence. In the afternoon, when we had started the caravan, I rode all over the country on every side looking for water, but could not find any, except a mere puddle where horses and cattle had pitted the wet mud with foot-prints. Into these holes a little water had collected, and we were fain to stoop down and drink with eagerness the filthy liquid that, at another time, would have turned my stomach. But we were happily getting out of the watery region, and before night we got into a yourt to make tea, and found delicious spring-water.

The camel that was drawing my cart did a very unusual thing during this evening. He set to kicking so violently that at first I was afraid he would smash everything to pieces, but, as every blow was delivered on the solid part of the machine, no damage was done, except to the camel's own legs. He would not desist until he had so mauled himself that he could hardly stand on his legs. And when the pain had a little subsided he would resume the kicking, but with less and less energy, until he was fairly defeated. During the fits he was dangerous to approach, for, by the formation of a camel's hind legs, the lower extremities spread out widely from the hocks, and the feet, in kicking, project considerably beyond the perpendicular of the shaft. Tellig did, in fact, get knocked over in this way. This was the only instance in my experience of one of these patient animals getting out of temper.

The face of the country was now fast changing its character, being broken up into irregular elevations, and was more grassy. We hoped the worst part of the desert had been left behind, as we gradually got into an inhabited region. Passing *Sharra-sharatu*, where there were many yourts, we proceeded to *Shibetu*, in the middle of a hilly country. Our next stage took us to the *Ulin-dhabha* mountains, the only ones worthy the name we had seen in Mongolia. The road rises gradually towards the mountains from 3700 feet to 4900 feet, which is the elevation of the pass. The pass is an easy one, and forms a deep cutting into the mountains. The pass opens out a fine valley on the north, which was alive with men and beasts moving about; yourts packed up and laid on the backs of cows, camels, &c., and on rude wooden carts; flocks of sheep, and droves of cattle being driven here and there. The Mongols were moving to winter quarters. In the summer season they spread all over the desert and find enough food to support their beasts, but in the winter they try to get into some sheltered place where there is enough grass to keep their beasts alive during those dreary months. The few touches of north wind we had lately felt warned the inhabitants of the steppes of the approach of winter, and of the necessity of seeking a more hospitable region.

Near *Bombatu*, where we halted, the grass was luxuriant, and our half-starved ponies enjoyed it thoroughly. But, unfortunately, when our beasts are in clover our men are fagged out. Tellig especially, who has had most of the work, is nearly done for want of sleep and from constant exposure on the back of his camel.

There was no end to the ox-cart caravans that passed us on the way to China. There are between 100 and 200 carts in each, and they followed so close on one another that it seemed as if there was a continuous line of them for the whole length of a night's march. Their tinkling bells have a strange, but not unpleasant, effect as they move slowly along.

On the 15th September the lama made an excuse of buying sheep for himself and us, to halt at 9 a.m. some miles south of the steppe *Guntu-gulu*. We had been but two days without meat, but the Mongols had eaten nothing for six days. We had made several ineffectual attempts to buy sheep, and that very morning we had concluded a bargain for one, but the owner in catching the sheep missed his mark as he sprang forward to clutch it, and fell sprawling on his face. Of course we laughed, in common with the Mongol spectators, and whether the fellow was angry at being the occasion of merriment to us, or whether he considered his accident as a providential intimation that he was to sell no sheep that day, I cannot tell; but he obstinately declined to have anything more to say to us on the subject of sheep-selling.

The pony I had got at Tsagan-tuguruk had gone all to the bad with his feet. The roads had been very stony all the way, and his hoofs were too far gone to bear rough travelling. I bartered him, therefore, for two good sheep, and now I had only the skeleton of Dolonor left.

High mountains appeared fifteen miles east of us (if one

may venture to estimate distance in such a country), and we began to hope for something like scenery. It blew fresh and cold from S.-W., and in the afternoon it came round to N.-W., a regular *choinar salchin*, or north wind, a word of horrible signification to Mongols. And if dreaded in September what must it be in January ? I often wondered how the wretches get through their dreary winter. They are taken very suddenly with these cold northers. The day may be fine, and almost oppressively warm. A cloud comes over, and drops as much water as you would get out of a watering-pan. Then the north wind pipes up, and in a few hours you have made the transition from a tropical summer to worse than an Arctic winter, for the biting wind cuts into the bone.

In the face of a sharp norther we entered on the steppe *Guntu-gulu*, which seemed to be about five miles broad, but it proved the best part of a day's march, so deceptive are distances without prominent marks. A scene occurred in the steppe which delayed us a night, and might have proved serious enough to arrest our progress altogether. One of our guns went off in the cart (we always kept them loaded and handy), the charge went through some bedding, then the wooden back of the cart, and ricochetted from a wooden bar outside, miraculously clearing the camel that was following within two yards of the cart, and describing a curve over the whole line ; one of the pellets hit the lama who was bringing up the rear, at a distance of full sixty yards, and made a groove on the outside of the flap of his ear. It bled profusely ; in fact, the first notice he had of the injury was the streams of blood that suffused his neck and shoulders. He roared in terror, thinking he was *at least* killed ; stopped the caravan ; dismounted from his camel, and committed himself to the care of Tellig and the Kitat lama. The tent was hastily put up, and all made ready for a halt. Tellig and the others were greatly alarmed, and disturbed in their

K

minds, and we were somewhat uncertain of the view their superstitious fanaticism might lead them to take of the affair. Luckily we had just got clear of another very large caravan, and were spared the officious assistance of a crowd of people. There was a pool of water close by, and we sent for repeated supplies of it, washing the car, and letting it bleed freely. The wound was nothing at all, but the profuse bleeding frightened the Mongols. Our policy was to look wise ; and my companion being provided with a neatly got-up little case containing various articles of the *materia medica*, it was produced, and inspired a proper amount of blind faith in the minds of our Mongol friends. The wound was washed with arnica, and a piece of sticking-plaster put on it so successfully, that it completely stopped the bleeding, and made a very neat finish. The Mongols looked on with much wonder and reverence at our proceedings, and if any idea at retaliation for the injury had crossed their minds, it was now giving place to a feeling of gratitude for our surgical assistance. The lama was helpless from fright, and we had him lifted to his tent, where we made him recline on a bed that had been extemporised for him with boxes and things packed behind him on the windy side. A towel was tied round his head to keep the cold out, and he was made as comfortable as our means would allow. He looked sad and woe-begone, and we could with difficulty suppress a smile at the utter prostration of mind that the sight of his own blood had induced. He now imagined he had pains in his head, throat, and chest, and seeing him so entirely a victim to his fears, we were obliged to humour them a little, prescribing for his various symptoms with great care. The first thing we ordered him was a measured glass of brandy, knowing him to be partial to that liquor. This roused him a little, and his pluck began to return. We then prescribed tea, which was soon made, and, as he improved in spirits, we ordered mutton, knowing they had some scraps left from their morning's feast. All that done, we allowed him to smoke, and finally prescribed a good night's rest. In the morning we inquired for our patient and found him well, but much inclined to remain in his shell till the north wind was over. This was a little too much of a good thing ; so when we had carefully examined him all over, and scrutinised all his symptoms, we were compelled to pronounce him fit to travel. He could not get out of it, but reluctantly mounted his camel, his head still tied up in a white towel, to the wonderment of the wandering Tartars we encountered on our march. It certainly never was my fortune to be so well treated by a doctor, but as the faculty in this country depend so much on popularity, a similar mode of treatment with the majority of their patients would be well worth their consideration. I may here observe that the Mongols have their ears very protuberant, like an elephant's.

The accident to the lama was a godsend to us in procuring us a night's rest. The wind blew mercilessly across the steppe, so that sleeping in our carts with their backs turned to the wind, we could not keep warm. What it would have been, marching in the teeth of it with our front exposed, may be imagined by those who have experienced these cutting winds, for the fronts of our carts were, with all our care, but indifferently closed by sheets of felt, fastened as securely as we could manage, but utterly ineffective to keep out a gale of wind.

Most of the steppes in the desert are inhabited by a small marmot, like a rat, which burrows in the ground. Its custom is to sit on its haunches (it has only a rudimentary tail) beside its hole, uttering a chirping noise when alarmed, and then dropping into its hole, turning round immediately with only its head out to see if the apprehended danger is imminent, and then disappearing altogether. Each hole has several roads to it, extending to about twenty or thirty yards from the hole. The little animal seems never to stray from the beaten track, and is so secure of reaching its retreat, that it will allow you almost to tread on it before it begins to scamper home. Where these animals abound, the ground is furrowed in all directions by their roads. On the margins of their holes a heap of grass and herbs is piled up, which Huc thought was for the purpose of sheltering the animals from the winter winds. I have too much faith in their instinct to believe that, however, for, once in their burrows underground, no wind can touch them. It is more probable that the stores of vegetable matter so collected are intended for winter forage, which they collect with great industry during the autumn. Our ponies were very fond of nibbling at these heaps of drying grass, and turning them over with their noses, a practice which we did our best to discourage. It was in fact a kind of sacrilege to destroy wantonly the stores of food that these interesting creatures had with so much forethought and months of patient labour accumulated against the evil day.

In Guntu-gulu we met with another marmot of nearly similar habits, but much larger. It is in size and colour like a hare, but heavier and clumsier in its movements. Its burrows are as large as a rabbit's. It is found at a considerable distance from its hole, and is more easily alarmed than its neighbour, because less easily concealed. When slightly alarmed, it makes rapidly for its hole, and there sits till the danger approaches too near. Then, cocking up its short tail and uttering a chirp, it disappears into its hole. We could never get within shot of these animals. As to the little fellows, we got so close to them that it would have been cruelty to shoot them, as we had no means of preserving the skin. The larger ones burrow in stony places, and with their short legs, strong claws, and wiry hair, somewhat resemble the badger or racoon. They might be the *Lepus pusillus*, or "calling hare," if it were not that that species is positively said never to be found farther east than the Oby.

The wind lulled at sunset, and we had a fine frosty night. The morning of the 17th September showed us the first *bonâ fide* ice, and from that time we had frost during all the remainder of the journey. It was a moonless night, the roads were indifferent, the Mongols hungry and tired, and they therefore took it on themselves to halt for some hours before daylight to make tea near *Khulustu-tologoi*. From there we crossed the steppe *Borelju*, meeting the usual array of ox-cart caravans, and encamped at 10 o'clock near the entrance to a pass leading through a ridge of hills. The sharp clear outline of *Bain-ula* (rich mountain), ten to sixteen miles distant on our right, and the modest elevations at the foot of which we were encamped, made a pretty bit of scenery after such a monotonous succession of steppes. We had now been twenty-two days in Mongolia, and had become strongly imbued with the habits of the people we were living amongst. To have imagined that we were *travelling* at such a slow pace would have been misery. But there was nothing to make us believe we were travelling. Now and then a vague idea would cross our minds that some day we ought to see Kiachta, but that was of short duration, and our daily routine all went to keep up the illusion that we were dwellers in the desert. There was nothing to mark our daily stages, no church spires or road-side inns, not even a mile post. Those fine euphonious names of places I have given indicate nothing. They might with as much propriety be given to various parts of the ocean. We had entirely identified ourselves with the wandering Tartars, and were content to live in the desert with much the same feeling that the Israelites must have experienced during their desert journeyings, that there was a promised land dimly figured out to them—that is to say, their apprehension of the reality of it was dim; but the thought of ever arriving there had but slight influence on their daily life. The regular supply of manna was to their minds much more important than the bright future to which their leaders looked forward. And so it is with the greater part of mankind.

With all its drawbacks, there is a charm about desert life which is worth something to a man who has undergone the worry of incessant occupation. You are safe there from the intrusions of mail steamers and electric telegraphs, and "every day's report of the wrong and outrage with which earth is filled." The longer you live in such quiet solitudes the more independent you feel of the great struggling world without. It is a relief to turn your back on it for a while, and betake yourself to the children of nature, who, if they lack the pleasures, lack also many of the miseries, and some of the crimes, which accompany civilisation.

The day turned out very warm, so much so, that we were glad to get shelter from the sun under our canvas until 3 o'clock, when we were again in the saddle. The pass proved a fine valley, rich in grass. Another long string of caravans was met with, most of the carts empty, and bound from Urga to Dolonor. Why they were empty we could not ascertain, but conjectured that they could not get loaded before winter, of which the late severe weather had given them warning, and that they were bound at all hazards to get home to winter quarters.

Some days before this we had picked up a young pilgrim, a lama, on a journey to the great lamasery at Urga, there to pass a certain time in study. The boy was performing a journey of between 200 and 300 miles alone and on foot. He carried nothing in the world with him except the clothes on his back and a few musty papers containing lama prayers, carefully tied up between two boards which he carried in his bosom. He had no provisions with him, still less any money, but depended solely on the well-known hospitality of his countrymen for his daily bread and his night's lodging. I thought there was something heroic in a boy of fifteen undertaking such a journey under such circumstances, but the Mongols thought nothing of it. Our caravan offered him a good opportunity of performing his journey comfortably, which he at once and without ceremony availed himself of. His first appearance was in one of our halts, where he was discovered in the tent of our Mongols, as if he had dropped from the clouds, and our three Mongols had thenceforth to fill two extra mouths, which must have been a considerable tax on them. The boy was at once placed on our effective staff, and we christened him *Paga-lama*, or "Little Lama," a name not much relished at first, but he soon became reconciled to it. The little lama had left his mother's tent in summer, a few days before; winter had now overtaken him—for there is no autumn or spring in Mongolia—and he was all too thinly clad for such inclement weather. Our lama, seeing the boy pinched with cold in these biting north winds, with the genuine hospitality of a Mongol gave up one of his coats to him, thus unconsciously practising a Christian precept to which few Christians in my experience pay so much practical respect. The little lama's loose leather boots, and particularly the felt stockings inside of them, were considerably travel-worn; and, with all his management, he could not keep his red toes covered from the cold. But he was patient and enduring, and very thankful for what he had got. He had no more long marches to make on foot, for our lama generally contrived to put him on a camel.

On the morning of the 18th of September, we found ourselves starting from a halt at 6 o'clock, which caused a row between us and the Mongols; for though the night had been cold and dark enough to give them an excuse, we admitted no excuses for extra stoppages, and we had been stopped most of the night. It was a cold, raw morning, with a heavy leaden sky, and a fresh southerly wind, very unusual weather in Mongolia. We soon came to a point where the road seemed to terminate abruptly on the brow of a precipice, and it was now plain that we could not have proceeded further without good daylight. From our elevated position we came suddenly on a view of scenery of surpassing magnificence. An amphitheatre of mountains lay before us, rising up in sharp ridges, and tumbled about in the wildest confusion, like the waves of the sea in a storm. The crests of many of them were crowned with patches of wood, and to us, who had lived so long in the flat, treeless desert, the effect of this sudden apparition was as if we had been transported to fairy land.

We had to cross a wide valley that lies half encircled at the foot of the mountains, and our descent was almost precipitous for 500 feet. We had to get out and walk, and the camels had enough to do to get the empty carts down safely.

On the top of the high ground, and at the beginning of the descent, is a large *obon*, or altar, consisting of a cairn of stones. There are many of them in different parts of Mongolia. They are much respected by the Mongols, and have a religio-superstitious character. It is considered the duty of every traveller to contribute something to the heap, the orthodox contribution being undoubtedly a stone. Our lama seldom troubled himself to dismount, and find a stone, but contented himself with plucking a handful of hair from the hump of his camel, and allowing it to be wafted to the *obon*, if the wind should happen to take it there. At the same time he saved his conscience by mumbling a few words from the form of prayer prescribed for such occasions. At the more important *obons*, however, such as the one which has led to these remarks, which are always placed at difficult or dangerous passes, he rode a-head of the caravan, dismounted, and with solemn words and gestures propitiated the good genius of the mountain. The Mongols have a great horror of evil spirits, and have strong faith in the personality, not of one, but many devils. In this respect, they are like the Chinese Buddhists, but I never could detect that they worshipped the devil, as their neighbours do, the whole drift of whose religious ceremonies always seemed to me to be to charm away or make terms with evil spirits. This is, of course, only negative evidence as regards the Mongols, and that from a very slight experience, but the tone of religious sentiment among them is more healthy and elevating, encouraging the belief that devils are not among their objects of worship. They don't speak of the *tchutgour*, or devil, in the same flippant way as the Chinese do of their *kwei*, and although they attribute diseases and misfortunes to *tchutgour* influences, only to be counteracted by lama incantations, they hold that good men, and especially good lamas, never can *see* a *tchutgour*. I have tried to joke with them on the subject, and turn their *tchutgour* notions into ridicule, but the Mongols, though easily amused on any other subject, were sensitively anxious on this, and never spoke of it without serious concern. The rapid and complete recovery of our lama from what seemed to him and his friends a deadly wound, was the cause of no small congratulation to them as establishing the moral excellence of his character, by means of a severe ordeal—as it were a hand-to-hand contest with the powers of evil.

As we advanced across the valley a few drops of rain fell. A halt was summarily ordered, and the Mongols began to run about, hastily unloading camels and unrolling tents, with horror depicted on their faces, muttering to themselves, "*borro beina*," "the rain is coming." There is so little rain in Mongolia, that no great preparations are made for it, and a smart shower disconcerts travelling Mongols as if they were poultry. Before our tents were got up, the rain was falling heavily, and we were all well drenched, but when we had got safely under the canvas, the real misery of our situation flashed upon us—the argols were wet, and we could get no fire! The poor Mongols resigned themselves to their fate with enviable philosophy, looking on their misfortune as one of the chances of war. We were not so well trained in the school of adversity, however, and could not tolerate the idea of sitting in our wet clothes during that cold, rainy day. Besides, past experience had taught us to look for the dreaded north wind after rain, and how could we abide its onset in such a condition? There was but one source from which we could obtain fuel, and that was to break up one of our cases of stores, and burn the wood. This was also wet, but not saturated like the argols, and after some difficulty we lighted a fire in our tent, and gave the Mongols enough to make them a fire also, by which to boil their tea. We were richly rewarded by their looks and expressions of gratitude for such an unexpected blessing. The rain continued all day till sunset, when it cleared up, and the wind came round to N.-W., piping up in the usual manner. We got our tent shifted round, back to wind, and made ourselves exceedingly comfortable. With waterproof sheets and a light cork mattress, the wet ground was of no account, and we could always manage to keep our blankets dry. In the morning the ground was white with snow, and the north wind blowing more pitilessly than ever. A few driving showers of snow fell for some hours after sunrise, and we waited till 10 o'clock before resuming our journey towards the mountains *Tsagan-dypsy* which bounded the plain in our front. *Tsagan* meaning "white," we thought the name highly appropriate, as we gazed the live-long day on their snow-clad slopes. It was a trying day to all of us, and I never suffered so much from cold. The sun seldom showed his face, and the air was charged with black, heavy snow-clouds, which only the violence of the wind prevented from falling. It was impossible to endure the wind, either in cart or on horseback. There was nothing for it but to walk, but that was no easy performance in the teeth of such a gale, and we were fain to take shelter behind the carts, supporting ourselves by holding on to them. I estimated that I walked twenty miles in that way. The camels breasted the storm bravely, and even seemed to enjoy it. The Bactrian camel, at least the Mongol variety, is peculiarly adapted for cold climates. In a hot day he is easily fatigued, and seems almost to melt away in perspiration under his load (hence our constantly travelling at night, in the early part of our journey, and resting in the heat of the day), but in cold weather he braces himself up to his work, and the colder it gets, the better he is.

We were entertained by the few travellers we met with alarming accounts of the state of the river Tolla, which was said to be in flood, and impassable. We paid little heed to such Job's comforters, knowing the Asiatic proneness to figurative language; but our lama was disconsolate, and began to look like a man who feels that some great calamity is hanging over him.

On gaining the Tsagan-dypsy mountains we enter a long, narrow, but very pretty valley, watered by the small river *Kul*, which runs into the *Tolla*. The mountains on both sides of us were well wooded, chiefly with fir with yellow feathery leaves, and small birch. The fir grows to no great size, probably because it is in too great demand for sale in China. Several wood-cutting stations were observed in this valley of the Kul, where the timber is collected and the ox-carts loaded, of which we met so many in the desert.

With the woods, several new birds appear, conspicuous among which are magpies, jackdaws, and pigeons.

The *Yak*, or "long-haired ox," or "grunting ox" (*Poëphagus grunniens*), also now appear in considerable numbers. They are smaller than the average Mongol ox, but seem to be very strong and hardy. They are used solely for draught purposes. It has been supposed that these animals are peculiar to Thibet, but they appear to be also indigenous in Mongolia.

Passing through the Kul valley, our lama purchased two small trees for firewood, giving in exchange half a brick of tea. It was joyfully intimated to us that we should want no more argols, but should find wood all the rest of the journey. The intelligence pleased us not so much on account of the prospect of a more civilised fuel to burn than argols, for, cooking as we did, in the open air, there was not much to choose between the two; but we received it as a tangible evidence that we had really passed the great desert, and were henceforth to travel in a country of mountains and "shaggy wood."

CHAPTER IX.

URGA TO KIACHTA.

JUST as we came in sight of the river *Tolla*, and with our glasses could make out the houses in the Chinese settlement of *Mai-machin* beyond, a heavy, blinding shower of snow came on, which neither man nor beast could face, in the teeth of such a wind as was blowing. The camels were halted and tents hastily pitched, but not before the ground was covered with snow. The storm did not, however, prevent visitors from coming to us from the numerous caravans that were encamped round us in the valley. Eager inquiries were made as to the state of the river, and the information received was to us more gloomy, because more definite, than before. The stream was very rapid, and the water very high. The only boat they had fit to cross it had been swept away by the force of the current, and in an attempt to ford it, two men and a horse had been drowned that very day. Our informants were in a similar predicament to ourselves, and some of them had been waiting several days for an opportunity to cross.

We could no longer discredit these statements, and we acquiesced in our adverse fate to the best of our ability; but it was sorely trying to our patience to be stuck there in sight of *Urga*, the first great break in our journey through Mongolia, with only a little bit of a river between. We were consoled as usual under such circumstances by a good dinner, to the preparation of which we always devoted special care, when we were stopped by compulsion. A few hours' kindly converse with the Mongols in their tent served to while away the long evening. They are, in many things, very much like children, and easily amused. Our simplest plan was to select one of the company, generally the Kitat lama, and make him the subject of a series of imaginary stories that we had heard of him in distant parts. The Mongols are always ready to enjoy a joke at the expense of their friends, though the individual directly interested does not seem to appreciate it. It is a very tender point with a lama to be asked how his wife and family are, as their vows exclude them from matrimonial happiness (or otherwise). They have a long list of stereotyped salutations, which are hurriedly exchanged by travellers as they pass on the road, and more deliberately and sententiously delivered on entering a tent. Tender inquiries after the flocks and herds, wives and children, are among the number, but the latter of course is never addressed to lamas. We, in our ignorance, were not supposed to know the lama *régime*, and we could always shock the feelings of a strange lama by asking after the *chuchung* (wife), and thereby raise a laugh among the listeners.

During our night encampments it was considered necessary for one of the party to keep watch and ward over the goods and chattels, for the Mongols are not so honest as they usually get credit for. Foreigners are disposed to put more confidence in them than they do in each other, and they must surely know their own countrymen best. If a Chinaman were asked what he took such precautions for, he would probably say against wolves and tigers; but the plainspoken Mongols bluntly tell you that thieves are their bugbear. The expression they generally use for thieves is *mochung*, "bad men," and it is questionable whether they recognise any other kind of badness. They don't break up the night into different watches, but one keeps guard the whole night through, the others taking it in turns on subsequent nights. The lama, by virtue of his position as head of the party, gave himself a dispensation, and the onus of watching fell on Tellig and the Kitat lama. When we had strapped down the door of our tent, made all snug for the night, and retired under the blankets with a book, a candle burning on the ground, we used to receive visits from Tellig in his rounds. Lying down on the ground, he would insinuate his large bullet head under the curtain of the tent, and scan us carefully to see if we were asleep. If awake, he would ask us for a light to his pipe, and for permission to smoke it in the tent, as, in the high wind, it would be difficult to keep it alight outside. He would then lie and smoke with half his body inside the tent and half out, and on such occasions he would become very confidential, giving us most interesting accounts of his family affairs. He had a yourt near Tsagan-tuguruk, and in that yourt he had a wife that he was greatly attached to, and two boys that he was very proud of,—one four years old and the other two. He had moderate possessions in cattle, which, in his absence, were cared for by his brother. He had been a long time separated from his family, and while we were at Tsagan-tuguruk he had stolen a few hours to ride over and see his "chickens and their dam"; but our impetuous haste to get away had cut his visit very short. Tellig's story brought qualms of compunction to our mind for what now seemed inconsiderate treatment; for he had, from the first, had all the hard work, and none of the indulgences; moreover he had always done for us cheerfully what he was in no wise bound to do.

The wind continued to howl eerily the whole night, and our canvas flapped about like the sails of a ship in stays. The morning was still bitterly cold, and the sky darkened by heavy snow clouds driving furiously. It required no small resolution to turn out of our warm beds that morning; and I am sure if either of us had been travelling alone, he would have been inclined to lie quiet till called for. But we were each afraid of showing the white feather, and of being twitted with impeding the progress of the journey; we therefore mutually forced ourselves to get up. The Mongols were making no move. As for Tellig, he had just gone to sleep after his night's watching, and it seemed nothing could ever be done without him. With considerable trouble we overcame the *vis inertiæ* of Mr. Lama, and persuaded him to ride down with us to the bank of the river to reconnoitre. The horses were brought in from the hill-side where they had spent the night trying to pick out a few blades of grass from among the stones. My "Dolonor" looked down in the mouth, and did not snort at his master, which heretofore he had never failed of doing on every occasion. The poor brute was completely doubled up with the cold, and could hardly move one leg past another. I immediately presented him to a Mongol, but I am afraid, with his old age and miserable condition, he could not last many more such nights.

A great concourse of people were assembled on the bank of the *Tolla*, many who wanted to cross, and many hangers-on, who make a living by assisting travellers to cross the river. Mongols kept riding backwards and forwards between the river and the various caravans encamped in Kul valley, all bent on the same errand as ourselves. But there was no crossing the Tolla that day. The stream was foaming and roaring like a cataract, with a current of nearly seven miles an hour. It was deep enough to take a man up to the neck, and the bottom was strewn with large round pebbles, making fording difficult, even had the current been moderate and the water shallower. What the boat was like that had been swept away I cannot say; but there was only left a raft made of hollow trees lashed together, and, in the present state of the river, inadequate to any purpose whatever. In the motley crowd there assembled, every one had some sage advice to offer; communications were carried on at the highest pitch of many stentorian lungs, and the place was like another Babel. All concurred in the impossibility of crossing; some thought it would be practicable to-morrow, others were less hopeful. There was nothing for us to do but to admire the truly magnificent scenery with which we were surrounded. The valley of the Kul runs north, and enters the larger valley of the Tolla at right angles. The general aspect of the mountains that overhang Urga is bare, the woods being scattered in small patches. The Tolla rushes out of a gorge in the mountains to the east, and is completely hidden by brushwood and willows, until it debouches on the opening formed by the Kul, its tributary. The Tolla hugs the left side of the valley, leaving a wide flat on the right, over which lies the road to *Maimachin* and *Urga*.

The day continued black and stormy till sunset. In the evening the wind moderated, and at night the stars shone out in all their splendour. The morning of the 21st of September was charming, a bright sun and a blue sky, with hard frost on the ground. The air was still, and the concert of mingled sounds, of cattle lowing, dogs barking, and the general hubbub among the wild Mongols who were in motion in all quarters, was soothing to the feelings. It felt like a summer day, in spite of the hard crust under our feet. I am persuaded that unbroken fine weather would become very tiresome and monotonous; it can only be thoroughly enjoyed by contrast with stormy antecedents.

We again left the caravan to ride to the river, and, like Noah's dove, we returned with the olive-branch in our mouth. The waters had subsided a little, and some camels had actually crossed. There was no doubt of it, for we saw them with our own eyes standing dripping on the bank. The lama of course made difficulties, but we forced him to the attempt, and got the caravan moved down to the water by 2 o'clock. There were two reasons why he felt reluctance to force a passage to-day; first, we had our carts to get through, which was, of course, much more difficult, and even risky, than merely walking a camel through the water with a load on his back. This objection we met by offering to leave our carts behind. The next objection, which the lama did not think it judicious to name to us, but which was nevertheless to him the more cogent of the two, was that he would require many assistants, and in the present condition of the ford, with so many people waiting to cross, they exacted onerous terms for their assistance; for even the simple unsophisticated Mongols understand the mercantile laws of supply and demand.

The regular ford was still too deep, and a more eligible spot was selected, half a mile higher up the stream, where it is divided into three branches, with low flat islands between. The three branches make up a breadth of several hundred yards, and the opposite shore is concealed from view by the small trees and underwood that grow on the islands. The scene at this ford was most animated and exciting. Before proceeding to do anything, a great deal of jabbering had to be gone through, but once the plan of action was settled, our assistants set to work energetically. The two ponies of my companion were taken possession of, each bestridden by a Mongol, with his nether garments either stripped off altogether, or tucked up to his hips. Each took the nose-string of a camel and plunged into the ice-cold water. The camels were wretched, turning their long necks every way to avert their timid eyes from the water, of which they have an instinctive dread. Moral suasion is vigorously applied to a

FORDING THE POLLA NEAR URGA. (Page 117.)

camel's hind-quarters by half a dozen men armed with cudgels, but he still hesitates. The pony in his turn gets tired, standing in the cold water, and tries to back out just as the camel is feeling his way with his fore feet. The rider is equally impatient, with his bare legs dangling in the water, and plies his steed vigorously with his heels. It is all a question of time, and both animals are eventually launched into the stream. The camel's footing on the loose slippery stones is very insecure, and when the deep part is reached, it requires all his strength to prevent the current from floating him clean off his legs. He knows his danger, and trembles in every muscle. The same struggle occurs at each of the three branches, and we all watch the progress of the first detachment with breathless anxiety, as we see the pony gradually sinking till only his head and shoulders are above water. When they are safely landed on *terra firma*, the two camels are unloaded, and brought back in the same way to fetch the two carts. The carts have in the meantime been emptied of our bedding, and various small necessaries we usually kept there, which are lashed up in bundles, and covered with waterproof sheets, ready to put on the back of a camel. The passage of the carts was the most ticklish business of all. They were all wood, except the iron-work about the wheels. Would they sink or swim? If the latter, it would be impossible to cross them in such a current. One was actually floated away, camel and all, but luckily fetched up on a shoal place lower down, whence it was recovered with slight damage. We crossed with the last batch, two on a camel. A Mongol sat behind me, and made me lean over against the current, to give the camel a bias in that direction; but I confess to having felt momentarily nervous, as the poor beast staggered and hesitated in a strong eddying current that almost carried him off his legs. Four hours had been occupied in crossing the Tolla, during all which time the two ponies and their riders were in the water. The men's legs had become a bright red colour, and their teeth chattered audibly ; but they were cheery and light-hearted, and only laughed at their hardships. A dram when it was all over made them as happy as kings. They are undoubtedly a fine hardy race, these Mongols; no wonder that they make such admirable soldiers. All sorts of people were crossing the Tolla with us, among whom were some very old men travelling on horseback. One old woman I observed also, infirm and almost blind, crossing on a pony, her son riding alongside of her and holding her on. These people all take off their boots and trowsers, and carry them on the saddle to put on dry at the other side.

We were now a good mile from the road, and it was getting dark. We could not travel further that night, and did not wish to put up our tent. We therefore accepted an escort, and the proffered hospitality of a Mongol, and galloped to his yourt, which was near the Urga road. The plain is grassy, but rather stony, and intersected by many small watercourses running out of the Tolla. Our host was none other than the *Kitat*, whom we had so summarily dismissed, or at least compelled to send in his resignation, at Tsagan-tuguruk. He received us with open arms in his yourt, and commended us to the good offices of the lady who presided over the cauldron. Whether she was his own wife, or somebody else's wife, we could not clearly determine, but she performed the household duties with exemplary assiduity. A piece of a sheep was immediately put on the fire, while the Kitat and the wife plied us with milk and cheese, and did their best to entertain us with their lively conversation, which turned chiefly on the passage of the Tolla, with an occasional allusion to Tsagan-tuguruk. We, all the while, tried to analyse the motives that actuated the Kitat in going out of his way to show us such civility, seeing we had last parted with him on very indifferent terms. Did he intend to heap coals of fire on our heads? or to show us that Mongols bear no malice? Or was he proud to show his friends that he had such distinguished guests in his tent? I believe he was moved by none of these considerations, but simply by the feeling of true hospitality that is natural to all Mongols. It turned out that the feast our host had prepared was solely for us, for he himself was already engaged to dine with our lama and his Tolla-river friends when they should come up. We were visited by many Mongols, some of whom appeared to belong to the family, and spent a very pleasant evening. When bed-time came, and the fire was out, the hole in the roof was covered over, and the yourt was cleared of all but ourselves, the Kitat and the lady.

Many valuable hours were lost next morning in settling with the Mongols for their services of the preceding day. It cost three taels in all—about a guinea—a sum which seemed to our lama exorbitant, and caused many rueful shakes of his shaven head. During the bustle of preparation, a heartless robbery was committed on me. A small pic-nic case, containing a drinking-glass, knife, fork and spoon, was stolen out of the cart. If they had stolen a horse, or our tent, or box of Sycee silver, I could have born it with equanimity, but the loss of articles so constantly in use was hard to bear. I missed them every hour of the day, and it was of course impossible to replace them. I was compelled, on emergencies, thereafter to use the *ei-iga* of some stray Mongol, which went much against the grain. They are so uncleanly in their habits that their wooden cups get frequently encrusted with dirt. Their usual mode of cleaning them is to give the inside of the cup a scrape with the back of the thumb-nail, or, when they mean to be very particular, they clean their cup in the same manner as a dog cleans a plate.

Having bought another pony for myself from the Kitat,

first, because I wanted it; and second, because I wanted to acknowledge his hospitality, we formed the order of march, which was this : Tellig, mounted on a pony, to accompany us and pilot us to Maimachin and Urga, and then follow after the caravan, which was to take a short cut from Maimachin and cut off a corner at Urga, not passing through the town at all. Maimachin is a Chinese commercial settlement about two miles from the ford of the Tolla, established, as the Mongols believe, for the purpose of swindling them. It is a unique-looking place, built of wood for the most part, the outer wall enclosing the whole, as also the fences round each compound, being made of rough poles placed uprightly and close together. It is entered by a gate, which has the appearance of being in constant use. The mutual jealousies of the two races lead them both to seclude themselves for their own protection. The Chinese shopkeepers in the settlement are well-to-do people, mostly, I believe, Shansi men. We rode about the streets for some time trying to find a few necessaries we required, but were not very successful. At last we stopped at a blacksmith's shop to try and get our ponies shod. The artisan to whom we addressed ourselves did not understand us, but ran into the next shop and brought out a well-dressed young fellow, who at once addressed us in Russian. He could not comprehend our ignorance of that language; but he soon condescended to speak Chinese, which a Chinaman never will do if he can get on in any other language. We could not deal with the man, however, and being short of time we yielded to Tellig's importunity, and turned our heads towards Urga. The streets of Maimachin are canals of black mire, and so uneven that our beasts could with difficulty keep their legs. We were heartily glad to get out into the open air again.

On the way to Urga we passed a large house nearly finished, on a rising ground, and in a fine commanding position. It is the house of the Russian consul; but Tellig would not have it so,—said he knew the Russian house, and would take us there all right. He certainly did take us to a Russian piggery, where a few so-called merchants lived in the most barbarous and filthy condition. We could not even communicate with them, except in the little we had picked up of the Mongol language. To see the consul we had to go all the way back again to the big house we had passed. Mr. Shishmaroff, the vice-consul in charge, received us very hospitably, and treated us to a civilised breakfast on a clean white tablecloth. It was a greater luxury to us than probably even our host imagined, for we had not seen an egg for twenty-seven days, there being no fowls in Mongolia. Mr. Shishmaroff must lead a very solitary life in Urga, having no one with whom to associate but the high Chinese mandarin and the Mongol deputy-khan. His house-supplies are, for the most part, brought from Kiachta, the Russian frontier town, 175 miles distant. The Russian government keeps up a considerable establishment at Urga, the consul having a body-guard of twenty Cossacks, besides the twenty Russian carpenters who are at work on the new house, and other hangers-on. The object of such an expensive establishment, at a place like Urga, where Russia has no interests whatever to protect, can only be divined by the light of its traditional policy of progress in Asia. It has long been considered* that the Khingan chain of mountains running east and west past Urga to the head waters of the river Amoor forms the "natural boundary" of Siberia, and consequently advantage has been taken of disputes between the Mongol khans of former times and some Russian merchants who had penetrated as far as Urga, to gain a foot-hold there, which will certainly never be relinquished until the whole tract of country enclosed by these

* See Bell of Antermony.

mountains and by the river Kerulun, the head stream of the Amur, to Lake Hurun or Dalainor, has been annexed to Siberia. After that, the "natural boundary" will be discovered to lie still farther to the south. Russia is in no hurry to enter on the possession of this new territory, but, in the mean time, the country has been surveyed, and is included in Russian maps of Eastern Siberia. The transfer will be made quietly, and without bloodshed, when the favourable moment comes, for none understand better than Russian diplomatists the *suaviter in modo* when it suits their purpose. No one will be much a loser by the change. The Emperor of China will lose his nominal suzerainty over a country that even now probably costs him more than it is worth. The Mongol tribes, with their chiefs, would merely become subjects of one autocrat instead of another; but everything else would probably go on as at present until time brought gradual changes. The Chinese merchants don't care a straw about who is king as long as they are left to their peaceful occupations; and the Russian government is too enlightened to throw any obstacles in the way of a trade which has done more than anything else to develop the resources of the Siberian deserts.

The name, *Urga*, or the camp, is not in common use. The Mongols call it *Kuren* or *Ta Kuren*, which Huc translates the "great enclosure." The situation of the town, or camp, or whatever it may be called, is romantic in the extreme. It stands on a wide plateau about a mile from the Tolla. Behind the Kuren is a bold and rugged mountain range which shelters it from the northerly gales, while in front there is never wanting a pleasing prospect for the eye to rest upon in the roughly wooded mountains beyond the Tolla, that hem in the valley of that river. The river itself is hardly seen from the town, being concealed by the growth of brushwood on its banks and on the low islands that lie in the stream.

The population is scattered over the plateau, without much reference to regularity of arrangement, and instead of streets the dwellings of the Mongols are separated by crooked passages. The only buildings in the place are temples, official residences, and the houses occupied by Chinese or Russians. The Mongols live in tents, as they do in the desert, with this difference, that each family surrounds itself with a wooden palisade as a protection from thieves, who are numerous among the pilgrims, who resort on pious missions to the Kuren.

A man was found to shoe our ponies, which he did well and expeditiously, and at a very moderate charge, about half the sum demanded at Maimachin. The shoeing-smith was a Chinaman—of course—for it seems the Mongols never do, under any circumstances, shoe their horses. They have no hard roads, it is true, to contend with, but even the gravelly sand of many parts of the desert does sometimes wear down the soles of their horses' feet, and particularly the toes, until the animal becomes useless. They seldom allow them to get so bad as that, however, as the large herds they possess afford them the means of frequently changing their saddle-horses.

There are no shops in the Kuren, that being contrary to the Mongol nature. All things necessary for desert life are to be purchased for bricks of tea in a large open space where a great bazaar is held under booths, principally by Mongol women. There you may purchase horses, cattle, tents, leather harness, saddles, beef, mutton, caps for lamas or black men, female ornaments, felt,—in short everything within the scope of Mongol imagination. Our small purchases were effected very satisfactorily—no attempt was made to impose on us because we were strangers, and we had reason to congratulate ourselves that we were not at the mercy of Chinese. In nothing is the contrast between

Mongols and Chinese more marked than in the common honesty of shopkeepers or hawkers. It may indeed be said with truth that mercantile honesty allows a man to get as much as he can for his goods, but it is very doubtful whether such a maxim can properly be stretched so as to justify a shopkeeper in taking a customer at a disadvantage.

The nucleus of the Mongol settlement at Urga is the Great Lamasery of the Guison-tamba or Lama-king of the Mongols. In this monastery, and in the minor ones round it, it has been said that 30,000 lamas reside, which estimate, however, must be received with caution. The two great lamaseries of Dobodorsha and Daichenalon are built in an indentation of the mountains that form the northern valley which opens into the valley of the Tolla at Urga. As our route from Urga lay on the slope of the opposite side of the valley, and our time was exhausted, we had not the chance of visiting these temples. The buildings are of vast extent, as plain almost as if they were barracks; but what ornamentation there is about them is quiet and in good taste. They differ considerably from the Chinese style of architecture, and are no doubt Thibetan. An inscription in the Thibetan language has been placed on the slope of the hill above the monasteries. The characters are formed by means of white stones, and the size of them is such as to render the writing perfectly legible at the distance of a mile.

All good lamas esteem it an honour to be able to say they have made a pilgrimage to the Kuren, and these devotees come from enormous distances—some from the Manchurian wildernesses in the far east, and others from the frontiers of Thibet.* There are many small shrines on the plateau on which the town stands, erected for the convenience of those ascetics who are desirous of commending themselves to the

* Huc.

favour of Bhudda and to the respect of their fellows. I observed one of these deluded people performing a journey to a shrine, which was then about a quarter of a mile from him. He advanced by three measured steps one stage, made sundry prostrations, falling flat on his face on the stony ground, repeated prayers, and then advanced again. I know not from what distance he had come, or how long it was since he had commenced this slow and painful march; but, on a rough calculation, we made out that it would take him two days more, at the same rate of progress, to reach the goal.

The Lama-king of the Kuren is regarded by the Mongols as a god. He can never die—he only transmigrates. The whole of the Kalkas tribes are under his sway, and this personage is consequently an object of constant jealousy to the emperors of China, who keep an anxious watch over his proceedings. The lama system has been greatly humoured by the Chinese emperors from early times, and the theocracy of Mongolia and Thibet is mainly of their creation. The secular sovereignty of these nations became spiritual by an accident or an after-thought, and does not, like the Japanese, trace back into the dawn of history its descent from the gods. The last independent king of Thibet finding himself in great trouble from within and from without, escaped from the cares of government by becoming a lama. This happened about the year 1100 A.D., and, in a few years afterwards, Thibet became subject to China. When Kublai became Emperor of China he made a lama of Thibet king, and the kings who succeeded the Mongols in China followed up the idea of conciliating the lama power by making eight of them kings. These afterwards (A.D. 1426) took the title of grand lama, and the chief of them became the Dalai-lama of Thibet,* who from that

---

* Histoire des Huns, De Guignes, Paris, 1756.

time to this has been the head of the Bhuddist religion and the vassal king of Thibet. It would have been impossible, under any circumstances, for the Dalai-lama to have maintained a real surveillance over the widely-scattered tribes who acknowledged his spiritual sway; and in fact his authority over his distant dependents began to be greatly relaxed from the time that the emperors of China completed the subjection of all the tribes who now inhabit what is called Chinese Tartary. The Emperor Kang-hi, under whose reign this was accomplished, promoted the independence of the lama-king of the Kalkas with a view to severing the tie that bound them to their neighbours the Eleuths or Kalmuks, and in order to accustom the vassal chiefs of the various tribes to look more and more to the Chinese emperors for government and protection. By this wise policy the Chinese government sought to divert the Mongols from forming any combination which might threaten the stability of the foreign rule to which the tribes had just been subjected. The Chinese ambassadors at the court of the Dalai-lama, men of great talent, and trained in diplomatic subtlety, furthered these purposes of their government by holding in check the pretensions of the Dalai-lama, while appearing to support him, and, by indirect means, neutralising his authority whenever the exercise of it seemed to clash with the Chinese policy. The lama-king of the Kalkas has therefore become virtually independent of his spiritual superior at Lassa, for whom he has about the same regard as Napoleon has for the Pope.

The "Urga" of the Kalkas has not always been where it stands now. In 1720,* it was on the river Orkhon, near its confluence with the Selenga, some distance north of the present Urga. But some time before that date the Kalkas had their head-quarters where the Urga now stands, for we

* Bell.

read* of the Eleuths having "destroyed the magnificent temple, which the Kutuchtu had built near the river Tula, of yellow varnished bricks," about the year 1688.

The mountain fastnesses of the Khangai range, stretching south-west from Urga, and bordering the great desert, are eminently favourable to the assembling of armies, and afford a safe retreat for fugitive tribes. The richness of the pastures, and the abundance of water supplied by the larger rivers, and by the mountain streams that are found in every ravine, afford sustenance for unlimited herds and flocks. The first Huns had their head-quarters not far from Urga long before the Christian era. The site of the old Mongol capital of Kara Korum is about 160 miles from Urga in a south-west direction. Thence the Mongols issued forth to conquer Asia and Europe, and thither they returned, when driven out of China in 1368, to found the new empire of the Yuen of the north, under a Grand Khan of the Kalkas. There also flourished Ung-Khan, celebrated in the 12th century, from his name having been used by the Nestorians as a stalking-horse for perpetrating what has generally been considered as a gigantic hoax on the Pope and various European sovereigns. The Nestorians caused it to be reported that they had converted this potentate and his subjects to Christianity; and that the Khan had been by them baptised under the name of John. Letters were written in the name of this "Prester John" as he was called, to his royal brethren in the west. These seem to have been credited as genuine, for more than one mission was despatched from European courts to make the acquaintance of this most Christian king. There is, perhaps, as much reason to believe as to doubt the conversion of this prince. These expeditions, if they failed in their main purpose, were

* Un. Hist., vol. iv. p. 77.

at least the means of giving to the world much curious information concerning the inhabitants of the Great Tartary.

"Prester John," or, to call him by his right name, Ung-Khan, was the most powerful Tartar prince of his day. Genghis, then called Temoujin, when a very young man, repaired to the court of Ung-Khan to seek aid to repress disturbances among his own tribes, and soon became commander-in-chief of Ung-Khan's armies, in which capacity he displayed the high military qualities which afterwards made him master of nearly the whole civilised world. He was a great favourite with the Khan, and all went on smoothly until the unlucky day when Ung-Khan's daughter fell in love with young Temoujin. The course of true love did not run smooth with him, for his rivals being fired with enmity, began to plot against him with the Khan, who in time yielded to their instigation, and betrayed his best friend. Temoujin remained true to his colours long after he lost the confidence of the Khan; but the discovery of a deeply-laid plot against his life at length brought him to an open rupture with his sovereign. They fought a pitched battle between the rivers Tolla and Kerlon, probably at a short distance eastward from the present Urga. Ung-Khan's forces had greatly the advantage in numbers, but the Khan was no match for his accomplished general. Temoujin gained a decisive victory. The Khan escaped from the field of battle, but was soon afterwards killed, and his dynasty destroyed. Temoujin now found himself master of the situation, and was installed at Kara-Korum in 1206, under the title of Genghis-Khan.

Having done our business at the Kuren, we started rather late in the afternoon in pursuit of the camels. The route lay about north through a valley. It was bad travelling, owing to the rough nature of the ground. It is naturally soft and boggy, and the melted snow in the low ground had greatly aggravated the evil. When past the great monasteries, we got on higher ground on the slope of the hills, but this was, if possible, more slippery than the low road, for the melting snow above kept up a continuous supply of moisture which made the road very difficult even for horses. We soon came upon the traces of camels, which we had no difficulty in identifying by the side-slips down the hill made by their broad splay feet. This is always dangerous work for camels, and we had some apprehension of accidents from "splitting," or dislocating the hip joints. We were in consequence not ill-pleased to come upon the caravan a little after sunset, encamped in a narrow ravine looking west, and at the foot of a steep pass. Several of the camels had fallen, but fortunately none were injured. It was a fine moonlight night, and we tried to get our people to proceed on the journey; but the camels could not draw the carts over the pass, steep as it was, and with such slippery roads. Bullocks had been sent for, and they were expected every hour, of course, but it might have been evident to us that they had no intention of coming before morning. Anyhow we would not be the occasion of delay, and therefore slept in our carts ready for a move at any moment. At daylight on the 23rd of September the bullocks came, two for each cart, accompanied by a young woman and a boy, who proceeded to harness them in a very slow and deliberate manner. The beasts did their work, but with difficulty, owing to the broken character of the road. On the top of the pass our lama paid his respects to an obon, by throwing a large piece of wood on it, and the bullocks took the carts safely down the other side of the pass, which was quite as steep as the ascent. We then proceeded with the camels through valleys and undulations, among fine mountain scenery, avoiding the main road, and striking off through various bye-paths, all apparently well known to our conductors. At 3 p.m. we halted off *Narim* valley to dine, intending to take advantage of the moonlight to resume our night travelling. But as bad luck would have it a snowstorm came on, and we had to remain where we were till morning. All hopes of mending our pace from Urga to Kiachta now vanished. We had already lost two good nights out of the four, or at most five days which is considered ample time for the journey; and if the stormy weather were to continue, which it looked very like doing, we might be the whole winter on the road. The beasts had little to eat but snow all night. In the morning the ground was white, but the storm was over. Our old enemy the wind began early in the day to stir the twigs of the trees, and though he came in like a lamb, we had but too sure a presentiment of what was coming. It blew fiercely all day, and we walked during the greater part of it. The slight covering of snow on the ground soon melted under the combined action of the sun and wind. The latter agency is certainly the more powerful of the two, when the atmosphere is above freezing temperature. Our nights were always very frosty, but the sun had still sufficient influence during the middle of the day to moisten the surface of the ground.

Over a steep pass and down into another valley we joined the main road, which is now very broad and good. Our march continued to be diversified by valleys and undulations, the scene constantly changing, and now and again opening out enchanting views of scenery, with every variety of rock and river, wooded hills and high mountain ranges tumbling on each other. The wind, that had blown bitterly cold all day, lulled at sunset; the sky continued clear, and we had a calm frosty night. Halted at 10 p.m. in *Gurun-dsata*, a broad rich valley, with abundant grass, and supporting vast herds of cattle, which the clear moonlight revealed to us. The beauties of this spot were only fully discovered at sunrise the next morning, which being calm and fine, we were in the best humour to enjoy the rocky, woody, and pastoral scenes around us. It was plain we had got into a country altogether different from the Mongol steppes. The valleys are all watered by streams, and the soil susceptible of high cultivation.

We are now frightened with another bugbear, in the shape of an unfordable river, the *Khara-gol*, or "black-river." It seemed we were destined to be delayed by every possible contrivance of nature, for these rivers are very rarely flooded. Were it otherwise, some device would certainly have been found to meet the emergency. It was all the more hard, therefore, that these paltry little Mongol rivers should get themselves up into such a state of fury just when we were passing through the country.

During our march towards Khara river, we struck the river *Boro*, a tributary of the Khara, which waters a fine broad valley containing the largest Mongol population we had seen anywhere collected in one place. As we followed the course of the Boro down the valley, we passed several apparently separate communities, all rich in cattle. A novel sight here met our eye, the cultivation of a coarse kind of rye, called by the Mongols, *boota*. They were harvesting this as we passed, carting it to the yourts in a rough sort of wooden cart, and stacking it up. This seems to show that the Mongols are not naturally averse to cultivation, when they are favourably circumstanced for carrying it out. Some of their tribes, such as those in Western Toumet, mentioned by Huc, do indeed systematically cultivate the ground. The sun had set before we got to the end of the valley, and we encamped in the evening not far from the left bank of the Khara-gol, sending out the lama with a native of the district to survey a crossing for the morning.

Early on the 26th we advanced to the river at a place higher up than the usual ford. Carts were unloaded, and the passage effected in the same way as the Tolla, but, the

M

river being much smaller, less time was lost in the operation. There is always a busy scene at these fords, particularly when a drove of cattle have to be got over. One poor man spent the whole morning in fruitless endeavours to drive half-a-dozen cattle through the river, but the neighbours at last came to his assistance, and led them through one by one.

There was a steep pass before us, a few miles distant, and at a yourt near the Khara four sturdy little yaks were engaged to get our carts over. A young lama courier, well versed in the Russian language, whom we found in the yourt, where he had spent the night, afforded us no end of fun all the morning. He was a great wag, and affected to be a man of the world, travelling constantly as he did between the court of Peking and Kiachta. He chaffed our lama more than he liked, criticising his cattle, and offering to buy him out. As a specimen of how these couriers do their work, this young scamp had not only spent the whole night in a yourt, but waited in the morning for our party, and kept company with us till near mid-day.

The pass is up a steep and rugged ravine, thickly wooded with white-skinned birch-trees. The trees do not grow to any size before they rot in the heart, and become hollow, when the wind blows them over. Few of them have a proper trunk, but two or three strong suckers shooting up from the root. It makes excellent firewood, but is unfit for any other purpose.

In the ascent the view is entirely shut in by the woods, but on the top, near the *Obon*, is a clear space, from which an imposing view is obtained of the hills and dales behind and before us, with the Boro valley spread out at our feet. In the descent we plunge again into the thick woods, emerging at the foot into a long valley leading to *Bain-gol*. This is a very small river, with soft, boggy ground on either side, very bad walking for camels. The river, like the others we had crossed, runs westwards and northwards. On the north side of Bain-gol we halted from sunset till midnight, and at daylight entered another fine, long valley, through which runs the *Shara-gol*, the "yellow," or "sandy river," for it may be translated either way. In this valley the grass grew more luxuriantly than we had yet seen. Crowds of Mongols were settled here, and the valley was covered with enormous herds of cattle. The people were busy cutting the long grass with scythes, which they handle very skilfully, and stacking it up round their yourts. This grassy spot was selected for wintering in, and is no doubt less populous in the summer season, when the grass is green and abundant in the country. A steep pass takes us out of this valley, but we still follow to the left the course of the river for some distance. We halted about 4 o'clock, the lama having ridden to a distant yourt to buy a sheep. He could not bring it with him, but must needs return to our tent, and send Tellig, who was a "black man," to fetch the sheep, thereby losing much valuable time. The lama notions on this subject are absurd in the extreme. They will not kill an animal, nor will they carry it to be killed. But they will bargain for and purchase the animal for the purpose of getting it killed, and they will eat it after it is killed, thus becoming "accessory after the fact," as well as before it. I never could understand the logic of this practical application of the doctrine of transmigration, for it always appeared to me that on the hypothesis of the soul of Bhudda or any relative being in captivity in the body of a sheep, it would be a simple act of charity to release it by procuring the transmigration.

It rained a little at sunset, but no gale of wind followed, as on former occasions.

At midnight we proceeded over a stiff sandy pass, and got the carts through by putting an extra camel to each of them. This was followed by another stiff pass, a little sandy, but road pretty good, and so on through the night, till we descended about 9 o'clock next day to the banks of the *Iro-gol*, a smooth flowing river, 100 yards wide, and ten feet deep. Seeing hosts of caravans on both sides of the river we expected to have to "wait a wee" before we could get across, but were agreeably surprised to find a passage ready for us in a few hours. Rafts made of hollowed trees lashed together transport the baggage, the camels and horses, unloaded, are led from the boats, and swim across. The current of the Iro was about three miles an hour. The right bank of the river at the place we crossed is a great flat, but the left bank is hilly and well wooded, and apparently closed in by bluffs on the right bank above and below us, for the river is very tortuous. It forms altogether a very pretty valley. We had to spend a good many hours basking in the warm sunshine, waiting for all the force to get over. When the caravan was ready to start we induced the lama to ride ahead with us through *Talabulyk*, taking a sackful of mutton to be boiled at some yourt ready for Tellig and his friend when they came up. By this means we saved much time, and gave the Mongols no excuse for another halt. One long march would bring us to Kiachta, and we were the more anxious to lose no time, because a storm, or some other unforeseen event, might delay us again. We travelled hard all night over rough roads, through dense pine forests, and shortly after daylight we came out on a rather sandy open space, across which, at a distance of eight miles, Tellig pointed out two white specks, informing us, with an air of triumph, that that was Kiachta. They were two of the church spires that form landmarks for all Russian towns.

Here we were, then, at last, on the 29th of September, at the end of a journey which had sometimes seemed interminable. Thirty-four days in travelling 780 miles! Think of that, ye who fly about the country in express trains. Of course the high Russian officials who pass occasionally between Peking and St. Petersburg have a quicker mode of getting across Mongolia. The post horses kept for the couriers are at their disposal, and by some pre-arrangement they have relays all the way, and so they travel in their own comfortable carriages from Kiachta to Peking in twelve days or so.

CHAPTER X.

MONGOLS—HISTORICAL NOTES.

A PECULIAR interest surrounds these wandering tribes of the desert. In them we see the living representatives of the ancient Huns, and of the yet more ancient Scythians. Of them came Attila, "the Scourge of God," who with his barbarian hordes shook the foundations of Europe in the fifth century, and accelerated the downfall of the old Roman empire; of them came also the redoubtable warriors who desolated Asia and Europe six hundred years ago.

The Mongol tribes are exceedingly conservative in their habits; their fashions never change. A description of their manners in the time of Genghis, or even of Attila, is equally applicable now. Everything goes to show that in the form of their tents, in their dress, their social customs, and their mode of life, the Mongols of to-day have changed but little since they first became known to history.

The early history of the Huns is involved in obscurity. They appear to have existed as a pastoral people, inhabiting the east of the desert of Gobi from about 1200 B.C., during which time they were frequently at war with the Chinese. The first authentic accounts of them date from about the year 200 B.C., when they greatly extended their empire, and became very formidable neighbours to China. It was in the third century before the Christian era that the Chinese built the famous wall as a protection from the inroads of the warlike Huns, who, notwithstanding, laid China under tribute.

Vouti, of the Han dynasty (died 87 B.C.), gained a bloody victory over the Huns, and was the first to break their power in China. He followed up his military success by the application of the craft for which his race was, even at that early date, distinguished. By diligently promoting dissension among the tribes he succeeded in severing many of them from their allegiance to the Tanjou, the title then adopted by the kings of the Huns. The Tanjou himself became afterwards a vassal to the Chinese emperors, and was fain to lick the dust for a dependent kingship.

About 100 years after the birth of Christ, the Huns were broken up and scattered. The Huns of the South, who had previously seceded from the main body, and had established their dynasty in alliance with China, held together till the year 216 A.D. The Northern Huns, being distressed by a great famine, were attacked by the tribes whom they had so long oppressed, and were compelled to seek safety in flight. From that era we must date the migrations of the Hunnish tribes. They were again subdivided. One branch wandered to the coast of the Caspian Sea, where they settled, and became modified in their character under the influence of a more genial climate; their nomad habits were gradually abandoned; and they became civilised. These were called the White Huns.

Another branch migrated in a north-westerly direction, and in their march had to contend with a more rigorous climate. Exasperated by their struggles with the elements and with many enemies, they retained all their savageness in their new settlement on the Volga. These restless warriors had barely secured their own existence in the west, when they began to attack their neighbours. After conquering the Alani, a nation only a little less barbarous than themselves, and adding to their own forces those of the vanquished tribes, the Huns became the terror of the Goths, and these also fell a prey to the invaders before the end of the fourth century of the Christian era.

But the power of these wandering tribes was always liable to be paralysed by the jealousies of rival chiefs. Their notions of government were crude; hereditary succession was held of little account among them. The Huns were only formidable to their neighbours when they were under the leadership of chiefs who possessed sufficient vigour to rise pre-eminent over all others, and the talent or the craft to secure to themselves absolute power.

Attila was one of these. The Huns were already in the ascendant when he came to the throne; but his genius, energy, and insatiable ambition soon rendered them the terror of all Europe, and himself the greatest barbarian that ever wielded the sceptre. Attila had a body-guard of subject kings. His effective force has been variously estimated at half-a-million and at seven hundred thousand men. He enriched himself with the spoils of all nations; yet in the height of his barbaric pride he retained in camp the simple habits of his ancestors. Having subdued every hostile tribe within his reach, and incorporated their armies with his own, he threw the whole weight of his forces on the corrupt and degenerate Roman Empire, which was brought to the feet of the conqueror and compelled to accept conditions of peace the most degrading that the insolence of the invader could dictate.

Desolation everywhere followed the march of Attila, for destruction was ever the glory of the barbarians. As the old Huns lived by predatory warfare, so the hosts of Attila were actuated, only in a higher degree, by the savage instincts of wild beasts. But their power only held together while there was food for pillage, and a master mind to direct their enterprise. And thus their reign of terror in Europe was of brief duration. A heavy debauch cut short the career of Attila, and he died an inglorious death in his own bed from the bursting of an artery. The empire of his creation collapsed after his death amid contending factions; and in A.D. 468, just fifteen years after the death of Attila, the empire of the Huns was utterly destroyed, and their name disappeared from history.

The shepherds tended their flocks in the steppes of Tartary, and 700 years passed away before another chief arose to summon the scattered tribes to his standard. During that period sundry insignificant dynasties succeeded each other on the outskirts of the Chinese dominions. The Turks also appeared in the interval, and established a formidable power, which lasted from the sixth to the eighth century. They issued from the Altai mountains, where they had served the Geougen Tartars who had overwhelmed the Huns after the death of Attila. The Turks, or Turki, reduced the Geougen, and, it is said, almost extirpated them. These Turks have been supposed to have been identical in race with the Huns who preceded, and the Mongols who followed, them.* But there is much reason to doubt their consanguinity.† The great skill in iron working for which the original Turks were distinguished, seems sufficient to mark a difference between them and the ancestors of the pure Mongols. They shaved the beard also in token of grief, and were considered by the Persians handsome men.‡ The Huns and Mongols had almost no beard, and in the eyes of all writers who have thought it worth while to describe their persons, they were remarkable for their deformity.

It would, however, be a hopeless task to unravel the descent of the various races miscalled Tartars. The old Chinese

---

* De Guignes. Hist. des Huns.   † Memoirs of Baber. Erskine's Introd.
‡ Un Hist. vol. iii. p. 365.

records have preserved little more than the catalogue of kings and battles, and of the rise and fall of dynasties. The Tartar powers that have successively risen up in Asia have never been composed of a homogeneous race. Their names, even, have generally been taken from some small tribe or family which accident rendered prominent ; and the names Tartar, Turk, and Mongol, have been perpetuated and misapplied to armies and confederations of mixed races. The wanderings of these mixed tribes, the dissolution of empires which arose among them, and the reconstruction of these empires under new combinations, have constantly tended to the amalgamation in blood and language of races distinct in origin, but following the same nomadic habits. Their mode also of dealing with prisoners of war, and the conditions which they imposed on conquered nations, conduced still more to the fusion and confusion of races. It was unusual with the Huns or Mongols to spare their prisoners, unless they could employ them either as slaves or soldiers, or make profit by their ransom. The men were massacred, and the eligible women were appropriated by the conquerors. A supply of women was exacted as tribute from subject states. This gross indignity was ruthlessly imposed on the Chinese ; and " a select band of the fairest maidens of China was annually devoted to the rude embraces of the Huns."* These practices must have tended greatly to enhance the perplexity of ethnologists in attempting to analyse the masses of men who, by the vicissitudes of war, were from time to time assembled under one standard, and received the name of the dominant family.

When the Huns appeared in Europe, however, they were portrayed by the Goths and Romans in graphic but distorted terms. Through the haze of these hideous caricatures,† and

* Gibbon, vol. iii. p. 363. † Ibid. p. 371.

the fabulous origin which fear and hatred attributed to the
Huns, we cannot fail to identify in them the form and features of the modern Mongols. Whatever be the descent of
the numerous Turki tribes, and whatever changes may have
been brought about by intermixture, change of climate, &c.,
in the pastoral peoples, the great race of the Mongols has in
the main preserved its manners and its characteristics through
all its revolutions and migrations, and has proved its unity in
blood with the Huns of Attila. The Mongols are certainly
far from being a handsome people, but the Romans, themselves models of symmetry, greatly exaggerated their deformity. The barbarians were esteemed so fiendish in their
aspect, that the Goths, to account for the phenomenon, were
obliged to invent the fable of the descent of the Huns from
the unholy union of Scythian witches with infernal spirits.
They were inhumanly ugly. Attila himself was hideous.
Yet that did not deter the young Princess Honoria from betraying, or feigning, a passion for him. That spirited lady,
with a courage worthy of a better cause, found means of
secretly communicating with the king of the Huns, and
urged him to claim her as his bride.

In the thirteenth century, Genghis became Khan * of all
the Mongols, who under him were once more the terror of
the world. Genghis had already conquered the Naimans, a
powerful people in their day; and invaded Tangout. When
he had assembled under his standard the tribes of his own
people and of the nations whom he had conquered, he was
impelled by his restless ambition to keep them in motion.
The lust of conquest became his ruling passion, and every
new trophy added fuel to its flame. He first invaded Kitai,
or northern China, overran the territories of the then powerful Kin, desolated their cities and villages, and massacred

---

* The title of Khan was first assumed by the Geougen, in the fifth century.

their people, and then retired to the river Tolla to recruit, having added to his army many Chinese of all ranks. The seven years' campaign in the west followed shortly after, during which Genghis conquered Persia and Bukhara, destroyed many populous cities, and put to the sword prodigious numbers of human beings. His lieutenants extended their ravages still further westward, while Genghis himself returned to his head-quarters at Kara-Korum. Kitai was again invaded, and Tangout subjugated. On the death of Genghis, in 1227, the succession to the Khanate fell to his son Oktai, who followed up the conquest of China according to instructions delivered by Genghis on his death-bed. But the empire had become so unwieldy, and the distances that separated the divisions of it so vast, that it could no longer subsist in its integrity. It was soon split up into sections, which were parcelled out to the descendants of Genghis. Some reigned in Persia, and some in Kapchak, a territory stretching from the Caspian Sea to Kazan, and covering a large portion of the steppe of the Kirghis. The little dynasty of the Nogai Tartars was also founded in Europe by a descendant of Genghis. The Tartar kingdoms of Kazan and the Crimea were both offshoots from the khans of Kapchak. Batou, Khan of Kapchak, or the Golden Horde, took Moscow and wasted the Russian provinces. Kublai, who succeeded to China, was the greatest of them all. In addition to that country, he possessed Pegu, Thibet, and the whole of Tartary; while Cochin China, Tonquin, and Corea paid him tribute. He was, moreover, acknowledged by all the other khans as their chief. But the whole continent of Asia lay between him and his vassals, and his suzerainty soon became a name only, and in course of time the form also was discontinued.

The Mongols were, however, incapable of maintaining a settled government. The expeditions to subjugate Japan having proved fruitless, there was no other country left for them to conquer; this quiescent state was unnatural to them, and Chinese culture demoralised them in less than a hundred years.

Russia was held by a tenure more suitable to the nomad habits of the Mongols. Armies had to be maintained, and the khans of the Golden Horde found occupation in keeping down the Russian princes. They therefore held their supremacy in Europe, until they did the work of their enemies by quarrelling amongst themselves, but their yoke was not finally shaken off till the fifteenth century.

Before the empires founded by the family of Genghis had been wholly broken up, another great Mongol conqueror appeared in the person of Timour, or Tamerlane. Born under happier auspices, and brought up in contact with more civilised people, Timour added to the native ferocity and the ambition of universal empire of his ancestors, the arts and some of the refinements of education. He was, moreover, a zealous Mahommedan, and drew from the Koran encouragements in his career of conquest, and excellent moral maxims which seemed in strange contrast with his life. In a military point of view, Timour's life was a brilliant success. Before his death he placed twenty-seven crowns on his head; he conquered India, and boasted that he had penetrated northwards to the region of perpetual day. His conquests outstripped those of Alexander. "On the eastern bank of the Hyphasis, on the edge of the Desert, the Macedonian hero halted and wept; the Mogul entered the desert, reduced the fortress of Batnir, and stood in arms before Delhi."* He captured Delhi, and "purified his soldiers in the blood of the idolaters." Timour, when he was seventy years old, resolved to re-conquer China, from which country

* Gibbon, vol. ix. p. 10.

the family of Genghis had been recently expelled. He despatched his armies from Samarcand for the expedition, but he himself died on the way, in 1405, and his empire fell to pieces through the incapacity of his sons.

Timour had perhaps the honour of shedding more blood than any of his predecessors; but, like them, he was incapable of governing what he had conquered. His boast that a child might carry a purse of gold from the east to the west, could be justified only on the supposition that he had pacified Asia by making it a solitude.

He was considered a usurper by the Mongols of his day. He made war on his own people because they were idolaters; yet the modern Mongols worship him, beguiling their long evenings in their tents by chanting invocations to his memory.

The next great Mongol who left his mark on the world was Timour's great-grandson Baber, who conquered Delhi in 1528, and founded there the dynasty of the Great Mogul. But Baber was ashamed of his descent, and despised the Mongol character. It was probably to his throwing off the barbarism of his ancestors, that his family owed the permanence of their Indian empire. The last scion of this royal house died in misery at Rangoon, in 1862.

On the disruption of the Mongol empire, founded by Genghis, and built on by his successors, the tribes who composed it were dispersed far and wide over Europe and Asia, from the Great Wall of China to the Volga and the Black Sea. Their dynastic divisions were numerous, but the Mongol blood was soon lost in many of these. The Khans were often followed into conquered territories by a small proportion only of their own race, sometimes by a few families, and sometimes by a few individuals only, their armies being mainly composed of alien elements. These handfuls of men soon lost their national characteristics under the influence of a settled life, and contact with races better trained in the arts of peace. The numerical superiority of the people among whom they lived, must necessarily have absorbed them; and it would be hard now to trace the Mongol blood in the descendants of the Tartars of the Crimea, of Kazan, of Nogai, or of Kapchak.

The homogeneous race of the Mongols may now be divided into the Kalkas, the Kalmuks, and the Bouriats. The Kalkas, who take their name from a small river rising in the Siolki mountains in Manchuria, are a numerous people, occupying the north of the Great Desert. They may be called the Mongols proper, if any are entitled to that name.

The Kalmuks, so nicknamed by the Mahommedan Tartars, inhabit the Russian province of Astrakhan. A remarkable exodus of these people took place in 1770-71, on which occasion half a million of the Kalmuks of the Volga fled from the tyranny of Catherine II., and directed their march eastward by the route by which their ancestors had so often travelled to Europe. During their eight months' pilgrimage they were goaded to despair by hunger, weariness, and savage enemies; and when they at last found shelter in the dominions of the Emperor of China, they had been reduced to half their number. The Emperor Kienloong allotted to them a settlement in the province of Dsungaria, on the north-west of the desert. The Eleuths on the south-east of the desert are also of the race of the Kalmuks. The black Kalmuks are settled near the sources of the river Obi, north of the Altai mountains.

The Bouriats in the Siberian province of Trans-baikal, although of true Mongol origin, do not appear to have been much mixed up in the military movements of the other tribes. They were nevertheless a warlike people, were subdued by the family of Genghis in the thirteenth century, and made a respectable stand against the Russians in the seventeenth.

There are other tribes of Mongols within the modern limits of China proper, though north of the Great Wall. Some of these till the ground, but they are principally kept up as the reserve army of China.

From the earliest times, these wandering tribes, when not united in a crusade against the human race at large, were constantly at war with each other. These feuds were continued with varying results for several centuries after their empire was broken up; but the adroitness of the Chinese on the one side, and the brute force of Russia on the other, have subdued the turbulent spirit of the Mongol hordes, who for the last hundred years have been quiet subjects of these two empires.

The Mongols, Kalmuks, and Bouriats are all Bhuddists, while the other Tartar tribes, with whom the Mongols have been associated in their wars, are almost all Mahommedans.

The history of the wars of the Huns and Mongols exhibits some curious psychical phenomena. First, we see these barbarous tribes, living in the most primitive condition, ignorant of everything beyond the range of animal instinct, vanquishing in fair fight the most warlike and civilised nations that then existed. By the weight of their masses, and the impetuosity of their onslaught, stimulated by the ferocity of fanaticism, the barbarians broke in on the old empires, which they overwhelmed like a flood. Civilisation bowed the neck to barbarism: matter triumphed over mind.

And yet the materials of which these formidable hosts were composed were in themselves feeble and innocuous. When we see the descendants of the Huns quietly feeding their sheep in their native deserts, harmless and kind-hearted, simple and contented, it is hard to conceive that out of such a race could have come the conquerors of the world. Their power indeed was a matter of pure accident, that is to say, it lay dormant until accident raised up men with ability to use it. The shepherds have little power of reasoning, and no notions of self-government; but they are willing machines in the hands of a man of strong intellect, who can exact from them the worship due to a divinity. Under such a leader they can be handled like a pack of hounds, with which they have a close affinity in the instinct of obedience and unreasoning courage: animal qualities which are invaluable to the schemes of the master-mind.

The heroes of the Mongol tribes have been few and far between. The marvel is that such a people could produce heroes at all. Their great conquerors were not men of ordinary ability, but of vast genius, rendered all the more conspicuous by their untutored barbarism. None but great minds could have controlled and directed the movements of such multitudes. The words of the khan were inexorable laws; without the ruling spirit nothing could be done. China was saved from a second conquest by the accident of the death of Timour; and it has been said that the fate of Europe at one time depended on the digestion of a barbarian under the Great Wall of China. Nor were the Mongol leaders animated by blind ferocity. They had an object in their wars, which was nothing less than the sovereignty of the world. Their courage was high, and they occasionally fought desperate battles. But that was not their usual custom. Attila, and Genghis, and Timour, all showed remarkable caution. They calculated the chances of a battle or a campaign with the deliberation of experienced generals, and declined engagements against heavy odds when they could effect a retreat without discouraging their troops. Attila, the rudest of them all, was a skilful diplomatist. He penetrated into Gaul, not so much by force of arms as by the craft he displayed in playing off one faction against another, and so distracting the counsels of his enemies.

The secret of the ascendency of the Mongol chiefs lay mainly in the skill with which they used the potent instrument of superstition. The shepherds, illiterate and brutish, had a blind awe of the supernatural, which it was the policy of their leaders to encourage. Attila became miraculously possessed of the sword of the Scythian Mars, and thenceforth bore a sacred character which was confirmed to him by his early successes. A divine origin was attributed to the ancestors of Genghis. He was styled the son of God, and was popularly believed to have been born of a virgin.* The Turks traced their descent from a youth who was nursed by a she-wolf, a fable probably borrowed from that of Romulus and Remus.

The kings of the Huns and Mongols excited the enthusiasm of their armies by the use of omens. When unfavourable to their plans, the omens were either disregarded or explained away by the chiefs, who were probably incredulous, but at all events possessed the resolution to rise superior to the oracles. Thus when Attila had raised the siege of Orleans, and was pressed in his retreat by a powerful army of Goths and Romans, the auguries were against him, and his troops were dispirited. But Attila, considering that a defeat would be less disastrous to him than flight, rallied the sinking courage of the Huns by an eloquent oration, in which, with consummate ingenuity, he turned the very advantages of the enemy into encouragements to himself. Their well-chosen posts, their strict alliance and close order, he affected to attribute to fear alone. He plied his people also with arguments from the doctrine of fate, and persuaded them that they were as safe in the thick of the fight as in

* Gibbon, vol. iv. p. 322, and note.

their own tents. In the desperate battle which ensued, Attila outdid himself in personal valour, and the Huns fought furiously; the slaughter on both sides was prodigious; but when night came Attila was fain to retire within his camp. The result of the action was nevertheless creditable to his sagacity, for he was still so formidable in defeat that his enemies compared him to a lion at bay, and they dared not renew the attack.

Timour, who lived in a more enlightened age, or rather among a more enlightened people, and was himself educated in Mohamedanism, rose to a higher flight in the use and contempt of auguries. Instead of examining the entrails of animals, he consulted the planets and the Koran. When marching on Delhi his astrologers could not educe any favourable indication from the stars, but Timour refused to hamper his plans by such considerations, telling his astrologers that fortune does not depend on the stars, but on the Creator of them.

The Huns and Mongols were distinguished from other men, chiefly by their waste of human life. They may be said to have depopulated Asia. The flourishing cities that once existed in the deserts of Tartary have been utterly destroyed; the history of many of them has been lost; and where large populations cultivated arts and industry, one may now see only the tent of a herdsman in the vast solitude. The savages boasted that grass never grew where the feet of their horses had trod, and that a horse might run without stumbling over the places where the great cities had stood. The conquerors built towers and pyramids of the heads of their enemies, that is, their prisoners—not soldiers only—but whole populations whom they massacred in cold blood.

But yet, though ferocious, the barbarians were not, strictly speaking, cruel. Their systematic slaughter must be otherwise accounted for, and in a way even more humiliating to human nature. The morality of the kings, khans or emperors may be assumed to have been on a par with that of the people; it was in intellect only that they were pre-eminent. Attila, in the midst of his sins against mankind, was accessible to pity. His own people loved him. Genghis aspired to the honour of a wise legislator, and primitive though his code was, his motives for devising it were honourable. He encouraged trade so far as he knew how; patronised the sciences, and favoured the missionaries of all persuasions. He was both just and generous, and if he had but governed, instead of killing, the people he conquered, it is possible that he might have been a benefactor to mankind. Yet, in three cities alone, Genghis caused more than four millions of people to be slaughtered.

But the strange paradox comes out in more vivid colours in the character of Timour, who, compared with his predecessors, was civilised and humane. Amongst his exploits was the massacre of one hundred thousand people at Delhi. He exacted from Ispahan a contribution of seventy thousand, and from Bagdad of ninety thousand human heads to build towers with. Although a Mahommedan he did not spare his co-religionists, but slew indiscriminately all who seemed to stand in his way. When he grew old, and was satiated with blood and glory, he repented. But his repentance was the most curious episode in the monster's history. He planned a pious mission to China, and in announcing his resolve to his council, he told them that the conquests he had made were not obtained *without some violence*, which had occasioned the death of a great number of God's creatures. To atone for past crimes he determined to perform some good action, namely, to *exterminate the idolaters of China*.*

By what law or standard of ethics can such an abuse of the

---

* Un. Hist. vol. v. p. 57.

moral faculties be judged? And how can such antagonistic traits of character be reconciled?

The Mongols did not practise the cruelties that have so often disgraced more refined peoples. Tortures were exceptional among them, perhaps because their invention had not risen to such a pitch. Noble captives were paraded in chains, but that was done rather to glorify the victor than to punish the victim. The Mongol massacres seem to have been dictated less by positive than negative considerations. Their low estimate of the value of human life lay at the bottom of it all. The slaughter of the population of a great city was no more in their eyes than the destruction of so many vermin. Their towers of human heads were to the primitive barbarians what the trophies of the chace are to sportsmen. Being guided by animal instincts alone, they were unconscious of any wrong. So low is the moral condition of uncultivated races, "the children of nature," that human feelings can only grow in them after ages of gradual education. The social virtues, and even the natural affections, are only developed in their full force by means of artificial or civilised life, just as the perfectability of plants is only attained by the aid which art gives to nature. So, then, the artificial state is in a sense more natural to man than the natural or primitive condition of savages. His moral nature needs culture as much as his intellect does; and artificial life alone can bring out man's natural qualities. The affections of the Huns and Mongols were little more than such as they possessed in common with the lower animals. They loved their children after a fashion, and sometimes they loved a favourite wife. But if we desire to test the quality of the paternal affection of such people, let us look at the half-tamed barbarian Peter the Great, who condemned and executed his own son, after inviting him to surrender under the promise of a full pardon.

The theory has been advanced that the exclusively animal diet of the shepherds rendered them ferocious,* and that their familiarity with the blood of their sheep excited their passion for the blood of their fellow-creatures. But neither of these hypotheses is founded on fact. The elaborate cruelties of the vegetarians of China and Japan supply a sufficient answer to the first. The Chinese have racked their ingenuity to multiply tortures, and a fat rice-eater will sip up his tea and fan himself with perfect *sang-froid*, while he causes the nails of a victim to be pulled out. When their blood is up the Chinese are as savage as the Mongols, and by so much the more cruel as their superior intellects supply to them varieties in the enjoyment of their blood-thirstiness.

To the second observation it may be replied that the professional butchers are not the least humane class of civilised society; their occupation does not impair their human sympathies. A wild beast may be excited by the taste of blood, but it is merely from the instinct that impels him to seek his natural food.

The brutalising influence of war itself is well known. To this rule there are few exceptions. Even among Christian nations, in whom the degrading tendency is counteracted by education and social culture, the hero of many battles is but too apt to value his men at so much per head. Barbarians, with no controlling power to check the natural bent of their passions, exhibit the full dehumanising effects of war. They glory in the mere shedding of blood, as a hunter delights in the death of his game. Yet this savage passion is far removed from simple cruelty, and may be quite compatible with a low form of goodness of heart.

* "Il est certain que les grands mangeurs de viande sont en général cruels et féroces plus que les autres hommes. Cette observation est de tous les lieux et de tous les temps ; la barbarie anglaise est connue."—Emile de Rousseau. Gibbon, iii. p. 350.

Although at first sight the simple life of pastoral peoples does not seem likely to produce a race of warriors, yet the very simplicity of their habits peculiarly adapts them for warlike enterprises. The incentives to war would not be wanting to wandering tribes with no fixed boundary; for they would be constantly invading each others' pasture grounds. Hence, the habits of predatory warfare would be induced. Their hardiness and endurance would enable them to sustain the fatigue of long marches, privations and exposure. Such a community needs no commissariat. Their food is the flesh of their cattle or horses, which, being accustomed to eat grass only, can always feed themselves on the way. Their tents might even be dispensed with, and the ground would serve them for a camp. Their indifference to life renders unnecessary any provision for the care of the sick or the wounded. They are not hampered in their movements by any tie to localities. The whole world is alike to them. Their life in war, involving the long marches and countermarches which wear out other troops, was little different from their ordinary habits in peace. Their enthusiasm made them formidable. Their ignorance rendered them unscrupulous. They destroyed the noblest monuments of learning and industry with the same wantonness that prompts a child to pull to pieces the finest piece of mechanism. They set no value on anything, and it was a pleasant recreation for them to destroy what they could neither appreciate nor understand. The spoils of civilisation allured them to new conquests. Victory inflated their fanaticism. Defeat subdued their spirit for the time, but they had always a retreat open in the deserts of Asia where they were at least safe from the retaliation of the civilised nations whom they had oppressed. In their career of devastation they were often stimulated by necessity. When their earlier successes had attracted great numbers to the victorious standard, it was impossible to maintain the vast multitude stationary. First, their pastures would soon become exhausted; and, secondly, their leaders could only maintain their own character and their ascendency over their followers by active operations. The alien troops, who entered largely into the composition of their armies, were always ready to secede from their forced allegiance. Any symptom of weakness or incapacity in the chief would be the signal for a general disruption. Out of this necessity for perpetual motion doubtless arose the Mongol vision of universal empire.

The military enthusiasm in the Mongols is only dormant, not dead. We have seen, four or five years ago, with what alacrity Sang-ko-lin-sin, himself a Kalka Mongol, and one of the forty-eight kings, brought a force into the field to bar our entrance into Peking, and with what zeal and energy the Mongol troops acquitted themselves. Given a sufficient motive, and a man to lead them, and the shepherds could soon be put in motion again. By nature they are faithful to their chiefs, and their head lama has but to hold up his finger to stir up the sleeping prowess of the shepherds. Nor is it likely that the sanguinary passions, common to barbarians, have been eradicated in the Mongols. Quiet and peaceful as they are among their flocks, they would be as fierce in war as in the bloodiest days of their history.

CHAPTER XI.

MONGOLS—PHYSICAL AND MENTAL CHARACTERISTICS.

THE following physical characteristics of the Mongolian race, by a gentleman who resided many years among the Bouriats in Trans-baikal, are equally applicable to the tribes in Mongolia proper, and to some extent also to the Chinese.

"The high cheek-bones; the oblique, elongated eye, dark and piercing; the flat nose, with compressed nostrils; the strong black straight hair; the large protuberant ears; the small sharp chin; the want of beard in the men, till late in life; the general gravity of expression, and cautious, inquisitive mode of address, are so many marks of this tribe of men, never to be mistaken, and never to be found so strongly developed in any other."[*]

There is nothing noble or generous in the Mongol character, and those tribes who have afforded the widest field for observation, are said to be naturally servile to superiors and tyrannical to inferiors.

Their *meanness* is remarkable. They are not too proud to beg the smallest trifle, and a man well blessed with this world's goods thinks it no disgrace to receive alms.

The habits they have inherited qualify them admirably for the lazy nomad life which they lead. But they have no heart for work in the sense of regular, steady occupation. Fatigue and privation they make no account of, but

---

[*] Scottish Congreg. Mag., Dec. 1841.

it goes quite against the grain with them to do a day's work. They sadly lack energy and enterprise, and are easily discouraged. The Mongols proper are seldom tempted to leave the beaten track of their pastoral life, and even the Bouriats, who live amongst Russians, and have incentives to exertion, show little disposition to depart in anything from their traditional mode of life. The Russian government has tried to make them farmers, but with very little success. Every Bouriat family is compelled by law to cultivate a few acres of ground. Government supplies them with seed, generally rye, on condition that an equal quantity be returned to the government granary the following year, or its equivalent in money paid. They are subject to bad seasons in those regions. A backward, dry spring, with no rain before June, is of not unfrequent occurrence; in such seasons the crops don't ripen before the autumn frosts come, and the year's labour is lost. The seed corn must, nevertheless, be delivered back to the granary, and the Bouriat agriculturist loses heart.

The cardinal virtue of the Mongol tribes is hospitality, which is as freely exhibited to perfect strangers, as to neighbours, from whom a return may be expected. Indeed, the nomad life would be intolerable without this mutual good-feeling and readiness to assist, to feed, and to shelter travellers. The absence of trades, and of the amenities of settled communities, renders the Mongol people mutually dependent, and hospitality becomes simply a necessity among them. At the pitching and striking of tents, at sheep-shearing and felt-making, the assistance of neighbours is required by all in turn. When cattle stray, the neighbours help to catch them. When a Mongol is on a journey in the desert, he is dependent on the hospitality of the families whose tents he may pass on his way, and he will always be welcome. The Mongols are also attracted to each other's quarters to hear news, or for the mere satisfaction of talking. In such a sparsely peopled country, this feeling makes a stranger all the more welcome.

Although rather addicted to petty pilfering, the Mongols are, in a general way, honest. At any rate, they will not betray a trust committed to them. The fidelity of servants is universal, and theft, robbery, and assault, are of rare occurrence among them. Their most prevalent vice is drunkenness; and, although drinking, and even smoking, are prohibited by the sacerdotal law, the living example of the priests is more powerful than the dead letter of the law. Those Mongols who wander to the frontier of China or Russia, supply themselves with tobacco, and distribute it to their friends in the desert. Every one carries a pipe with a small brass bowl, like the Chinese. A steel and flint are invariably attached to the tobacco-pouch. The Mongols also take snuff, using a stone bottle, with an ivory spoon attached to the stopper, after the Chinese fashion. Chinese liquor they use very sparingly, and only on great occasions of bargaining or merry-making. They use a spirit of their own very extensively, and as it is made out of milk, an article which is very abundant among pastoral people, their supply of the spirit is almost unlimited. They call it *ir'chi*, or in the Bouriat dialect *araki*, a name applied by the Mongols to all liquors indiscriminately. It is better known to Europeans by the name of *kumiss*. The following account of the mode in which the spirit is distilled from milk is interesting: "The milk, previously soured and fermented, is put into a large iron kettle, over which is inverted a wooden dish, fitted to the edge of the former, and luted with cow-dung. One end of a bent wooden tube is inserted into a hole in the inverted dish, and at the other end is placed a cast-iron pot to receive the liquid as it comes over. When the fire has made the contents of the kettle boil, the vapour is condensed within the tube, and passes into the receiving vessel in the form of ardent spirit."[*] The spirit is fit to drink whenever it is made, and as it is more than usually plentiful when the pastures are richest, that is the season of the greatest excesses. Any sort of milk may be used, but mare's milk is said to make the most approved liquor. The Mongols are inclined to be uproarious in their cups; and squabbles often occur, but they seldom come to anything very serious.

The morality of the Mongols is about a fair average of that of the rest of mankind, perhaps purer than that of more civilised countries. Their customs admit of polygamy, but it is too expensive to be very common, as each wife has to be in a manner bought of her father for a certain number of oxen, horses, or camels. They have a strong objection to marrying within their own families, or tribes, considering all the descendants of one father or head of a tribe as brothers and sisters, however distant their actual relationship may be. "So universal is this custom," says the writer already quoted, "that I never knew or heard of an instance of its being violated."

The lamas are all celibats, but seeing this class numbers one fourth or one fifth of the male population, it might safely be predicated of them that their vows are not strictly kept. As a matter of fact, the celibacy of the lamas is in very many instances a merely nominal thing. The lama may not marry, but he can take to himself a "disciple;" children will be born to him in the natural course of events, and no great public scandal will be excited thereby. Hence a standing joke among the laity is to ask tenderly for the health of Mrs. Lama.

The Mongol women are childishly fond of small orna-

[*] Scot. Cong. Mag., Feb. 1842.

ments for their hair. Any kind of tinsel, or small glass ware, is highly valued by them. Before marriage, the women wear their hair disposed in plaits which hang straight down. Ornaments of coral, or other articles, are suspended from the plaits. After marriage the hair is collected into two thick ties, one at each side, falling down over the front of the shoulders, and adorned according to the fancy or means of the wearer. They wear a kind of tiara round the head, which is ornamented with coral, glass, strings of mock pearls, or any kind of gaudy trinkets they can pick up. They also wear sometimes, instead of the ordinary cap, a coronet of soft fur, fastened round the head, and projecting over the brow, which gives them, at first sight, a rakish appearance.

The Mongols, one and all, evince great regard for decency in their dress and habits. Their inner garments consist of cotton trousers, tightly fastened by a scarf round the waist, and a long flowing robe of the same material. These are generally of blue. The long sheepskin is kept in reserve for night-work, or cold days. They never appear uncovered outside of their tents, even in hot weather. In this respect they contrast remarkably with all other natives in hot climates with whom I am acquainted.

In physical development, the Mongols do not rank very high. They are in stature below the middle height, but moderately stout. Short necks are common, but many thin, scraggy necks are also met with. They do not get corpulent like the Chinese. They look healthy and robust. Their muscular energy is rather low, which may be due to their avoiding all regular work, and partly perhaps to their exclusively animal diet.

Wrestling is one of their favourite amusements, and the trained wrestlers are proud of their skill in the art. A square-built lama challenged me to wrestle with him at Tsagan-tuguruk. There was a great concourse of people present, and to have declined the contest would have been as bad as a defeat. I therefore determined to risk the trial. I soon found that being totally ignorant of the art, I had to act solely on the defensive. After some ineffectual attempts the lama threw me. I had a firm hold of him, however, and we both came down together, the lama under. Having come out of the ordeal better than I expected, I had no wish to try another round, and the lama also had enough. It was my turn to challenge then, and considering that the honour of my country required it, I offered to box my antagonist, which honour he respectfully declined. This incident exhibited to me the muscular weakness of one of the best-made men I met among the Mongols.

But their weakest point is their legs, which are rarely exercised. The Mongols begin from their earliest years to ride on horseback. If they have but to go a few hundred yards, they will ride if possible, in preference to walking. They walk with the gait of a duck; indeed, were their legs good—which they are not—the heavy shapeless leather boots they wear would prove an effectual bar to walking. These boots come up near the knee, are made of nearly uniform size, so that the largest feet will go easily into any of their boots. Thick stockings are also used, and the foot has ample play with all that. They are nearly all bow-legged, a circumstance that might be explained by their constant habit of riding, or by the pressure that is put on them when infants to make them sit cross-legged, were it not frequently developed in children before the age when nurses begin to cross their legs. The phenomenon may nevertheless be the indirect result of both these causes. The habits of the tribes being fixed and uniform for many ages, the bow-legged tendency which these habits are calculated to produce, may have been gradually impressed on the race as a permanent feature, by the mystery of hereditary influence. Thus the peculiarity, although originally accidental, would become permanent and constitutional. The Mongol is rarely seen standing upright. He is either sitting on horseback, or crouching in a tent.

The Mongols are rather dark-complexioned; the face and hands, which are constantly exposed to sun and weather, are deeply bronzed; the skin is very coarse; the covered parts of the body are much lighter than the exposed parts, but among the men there is nothing like a white skin. The whitest of them are yellowish. During our ablutions the whiteness of our skins was a subject of constant remark among the Mongols, although the skin of our faces became, by constant exposure to the sun while in Mongolia, as dark as that of the Mongols themselves. The Mongols, nevertheless, have often a ruddy complexion, but it is uncommon among the men. The women are much fairer than the men, and are much less exposed to the sun, being mostly in the tents attending to household duties. Their faces, although rough and weather-beaten more or less, have all a "roseate hue." Old women frequently become pasty white in the face. Their children are born fair skinned, and with brownish hair, which gradually becomes darker as they grow up. Shades of brown are however not unfrequent even in adults, and a tendency to curl is sometimes observable. Their eyes are seldom quite black, but run on various shades of brown. The white of the eye is usually "bloodshot" in middle-aged men, probably from two causes, exposure to wind and weather, and the argol smoke of their tent fires. They live, without any inconvenience, in an atmosphere of sharp biting smoke, which our eyes could not tolerate. The small eyes of the Mongols are shaded by heavy wrinkled eyelids, which, in many instances, are permanently contracted, giving the eye a peculiarly keen expression, as it peers out from under the mass of soft muscle that surrounds it. This feature is entirely absent in children, and is no doubt produced in adults by exposure to glare and the habit of straining after distant objects in a dry sandy country.

The almost entire absence of beard is a remarkable feature in the Mongolians. As regards this and other marks of race, it may be useful to compare the Mongols with their near neighbours the Chinese. The two races have a sufficient number of broad characteristics in common to warrant their classification under one great type of mankind. But their differences are also well marked, and are deserving of attention. The northern districts of China are not very different from Mongolia in point of climate. Both have a short but hot summer, and an extremely rigorous winter, differing only in degree. Both climates are dry. The northern Chinese assimilate more closely than any other of their countrymen to the Mongol habit of life. They eat animal food rather extensively, and drink strong liquor freely. Yet in physical development they are further removed from the Mongols in some features than even the southern Chinese who live on rice, fish, and vegetables. In the matter of beards, which led to this comparison, the northern Chinese are in a marked degree more hairy than their southern compatriots, and these again than the natives of Mongolia. In none of them is the beard developed till towards middle life; yet they all attain the age of puberty earlier than Europeans. The beef-eaters of northern China are tall, muscular, and robust, as much superior to the Mongols as they are to their own countrymen who lead a different life. But with their animal diet the northern Chinese eat copiously of vegetable and farinaceous food, while the Mongols live almost exclusively on mutton.

The regularity of habits which prevail in settled populations may also have its influence in the general physical development of the people. The nomads have certain qualities cultivated to excess, and others almost entirely unused. The animal instincts are naturally found highly developed amongst the Mongols. The sense of sight is very acute in them; they are sensitive to indications of changes of weather, and so with various other instincts which to these wandering tribes supply the wants of a more artificial life, and enable them to exist in a state of nature. Individuality is in a great measure lost among such people. The habits and education of each individual among them are identical. Their pursuits are all the same. The very same faculties, both physical and mental, are kept in exercise among the whole tribe, and that through many generations, so that they have become hereditary, and indelibly imprinted on the race. A Mongol who was not a good horseman would be as anomalous as one that was inhospitable. The uniformity of life among the members of these nomad tribes, while it keeps back many faculties, the exercise of which is necessary to the existence of civilised people, also renders the type of whole tribes constant, so that no one individual differs greatly in external features from another. In civilised communities, where the division of labour has become so indispensable as to be in itself one great criterion of civilisation, a variety of types are evolved even in a single lifetime. A tailor can never be mistaken for a blacksmith, nor a soldier for a sailor; but tribes whose habits compel each family to be independent, as it were, of all the rest of the world, whose wants are limited by the means of supplying them, and among whom different occupations are almost unknown, do necessarily present a remarkable uniformity. It would be unsound to generalise too freely, and there are of course the individual distinctions of physiognomy as well marked as among other races, but these differences are more limited in their scope. Some trades are known to the Mongols, such as felt-making, tanning and dressing skins, iron, copper, and silver work,

o

saddle-making, &c. In more settled parts they also make harness, carts, and sledges; and printing from blocks, after the manner of the Chinese and Japanese, is also known among them. These arts are most cultivated among the Bouriats in Siberia, who, by their contact with the Russians, and from the nature of the country they inhabit, are thrown more in the way of artificial life than the desert tribes.

To the casual observer, at least, the Mongols do not present the same individual differences as their neighbours, the Chinese. In complexion they are nearly all alike, although the skin seems to get darker as the face becomes wrinkled with age, which might seem to favour the idea that the brownish skin of the Mongols is due as much to their habits as to their descent, or the effects of climate. But the causes which influence colour are very obscure. In Siberia, where Sclavonic races have been settled for nearly two centuries, living side by side with Mongol tribes, and exposed to the same climatic influences, these show no signs of variation from the complexion of their ancestors, as it is exhibited by their European representatives. Again, the Portuguese settlers in Macao, who degenerate very rapidly, become in two or three generations much darker in the skin than the native Chinese. It is not the smoky atmosphere of their tents that darkens the skin of the Mongols, for in that case, the women, who are more exposed to it, would be darker than the men, the reverse of which is the case. A comparison with the Japanese again would seem to show that exposure exercises at the most an insignificant effect in darkening the skin. The Japanese live much within doors, and are careful to protect themselves from the sun when they stir abroad by means of broad-brimmed hats and umbrellas. Great differences of complexion exist among them, whether regarded as individuals or classes; but it is safe to say they are on the whole quite as dark as the Mongols. The contrast between men and women is singularly marked, the women having fair clear complexions, often rosy. Yet the Japanese women are a good deal out of doors, and are fairer skinned than the Chinese women, who are only blanched by confinement to the house and exclusion from light and air.

The Mongols, although deficient in muscular energy, and incapacitated for sustained activity, are nevertheless gifted with great powers of endurance. I have already noticed their capacity for enduring prolonged fasts, and their ability to go several days and nights without sleep, with equal impunity. The sudden and important changes to which their climate is subject, are also borne without any great suffering. From a hot summer, they are plunged, with but slight gradations, into an extremely rigorous winter, when the temperature falls very low, and is accompanied by keen cutting winds, that sweep over the steppes with merciless fury, and from which they have no better protection than their tents.

The Mongol tribes stand low in the scale of mental capacity. Scattered over vast deserts, remote from civilised man, they are ignorant by necessity. Their intellectual faculties have no stimulus to exertion. Their aims in life, and their whole worldly ambition, are limited to flocks and herds. While there is grass enough to feed the sheep, and sheep enough to feed the men, they have little else to disturb their quiet equanimity. Thus they lead an idle careless life, free from thought and everything that might disturb the negative happiness they enjoy. This kind of existence is truly a low form, having more affinity with the animal than the mental side of human nature, while at the same time it is to be observed that they are almost entire strangers to the varied emotions that fill up the existence of a civilised being; so that both their intellectual and moral qualities are dwarfed and partially destroyed. The prostrate mental condition of the people predisposes them to the domination of superior minds, and when their highly superstitious tendencies are considered, it is not surprising that they are among the most priest-ridden races in the world. It is not easy to say why these people should be more easily imposed upon than others, excepting that ignorance is always found to go hand-in-hand with this mental weakness. The wild solitary life of the desert is also, no doubt, eminently favourable to belief in the supernatural and mysterious.

A man who frequently passes days and nights with no society, except the howling waste below, and the deep blue sky above, has his imagination set free from the trammels of the world of fact. He has no resources but in the spirit-world, and it is not unnatural that his fancy should people the air with superior intelligences, whose voices are heard in the desert winds or the rustling leaves of the forest. Under these conditions of life, the poor nomads are in a proper frame of mind to become the thralls of any one who will undertake to interpret for them the spiritual mysteries on which their imagination runs riot. The lamas fill this office, and are treated with unbounded respect by the masses. The religion of the Mongols is Bhuddism, a superstition which numbers more votaries than any other existing religion, true or false. But the fact is, they are Bhuddists only in name; that is to say, the laity are almost wholly ignorant of the doctrines of Bhuddism. Even the lamas have but vague and confused ideas about it. Their prayers are conned by rote, and these priests are generally ignorant of the Thibetan language in which they are written.

The Mongol religion may indeed be called Lamaism, its leading doctrine being faith, implicit and absolute, in the authoritative teaching of the lamas, and that not in any well-digested system of belief settled and fixed by the united wisdom of the sect, but in such interpretation of spiritual matters as any individual lama may choose to give. The gods are deified lamas. The Dalai Lama of Thibet is a god incarnate, as is also the Lama king of the Mongols; and even the ordinary lamas, whose name is legion, are considered as off-shoots from deity in a sense that entitles them to the worship of common mortals. The abstruse doctrines of the metempsychosis and the future state, are studied by the recluses who live in the retirement of the great monasteries, and spend their time in prayer and meditation. But the every-day lama, although he carries a pocketful of musty papers, in which the eighteen hells and twenty-six heavens are elucidated, cares little for these things. He has more practical matters to attend to than meditating on the Bhuddist notion of bliss consummated by absorption into Bhudda—complete repose—in other words, annihilation. His written liturgies are a powerful spell by which he maintains his moral influence over the people, and it is none the less powerful that neither party fully comprehends their meaning. More regard is paid to the quantity than to the quality of their prayers, and to facilitate their devotions an ingenious machine is in common use, consisting of a roller containing a string of prayers. This is sometimes turned by hand, and sometimes it is attached to a windmill! So long as it is turned round by some means, the efficacy of the prayers is considered the same. No doubt it is. The petitions are long-winded and multifarious.

The following, from one of the lama liturgies, is a specimen :

" From the fear of the king, from the fear of robbers, from the fear of fire, from the fear of water, from the fear of loss, from the fear of enemies, from the fear of famine ; of thunder, of untimely death, earthquakes, thunderbolts, of the king's judgment, of the tengri, of the loo, of wild beasts, &c., keep me and all men in safety."*

* First-fruits of a Mission to Siberia. Cape Town. 1847.

The general drift of their religious observances is towards securing immunity from the " ills that flesh is heir to," rather than towards providing for a future state. Both objects are aimed at, but the materialistic greatly preponderates. Medical knowledge is of course at a low ebb among these wandering people. The lamas are their physicians. When a child or a horse is taken ill, the ignorant people are taught to believe that an evil spirit is present, which can only be exorcised by the incantations of a lama. In every doubt and difficulty a lama is consulted. He is at once a detective officer, justice of the peace, priest and physician. His blessing is at all times efficacious. His power over disease is unquestioned. There is virtue for good or evil in all his acts. His authority to declare what is right and what is wrong is never doubted. The punishments he may inflict for violation of his precepts are borne patiently. In a word, the lamas are the beginning and the end, at once the ministers and the objects of religion to the simple Mongols. Their persons are held sacred, and they wear a sacred dress consisting of a red cotton garment with a collar of black velvet, and a cap of peculiar shape. Their heads are shaven all over, which is a sufficient distinction from the laymen, who shave the head only in front of the crown, wearing a tail like the Chinese. Wherever a lama goes he is received with open arms, and assumes the place of honour in any tent which he may deign to enter. The priestly tyranny of these functionaries opens a wide door to the most heartless knavery, and dishonest lamas who oppress and eat up the people are very common. Were the lama order restricted to one class of people, it is possible their victims might rise in rebellion against their assumption of authority. But the lamas are drawn from every tribe and household. The second son of every family is generally set apart from his birth as a priest. In childhood and youth he is regarded as a superior being in his parental tent. The place of honour is assigned to him from the time he is able to sit cross-legged. When an opportunity offers, the little devotee repairs to a monastery, where he may learn the Thibetan characters and the rudiments of the lama prayers. Great numbers of lamas reside permanently in these monasteries, which are supported by contributions from the people, or endowed by the Emperor of China. The lama unattached receives no pay, and has therefore to support himself, as the rest of his countrymen do, by feeding sheep and cattle. His special services are paid for according to his cupidity or the wealth of his employers. Many of them grow rich on the spoils of their deluded votaries. Some others, of ultra-nomadic proclivities, keep no cattle and own no tents. They simply roam about where fancy directs, and live on the people whose tents they pass. These are not much respected, but are, nevertheless, hospitably entertained wherever they go.

The spread of Bhuddism eastward over Mongolia, China, and Japan, the deep hold it has taken on the people of those countries, to the extinction almost of pre-existing superstitions, are most remarkable phenomena. Looking at the degenerate form of the religion that has sprung up in Mongolia, and the ignorance of the people, tending strongly to adherence to the dogmas of their fathers, it seems wonderful that Bhuddism should have had vitality enough to supersede the ancient Shamanism.

The Bhuddistic doctrines, involved and obscure as they are, certainly filled up a blank that must have been felt even among the most unthinking races, for Shamanism had no reference to a future life. In this respect Bhuddism is more elevating than Shamanism, and when first introduced into a new country, it was probably in a purer form, and untarnished by the many abuses that have grown out of it in its subsequent history.

Among the Bouriats, Shamanism was almost universal as

late as one hundred and fifty years ago. Up to that time it was the only superstition known to the northern nomads. The Shaman worship was directed to the material heavens and heavenly bodies—fire, earth and water, wild beasts and birds, and the malignant spirits of the air, called *tengri*. Its ritual consisted very little in prayers, but mainly of animal sacrifices. Some curious facts connected with the Shaman superstition are given by Mr. Swan in the " Scottish Congregational Magazine."

As a preventive against cattle being killed by lightning, a horse is devoted to the god of thunder—light grey or white being preferred. He is brought to the door of his owner's tent, and while the Shaman ceremonies are going on, a cup of milk is placed on his back. When the ceremonies are concluded, the horse is cast loose, the milk falls, and the animal is thenceforth sacred. No one may use him again, and, when he dies, his tail and mane are cut off and twisted into those of another horse, who, from that time, also becomes sacred to the god of thunder. They also had a ceremony of a scapegoat, which in its details coincided most singularly with that of the Levitical institution. The Shaman offerings usually consisted of three animals sacrificed at once—part of the flesh was eaten, and the rest, stuck on a pole, was consumed by crows or magpies.

Another strange practice of the Shamans, and one which is common also among the lamas, betrays the intellectual imbecility of the people who could tolerate and be deceived by it. To exorcise the evil spirit out of a sick person, an effigy of straw is made, and clothed in the garments of the patient. The priests proceed to kill the man of straw, then convey it away and burn it. The unsophisticated devil is supposed to be watching these proceedings, and to mistake the effigy for the sick person; so that when it is destroyed, this most accommodating spirit considers his own malignant purpose accomplished, and at once leaves the sick person, who thereupon recovers. It is even said that human victims are used for this purpose by the rich in Mongolia and Thibet.

The Shamans were simply sorcerers. Their ceremonies were wild fanatical ravings, and their ranks were usually filled by persons of diseased brains. The people generally were reluctant to become Shamans, and a severe illness was often held to be an intimation to the person affected of the desire of the Spirits that he or she should become a "medium."

The Bouriats learned Bhuddism from the Mongols, their kinsmen. About the beginning of the eighteenth century a mission was sent from Siberia to Thibet. The members of it returned as lamas and brought the paraphernalia of the new religion with them, built a temple, and set up Bhuddism. The Shamans were then gradually superseded by the lamas in the districts of Trans-baikal—sacrifices gave place to prayers—and a purely materialist superstition to one which recognised the necessity of providing against a future existence.

When, and under what circumstances, the Mongols proper embraced Bhuddism, is not so easy to determine. The Chinese received it in the first, and the Japanese in the sixth century of the Christian era; but it does not appear to have been known to the Mongols before the time of Genghis. It was probably during the wandering career of the hordes under his leadership, that the lamas insinuated themselves into influence over the untutored shepherds. The higher culture which they had acquired, even by their partial education, would mark them in the eyes of the rude Tartars as a superior order of magicians; and their ascendancy over the Mongol intellects would be natural and easy.

There are traditions of Lamaism in the district of the Ortous before the time of Genghis, but as that part of the desert had frequently been incorporated with China, the existence of Bhuddist monasteries there is not inconsistent with the supposition that the Mongol tribes became Bhuddists only after the wars of Genghis.

It would appear that Mohammedanism also was introduced into China by means of the armies of Genghis, which traversed Asia in every direction from the Great Wall of China to the Volga.

The Bhuddism, or Lamaism, of the Mongols, serves the important purpose of binding the tribes together by one common bond of union. The adoration they are taught to pay to their Dalai Lama is such as to give that personage a power over them greater, probably, than is exercised by any crowned head over his people. The Dalai Lama is the Pope of the Mongols. He is a valuable ally to the Chinese Emperor, and would be a dangerous enemy. When Russia comes to carry out any aggressive design in Mongolia, the Great Lama of the Kalkas will be the instrument used; and the Consular establishment at Urga, if it succeeds in gaining over the Lama king to the Russian views, will not have been kept up in vain. To conciliate this dignitary the Chinese Emperors liberally endow monasteries, and support and encourage Lamaism in every way possible;—but the Russian Emperors will find no difficulty in securing the attachment of the Lama when their plans are matured.

The Mongol people, though in a sense slaves or serfs to their chiefs, really enjoy every liberty. They pay tithes to their lords of the produce of their herds, but there is no exaction, and no apparent discontent. The forty-eight chieftains enjoy the Chinese title of *wang*, *i.e.*, prince, or king, and though tributary to the Emperor, they receive from him more than they pay. Their allegiance is, in reality, purchased by the Chinese court, and they are certainly faithful to their salt.

CHAPTER XII.

KIACHTA.

As we approached the Russian frontier we reflected on the savage condition in which we had been living for so long, and were not without some anxiety as to how we should brook the glimmering of civilisation which we might expect to find, even in that remote corner of Christendom. It was also uncertain what reception we would meet with from the Russian officials, for although we had every reason to anticipate cordiality and friendly assistance, still political complications in Europe might have altered the relations of either of our respective countries with the court of Russia, and difficulties might possibly be raised. I had not forgotten the advice of a Russian official, high in the confidence of his Government, to defer my journey till more tranquil times. While indulging in these vain surmises, a smart shower of snow diverted our attention to other matters.

The Chinese town of Maimachin has first to be passed through. It is surrounded by a modern palisade, and looks mean enough externally, but improves vastly on acquaintance. The streets are regular, wide (for China), and tolerably clean. The houses are solid, tidy, and tastefully decorated, with pretty little courtyards, and ornamental screens for their doors, &c. The Chinese settlers have evidently improved by contact with the Russians, for the style of their houses in Maimachin, where the Chinese are only sojourners away from their own country, is superior to what one usually sees, even in fashionable cities in China proper. The *yamun*, or Government office, is at the far end of Maimachin, and is presided over by a Mongol. Beyond the Yamun is an open square, which is considered neutral ground between Russia and China. On the Russian side of the square we pass through a gate and are in Kiachta, under the wing of the great Russian eagle, which we see paraded everywhere over our heads. The black and white posts, said to have been a pet fancy of that miserable pedant, Paul Petrovitch, that offend the eye everywhere in Russia; the elegant houses with white-washed walls and red or green roofs; the gorgeous churches with tall tapering spires; and the wide streets, with nobody in them, are all taken in at the first glance through the gateway, and establish it beyond doubt that we are really in the territory of the Czars.

With little trouble we found out Mr. Pfaffius, Commissary of the Frontier, an office established in lieu of the governorship which had been abolished. The Commissary received us in a very friendly manner, gave me some letters that had overtaken me from China, files of the "Times" newspaper up to the 5th of August, and finally, to my great joy and comfort, announced that he had instructions from his superiors to facilitate my journey homewards, in consequence of an application from Lord Napier to the authorities at St. Petersburg. Nothing could be more satisfactory, and we had only now to get lodgings and make ourselves easy for a little.

Kiachta itself is but a small place, and contains few inhabitants, except the Commissary and his dependents, and the Russian merchants who are engaged in the China trade. The general population lives at Troitskosarfsk, which is a good-sized town, about two miles from Kiachta. Thither we proceeded with our caravan, and soon fell into comfortable quarters by the kind assistance of my countryman, Mr.

Grant. The day was wearing on, and our Mongols were in a hurry to get back to their grazing-ground. The camels were soon relieved of their burdens, but we could hardly realise that they were now unloaded for the last time in our service. The lama called us to count over the packages, and see whether everything was right; he then received the balance of his contract money, and was off. We did not charge him the forfeit he was liable to for the four days' over-time. Tellig received a small present, which gratified him beyond measure, for he never considered that he had done anything to lay us under an obligation to him. We really felt sorry to part from our Mongols, especially the faithful Tellig, and we could not help commiserating them as we thought of the severe season they had to pass on those dreary steppes, so intolerable in September, that one would suppose flesh and blood could not withstand the cruel cold of winter. They had in view a return cargo from a Chinaman in Maimachin, and, after a few days' rest, they would probably be on the march again towards the Great Wall of China. They had no intention of laying up any part of the winter, that being in fact their busiest season, and they would be in Kiachta again about December. What a miserable life it seems to live day and night almost on the back of a stinking camel! And yet these people, in the midst of hardships, are as happy as the day is long.

One of our first objects of inquiry at Kiachta was a Russian bath, which we found in the house where we lodged, and anything so exquisitely luxurious I never experienced, burdened as I was with a month's sand and dust, which we had no efficient means of getting rid of in the desert. The Mongols, indeed, never attempt to wash themselves, being only too glad to get water enough to boil their mutton and make their tea, and that is generally carried from a considerable distance, for a yourt is never found very close to a well. I never could get an explanation of this, but presume it is so ordained by law, to prevent any one family from monopolising a well. Although the Mongols do not wash at all, they did not look so dirty as we did after twenty-four hours travel,—either the dust does not stick to them, or it does not show on their darker-coloured skins. Anyhow, it does not inconvenience them, and all the purifying I have seen them attempt is a rough wipe they occasionally give to their greasy mouths with the skirt of their garment, either calico or sheepskin.

We were agreeably surprised to find so much refinement in this outpost of Siberia. The houses are mostly large and comfortable. All are built of wood, and mostly of round logs dovetailed together at the ends, and caulked with moss, giving them a massive warm look, even from outside. Those of greater pretensions are faced outside with planed wood, painted white, which, with their red or green painted roofs, give a cheerful air to the whole place. The churches are a great ornament to the town. They are all three built of brick, and white-washed, the tall cupolas being painted green.

The streets are well kept, which is not difficult to do, seeing that the ground is dry, and there is no great traffic to cut up the roads. Several of the streets are provided with wooden side-walks, which are very agreeable to the feet where the planking is sound, but in many places it has given way, exposing dangerous pitfalls to nocturnal or inebriated pedestrians.

Every Russian above the rank of a *moujik* (peasant) drives in some sort of a vehicle; and there are all sorts in Kiachta, from the droshkie, pure and simple, drawn by one or two shaggy Siberian ponies, to the luxurious carriage of "the swell," mounting a coachman, and perhaps a footman in livery, and drawn by two well-bred showy little horses from the west. The Russians never ride for pleasure or exercise ; in this respect resembling the Chinese, who never ride, walk, dance, or do anything that they can afford to pay some one else to do for them. A few of the Kiachta notabilities, who have been put under strict regimen by their doctors, certainly may be seen in the afternoon taking a constitutional, closely muffled up in their fur over-coats, which they hug round them with both hands, greatly impeding the free movement of the limbs. Fast walking would, however, probably be considered derogatory to the dignity of their station. These solitary and sombre-looking figures, covered up to the eyes, look like assassins, and the imagination can easily picture to itself a dagger concealed under the ample folds of the cloak as they pace slowly along in the dusk on the open road between Kiachta and Troitskosarfsk.

The Russians generally have a lurking consciousness that they are but half civilised, and they are quite aware that they are so esteemed by the rest of Europe. Hence they are at unusual pains to maintain punctiliously the external forms of civilised life, mistaking the husk for the kernel. The tailors and milliners of Kiachta are as particular, and their customers perhaps more so, about getting the latest Parisian fashions, as their contemporaries in the most fashionable towns in Europe or even America. A morning visit in a shooting-coat to a merchant in Kiachta would grievously shock his sense of propriety, and if such an outlandish garb were to meet the ultra-refined eyes of his wife, the probable consequences to her delicate system are too serious to contemplate, albeit she is " fat, fair, and forty," and will challenge you in champagne on a proper occasion till all is blue. I had the misfortune to be the innocent cause of an alarming attack to a gentleman, who was civil enough to call at an unexpectedly early hour in the morning, by appearing before him in slippers and a Chinese sleeping-dress. The apparition paralysed him for two minutes, nor did he entirely recover his equanimity during the interview. It is this mistaken notion of what constitutes civilisation that induces the well-to-do Russian to wear expensive furs, simply because they are expensive, and to drink English bottled porter, not because he likes it, but because it costs twelve shillings a bottle.

In the streets and in the bazaar (Gostinnaidvor) a strange mixture of races is seen. The hairy, greasy, drunk-when-he-can Russian moujik; the small-eyed cunning Russian shop-keeper; a sprinkling of fine, dirty, rough-looking Bouriats, a Tartar tribe subject to Russia; a few Mongols who have business,—for their authorities, instigated by the Chinese government, are jealously watchful of their crossing the frontier,—and a few astute Chinese, the most business-like of the whole crowd.

The merchants of Kiachta are mostly reported to be enormously wealthy—several millions of roubles are not considered too much to ascribe to the most prosperous of them. These great fortunes are doubtless for the most part mythical, and as mammon is devoutly worshipped here, and the Russian " swell " has no qualities but wealth to recommend him to the respect of his countrymen, their reputed millions are merely a figure of speech, by which the public mean to express their appreciation of character. That the Kiachta merchants are, on the whole, wealthy, there is no doubt, and the most approved means for attaining that desirable condition seems to be to fail periodically. On those occasions the gentleman makes a journey to Nijni-novgorod and Moscow to see his creditors,—offers them fifty kopeks in the rouble or —nothing. The composition is accepted for various reasons: first, because it would be too much trouble to dispute it, and secondly, because the said creditors have made a good thing out of the connection, and hope to do so again. All this being satisfactorily arranged, the merchant starts afresh in the old line, having in the meantime added " house to house, and field to field." I would not be supposed to insinuate that this is a common practice in Kiachta, but some instances were pointed out to me of Crœsuses who had passed through the ordeal more than once, rising higher in public estimation each time, as their worldly prosperity increased. Large profits are made, or rather have been made, in the Kiachta trade, both with China and the west of Russia. Almost every merchant has a shop either in the bazaar at Troits-kosarfsk or in Kiachta, and their principle in business is rather to do little with large profits, than to accept smaller profits with a greatly extended trade. They don't seem to try to undersell each other, but rather combine to tax the public heavily for all the necessaries of life. The prices of nearly all articles in the shops are extravagant, even allowing for the expensive carriage their goods have to bear from the great distances most of them have to come. Were they to be content with such profits as would be considered ample in any other civilised country, they would place the necessaries of life, and even luxuries, within the reach of a vast number of people whose means do not at present admit of expensive indulgences, and thereby increase consumption to an extent that would in the long run bring them in greater aggregate profits than they now realise, and indirectly add to the general prosperity and well-being of the place. For one bottle of porter they now sell at three and four roubles, they would sell ten at one-and-a-half or two roubles; and so with other things. But the Russians have no notions of expansion, and the merchants are far behind the Government in commercial enlightenment. The recent measure of opening the Russian sea-ports to the import of tea direct from China, has utterly disconcerted the Kiachta people, who looked on the overland tea-trade through Siberia, with its sure snug profits, as part of their inheritance; and bitter complaints are heard on all sides at such an arbitrary interference with their prerogative. They considered themselves to have a vested right to supply the Russian people with dear tea for ever.

The Chinese of Maimachin are likewise reputed wealthy, and no doubt they are, to judge by their portly figures. This is considered a sure sign of prosperity in China, where rolling in wealth, and rolling in fat, are often considered synonymous terms. I have, however, known the criterion prove frequently fallacious. The Chinese merchants of Maimachin live there without their families, and consider themselves as mere sojourners, although many of them spend the best part of their lives there. They have an unconquerable aversion to moving their families from the spot where they and their fathers were born; and even within the bounds of their own country they rarely migrate for good from one district to another, unless driven to such a step by some potent cause, such as a visitation from the "rebels."

The Russians and Chinese are peculiarly suited to each other in the commercial, as well as in the diplomatic departments. They have an equal regard for truth, for the Russian, spite of his fair complexion, is at the bottom more than half Asiatic. There is nothing original about this observation, but it serves to explain how it is that the Russians have won their way into China by quiet and peaceable means, while we have always been running our head against a stone wall, and never could get over it without breaking it down. The Russian meets the Chinese as Greek meets Greek: craft is encountered with craft, politeness with politeness, and patience with patience. They understand each other's character thoroughly, because they are so closely alike. If some matter has to be negotiated, it is quite understood that each begins as far from the subject as possible : much conversation takes place on both sides; many pipes are smoked, and many cups of tea sipped, while they are beating about the bush. They receive each other's statements for what they are worth, that is, not as being intended to convey any definite signification, but as merely put in for the purpose of concealing their real purpose and to smooth the way to the object in view. Of course much valuable time is lost by this circumlocution, but it is a matter of apparent indifference to either party whether the negotiation is concluded in one day, or three days, or three weeks. They prefer their own way of dealing, and don't understand any other. When either Russian or Chinese meets a European, say an Englishman, he instinctively recoils from the blunt, straightforward, up-and-down manner of coming to business at once ; and the Asiatic either declines a contest which he cannot fight with his own weapons, or, seizing the weak point of his antagonist, he angles with him until he wearies him into acquiescence. As a rule, the Asiatic has the advantage. His patient equanimity, and heedlessness of the waste of time, are too much for the impetuous haste of the European. This characteristic of the Russian trading classes has enabled them to insinuate themselves into the confidence of the Chinese; to fraternise and identify themselves with them, and as it were make common cause with them in their daily life; while the European holds himself aloof, and only comes in contact with the Chinese when business requires it,—for all the rest, a great gulf separates them in thoughts, ideas, and the aims of life. The Russians and Chinese are equally low in their tastes ; intellectual and manly recreations are equally foreign to them, while eating and drinking, play-going and gambling, are the congenial amusements of both alike. I have been told that the Russian merchants of Kiachta, when they wish to treat each other to something worthy of a highly cultivated mind, order a Chinese dinner in Maimachin, a feast that most Europeans would rather undergo the incipient stages of starvation than come within the smell of. But in this and other things the Russians pay tribute to the superior civilisation of the Chinese, all the more genuine that it is unconsciously done. That the Chinese are the more civilised of the two, I am thoroughly convinced. Their notions of civilisation certainly run in a different groove from those of Christian nations, but it is a spontaneous growth, and genuine of its kind. But the Russians, after all that they have borrowed from their western neighbours, remain barbarians at bottom; and their living in large houses, and drinking expensive wines, serve merely to exhibit, in more striking colours, the native barbarism of the stock on which these twigs of a higher order of life have been engrafted. This does not, of course, apply to the educated gentlemen of Russia, the *nous autres*, who constitute a higher caste, and who have been largely leavened with foreign blood, but only to the middle and lower ranks. There is no middle class in Russia, as we understand the term, but there is a pretty large number of merchants who have risen from the condition of serfs, many of them very rich, and who must be taken to represent the middle class, but between whom and the gentlemen in uniform there is as impassable a barrier as between a merchant in Japan and a daimio. The Chinese far outstrip the Russians as a nation of shopkeepers, and in commercial matters generally have more enlarged and liberal ideas. Much of this is due to the non-interference of Government with trade. The restrictions of shops to one locality in Russian towns has its advantages and disadvantages; but the licence fees required for admission to the guilds, and for permission to open a shop in the bazaar, are so onerous as to exclude that class of small shopkeepers who are the life and soul of Chinese cities.

The largest building in Kiachta is called the Custom

House, but it is no longer used as such, all duties on merchandise having been recently abolished through the enlightened exertions of the present Governor-General of Eastern Siberia, who has done much to develop trade in his government. And truly the whole of that inaccessible region, including the Amoor provinces, is so ill-favoured by nature in its geographical position, and so thinly inhabited by a race who have had all enterprize ground out of them by centuries of oppression, that it is only by coaxing and nursing that prosperity can ever take root and flourish. The old Custom House is now occupied by the chief of *postes* and some other Government officials. It is situated on an elevation above the town and at the far end of Troitskosarfsk, at as great a distance as possible from the residence of the Commissary of the Frontier, who holds his court at the opposite extremity of Kiachta.

Having much business to transact at both these places, we hired a droshkie by the day at two roubles, an old shabby looking machine, very groggy on the springs, with two wild half-broken ponies tied to it with ropes, and an unkempt *moujik* on the box. In this turn-out we rattled along the dusty streets of Kiachta, passed by everything we saw excepting costermongers' carts. I felt very small, perched on the old rattle-trap, and had it not been for the " honour of the thing " I would infinitely have preferred walking or riding, but that was not to be thought of in a Russian, and especially a Siberian, town. Our reputation was at stake.

Kiachta lies snugly in a hollow between hills of sand and fir-trees, well sheltered from the northerly winds, and opening out southwards towards Mongolia. A small rivulet runs through the ravine, which turns west through the sandy plain on the Mongol side of the frontier, and falls into the general receptacle of the other rivers we had crossed. Kiachta and Troitskosarfsk are said to contain 20,000 inhabitants, who are pretty well supplied with provisions from the interior. Great numbers of peasants' carts may be seen in the morning bringing in the products of their farms and gardens to market. All the common vegetables are to be had in abundance; good beef and mutton of course, though the Russians, for some unexplained reason, eat very little mutton. The supplies for Kiachta come from great distances, and the peasants start from their homes long before break of day. They generally hunt in couples, the man with his sheepskin coat hung on him, leading the horse and riding by turns, while the good-wife, swaddled up into a round bundle of clothing, and booted to the knees, sits on the top of the cabbages. A large square in the centre of Troitskosarfsk is set apart as a corn and hay market, and is provided with sundry weights and scales sanctioned by the proper authorities. Here the vendors of agricultural produce assemble, and generally manage to get rid of their stocks by an early hour in the afternoon. Everything seems to be sold by weight in Russia, but they can hardly carry this to the same extent as the Chinese, who sell live chickens by weight, and by way of making up for any deficiency stuff their crops with sand, which adds an ounce or two to the aggregate weight, but produces death in a very short time. This trick used to be played off on masters of steamers, who thought to do a service to their countrymen at Shanghae, where provisions were at famine prices, by bringing a few hundred fowls from other ports where they were to be had cheap. The mortality in the middle passage was so great, however, that the second day generally threw a very different light on the venture.

Kiachta is also well supplied with excellent fish, the sturgeon among others, from the river Selenga, and it was here for the first time that we indulged ourselves in fresh caviar.

In this town there is a public recreation ground within a neat enclosure, where ladies promenade in the afternoon to inhale the fresh air, or exhibit the latest thing in bonnets, for Russians don't care much for air or exercise. Some retired nooks there are in the enclosure, suggestive of love-making at a more genial season, but they looked dreary enough in September, with a hard frost on the ground, and snow on the neighbouring hills. The whole goes by the name of "the garden," and in the three short months of summer it may possibly show something to justify this appellation. The mere attempt at gardening under such difficulties as a Siberian climate imposes, is creditable to the enterprise of the Kiachtaites, and it were much to be wished that the sun would shine on their efforts. The severity of the weather drives those who have a taste for flowers to cultivate them in their houses, which they do very successfully. Many of their rooms are like greenhouses, furnished round with large flowering shrubs in pots, very pleasant to the eye, whatever may be the effect of so much vegetation on human health. The plants are put out into gardens during the short summer, and withdrawn to the warm rooms when the chill winds give notice that winter is near.

The climate of Kiachta is very cold in winter, and pretty hot in summer. The air is very dry, soil sandy, and little or no rain or snow falls. It lies in lat. 50° 15', and at an elevation of 2200 feet above the sea. The population is reputed to be healthy, and old people of eighty and upwards are as lively as crickets. The houses are very comfortable, so far at least as warmth constitutes comfort, and in severe climates it is undoubtedly the first essential. The massive wooden walls well caulked with moss, which is said to be better and more lasting than oakum, are well adapted to exclude cold. They have all double windows a few inches apart, with the space between filled with cotton wool along the sill. The rooms are heated by large closed stoves or ovens, which are used for cooking as well as warming the house. In general, one stove is made to heat several rooms, being built into the corner presenting one face to each apartment. The great drawback in all this is the absolute want of ventilation, which was to us very trying and disagreeable, but the Russians are accustomed to live in health in the close stuffy atmosphere of their houses. The temperature of their rooms is kept up to about + 16° Reaumur (68° Fahrenheit), and varies but little from that range. They use a great deal of firewood, which is cheap in the neighbourhood of those vast primæval forests, and in the yards of Kiachta immense stores of this fuel are piled up for winter use.

The Russian manner of living was not quite suitable to us, although more regular than we had lately been accustomed to. They eat but one meal a-day, and that about twelve or one o'clock. The everlasting samovar fills up the morning and evening with its incessant bubbling and spluttering. Much tea-drinking is calculated to take the edge off a ravenous appetite, and in addition to the fluid we were fain to eat all the little cakes that usually accompany the samovar, in order to tide over the long twenty-four hours that interfered between regular meals. The stock dish of the Russians is a vegetable soup, with beef boiled in it. It is called *shtchee*, and is good or bad, according to the materials available for its manufacture, and the skill of the cook. Our cook in Kiachta was a lady of the mature age of eighty-two, who was justly proud of her attainments. The *shtchee* is enough of itself to make a substantial meal, as the *bouilli* is served up with it; but it is generally followed by a solid piece of roast beef. The bread is very good and white, but a strange custom prevails of putting black bread on the table along with the white, for the apparent purpose of showing off by contrast the extreme whiteness of the white, for no one ever touches the black when he can get the other. The real black bread is heavier, and as clammy as if potatoes entered largely into its composition. It is used almost exclusively by the peasants, and is doubly economical, being in the first instance cheap in price, and moreover a very little of it goes a long way, as it resists digestion as long as a hard-boiled egg. The black bread used by the well-to-do classes is a compromise, and is of a black-brown colour, known as *demi-blanc*.

The Kiachta community is for the most part permanent. The official portion of it is of course migratory, as the Government *employés* look for promotion to other regions, but some of them also settle down in Kiachta and found families. Many of the merchants also move westward, or intend to do so, but the whole substratum of peasants, artisans and tradesmen is a settled population. They talk little of Petersburg and Moscow, and when they do, it is with a kind of distant awe, as if these holy places belonged to a higher world. Irkutsk is the centre of their thoughts, the pivot on which they move. Whatever is defective in Kiachta is sure to be found in perfection in Irkutsk ; the best hotels, horses, carriages, doctors, houses, churches, shops—everything—are there. A journey to Irkutsk is not an unfrequent occurrence, but a journey to Moscow is something to be talked about on every convenient occasion for the remainder of one's life-time.

The town was founded in 1728, as an *entrepôt* of the caravan trade with China, and to that alone does it owe its importance. Tea has always been much the largest item in this trade, and although Kiachta must continue to command the trade between China and Eastern Siberia, the direct importation of sea-borne teas to the Baltic ports cuts off an important source of prosperity from Kiachta. The mercantile community have, up to last year, endeavoured to compete with their rivals, and pushed into China to purchase the tea in the same markets; but the conditions of the trade are so much altered that they are deprived of their former facilities for bartering Russian produce, and in other respects the caravan trade is too heavily weighted ever to compete successfully with the long sea route. Even in Russia, wedded as the masses are to prejudice, common sense must gain the day in the end, particularly where roubles and kopeks are in question.

We did not grudge ourselves a few days' rest at Kiachta, considering we had accomplished the most tedious part of the journey, and henceforward would get over the ground as fast as horses' legs could carry us. But no such luck was in store for us. The first news we had from the commissary and others, was that the whole country between the shores of the Baikal lake and Kiachta was inundated by the flooding of the river Selenga. It seemed that our adverse fortune was to follow us along the whole journey. We need not have been surprised, however, at the intelligence we received of the condition of the Selenga, since into it all the rivers we had crossed in Mongolia discharge themselves. The post from Europe was long overdue, and no news had been received from the Baikal for ten days. We were constrained perforce to remain quiescent until the waters should subside, and a day or two after our arrival a courier who came with the missing mail reported a slight improvement in the communication, he having succeeded in carrying the mail in small boats from station to station. Our time was not, however, misspent, for we had a number of preparations to make for our journey. In the first place we had to exchange our Chinese silver into Russian paper money. We were prepared of course to lose on this operation, but were agreeably surprised to find we had got off with only about one per cent. For one tael of sycee we received $2r.\ 15kop.$, which, at the then value of three shillings to the rouble, gave us $6s.\ 5\frac{4}{10}d.$

for our tael, which was worth roundly 6s. 6d. We had then our ponies and carts to dispose of, and my pony was quickly sold for ten roubles, of which my share was eight, that is twenty-four shillings for what cost thirty-two,—so far so good. But, when we came to offer the carts for sale, difficulties presented themselves. No one had ever heard of such articles being sold in Kiachta. This seemed strange, for the Chinese—if not the Russians—use no other conveyance in their frequent journeys to China. The carts are made only in China, and therefore ought to be at a premium in Kiachta. But the Russians were not to be reasoned with in this way, but maintained that it was hopeless to attempt to sell our carts, and we abandoned the idea. We happened, however, to mention the subject to some Chinese in Maimachin, and having persuaded them to come to Troitskosarfsk, and see the articles, we concluded a bargain, on the eve of our departure, for sixty-five roubles, about half what they cost.

It was necessary to our comfort to purchase a *tarantass*, or large travelling carriage. It was possible to travel without one, using the *kibitka*, or small carriage, provided at the post-stations; but that mode of travelling involved the annoyance of changing at every station, which, with our huge amount of baggage, would have been intolerable. We had some trouble to find a tarantass, and when we had got one it was not quite what it should have been—indeed we should have done better to have used the post kibitkas as far as Irkutsk, and bought a tarantass there, where we would have had a better selection.

In Maimachin we purchased some goat skins, with hair twelve inches long. These we had sown together into a sack for each of us to put our legs into when sitting in the carriage; a very simple contrivance, well worthy of the attention of all travellers in those regions in cold weather, and which contributed in no small degree to our comfort on the road.

The remnant of our stores, &c., tent, saddles, and such like, had to be abandoned in Kiachta, and we could only make room in the tarantass for a little brandy, and some tins of bacon, and smoked tongues. Hitherto we had trusted nothing to the chance supplies of provisions that might be found on the road; but now, being in a civilised (?) country, we depended solely on its resources, such as they were.

We had no trouble with our papers in Kiachta, and our luggage was never looked at; neither did we require to take out a Russian passport, but merely had to get our Peking ones viséd for Irkutsk by the master of police, which formality enabled us to obtain from the chief of the posts a *padaroshna*, or pass for post-horses, which are entirely under Government control. In addition to this, Mr. Pfaffius supplied us with a special pass, to give greater effect to the padaroshna, and to ensure us proper attention from the various station masters as far as Irkutsk. This document was to be exchanged for a similar one, which we hoped to obtain from the higher authorities at the provincial capital. We experienced the greatest civility and ready assistance from all the Russian officials with whom we came in contact in Kiachta, and the bugbear of troublesome interference by the authorities vanished away.

We soon got tired waiting for better news of the state of the roads between us and Lake Baikal, and determined to start on the 7th of October at all hazards. The steady frosty weather, with occasional falls of snow, gave us warning of winter, and of the uncertainty of getting our heavy carriage over half-frozen rivers. Every day was important at such a critical season, and the motherly counsels of the good old lady we were living with, to postpone our journey till December, when the snow roads would be in perfect order, only made us the more impatient to be off. Had we stayed another day we might have been tempted to give ear to these reiterated remonstrances against tempting Providence by starting at such a time.

Some hours were occupied in loading our tarantass, for we discovered to our dismay that the machine, large as it was, was still too small for our baggage and ourselves. After several attempts to dovetail unwieldy boxes into corners and use up all smaller articles as broken stowage, we eventually succeeded, between the inside and the outside of the machine, to get everything on board, and with a severe struggle we squeezed ourselves in, horizontally, between the baggage and the hood of the conveyance. Our padaroshna was for three horses, but when the driver brought them to be harnessed, and saw the load he had to drag, he at once protested against going with less than four. We felt that he was quite right, but to establish a character it was necessary that we should be firm at the outset. To have admitted the necessity for four horses would have exposed us to all manner of impositions at the successive stations, where our ignorance of Russ would have placed us at the mercy of every ruffian of a postmaster. With great misgivings, therefore, we started with our three horses, driven by a Bouriat *yemschik*. The tarantass is a strong roughly made four-wheeled carriage, placed on poles, which rest across the two axletrees. The poles are made of soft wood, but have some spring in them, and the tarantass is at least more comfortable on rough roads than a Chinese two-wheeled cart. The hood comes well forward, and with an apron that comes up nearly to the top, and a curtain that can be let down from the front of the hood, the tarantass can be pretty well closed in.

The "horses" are only ponies, a little over thirteen hands high, strong shaggy little brutes, full of beans and of great endurance. They are harnessed, or rather tied, to the vehicle, or, as the Russians like to call it, the *equipage*, in the loosest possible manner. A stout steady one is put in the shafts without any traces, the collar being secured to the forward part of the shafts by strong leather bands. A wooden tree arched over the collar and fixed to the shafts by its two ends, has a bearing rein running from the top, and kept rather tight on the horse's mouth. A bell is also suspended from the top of this cumbrous-looking apparatus, which denotes to all whom it may concern that it jingles over a post-horse. The bell is an intolerable nuisance on the road, but it is of some use in arriving at a station to announce the important event to the station-keeper, who peradventure may be asleep.

The other horses are attached by rope traces to the axletrees, or any part of the outside of the tarantass which may be available for making fast a rope. Each horse is independent of the others, and any, except the middle one, may get off the road, kick, fall, or do what he likes, without disturbing the general equilibrium. The favourite number of horses in Russia is three, which they call a *troilki* —they all go abreast, whether the number be two or six. Everything about the "turn out" is of the loosest and rudest construction—the wheels have plenty of scope, and oscillate three or four inches on the axle, so as to be easily oiled. Something is constantly going wrong—the wonder is that the whole arrangement does not break down on the road beyond the hope of remedy; but the Russians are very clever at making shifts, and with the constant demands that are made on their resources, their talents are kept in full exercise.

CHAPTER XIII.

KIACHTA TO LAKE BAIKAL.

WE got out of Troitskosarfsk about three o'clock in the afternoon, for as we intended to travel as the Russians do, night and day, it made no difference at what time of the day or night we commenced the journey. The first stage led us over rather hilly roads, in many places heavy with sand. The hills around have a sandy appearance, but after crossing the first ridge we opened out fine broken scenery with richly wooded heights. Our *yemschik*, or driver, being a Bouriat, we were able to converse with him in his mother-tongue, for though the Bouriats grow up speaking Russian, they preserve their own domestic institutions, and among themselves speak their own language, which, with some slight differences, is identical with that spoken by the Mongols of the Great Desert.

The first station we arrived at was Ust Kiachtinské, which is a fair-sized village of small wooden houses, with a very neat little church. We were prepared for all the horrors of a Siberian post-station, but found instead a new station-house, well kept and scrubbed inside, warm and clean. It is twenty-three and a-half versts, or nearly sixteen miles, from Troitskosarfsk. Our doubts and fears regarding our ability to deal with Russians, of whose language we were ignorant, awed us into great circumspection at this, the first point where we were left to our unaided resources. Our first anxiety was to maintain our prestige among the Russians, for, that failing, we should have been helpless indeed. The only sure way of saving our name under the circumstances was to decline all discussion, and as far as possible hold our tongues. This succeeded very well at Ust Kiachtinské—four horses were put to our tarantass, and no extra fare asked. The post had left that day, and the poor jades allotted to us had already performed one stage over very heavy roads, and were in no condition to drag our unwieldy equipage. Our Bouriat yemschik had not gone very far over the soft sand before he discovered this, and after exhausting all his persuasion to no good purpose, he sent a message to the station by a chance Russian whom we met on the road. In answer to this a fifth horse was sent from the post-house. The yemschik resumed his efforts to proceed, and by dint of yelling, carressing, and whipping, we got along a few miles further. A nasty steep hill lay before us, and arrested our progress finally for the night. When the yemschik had bawled himself hoarse, and had goaded his horses to despair, he entreated us, first in Russian, and then in Mongol, to get out and unload the carriage. It was a cold dark night, and we were warmly wedged into the carriage in a way that if we got out we could never have readjusted our beds in the dark. Finding us deaf to remonstrance, our poor yemschik took the horses out and let them graze—made a fire for himself of the end of a fallen tree, and waited patiently for morning.

When daylight came we found ourselves in a thick wood, half way up the hill. An hour and a half was spent in unloading and getting the vehicle over the hill. After which we proceeded slowly to the station Piravolofské, which we reached at 8 o'clock. On the road we passed several villages, with some cultivated enclosures farmed by Russians, who also keep a good many cattle.

It was plain that we could not go on so heavily laden, for even if horses could draw our tarantass, the machine itself would certainly break down, and we should run the risk of being wrecked on the road beyond the reach of assistance. We therefore determined if possible to secure an extra carriage at Piravolofské. To this the station-keeper demurred, and told us that with only one padaroshna it was impossible to horse two equipages. The pass from the commissary was efficacious in removing his doubts, and after expending all his eloquence in proving the impossibility of complying with our request, he quietly ordered a *kibitka*, into which we transferred a portion of our dead weight, and we went on our way rejoicing. The roads were rather sandy and a good deal up and down hill. At 2 o'clock we passed Paravotné station, where we had *shtchee*. We then proceeded by a good road up a long valley through which runs a tributary of the Selenga. Turning with the river into another valley to our left, we again encountered sandy and hilly roads. We soon struck the Selenga, a fine deep river, running through a wide valley, hemmed in by steep and well-wooded hills. A ferry-boat which was in attendance carried us across easily, horses, carriages, and all. The people who manned the boat were Russians and Bouriats, some of them showing unmistakeable marks of mixed blood. The river had fallen about twelve feet by the marks on the rock. A few miles from the ferry lies the small, but rather pretty town of Selenginsk. It has commodious barracks, one fine church, and some good houses. The station-master at Selenginsk was an old, fat, consequential and surly fellow. His room was adorned with some poor pictures, among which was an engraving of Catherine II. The companions of his solitude were a wretched-looking girl, maid-of-all-work, and a small cur, trained to perform certain tricks before travellers, on whom it seemed to depend for its daily bread. This old fellow was too important a personage in his own estimation to allow us to pass without challenging our right to the two carriages, but by dint of holding our tongue we conquered his objections as effectually as if we had greased his palm with roubles.

Night was on before we got away from Selenginsk. At 11 o'clock we passed Arbusofské, and at 5 next morning we passed Nijni Ubukunské. A bitterly cold morning was the 9th of October. Passed through a well-peopled valley, in good cultivation compared with what we had seen, though still far short of what it might be. The valley runs northeast to Verchne Udinsk, a considerable town. We did not go round by that town, but turned off at Mohinski into a valley on our left, and struck the Selenga again, keeping on the left bank of the river. We now began to experience the effects of the recent inundations. Although the flood had abated very much, the water in the river was still high, and the flat banks were great marshes. The road had been almost obliterated by the flood, and new tracks had been struck out through the driest parts, over large boulders, deep holes filled with water, and heavy mud. The horses floundered, but struggled bravely, and the yemschiks vociferated for miles, through this impracticable compound of land and water. We were five hours in going sixteen miles.

The valley narrows to a steep gorge through which the Selenga forces its way under a shade of overhanging trees that almost conceals it from view. The river was running about four miles an hour, but so smoothly and silently, that the current would have been hardly perceptible but for the floating branches of trees borne on its surface. The scenery is most beautiful. The perpendicular walls of rock that form the gorge are thickly wooded with pine and birch, which, combined with the willows that grow in great luxuriance on the low banks of the river, and seem to stretch their branches almost across the water, give quite a tropical appearance to the valley.

The road through the gorge is scarped out of the rock, and

rises to a good height above the river. It is narrow in the parts which are entirely artificial, so narrow that in some places there is not room for two vehicles to pass. The grandeur of the scenery faded away before our eyes as we looked down from the height into the deep abyss below. The edge of the precipice is guarded by a rough, strong, wooden parapet, without which, restive horses and drunken yemschiks would inevitably be immolated by the score at this dangerous place.

At 3 p.m. we arrived at Poloviné station, simultaneously with a number of other travellers from various quarters. The long interruption of travelling from the flooding of the country, had accumulated a great many on the west of Baikal lake, and now they crowded on all at once. Amongst our fellow-travellers were several government officers, and two loquacious Poles from Irkutsk. The station could not furnish horses for half of the number, and as we had all arrived together, it was a question who should get them. We required seven for our two carriages in the then state of the roads, and it was no small satisfaction to us to find that the postmaster assigned to us the precedence. The government officers made no remark, but simply ordered the samovar to make tea. The Russian travellers also took it very quietly. But the two Poles were not so easily appeased. We could glean a few words from the volleys of abuse with which they indulged themselves, the gist of which was anathemas on the Russian government, the postal system, and things in general, winding up with a threat to set up a "republic" in Siberia. Leaving our exasperated friends to digest the venom of their spleen, we rattled away over good roads along the left bank of the Selenga, till we arrived at dusk at the post station of Ilyensk, six versts short of the town of that name. The postmaster here was an old sergeant who kept house with his aged wife. She seemed to be a good sort of woman, for the house was in capital order, the wooden floor clean scrubbed, and the walls beautifully white. Tables and chairs were in the like good trim, as were also the pots and pans and crockery. The sergeant received us with open arms, and was obsequiously civil. It is probable that the yemschiks who had conducted us from Poloviné had passed the word to him of our being distinguished personages, whom all good post-masters delighted to honour. When the little man had acquitted himself of his bowing and scraping, he began to expatiate on the coldness of the night and the badness of the road that lay before us. The end of it was that he pressed us, with his most winning grimaces, to make ourselves comfortable under his roof for the night, and proceed at daylight next morning towards the Baikal. We were but too willing to listen to the voice of the charmer, for experience had taught us that night travelling in Siberia is no great luxury. Having therefore satisfied ourselves that we should be in good time to catch the steamer on the Baikal, which makes two trips a week, we resigned ourselves with a good conscience to the kind solicitations of our host. When supper was over and bedtime came, visions of Russian vermin began to haunt us, and seriously disturbed our prospects of rest. The most careful scrutiny of the apartment, however, led to no discoveries of a disagreeable nature, beyond the shoals of small cockroaches which the heat of the room brought out in high condition. These animals are inoffensive enough in their habits, but restless, and ever on the move, running to and fro over the room and everything in it. They emit a fetid odour, which is the most unpleasant thing about them, particularly when you inadvertently crush them. But the close, oven-heat of the room itself was in my case a sufficient objection to sleeping there, and the tarantass was to me the more attractive dormitory of the two. Indeed, when well wrapped up with furs, and only a part of the face exposed to the frost, the tarantass affords sleeping accommodation that might well be envied by a king, provided always there is no jolting over rough roads to disturb the sleeper.

The jingling of bells at various periods of the night announced the arrival of other travellers, and in the morning we found that one party of Russian officers, whom we had left drinking tea at Poloviné, had come and gone without stopping at Ilyensk. Another party of merchants had arrived later, and were all ready to start again when we got out of bed. We were naturally, though perhaps unjustly, suspicious of the Russians, and the first thought that flashed across our minds, on surveying our situation, was that we had been duped by the post-master into remaining all night at Ilyensk in order to let the others get a clear start of us on the road. It was of the last importance to reach the shore of Lake Baikal, from which we were still ninety versts distant, in time to save the steamer, and in the bad state of the roads it was impossible for us to calculate the length of time we should require to travel the distance. The advantage we had been induced to yield to our fellow-travellers might prove fatal to our own success, for although horses would be kept for us at Ilyensk, there might be a scarcity at the following stations, and our neighbours having the lead might take every available beast, leaving none for us. Under such circumstances the old sergeant was regarded with very different feelings from those we entertained of him when we retired to rest the night before. He did not escape a fair quota of abuse, but he still protested that his intentions were honourable. Great haste was made to get our horses in, and we had faint hopes of overtaking some of our friends.

The road from Ilyensk was good for fifteen versts, and quite level. Beyond that it had been completely destroyed by the recent floods, and the country was full of lagoons. The bridges were washed away, and their *débris* were scattered about over the fields. The main road was quite impracticable, and by-paths were struck out wherever the fancy, or topographical knowledge of the yemschik directed him. It was a wild chase for many weary miles, through great sheets of water, over high banks, and wide deep ditches, which were charged at full gallop, the lumbering machine being got over apparently by the sheer force of momentum. We then plunged into a dense forest where a lane had been cut out, leaving the stumps of the trees still sticking up. The ravines had been roughly bridged over with new-cut trees, overlaid with branches. This road, besides being as rough as wheeled carriage ever travelled on, was very circuitous, and our stage of twenty-four versts by the main road was stretched out to not much short of double that distance by the tracks we were compelled to follow. It says something, however, for the energy of the government, that the emergency should have been met so promptly. Their postal communication had not been interrupted a fortnight before this new road had been cut through the wood, on the slope of a hill above the reach of inundation.

Changed horses at Tarakanofské, a small miserable station, and at 1.30 reached Kabansk, a neat town with a pretty church. Here we dined, and proceeded at 2.30. The high mountains west of the Baikal were now distinctly visible. At the next station, Stepné-dvaretské, the postmaster was a Pole, a fine old gentleman, who was exiled under Nicholas in 1854. He appeared very anxious to talk about the affairs of Poland, but we had not acquired enough Russian to make conversation very interesting to either party, and besides we were in a hurry, and daylight was fast failing. The old fellow exulted in the expectation of foreign intervention in Poland, and became radiant with delight when we revealed our respective nationalities.

After leaving Stepné-dvaretské we soon reached the shore of the lake, when we turned to the left, and followed the coast-line, through occasional thickets and wide lagoons, till we reached Pasoilské, the terminus of the Trans-Baikal post-road. The station-house was full of travellers waiting for the steamer to cross the water. The fixed time of her departure was 9 o'clock the next morning, and the crowd of travellers spent the night in the post-house. No beds, and few seats are provided at these places. Men, women, and children roll themselves down on the floor indiscriminately, and sleep soundly through the incessant turmoil and noise that would make night hideous to nervous people. It is often impossible to thread one's way into the dormitory without treading on half the people who are sleeping among the bundles of clothing that cover the floor; but aggressions of that sort, being of common occurrence, are borne with stoical indifference. I slept as usual in the tarantass, and was lulled to sleep by the harmony of a howling wind, and the loud murmur of the waves of the lake that washed the sandy beach within a few yards of me.

The Selenga is formed in Mongolia by the junction of a number of small streams south of Lake Kosgol, 230 miles south-west from Kiachta. It is afterwards joined by the Orkhon, and its tributaries from the Kinghan mountains. The length of this river has been computed at 300 miles, which is probably near the mark. It is singularly rich in fish, among which is the sturgeon. The fisheries are a great blessing to the people who inhabit the valley, among whom fish forms a staple article of diet.

The Selenga falls into the Baikal, by several mouths, about twenty miles north of Pasoilské. That part of the coast would not be so convenient for the steamer to cross at, and would moreover make the crossing so much longer. But as the Selenga itself is navigable, by properly constructed vessels, from its mouth to a point higher than Selenginsk, the steamer route may possibly be eventually diverted to the river.

The valley of the Selenga is hemmed in to a narrow compass by mountains as far down as Ilyensk. Thence, downwards, the two mountain barriers diverge gradually, leaving a fine open valley, which widens to about forty miles on the coast of the lake. This valley supports a pretty large agricultural population, and the peasants seem all well-to-do. Agriculture is certainly not in an advanced state, if Europe be taken as a standard, but still a large portion of the valley is enclosed and cultivated; weeds are kept down; and stubble looks like stubble, and not merely grass of a different shade of colour from the surrounding pastures, which is the characteristic of the fields nearer Kiachta. The soil is light, dry, and friable; furrows don't hold their shape. The crops are chiefly cereals—wheat, barley, rye, and oats.

There is an immense tract of uncleared country in the Selenga valley, only wanting hands to fell trees and bring the soil under the plough, to make this a rich and fertile region. The slopes of the hills are also capable of cultivation, but centuries will probably elapse before they are required. In the meantime, both hills and plains bear magnificent crops of timber, which will keep the Siberians in fuel and building material for a thousand years to come.

Cattle are abundant, but under-bred and rather small. The milk cows are poor, which is singular considering that milk is such a valuable item in the subsistence of the people. They have a good hardy breed of sheep, which are nearly all black. Pigs are also very common in the villages. They are a peculiar breed, very active, do not grow to any size, rather long in the legs, and bristly. Their owners do not seem to feed their stock much, if at all, and consequently the animals have to follow their own instincts of self-preservation. They may be seen in the morning trooping it down the street at a steady trot, turning neither to the right hand nor to the left, until some edible substance arrests their attention. They are not very particular about what they eat, and they manage, by dint of rapid movements, to eke out a subsistence off the odds and ends to be found in the streets, and the roots they can burrow out of the fields. Many of these Siberian pigs are of a brown colour, which is uncommon in the porcine race.

The dogs of Siberia are of the ubiquitous breed which is common all over China, Japan, and many other countries, and is nearly akin to our own collie dog.

CHAPTER XIV.

LAKE BAIKAL TO IRKUTSK.

THE post-house of Pasoilské was all alive at an early hour on the 11th of October. Cart-loads of wood were piled on the fires. All the samovars were in requisition at once, and the company waited patiently, or impatiently, for their turn to come, for a Russian is very useless until he has guzzled three or four tumblers of tea. The "postilions," as they call the soldiers who travel with the mail-bags, and other hangers-on, generally came off best. Their instinct leads them to make friends with kitchen-maids, and the kitchen being their centre of attraction, it goes hard if they don't get their tea in good time.

The kitchen was the only place where one could get a wash, which is a difficult operation to the unskilful. No basin is provided, but an urchin, or a robust maiden, holds a pitcher of water, the contents of which you receive by instalments in the hollow of your two hands, and with good management you succeed in getting a few drops to your face.

While we were all stretching our necks to catch a glimpse of the steamer, every moment expected to heave in sight, an officer gave us the valuable hint that our tarantass could not be embarked at Pasoilské, there being no boat there capable of conveying it to the steamer. This was unwelcome intelligence to receive at the eleventh hour, but it was confirmed by the post-master who, however, had told us a different story the night before.

The "shipping port" was nine versts further south, and thither we had to transport our carriage. It was off the government post-road, and private horses had to be hired at rather an exorbitant rate. But there was no time to lose, and the Russian had us on the hip, an advantage which none know better how to turn to account. The road runs along a narrow sand-spit between the Baikal and the inner lagoons. It is very heavy, and the water has broken in on it in some places. The sand-spit runs out to a point forming a sheltered harbour inside for vessels of light draught. The entrance round the point has a shoal sand-bar, somewhat dangerous, running across it. Several Russian barges, rigged very much like Japanese junks, with one enormous mast placed near the centre of the vessel, and of about 150 tons burthen, lay aground discharging their cargoes on the shore. Several more were lying at anchor in the harbour. These vessels are of the rudest construction, and the most primitive model— very short, enormously high-sided, and of great beam. They have preposterously large rudders like the Chinese and Japanese junks. Their "lines" are so imperfect that no ordinary rudder would steer them. They must be incapable of any nautical movement except running before the wind. They carry large crews, chiefly Bouriats. Their heavy mainsail and rudder necessitates plenty of hands, and when in harbour (where they seem to spend most of their time) the large crew is useful in loading and discharging cargo.

When we consider the kind of craft, and the quality of their crews, by which the Baikal has been navigated, it is easy to account for the terrible stories of the storms that frequently spread destruction over the surface of the lake. That the lake, like other lakes similarly shut in by high mountains, is subject to sudden and violent storms, fraught with danger to crazy barks and unskilful navigators, there can be no doubt ; but we had occasion to observe that a very gentle zephyr indeed is accounted a storm on the Baikal. It is said that a peculiar phenomenon is sometimes observed in the lake,—a wave, or succession of waves, bubbling up from the bottom in the calmest weather as if moved by submarine influences. But it is not likely that this, or other anomalous convulsions in the waters of the Baikal are of frequent occurrence. But, although such phenomena have no doubt fortified the popular superstitious dread with which the lake is regarded, it is of the wind-storms that the Russian sailors and travellers are so apprehensive.

There is only one house at the port, which belongs to the company who own the steamers, as also many of the sailing craft that cross the lake. In the house we met but one traveller, all the others having stopped at Pasoilské to join the steamer there. There was a large concourse of people, however, engaged in landing and shipping cargo, and the scene was most animated. The sand-flat was covered with merchandise, in bales done up in cow-hides, casks, and all manner of packages—that from the west waiting to be carted away to the post-road for China or the Amoor river,—and eastern produce, principally Chinese, waiting shipment. The people moved about with more business-like energy than we had yet observed amongst Russians. The whole traffic with the Amoor crosses the Baikal here, as does also that with the south-eastern provinces of Siberia, which includes all Russian trade with China, excepting what finds its way to Semipalatinsk, further west on the Khirgis steppe. Large caravans of one-horse carts, laden with merchandise, are constantly met with on the post-road. The heavy portion of the trade naturally goes eastward, for all the clothing, all the luxuries, and much of what may be considered the necessaries of life of the Siberian cities, are supplied from Western Russia. Siberia has not much to send in return, except furs, the precious metals, and Chinese produce.

While we were waiting for the arrival of the steamer, we were roused by a wild kind of chant outside, and presently a procession of three Russian priests, with long hair and long beards, came into the room where we were sitting, and after doing reverence to the picture of the saint, stuck up in a corner of the room, they besprinkled the apartment with holy water, and retired. It was Sunday, and this imposing ceremony served to remind the Russians of that circumstance.

An officer from the Amoor country showed us great civility here, and made the time pass very pleasantly. He was worn with hard travelling, having ridden a long distance through forests where no proper road had yet been made. The usual way of travelling up the Amoor is by steamer, as far as the navigation is practicable, which is as high as the junction of the Shilka. But the steamers often tow huge barges, laden with grain, which greatly retards their progress, and besides, they are almost constantly breaking down. So that, where time is important, the shortest way is to ride until the regular post-road is struck.

This gentleman gave us some interesting information regarding the new road now being constructed by the government from Irkutsk to Kiachta, round the south end of Lake Baikal. The present route across the lake is very inconvenient, and not always safe. In summer and winter the communication by the lake is pretty regular ; but during the interregnum between the seasons it is very uncertain. When ice is forming on the lake it is always doubtful whether the steamer can cross with safety, and she is probably laid up for the winter sooner than is really necessary, from fear of being nipped by ice. Again, when the ice is melting, it would be hazardous to leave on the surface the post-stations which are used in winter traffic, for on such a large sheet of water, exposed to gales of wind, the ice may break up suddenly when thaw has once set in. This has actually happened: on one occasion a sudden break-up in the ice submerged a post-station with all the men, horses, &c., belonging to it. Thus the post establishments will generally be cleared off in spring, some time before the navigation is open. The inconvenience of depending on this one route for the transport of merchandise and gold has long been felt by the government, but the nature of the country on the southern shores of the Baikal presents almost insuperable difficulties to road-making. The precipitous mountain ranges in that region are at present impassable, except on foot or horseback, and dangerous even then. Our informant once tried it in winter, and had to abandon his horse to perish in the snow, saving his own life with difficulty. The road now being made is scarped out of the rock in the same way as the one I have described in the gorge in the Selenga valley. It is only worked at in winter when the peasants are frozen out of the mines and fields. One of the means employed to split the rocks, is to make enormous bonfires of trees when the temperature is very low ($-30°$ to $-40°$ Réaumur), the action of heat on the stone causing huge masses to crack, and enabling the workmen to dislodge it. This is necessarily a slow process. Several years have already been spent on it, and a good many more will elapse before the work is completed. When this road is finished it will materially shorten the distance between Irkutsk and Kiachta.

At noon a white column of wood-smoke on the horizon announced the approach of the steamer, and in a couple of hours she came-to off the port, dropped a barge which she had towed across, and proceeded to Pasoilské to embark mails and passengers. Her return was expected at 4 o'clock, but she did not appear till 6. It was then getting dark, and to our surprise it was unanimously pronounced too stormy for us to embark that night. It was even hinted that the steamer might run across to the other side of the lake where there was good shelter, and return next day to take us across. It was vain for us to remonstrate against this folly, though the wind was so light that we really could hardly tell which way it was blowing—with a chorus of bawling Russians all speaking at once. We had but to wait, and it was some consolation to us to hear the steamer's cable rattling through the hawse-pipe. She had dropped anchor in the offing, and, unless the "gale" increased, would remain there till morning.

The rates of passage by steamer across the lake are eight roubles first class, and five roubles deck passage, say twenty-four and fifteen shillings respectively. Distance about seventy miles. No table is kept on board. The freight on our tarantass was twenty roubles. Freight on general cargo is thirty kopeks per pood, equal to sixty shillings per ton. There seems to be no fixed rule as to passengers' baggage, but the agent is always open to an "arrangement." We were to pay the regular freight on ours, and the agent, to save himself the trouble of weighing it, asked us how much we had. I forget what the quantity was, but say it was ten poods. "Oh, then we will call it fifteen," said the agent. Our indignation was of course roused at this. We appealed to the Russian officer before mentioned, who laid it on so smartly to the agent for first asking us for the weight, and then assuming that we were necessarily trying to cheat him, that the wretch got frightened, and took our baggage free. This afforded the officer an opportunity, which the higher classes in Russia never let slip, of commenting on the low state of Russian morality, that is, of the merchant and moujik class, as distinguished from *nous autres*.

In the early morning the hive was all animation again. The clumsiest of boats were manned by crowds of Bouriats, with short paddles, to tow out to the steamer two of those huge barges that were lying in the harbour. The steamer was unable to approach nearer the shore than half a mile, owing to the shoalness of the water. The towing business pays the steamer well, and there are always numbers of sailing craft waiting at both ends for their turn to be towed across. Time is no object with them, and they miss many opportunities of sailing over with a fair wind, while waiting for the steamer to tow them. The trade is highly remunerative, as at present conducted, but it would pay much better to keep a smart steamer running regularly with mails and passengers, and a good tug to do nothing but tow barges. Half the number of these would then do as much work as the whole fleet does at present. A little healthy competition would work great results, but the Russians are fonder of combinations and monopolies than competition.

When the two barges had got their hawsers on board the steamer, one of the boats embarked our tarantass and ourselves, with a few other passengers who had turned up, and by eight o'clock we stood on the deck of the *General Karsakof*, so named after the present governor-general of Eastern Siberia. She is a rare specimen of naval architecture, and might have been built any time the last hundred years. Roughly put together, clumsy and unshapely, she would be a curiosity in any other part of the world ; and for dirt I am certain she has not her match. The engines, which are of fifty horse-power, are the only redeeming feature in the vessel. They were made by an Englishman in Western Siberia. It is no doubt a great thing to have floated a steamer at all on the Baikal lake, but while they were about it the builders might have produced something more ship-shape. The *General Karsakof* and her sister ship are coining money for their owners, however, and *they* have no reason to be dissatisfied with their property.

We made but slow progress with the two lumbering barges

in tow. There was a slight head wind at first, and our speed was about one mile per hour. Latterly the barges made sail, and we got on better.

Our course lay obliquely across the lake, about W.S.W. towards Listni-nijni at the head of the lower Angara. Had the weather been less severe we should have been tempted to keep the deck, and enjoy the sublime scenery with which we were surrounded. Both shores of the lake are very mountainous, those on the south-eastern side being highest, and covered with snow down to the water's edge. There was very little snow on the western side, the snow showers up to that time having been very slight and partial. The water of the lake, away from land, is of a very deep blue, almost black. Its depths have never been fathomed, probably from the want of proper tackle, for I am not aware that any ocean-sounding apparatus has ever been used on the Baikal. It has been said, I know not on what authority, that "no bottom" has been found at three thousand fathoms; but much that has been said of the Baikal is exaggerated, and I greatly doubt whether such a depth has been satisfactorily established. I was informed by a gentleman on the spot, personally acquainted with that part of the country, that the deepest soundings yet obtained in the lake were two hundred fathoms, and that beyond that depth nothing was known. It is only in a few places where soundings have not been taken.

The lake is over 300 miles in length, averaging about thirty in breadth; it covers a surface of 11,000 square miles, and is 1300 feet above the sea level. It is fed by two considerable rivers, the Little Angara on the north, and the Selenga on the east. It has only one outlet, the Great Angara, on the west, which drains the waters of the lake into the great river Yenisei, and that again into the Frozen Ocean. It is estimated that the water so drained out of the lake does not amount to more than one-tenth of the quantity poured into it. This estimate may be a little wide of the mark, but there can be no doubt of the fact that the lake receives a large surplus of water above what it gives out, which the quantity lost by evaporation must be utterly inadequate to account for. The level of the water fluctuates only a few feet between seasons.

Baikal is a Mongol name. In saintly Russia it is called the Holy Sea, and among the peasant navigators it is considered high treason to call it a lake.

So much for the much be-written Baikal. To return to the *General Karsakof*. She is puffing and spluttering, with no apparent result but the rapid diminution of the pile of firewood which cumbered her deck. The passengers, mostly on deck, wrapped in huge furs, sit patiently wherever sitting-room can be found, facing the keen air with unruffled equanimity. Their noses look a little blue, but what of that?—every other portion of their body is warmly covered. The saloon, so called, is under deck, cold and cheerless. It was occupied by a few Russian officers and ourselves, who, between intervals of sleep, called for the samovar, and sipped tea *ad libitum*, the only kind of entertainment the steamer seemed capable of providing. All travellers in Russia carry their own tea and sugar.

I presume some one navigated the steamer, but I never could discover who occupied this important post. She was steered mostly by Bouriats, who take it very easy, sitting all the time on neat little stools to that end provided.

We succeeded eventually in reaching the western shore. We were eighteen hours crossing, the distance being seventy miles. A good little harbour, with deep water, shelters the steamers at Listni-nijni. A pier has been built for the vessel to go alongside, and everything would be perfect were the easterly shelter a little more complete.

The captain of the steamer now appears on the scene to superintend the disembarkation. He is charged by government with the examination of the padaroshnas of passengers, which gives the authorities a check on any unauthorised persons going about the country.

It was 3 o'clock, and a bitterly cold morning, when we landed in the government of Irkutsk, but, as the steamer had been expected, there was no difficulty in getting horses at the station. A few versts beyond the station we observed a great bonfire blazing on the road-side, and certain wild-looking figures gliding about between the fire and a small hut close by. On reaching the spot, we detected a black and white bar suspended across the road, intimating that we were under arrest for the time being. The unearthly figures that reflected from their faces the fitful glare of the burning logs resolved themselves into men, clad in the grey great-coat of the Russian soldiers. Our luggage, it seemed, had to be examined here, which involved the torture of turning out of our warm berths. The officials were inexorable. Not knowing who was chief,—for as usual they all spoke at once, and every one seemed more officious than another,—we did not know whom to bribe; and, after turning out of our tarantass, we were not at all in a humour to bribe anybody. The officers of the customs, for such we assumed them to be, took plenty of time to turn over our boxes before opening any of them, but finding at last that the coveted coin was not forthcoming, they opened one or two packages for form's sake, repacked them, and performed the ceremony of putting a seal on them. We were then furnished with a certificate, which we were instructed to produce at Irkutsk, failing to do which it would be the worse for us. We never did produce it, and never were asked for it. Indeed this was the first and last time our baggage was looked at during the whole journey through

Siberia and Russia. The other passengers by the steamer came up after us, and passed the barrier without stopping. We should have done the same, no doubt, had we been better acquainted with the language.

The country west of Baikal, like that east of Baikal, is a vast forest, but not so mountainous. Between the lake and Irkutsk there is a great deal of cleared ground, and a considerable population. The Russian cottages are bare-looking, but neat and substantial. Their cattle-yards are mere open wooden palings, unsheltered and dreary-looking.

The road runs along the right bank of the Angara, the river that runs out of Lake Baikal, and falls into the Yenisei, about 1200 miles below Irkutsk. The water of the Angara is perfectly clear.

From the Baikal to Irkutsk we pass through a very fine country, whether regarded from a tourist or agricultural point of view. The cleared portion is in an advanced state of cultivation, carefully fenced, and very fertile. The people have more of the appearance of men who mean to make a living out of the soil, than any we had seen further east. The bold mountain scenery of the environs of the lake has disappeared, giving place to richly-wooded undulating hills, which are shown to great advantage by the intervals of villages and ploughed land. The rapid river flowing between steep banks, generally covered with trees or brushwood down to the water's edge, works its way circuitously through the hills, and gives a finish to as fine a bit of scenery as can anywhere be seen.

The road to Irkutsk is in capital order. Our horses were good, and our yemschiks willing, and by 11 o'clock we had rattled over the forty miles between the Baikal and Irkutsk. This distance is divided into three stages. At the last station the post-master was a German, of a Jewish cast of face, who seemed to be hired to tout for the Amoor Hotel in Irkutsk, which is the most popular with strangers. We had been specially warned against this establishment, and had the address of another, Metzgyr by name, which our yemschik pretended to know, and we started on our last stage with the understanding that we were to be conveyed to Metzgyr Hotel.

CHAPTER XV.

IRKUTSK.

THE sun shone brightly on the domes and cupolas of Irkutsk when they burst on the view; the effect of the dazzling white walls and bright green roofs of the churches was strikingly beautiful. Before entering the town, our yemschik descended from the box, and tied up the bells of the horses, in deference to a municipal law of the town, and in mercy to the inhabitants.

The streets of Irkutsk are straight, wide, and well kept. Indeed the main streets are too wide, and have always a more or less desolate appearance.

Our yemschik was again catechised about Metzgyr Hotel, but, after all, drove us into a hotel which, after unloading our gear, turned out to be the Amoor. The combined action of two conspirators was too much for us, and we had but to make the best of our situation. We were indeed too travel-worn to be particular about our quarters. A room was allotted to us, facetiously said to contain four bed-chambers. On inquiring for the said chambers we were pointed by the *maltchik* (boy) to certain corners and recesses, in which, by skilful dove-tailing, it was certainly possible to find sleeping-room for four people. Beds there were none, but there was a good solid floor, a plain hard sofa, three chairs, and a table. There was no fire-place in the room, the temperature being kept up by blazing furnaces opening in the corridor. The windows were hermetically sealed for the winter. Our first and last sensation, during our occupancy of that apartment, was suffocation, only to be relieved by active out-door exercise. The room was adorned by a few pictures, and a large placard, framed and hung up in a conspicuous place, advertised the *prix-courant* of liquors, cabs, billiards, and viands. Here we found *côtelettes* and *bifsteks*, admirably adapted to the Russian spelling.

The attendance was of a very mean order. An unkempt urchin in tattered habiliments, did the duty of maid-of-all-work, always in the way when not wanted, now and again disturbing the time-honoured dust of our fusty chamber by besoms and dish-cloths, but never to be found when he was required. No bells are provided for the convenience of visitors, and you may roar yourself hoarse with cries of *maltchik* or *tchelavek!* before any one will deign even to answer *sey tchass!* This word, literally interpreted, means directly, but it may be more practically translated to-morrow, or next week, or when convenient. It is only thrown out to allay your impatience, and keep you in play while the tchelavek is eating his dinner, or gossiping with the cook. No progress can be made till you have discovered his retreat, when the *à posteriori* argument of boot leather may be applied with good effect. This is the only form of entreaty that can impress a low Russian with respect, and one application will generally suffice.

All things considered, there is not much to complain of in the culinary department, but the service is enough to blunt the keenest appetite in the world. Everything is cold, dirty, and miserable. A good beefsteak is put on the table hot, but you have to wait twenty minutes for something to eat with it; then knives and forks are wanting, and when you flatter yourself all is in order, and you begin your dinner, salt is found to be missing. All that can be tolerated, but oh take care of the eggs! In Siberia they keep a stock of these in a fossil state for the entertainment of the unwary, for probably no Russian would be so green as to ask for them. At first we doubted whether Russians recognised any difference between a new-laid egg, and one that had been addled for six months. But, whatever their own proclivities may be, they do know a fresh egg when they see it. We succeeded at last in getting some only "suspicious," by taking hold of the boy in a menacing manner, and vowing that we would dash in his face every bad egg he should bring to us.

In a building separate from the hotel is a dining-room and tap-room, as also a billiard-room, with two tables. This part of the establishment is almost entirely monopolised by military officers, who play billiards all the morning, dine at the table d'hôte at 2 o'clock, and continue billiard-playing all the afternoon. Their billiard-cues have no leather tips, and the one table we attempted to play on was so uneven, from about twenty patches in the cloth, that we soon tired of seeing the balls steeple-chasing across the table. The dining-room is a large oblong, the walls covered with pictures of gentlemen in cocked hats and epaulettes, in a very low gaudy style of art. In the centre of one wall is a full-length portrait of the present emperor, which, with all its artistic defects, is nevertheless a fair likeness of his Imperial Majesty. The Russians are a loyal race, and naturally fond of pictures, whether of saints, or tsars, or heroes.

At the Amoor Hotel, I was greatly pleased to meet a friend and countryman who was travelling from St. Petersburg to China. The effect of this unexpected meeting was exhilarating, and I don't know whether it gave us most pleasure to recount the circumstances of our journey from China, or to hear our friend's experiences of that part of the road homewards which still lay before us. We certainly had no comfortable news to give each other. In exchange for the horrors of the road through Western Siberia, we threw in the picture of what a month's ride across the Mongolian steppes in November would be.

Irkutsk is a town that will bear a close inspection. The houses are all large, and as handsome as wooden buildings can well be made. The sombre hue of the external walls is the only unsightly feature about the place; but the general aspect of the town is so well relieved by the numerous handsome churches and other public buildings, that the whole effect is pleasing. The streets are adorned with many fine shops, where every European luxury is obtainable for money. Tailors and milliners are very fond of parading flourishing sign-boards in French, and even in that remote corner of the world, Paris is looked to as the seat of fashion. The *gostinnoi-dvor* is well supplied with all the staple articles of merchandise, including every variety of fur. We purchased very good Congou tea in the bazaar at 1 ruble 35 kopeks per pound, equal to four shillings.

Bakers are in great force in Irkutsk, many of them Germans. *Frantsooski khleb* (French bread) is all the rage in Siberia, and this sign is adopted by all bakers indiscriminately. The "French bread" is simply white bread made into rolls. It is very good, and being unobtainable in the country villages, travellers carry a supply with them from one town to another.

The tobacconists of Irkutsk are famed in Eastern Siberia for their "papiros," or paper cigars, which they make out of Turkish tobacco. The Russians, almost without exception of age or sex, smoke quantities of tobacco in the shape of papiros. In Irkutsk itself, however, "Moscow" is considered a better brand for papiros than "Irkutsk."

The prison occupies the corner of two streets. It has one iron-grated window facing the street, at which the prisoners are always to be seen clamouring for alms. The Russians are very charitable and give a great deal to these prisoners. It is very common also in the streets for passers-by, especially old ladies, to stop the convicts who are employed under a guard of Cossacks in carrying water, &c., and give them money. This is so much a matter of course that when any well-dressed person, suspected of being charitably disposed, is seen approaching a convict, the Cossacks halt by instinct.

Every resident in Irkutsk who can afford it keeps a carriage. Their horses are very showy in harness, and there are enough of them generally to be seen in the street to be an ornament to the place. The droshky service is also very good. The drivers always go fast and their horses are generally fresh and fiery.

There are several good libraries in Irkutsk, branches of scientific societies, a theatre, a newspaper, and other concomitants of cultivation. On the whole, I confess that my preconceived notions of Siberian life proved utterly fallacious. I had pictured to myself a barren, inhospitable climate, unfit for the habitation of any except those who were compelled by law to exist there, and who necessarily had to suffer every privation. Instead of that, I found settled communities, not only enjoying all the amenities of civilised life, but living in expensive luxury, and many of them in extravagance.

Irkutsk, like most other Siberian towns, is named after a river. It has a settled population of 23,000, but in winter, when the gold-washing ceases, the population is swelled by the addition of about 4000 miners, who pass the winter in town, and manage to spend every farthing of their earnings before the mining season comes round again. The town derives great importance from its being the residence of the governor-general and the capital of Eastern Siberia, which not only includes the Amoor country, but that large tract recently acquired from China, and now called Primorsky, or the Maritime Region. The heads of the police, military, financial, and post departments, have their offices in Irkutsk, which not only gives a tone to society, but keeps a large substratum of subordinate officers, with their families, about the place, and indirectly tends to promote the general prosperity. An archbishop also resides in Irkutsk.

On the second day of our stay in Irkutsk we visited the governor-general, and made the acquaintance of the chief of police, who put our papers in train. The governor-general holds a levée once a week, which happened to be on the day of our visit. About twenty persons in full dress presented themselves, including a number of officers, among whom we recognised with difficulty some of our late fellow-travellers. A number of peasants were assembled in the hall long before the appointed hour. They wore the most woe-begone visages, and each seemed to have his own special grievance. Each was armed with a scroll of paper, probably a petition, that he had got some one to write for him. These petitions were being patiently examined by an aide-de-camp, who seemed to decide on which were fit to be presented to his chief. The governor-general of Eastern Siberia has no sinecure. He has on his shoulders the affairs of a region larger than the whole of Europe, and which is yet but in the infancy of its development. The population is certainly scant, but it is composed of heterogeneous tribes, and the mere scarcity of population enhances the difficulty of general progress. A scattered population is, *ipso facto*, deprived on the one hand of the great stimulant to improvement which rivalry imparts to large communities, and on the other, of the facilities for carrying out the aspirations after better things which it may have. These disadvantages are a serious obstacle to any people, but to a race not naturally progressive, they are doubly so. Russia is not one of those countries where government ought to hold aloof from the affairs of the people. It may greatly err in doing too much;

but something it must do if Russia is to follow even at a great distance in the march of development. The people will not put the government in motion, but the government must lead the people in every step. In Eastern Siberia there is vast scope for the energy of a man of administrative ability and singleness of purpose. Untold wealth lies under its soil. With its iron and coal and lead, and the natural fertility of a large portion of its soil, it might by well-directed enterprise, become to a great extent independent of the world; while the fine rivers that traverse the country offer means of water-communication perhaps unequalled, certainly unsurpassed, in any other country. Very much has been done of late years to utilise these natural privileges; but much more remains to be done. And it depends greatly on the governor-general, whose vice-regal power is almost as absolute as the sway of the Tsar himself, whether the commercial and productive resources of those regions will continue to develop under the same enlightened impulse as heretofore.

Another element of the importance of Irkutsk is to be found in the circumstance that it is the commercial centre of Eastern Siberia. The houses of business of the out-stations, such as Kiachta, have mostly their head-quarters in Irkutsk. It is the principal dépôt on the highway between Western Russia, and China and the Amoor provinces; and a great deal of wealth has been accumulated there by persons engaged in trade.

The manufactures of this place, and indeed of Siberia generally, are insignificant and hardly worth alluding to. Manufactures of all kinds in Irkutsk employ a few hundred workmen, the principal works being in leather and soap. In a country so rich in minerals this need not be so. It only needs an enterprising population to turn the resources of the country to account, and cheapen many of those articles of daily consumption which the land carriage from Europe makes so exorbitantly dear in Siberia.

This, and the other great towns in Siberia, are well provided with educational institutions, and every good family employs private tutors and governesses. Education is prized by the higher classes, but utterly neglected by the lower, which include, generally speaking, the merchants. The society of Siberia is, on the whole, as good as in Russia proper. The higher class are generally of the Russian nobility, who, either to retrieve their broken fortunes, or with a view to more rapid advancement in rank, go out to Siberia to fill high official stations. Three, and in some cases two, years of public service in Siberia count for five years in Russia. There are other inducements to men of rank and intelligence to seek their fortunes in Siberia, among which may be named the greater scope for ambition which a half-settled country affords, and the freedom from the curse of cliques and intrigue which exist in Petersburg, and which only a few can hope to turn to their own advantage. A man's individuality counts for more in a country where he meets few of his peers, and that consideration may possibly weigh with some of them.

Many of the proprietors of gold-diggings are scions of the highest class of Russian aristocracy. These, and most of the officials, have generally their families with them in Siberia; and although they never lose their hold of Russia, practically Siberia is their home. They spare no expense in the education of their children, and hence the amount of both native and foreign talent that is employed in teaching. Foreign artists and men of science are frequently to be met with in Siberia, and are much sought after and hospitably entertained in the highest circles. The educated Russians, being conscious of their native deficiencies, have a high appreciation of talent, whencesoever it comes. Of late years Siberian society has received large accessions of educated people in the Polish political exiles, who are mostly students and professors in the universities, members of the Roman Catholic priesthood, and artists.

But what has done more, perhaps, than anything else to give a high tone to the upper classes in Siberia, and to stamp their manners with elegance, is the thirty years' residence of the political exiles of 1825, so-called Decembrists. On the day of the accession of the late Emperor Nicholas, a widespread conspiracy against him was discovered before it was quite ripe for action. Growing out of the general discontent which had hatched the abortive plot against the life of Alexander I., it assumed a definite shape and formidable magnitude, during the three weeks' interregnum which occurred between the death of Alexander and the accession of Nicholas, during which time Nicholas had been coquetting with the crown, before formally intimating his acceptance of it. The army was involved, and many of the officers of the Imperial Guard were deeply committed. The premature discovery of the conspiracy disconcerted the most active leaders of the malcontents, and when the crisis came, the rebellious troops were reduced by whole regiments who backed out at the last moment, and the few thousands who were left found themselves deserted by many of their officers. The forlorn hope assembled in St. Isaac's Square on the 26th of December, and the very first act of Nicholas's reign was to blow the insurgents to atoms with artillery, and cut up the flying remnant with cavalry.

A fearful day of reckoning followed this ill-fated attempt. A searching inquiry was at once instituted, conducted by commissioners. It lasted nearly half a year. Instigated by fear, and the thirst for vengeance, the government interpreted the most trivial circumstances into treason. The leaders of the insurrection were mostly young men of good families, but they were indirectly encouraged by noblemen of great wealth and power. All this was ferreted out in the protracted investigation. The end of it was the capital punishment of a few of the most active instigators of the plot, and the exile of the rest to Siberia.

Among these exiles were many members of the highest aristocracy. Their wives in most instances followed them into Siberia, which they were permitted by government to do, on certain conditions. One condition was, that the wives of exiles should come under an obligation never to return from the land of their banishment. Another was, that all their correspondence should pass through the hands of the governor-general in Siberia, and the ministry of secret police in St. Petersburg. This latter condition their ingenuity enabled them easily to evade. These ladies, among whom were princesses, countesses, and others of rank, fortune, and refinement, soon began to be influential in Siberia. Their husbands, who had been condemned to labour in the mines for various terms, some to ten, others to twenty-five years, and some others for life, were never detained much more than one year at any of their penal settlements. None were ever compelled to labour at all, except a few who were refractory, or who had committed misdemeanours while in Siberia. As time wore on, and the fury of the government abated, the interest of the friends and relations of the exiles induced the governor-general of Eastern Siberia to look favourably on them. They were then permitted to reside in, and to register themselves as residents of, various villages in the different provinces of Siberia. It was not long before they were allowed to reside in the larger towns, and once there, they soon built for themselves elegant houses in such places as Irkutsk, Krasnoyarsk, and Yeniseisk, where they lived openly and in comparative comfort, and took up their natural position as the *élite* of society. But though fortune seemed to smile on them, the exiles were politically dead, that being the inexorable sentence of the law which drove them from their native country. Children were born to them in Siberia, but although they took up the position in society which their birth and education entitled them to, they were, nevertheless, in the eye of the law, illegitimate, and incapable of enjoying any social or political rights. The sins of the fathers were visited on the children to interminable generations. Not only could the children of exiles not inherit their father's hereditary titles, but they were debarred even from bearing their own family name! And they inherited their parents' exile in never being permitted to return to Russia. This has, no doubt, been in some instances evaded, by daughters marrying Russian noblemen, and returning to Russia under cover of their husband's names, but such procedure was nevertheless strictly against the law.

Thus did the Decembrists expiate their political offences in their own persons, and in their descendants', for full thirty years, until the accession of the present emperor. As the iron rule of Nicholas was inaugurated by an act of crushing severity, so the milder sway of Alexander II. was marked at its outset by an act of mercy to the exiles of his father. A free pardon, with permission to return to Russia, was granted to all the survivors. Their children, born in Siberia, had their father's hereditary honours and full political rights restored to them. It is by such measures as this that Alexander II. has made his name respected and beloved by his people.

The influence of political exiles of various periods has made an ineradicable impression on the urban communities of Siberia, but the Decembrists, from their education and polish, have certainly done most to form the nucleus of good society there.

The mercantile class in Siberia, and indeed all over Russia, stands decidedly low in the social scale. A merchant, though enormously rich, and doing a very large business, is essentially a huckster. In manners they are little removed from the common peasant, from which class they have generally sprung. They are for the most part illiterate themselves, and, until very lately, have been incapable of appreciating the advantages of education for their children. They are widely separated from the upper classes, who regard them with unmixed contempt. The line of distinction between the nobility and the substrata of society is more broadly drawn in Russia than in any other country, excepting in the empire of Japan, where, however, the mercantile, and classes in our estimation below them, are well educated. This distinction of ranks is undoubtedly a relic of barbarism, but whether the mean tastes of what ought to be the middle classes in Russia be the cause, or the effect, of their relatively low status in society, they both mutually act and re-act on each other as cause and effect, and so the evil constantly perpetuates itself.

While resting in Irkutsk, we employed ourselves casting about for means of attaining the maximum of comfort, that is to say, the minimum of hardship, for the remaining part of the journey. We had learned the mode of travelling, and thought we knew exactly where reform could be applied with most effect. The greatest annoyance the traveller experiences in Russia and Siberia, is the necessity of paying horse hire at each station. It is bad enough during the day, but to turn out of a warm nest two or three times in a night, to banter postmasters and yemschiks, settle your fare to the next station, and see that your wheels are oiled, is simply intolerable, especially when the thermometer is anything you like below zero. The postmasters, with the most laudable desires possible, cannot cheat you. In every station is exhibited a placard, framed and glazed, signed and sealed by high functionaries, stating the distance in versts to each of the two nearest stations, and the fare in roubles and in kopeks, which, in Eastern Siberia, and also as far west as Tumen, is one kopek and a-half per verst per horse, that is, a little over three farthings per mile. Besides this, you are expected to pay twelve kopeks, or fourpence, for oiling wheels, which is necessary, on an average, at every third station. Then, if you use a post-carriage, or *kibitka*, another fourpence is due for that at every station. The drink-money, or *narodku*, due to the yemschik, must on no account be forgotten, for the speed with which you will be driven on the next stage will bear some proportion to the amount of drink-money which you are reported to have given for the preceding. Money does not always procure speed, but speed will always draw money. In the anxiety to award the due meed of merit a nice estimate must be made of the value of the service rendered, and the reward fixed at ten, fifteen, or twenty kopeks, or nothing at all, as the case may require. The condition of the roads and horses, over which the yemschik has no control, must be carefully weighed in this important calculation. But while nobody can attempt to cheat you with any decent prospect of success, it is always open to the station-keeper to say he has no change to give you. To meet this dodge you must carry a bag of coppers, which, unless it weighs nearly a hundred weight, will not last you from one town to another where alone the coin is procurable. Then, again, it was not to be denied that our knowlege of Russian was too limited for our purpose, in the event of our getting into any real difficulty, from the thousand and one accidents to which travellers in such a country are liable.

We contrived to magnify all these imaginary difficulties in our own eyes, when a young Russian, bearing the German name of his father, Schwartz, waited on us to offer his services on the road as far as St. Petersburg. He had literally devoured his patrimony with riotous living, and had been in all employments, from clerk in a government office in Irkutsk, to actor in the provincial theatre, and was now bent on returning to his family, like the prodigal, as he was, without a shirt to his back. His antecedents were nothing to us: seeing he was a Russian, spoke German perfectly, French intelligibly, as also a few words of English which he had picked up from grooms in St. Petersburg. We settled with him at once, giving him fifteen roubles down, to furnish him with clothes to cover his limbs from the cold—for the rest he was to work his passage to Petersburg. An agreement was duly drawn up and signed, and, to conform to Russian formalities, it was certified by the police, on which a special passport for him was issued. When all was in order, a creditor of Schwartz's appeared, and lodged a claim against him for the sum of ten roubles, which we had of course to pay, or forego the valuable services of the scamp. The ten roubles was not very alarming, but the number of similar demands that might follow, inspired us with sore misgivings on Schwartz's account. The more we actually paid for him, the stronger arguments we should have to go on paying. To save the equivalent of the fifteen roubles we had already given him, it was well worth while to pay other ten. But when we had spent twenty-five roubles on him, we should only have a stronger reason to pay twenty more, which, at that stage of the proceedings, would be evidently throwing good money after bad. After grave deliberation we determined, illogically as I confess, to pay the ten roubles demanded, and stop there. By good luck we were not called upon for more roubles. But our experience with Schwartz proved so unsatisfactory, that it would have been an economy to pay a hundred roubles to get rid of him. He was a trouble and a dead loss to us from first to last. His only real use was, as a standing butt for invective. His follies were, at the same time, aggravating and amusing. When he left at a post-station some of the things of which we had given him charge, it was a solace to us to know that he had also lost an extra pair of his own boots. And when we missed a preserved ox tongue, which had been put into water to soak at a previous station, it relieved our resentful feelings mightily to make Schwartz go without his dinner.

Snow fell in Irkutsk on the 17th October, and for two days, sledges were at work in the streets. The sun was powerful enough on the 18th to melt it a little during the middle of the day. But still there was the snow, a fortnight before its regular time, and we were just too late to be able to get over the rivers while they were still open for boats. It was an early winter in Eastern Siberia: that world-renowned individual, the "oldest inhabitant," only recollected one season in which snow-roads were practicable in Irkutsk as early as the 1st October, Russian date, or 13th, new style.

The 19th was a fine hard morning, with a sky slightly overcast; and on that day we resumed our nomad life, after six days' rest.

The River Angara flows through Irkutsk, but there is only a small portion of the town on the left bank. The Irkut, rising in the mountainous region near Kosogol, on the frontier, south-west of Irkutsk, falls into the Angara opposite the town. The post-road crosses the Angara below the confluence. The crossing is effected by means of a most efficient floating bridge, which consists of a boat held by a strong warp to an anchor dropped about 500 yards up the stream in mid-channel. The slack of the warp is buoyed up by three boats at equal intervals. In crossing, the boat's head is pointed obliquely across the stream by means of a large oar over the stern. The strength of the current does the rest. The boat swings on her anchor until she is laid alongside the landing on the opposite bank. The boat is double-bottomed, with a spacious platform on deck, and a moveable rail on each side. There is room on deck for three or four carriages to stand, and the passage is effected without taking the horses out. The Angara flows as clear as crystal out of the Baikal, and maintains its purity after receiving the Irkut. It is deep at Irkutsk, and the current is nearly six miles an hour.

The town again appears to good advantage from the left bank of the Angara. The river banks are in themselves rather picturesque, and when the water, the pretty white spires of the town, and thick woods around, are combined in one view, the effect is beautiful, and the traveller retains a pleasing impression of Irkutsk.

CHAPTER XVI.

IRKUTSK TO KRASNOYARSK.

For the first two stages from Irkutsk we caught occasional glimpses of high mountain ranges at a great distance to the south-west. But the dense forest soon shut in our view. The roads were tolerably good, and we rumbled along expeditiously and comfortably. The country maintains the same characteristics as already noted—thick woods for the most part, with clear patches here and there, and villages at intervals of a few miles; while its surface is pleasantly varied with hill and dale, and if only there were less forest to enable one to see round him, it would be a very cheerful drive. Innumerable small rivers have to be crossed in ferry-boats, which help to break the monotony of the journey. Reading is next to impossible on Russian roads, and the art of sleeping—when there is nothing better to do—is a most valuable accomplishment to the traveller. We had attained considerable proficiency in this, and I have been ferried across a river amid the hubbub of taking out and putting in horses, and rolling the carriage into and out of the ferry-boat, without suffering any interruption of a profound slumber.

Being eager to make up lost time, we drove our yemschiks hard with drink-money, and they certainly responded heartily to the stimulant. The roads are very steep, and nothing has been done in the way of cuttings or embankments. The ravines have generally small streamlets running along the bottom, which is ragged and broken. These are bridged over in a rough-and-ready manner. But the ascents and descents are fearfully steep. When a heavy carriage starts down a hill with three rats of ponies in front of it, one only bearing the weight of the vehicle, no earthly power can stop it. The drag on the wheel is of little use. The only safety is in the plan the Russian drivers adopt of going full tilt from top to bottom, to the delight of Siberian ponies—dashing over the wooden bridge like madmen, and halfway up the opposite hill before they draw rein. There is a fascinating excitement about this mode of charging a ravine which kills all sense of danger, except, perhaps, when the road is slippery with snow, well polished with sledges. Under these circumstances it is only the more necessary to urge the beasts at top speed; but a qualm of nervousness will occasionally rise, unbidden, until you have learned to confide implicitly in the infallibility of the yemschiks and their high-mettled steeds.

The ponies are always in prime condition for work. Little or no attention is paid to them in the stable or out of it, but they have always as much corn as they can eat, and they are notoriously good feeders. They are capable of a great amount of continuous hard work. On an average every one of them travels two stages a day, both ways, for they always return to their own station. That is equal to about forty miles with a loaded carriage, and the same distance back, with an empty one, on the same day. When the roads are tolerable they go at a good speed. We have travelled eighteen miles at a stretch within an hour and a half. The roads seldom admit of this rate of travelling, however, being generally, saving the bridges and the original cutting through the woods, left pretty much to nature.

Along the whole length of the post-road the distances from station to station are marked at every verst by wooden poles, painted black and white; and at each station a high post indicates the distances from the chief towns. A feeling of depression always came over me on spelling out the interesting word St. Petersburg, and finding it was more than 6000 versts or 4000 miles off. It was a tedious business to reduce such an imposing figure as that. After Irkutsk we had got it under the 6000. When wearied out with rough travelling, the few versts to the next halt were painful enough, and on such occasions the 5000 odd were really appalling.

We never stopped by day or night, unless compelled by force of circumstances. Our meals were consequently uncertain and irregular, both as to time, quantity, and quality. At most of the stations shtchee and beef could be had about mid-day, though unless it was ready we did not wait for it, but pushed on, trusting to what we might pick up in a chance way, and having our small stock of preserved meat to fall back upon, should everything else fail. Twice a day we drank tea. The Russians lose a great deal of time in tea-drinking at the post-stations. Give them plenty of tea, and they care little for food. Indeed they encourage the habit partly to blunt the appetite. It suits their constitutions, but it certainly did not answer with us, to be jolted and tumbled about on bad roads with a stomach full of fluid. Besides the loss of time was an object to us, but of little account apparently to the Russians. A sufficiency of solid food can be disposed of in a very few minutes, not so boiling tea, and I have constantly seen Russians slowly sipping quarts of the decoction long after their horses were ready for the road. In a very cold night the hot tea is no doubt acceptable, but one tumbler of hot grog is worth a gallon of tea, and occupies less time and less room.

After three days and nights' travelling we arrived at the Birusanskaya station, distant from Irkutsk 638 versts, or 426 miles, which was very fair going, all things considered. In that distance we had only passed one town—Nijni-udinsk. Birusanskaya stands on the right bank of the river Birusa, which, at this part of its course, divides the government of Irkutsk from that of Yenisei. This river, as well as those crossed to the eastward, rises in the mountain ranges near the southern frontier of Siberia. They all flow northward, and fall into the Angara, before its junction with the Yenisei.

At Birusanskaya we were told that the river was impassable on account of the ice, and that there were no horses, with a number of similar stories, more or less true. It was night, and we were not the only sufferers; so, as soon as we had fairly exhausted all the persuasive means at our disposal, we quietly went to roost like the rest. At 10 o'clock next morning we were furnished with horses, and drove to the river. It was fast freezing over, and at the regular crossing there was too much ice at the edges to admit of the ferry-boat's "communicating." Another crossing had therefore to be used, where there was no proper road on either side of the river, and which consequently involved much loss of time. On leaving the river, and before joining the post-road, a tract of prairie ground had to be crossed, all holes and hillocks, and anything but an eligible road for wheeled carriages.

The distance from home seemed to diminish suddenly as we came in sight of the telegraph wires which had been carried as far as the river Birusa. The posts were put up at some parts of the road eastward. Coils of wire were lying at every station, and the workmen were busy stretching and carrying it on. The posts are tall rough spars, placed at intervals of one hundred yards, and only two wires are used. The telegraph was completed to Irkutsk in December last.

A marked improvement in the roads was observable in the government of Yenisei. They had been macadamised, and although the stones had been overlaid with a coating of mud during the early part of autumn, it was not so deep as to become very rough with traffic. In some parts a thin covering of snow lay on the ground, and sledges were in use in such places.

In the middle of the night (a very cold one) of the 23rd October, we arrived at the river Kan, which, from the town of Kansk, flows nearly west, and joins the Yenisei north of Krasnoyarsk. The ferrymen were all on the opposite shore with their boats, and of course asleep, and we were anything but sanguine of rousing them. We called lustily, but the echo of our shouts alone responded, as if in mockery. " You may call spirits from the vasty deep," &c. But either we must get over, or shiver on the banks of this river Styx till day-light. Fortunately the yemschiks were as impatient as ourselves, and possessing stentorian lungs, they plied them vigorously, until at last a gruff response from the log-hut on the other side was vouchsafed. Then some low mutterings were heard (for the air was so still and frosty that you might have heard a pin fall), then a little rumbling of oars and heavy footsteps on the loose deck-boards of the ferry-boat, some splashing in the water, and in due time the boat itself, with the grim ferrymen in beards and sheepskins, was seen approaching us. The town of Kansk is a verst and a half from the ferry. The sharp air had affected all and sundry at the post-station of Kansk, for a deep sleep had fallen on them. With a little perseverance we knocked them up, in anything but an amiable frame of mind, and it was near 4 o'clock, a.m., before the sleepy yemschiks had got the horses in.

We had picked up a fellow-traveller the day before, and arranged to travel in company, if possible, as far as Tomsk. He was carrying gold from Irkutsk to Barnaul, which is the great place for smelting it. Our first introduction to him was at the Birusa river, which he excited our jealousy by crossing in advance of us. To get a rise out of him we promised extra drink-money to our yemschik if he would pass him, which he did. The Russian was annoyed at being passed, and at the next station he recorded his grievances in the book kept for that purpose. We left him there drinking tea, and soon after we missed some things which we had in the hurry left behind. Our new friend came up with us at the next station, and brought with him the missing articles. This began to make us feel kindly to him, and as we encountered him at every station, we soon got intimate, and he ended by proposing to keep company with us, dining and drinking tea together. His name was Vasil Vasilovitch Something or other (I never could catch his family name), but as his talk turned greatly on the charms of Barnaul, we gave him the nickname of Old Barnaul. He tried hard to speak French and English, but as he had only acquired about ten words of the former, and five of the latter, we could only get on with a conglomeration of Russian, French, and English, or through the interpretation of Schwartz. "*Prendre thé*—very good," was about his highest effort in philology. Old Barnaul talked much of San Francisco, whither he had been carried as a prisoner on board H.M.S. Pique, during the Crimean War. He was captured at Sitka, and after spending some time at San Francisco, studying American character, and acquiring his modicum of the English language, he found his way back in an American vessel to Sitka. Old Barnaul had a cossack in full accoutrements, *i. e.*, armed with a long sword, a most kind, good-natured Russian soldier, who was infinitely more useful to us than the empty-headed Schwartz.

Travelling in company has its arguments *pro* and *con*. First, *pro*—you have the chance of exciting in the respective yemschiks the noble ambition of landing you first at the next station, by holding out the promise to each of extra drink-money if he wins. This is also exhilarating to yourself, as in every stage of the journey you have the excitement of a race to beguile the tedium of the way. Then, by preconcerted arrangement, you determine at what station you will dine or drink tea, so that whichever of you arrives first can make the necessary preparations. Second, *con*. You throw a heavier burden on the yemschiks at the stations, and thereby protract the usual time required to change horses. And you run the risk of stopping the whole party by the greater number of horses you call for all at once, for there may often be horses for one traveller, where there are not enough for two. On the whole, it retards progress, just as in the case of vessels keeping company on the water, the speed obtained is somewhat less than that of the slowest of the convoy.

To the west of Kansk, the country is nearly cleared of wood, and is for the most part rather flat. Cultivation becomes more general, and the clear view occasionally obtained over the bare country, revealed many large villages dotted here and there.

The wind rose early in the day, and sent a cold chill through us as we drove up in its teeth. While halting at a station, a smart shower of snow fell, and caught our tarantass, half-open in front, and face to wind. It was fast filling with snow, and we rebuked Schwartz for his negligence. He at once transferred the responsibility from his own shoulders, by going out into the yard and kicking the first yemschik he met, which seems to be the most civil kind of salutation a Russian moujik expects. When the shower stopped, it was not difficult to shake out the snow from our blankets, and what was left was no great inconvenience to us, for the air was too cold to allow it to melt. The road was kept clean by the wind, which drove the snow before it like fine sand drift. But the wind was a sad inconvenience to us, and this was perhaps the only day on which our heavy furs and blankets were inadequate to retain warmth. The roads were excellent, however, and we went merrily along. We found the inconvenience of travelling with Old Barnaul, on coming to a station where horses were obtainable for us, being privileged, but none for him. The "cold without," and a good dinner within, induced us to wait a few hours until he could get horses. Besides, the Yenisei river was before us, and we were assured that the passage could not be effected in such a wind.

Very late at night we reached Basailsk, a station ten versts short of the Yenisei. There we remained all night, and next morning drove on to the river. Here was one instance, out of many, of the absurd situations that have been chosen for many of the post-stations in Siberia, with reference to the rivers. The station is nearly always placed at some distance from the river, sometimes only one or two versts. Horses have to be harnessed and driven to the river, there unharnessed again, transported across the water, and put to again on the other side. This extra work and loss of time would be saved by placing the station on the bank of the river, and so by having one on each side, the horses need never be ferried over at all.

The Yenisei is a noble river, the largest in Siberia. Its banks are bold, but very bare, while the lack of timber, and general baldness of the country, give the scene a bleak and inhospitable aspect. The sprinkling of snow that hung about the crevices served to intensify the gloom.

It was questionable whether we could cross the Yenisei in the face of the wind, which blew in strong gusts from the north-west, but we managed to get our establishments into a boat, rather small for the load she had, but quite large enough for the power available to propel her. She was headed straight across the stream, pulled by four men in the bow, and steered by the usual rudely made oar over the stern. They made very little way with her, and when we had reached the right bank of the river, we had dropped about a mile down stream. A horse was ready on the other side to tow the boat up to the proper landing-place. A rope was passed ashore, but before it was properly secured to the horse, the end slipped, a gust of wind caught the boat, and she was blown from the shore. This was too good an opportunity for jabbering and gesticulation to be lost on our lusty crew, and accordingly to this luxury they abandoned themselves, while the unfortunate boat, bearing us, the unfortunate passengers, was being blown out to the middle of the stream by the wind, and at the same time gliding swiftly down the river. When the crew had recovered themselves a little, they hesitated about which shore they ought to make for; and at last concluded it would be best to go back again to the left bank, which we reached at a point three miles below our original starting-place. The men landed, and went to the town to fetch horses to tow the boat up again. We walked to the town also to seek some shelter from the biting wind, and wait the arrival of the boat. She got up at noon, and we made a fresh start to cross, which was successfully accomplished the second time. A used-up team of horses awaited us, and we travelled slowly to Krasnoyarsk.

Amid a great deal of grass and waste land, the country round Krasnoyarsk is well cultivated, but very bare. The town is situated on a raised plateau in a large valley. Like other Siberian towns its streets are wide, straight, and clean, with dull-looking wooden houses, and handsome churches. There is something incongruous in this combination. The churches are undoubtedly highly ornamental to the town—it would be poor indeed without them—but the contrast between their snow-white walls and spires, and the earth-colour of the houses, is too great. They seem to have no connection with each other.

Krasnoyarsk, though the government town of Yeniseisk, is comparatively a small place, its population being something under 10,000. As an exception to the general rule, its name is not derived from a river, but means " red cliff."

The station-master at Krasnoyarsk combines with his official duties the business of hotel-keeper, an arrangement admirably convenient for travellers. The station hotel is a very good one from a Siberian point of view, and we were induced to shake down in it for the night from a variety of reasons, chiefly because we were very tired, and it was snowing heavily.

Other travellers from the west were there at the same time, and we were entertained by their accounts of the state of the roads from Nijni-novgorod. It was amusing to hear the different reports of travellers, and compare them. Most of them were absolutely contradictory, and we were constrained to come to the conclusion that Russian travellers fill up the blanks in conversation with whatever comes uppermost, without taxing their memory to the extent necessary to give an accurate statement of their experience.

The amount of attention which the efficient management of the hotel exacted from the landlord left him no time for the duties of his less remunerative position of postmaster. All the postal arrangements were in dire confusion in the morning, when we wished to start on our journey, yemschiks drunk, and no one at his post. We lost the whole morning waiting for horses, which was so vexatious that we resolved to record our complaint in " the book." At every post-station a black book is kept in a corner of a room on a small table, to which it is attached by a cord, and sealed. It is open for public inspection, and every traveller has the privilege of writing in it any grievance he may have suffered from inattention, incivility, or unwarrantable delay on the part of yemschiks or postmasters. The director-general of posts makes a periodical tour, and examines the black book of every station. The complaints of government couriers are, perhaps, the only ones that excite much attention. Everything else in the posting system is made subordinate to the rapid despatch of government intelligence. Horses can never be refused to a courier on any pretence whatever, for the station-keepers are obliged, at all times, to keep a certain number in reserve for such emergencies. When news of importance has to be transmitted, it can be done with very great rapidity by means of an *estafette*, which will carry news from Kiachta to St. Petersburg, a distance of over four thousand miles, in less than twenty days.

The rapidity with which the Russian government has, on certain occasions, obtained important news from China, proves the efficiency of the courier service. The signing of the treaties at Tientsin in 1858, and the Taku disaster in 1859, were known at St. Petersburg some two weeks before the official despatches reached this country. And now that the telegraph has been extended to Irkutsk, the Russians receive news from the Chinese commercial ports, on the direct steamer route, a good many days earlier than we can, even by telegraph from Suez. The capture of Nanking, for example, was reported in England *viâ* St. Petersburg on the 11th September, while our Suez telegram did not reach till the 23rd.

CHAPTER XVII.

KRASNOYARSK TO TOMSK.

IT had snowed all night in Krasnoyarsk, and sledges were actively employed in the streets next day. The conveyance given to us for our extra baggage was a sledge.

Old Barnaul could not get horses, so we left him behind. He managed to hire private horses for one stage, and came up to us at the next station.

The roads were good, but yemschiks sulky, and we were driven along at a snail's pace. When drink money was asked for, we upbraided the yemschik for his contumacy. He appealed to the "regulations," which only authorise a speed of eight versts per hour. We had nothing to object to this. But as the yemschik defended himself by the strict letter of the law, we could avail ourselves of it also, and there was nothing about drink money in the "regulations."

The wind had fortunately subsided, but the cold was intense. The country west of Krasnoyarsk continued very bare. The crisp snow made travelling easy, and later in the day we managed to mend our pace, making good way during the night, and arriving early on the following morning at the town of Achinsk, 166 versts, or 110 miles, from Krasnoyarsk. There are two pretty churches in Achinsk, and the houses are rather handsome for a small town of two or three thousand inhabitants. It is situated near the river Chulim, which trends westward and joins the Ob. Achinsk is the last town of the government of Yenisei, and also stands on the boundary line between eastern and western Siberia.

The country is more woody near Achinsk, and game of various kinds is abundant. We here for the first time tasted the *ryabchik*, a bird something between a pheasant and a partridge in size and in flavour.

While at Achinsk we were bluntly told we could not cross the Chulim, owing to the quantity of floating ice. The river is one verst and a-half from the town. The postmaster offered to drive us there, but said we should have to come back, unless we chose to encamp on the bank of the river. When we did get there, we succeeded, after a long debate, in inducing the boatmen to ferry us over. But for a full hour they stoutly refused to take the tarantass. The large boats had been laid aside, and smaller and more handy craft, better fitted for threading their way through thick blocks of ice, were being used. With patience, however, we gained our point, and got tarantass and all across the river, though not without considerable difficulty and danger.

We now entered the government of Tomsk, a fact of which the state of the roads would have been sufficient evidence. All through the government of Yenisei, a distance by our route of 350 miles, the roads are well kept up, with side drains and cross drains to keep them dry; but in Tomsk government the roads were far worse than nature made them, for traffic had ruined them and made them all but impassable. During the wet weather of early autumn they had been a mass of soft mud, which was cut up by wheels and horses' feet to a fearful extent. The frost caught them in that condition, and the result can be more easily imagined than described. The main road had been in fact abandoned, until enough snow should fall to fill up the inequalities; and in the meantime by-roads had to be struck out through the forest, that being the only practicable means of travelling at all. It is considered that between the autumn and the snow there are "no roads," and no Russian travels at that season unless under the most urgent circumstances. In the post regulations it is laid down that travellers can demand to be driven at the rate of ten versts per hour in summer, eight in autumn, and twelve in winter, from December to March. These rates are, in practice, greatly increased in summer and winter, but, in the month of October, it is hard work to average even the government speed. The state of the road beyond Achinsk had necessitated the subdivision of the stages, by erecting temporary intermediate stations. The whole of the arrangements were in confusion; so much so that after an early breakfast in Achinsk, we found no opportunity of dining till near midnight.

The cold continued very severe. Our freezing breath kept our faces in a mass of ice, large icicles formed on the horses' muzzles, and they were white all over with hoar frost, formed by the perspiration freezing on their hair. Our bread, and everything we had, was frozen through.

As we toiled on, painfully and slowly, on the 28th of October we met travellers who assured us of the impossibility of crossing the Kiya river at Mariinsk. We had learned, however, rather to take courage from this kind of Job's comfort with which we were so often entertained on the road; and we did not hesitate to advance to the river, which we reached at seven in the evening. An hour sufficed to persuade the ferrymen to tempt the crossing, and another hour saw us over the water and in the town of Mariinsk. We were fain to rest our aching bones a little, and finding a very civil but garrulous postmaster, a Pole, we dined comfortably at the station, and started again at midnight.

On the preceding night we had come to grief, by the wheel of our tarantass sinking into a pit that had been dug for a telegraph post, and then filled with snow. With the assistance of a peasant whom chance threw in our way, and a stout pole for a lever, the vehicle was extricated; but we had not gone two stages from Mariinsk before the same wheel fell suddenly to pieces without any immediate provocation. We were a number of miles from any station when this accident occurred, but the yemschik, being no doubt accustomed to similar mischances in driving four-wheeled carriages through tangled woods, proceeded at once to put us in temporary travelling order. He cut down a pretty stout tree, one end of which he laid on the axle of the fore wheels, while the other end rested on the ground behind the carriage. This formed a bridge for the axle of the hind wheel (the broken one) to rest upon, and by that simple expedient we got safely to the station, Berikulskoé. The accident delayed us a whole day at the station. Old Barnaul parted company with us to proceed to Tomsk, which was then only 120 miles distant. On entering the village, a blacksmith, spying our condition, and smelling a job, followed us to the station. We settled with him to repair our wheel, which was equivalent to making a new one all but the tire, for the sum of six roubles, and it was finished in the afternoon.

At this point we discovered that our special pass had been left five stations behind us. It was a serious matter to lose a document so essential to inspire postmasters with respect, and we wrote to the station where we supposed it had been left, requesting it might be forwarded to us. During the day, however, the post from Irkutsk passed, and brought us the paper, for which delicate attention we felt duly grateful.

From Berikulskoé we resumed the circuitous tracks through the forest. During the night our yemschik contrived to drive us up against a tree, to the irretrievable injury of the hood of our tarantass. Misfortunes seemed to come thick upon us and our ill-fated tarantass. Indeed, considering the terrible ordeal it had passed through, it was surprising that it had held together so long. Apprehension is lively in the dark hours, and visions of a final break down haunted us all that night, as we threaded our way in the deep shade of the forest, pitching and rolling like a ship in a storm. Our minds were sensibly relieved on reaching the town of Ishimskaya, at daybreak on the 30th of October.

Here we found Old Barnaul and his Cossack sleeping soundly on the boards. He had arrived the evening before, but had allowed himself to be cajoled into resting all night, and now it was too late to cross the river. The post that had passed us the day before had crossed the river in a boat at midnight, but since then the ice had set in so strong that the passage was impossible. It was therefore necessary to wait at the station till the ice on the river was strong enough to bear horses and carriages.

The station-master was a Pole, a very good sort of fellow, who would talk on any subject but Poland. He was something of a sportsman, possessed two old guns and some underbred pointers. His wealth consisted in three curious old-fashioned watches, which he offered for sale. One was by Dent, and he informed us he had bought it of a traveller for 125 roubles.

As the force of circumstances compelled us to spend the day at Ishimskaya, we endeavoured to make the most of it, and tried to induce the postmaster to accompany us on a shooting excursion. This he declined, but proffered us all the topographical information necessary to enable us to find the game for ourselves. So armed, we plunged into the woods, and beat about for hours among the snow without the satisfaction of seeing a feather, or finding traces on the snow of anything but vermin. We returned about sunset, tired and cold, spite of all our walking, and an irreverent magpie, on the outskirts of the town, paid the penalty of our disappointment.

The delay at this outlandish place was the more vexatious that it was within less than a day's march from Tomsk, where we purposed resting a day or two to refit. On the second morning we again stirred up the postmaster, but he absolutely refused to attempt the crossing with our tarantass. One traveller had come to grief that same morning trying to get a carriage over the ice. We resolved, however, to go without the tarantass, packing up a few necessaries in a small sledge, which we had drawn over the river by one horse, two more being sent from the station and put to on the other side. Old Barnaul accompanied us. The tarantass we left behind in charge of Schwartz, with orders to follow on as soon as the ice was strong enough to bear the carriage. Let it not be supposed that the same place that was open for boats on the 29th of October was frozen strong enough to bear horses and sledges thirty-six hours afterwards. When the river is freezing the ferry is removed to some distance, where a passage is kept open as long as possible by the constant traffic of boats. During that time the usual crossing at the post-road is left to freeze quietly, so that by the time the temporary ferry is no longer practicable, the ice at the regular ferry may be thick enough to bear the traffic.

Old Barnaul managed to slip on the ice and fall into a hole that had been broken by the horses' feet. A more miserable-looking object, on his emersion from the cold bath, I never saw. In the sledge his clothes became sheets of hard ice, but we were, fortunately for him, delayed for want of horses at the second station from Ishimskaya, so that the old man had time to melt down his congealed habiliments.

A good deal of snow fell during the day, but still the roughness of the road was but slightly mitigated thereby.

The sledge was comparatively easy, however, the runners lying on two or more hillocks at once, instead of jolting up and down each separate lump, like the wheel of a carriage.

During the night we were again stopped, with a number of other travellers, for want of horses, and it was 3 o'clock on the morning of the 1st November ere we entered on the last stage before Tomsk. Our sledges were quite open, and we could but abandon ourselves to the enjoyment of a night scene more gorgeous than fancy ever pictured. The snow had ceased falling, and the sky was clear and cloudless. Not a breath of wind stirred. It was a little past full moon, and the pure white surface of the ground sparkled in the bright moonlight as if it had been strewn with diamonds. Some of the finest constellations were high above the horizon. Orion, Taurus, and Gemini were conspicuous; and Sirius was never seen in greater splendour. Towards daybreak, Venus appeared in all her glory, and completed the most brilliant group of celestial phenomena the human eye ever rested on. There is a peculiar transparency in the Siberian sky, both by night and by day, but it needs a still frosty night to show it off to its best advantage.

Long before daylight we passed numerous trains of peasants, with their sledges, driving towards Tomsk with their daily supplies of provisions for the market.

Before sunrise we entered the town of Tomsk, and were not sorry when Old Barnaul conducted us to a lodging-house, where we could thaw ourselves and take rest. We were made excessively comfortable there by the old lady and her daughters. The *cuisine* was excellent, attendance good, and charges very moderate. Our room was adorned with a number of pictures. Christ and the apostles, with some others of saints, were most conspicuous. A view of Kazan, the column of Alexander at St. Petersburg, coloured German lithographs of the bombardment of Sevastopol and the battle of Inkermann, and, finally, a certificate, signed and sealed, purporting that the old lady had made a donation to "the Church" in 1846. Great value appeared to be set on this document, but whether the lady regarded her good deed as laying up treasures in heaven, or thought the evidence of it, given under the hands of holy men, to be proof against ill luck, is not easy to say. It is difficult to separate the religion of Russians from the gross superstition with which it is mixed up. The upper classes, as a whole, keep aloof from religious observances, while the peasant class are constantly crossing themselves to churches and saints, and never will enter a room without uncovering the head and doing reverence to the picture of the saint that always faces them as they enter the door. Many excellent men are to be found in the Russian priesthood, but as a class they certainly do not stand high. The Russian government has always used the clergy to work on the illiterate masses by means of their superstitious fanaticism. The cross was borne in front of the troops in St. Isaac's Square when Nicholas put down the insurrection of 1825. And the Empress Catherine II., whose life was the reverse of all piety, invoked the protection of the saints in order to excite the enthusiasm of the people. The Russian peasants are pharisaical in their observance of saints' days and fast days, but their sense of religion stops there. A characteristic anecdote, illustrative of the religious sentiments of the Russian moujik, was told us at Tomsk. A moujik killed a traveller on the road, and robbed him. In his pocket was found a cake made with fat, which the moujik, being hungry, was preparing to eat, when he suddenly recollected that it was a fast day, on which it was unlawful to eat animal food. His religious creed, which placed no obstacle in the way of murder and robbery, was inexorable in the matter of eating meat on a fast day.

Tomsk is not equal to Irkutsk in size or population, and lacks the mathematical symmetry which distinguishes the latter town. The buildings in Tomsk are also less elegant, but they have an air of more homely comfort than those of Irkutsk. Its architectural defects are, however, amply compensated by the superior advantages of its site, as it is built upon several hills, sloping on one side to the river Tom, and on the other side forming deep ravines, which gives the town a picturesque and even romantic appearance. A good many houses are built of brick, which the Russians call *stone*. On the outskirts there are great assemblages of small, miserable-looking, wooden huts, which help to disfigure the town. The principal houses are insured against fire, and the emblem of the "Salamander" Fire Office, nailed on the outer wall or over the door, meets the eye everywhere. Fires are by no means common, which is surprising considering the combustible material of which the cities are constructed, and the necessity of keeping up large fires during at least six months of the year. Nor do the inhabitants display any extraordinary caution in their habits, for though smoking in the streets (where it could not possibly do any harm) is strictly prohibited in Russia and Siberia, smoking within doors is universally practised by all classes.

Tomsk has been considered the coldest town in Siberia on the same parallel of latitude. The temperature in winter is as low as $-30°$ to $-40°$ Réaumur ($-35°$ to $-58°$ Fahrenheit), but it is becoming milder. An English lady, who had resided there a dozen years, informed us that during that period a marked improvement in the climate was noticeable. The extension of agriculture has probably been the means of producing this change. During our stay in Tomsk the thermometer showed $-8°$ to $-13°$ Réaumur ($14°$ to $3°$ Fahrenheit).

Excellent water is procured from the river. Water-carrying is quite a trade, employing a number of people from morning till night. A large hole in the ice is kept open, whence the water is carried up the steep bank in buckets, and conveyed through the town in carts, which are kept perfectly water-tight by the thick coating of ice that accumulates from the water dropped in filling.

All classes in Siberia are careful to cover themselves well from the cold. Wealthy people muffle up in expensive furs, and the peasants attain the same end by means of sheep-skins or deer-skins, which cost very little. No peasant is so poor as to be without very substantial gauntlets, made of stout leather with some warm substance inside, which protect both hands and wrists. They make little of the cold, however, when their avocations necessitate the endurance of it. In Tomsk, for example, it is not uncommon for the women to do their washing on the ice. Cutting a hole with an axe, they will stand or kneel over the water till their work is done, without even the appearance of hurrying. How they escape frost-bite it is hard to understand.

A few boys were seen skating on the river at Tomsk, but so few in number, and so grave in their demeanour, that it was sad to see them. Elsewhere we had observed skating in a small way, and in some villages small sledges even were used as playthings for children, but all so demurely as to be suggestive of the absence of real enjoyment. It may be that the Siberians make little of the ice because they have so much of it. But all roystering games in which the exuberant spirits of youth in other countries delight, are conspicuous by their absence in Siberia, and the *genus, little boy*, may almost be classed among the extinct mammals. So much the worse is it for the country. The youth who grow up without a taste for manly exercises are very likely, in maturer years, to betake themselves to in-door recreations of the most unprofitable kind.

Many of the largest mining proprietors have their town residences in Tomsk, and about four thousand workmen are in the habit of wintering in the towns, and spending their earnings there. I will here note a few particulars relative to mining in Siberia, supplied by a gentleman of extensive personal experience in that department. Siberia is rich in nearly all mineral treasures; but little attention has been paid to any but gold and silver, and even few of the latter mines have been worked. The richest gold-diggings that have ever been worked in Siberia are situated in the northern part of the government of Yeniseisk, but they are now nearly worked out. Very rich diggings, or mines, have also been worked in the Altai-saian chain, or "White Mountains," in the south of the same province, on the Chinese frontier. Within a recent period, gold has likewise been worked in the northern part of the government of Irkutsk, and in the Trans-baikal regions, which have only lately been thrown open to private enterprise. Within the last two or three years, gold discoveries in the Amoor districts have attracted thither many exploring parties, but I have not ascertained what success has attended their efforts.

Gold-diggings are to be met with in nearly all the uninhabited parts of Siberia. But in western Siberia the gold-fields are almost worked out, so that they are now of little value, and are carried on only in a small way.

In the Kirghis steppe there is one very rich silver mine, called the Zmeiewskoi, the property of a private family in Tomsk, the descendants of the first discoverer of gold in Siberia. This gentleman turned his discovery to good account. He was the first who worked gold-diggings in Siberia, and obtained many immunities from the government, who have always eagerly promoted the working of that metal. In his lifetime, he amassed a colossal fortune, and at his death, left mining property of enormous value. His successors, however, contrived to dissipate their inheritance by various means; but the silver mine in the Kirghis steppe has once more raised them to affluence.

The government gold, silver, copper, and iron mines are worked by criminals, condemned to hard labour, after having undergone corporal punishment for capital offences. They receive no pay for their labour, but only food and clothing enough to keep body and soul together. The works are all under the control and management of officers trained in the mine corps, called Mining Engineers. These officers are strongly imbued with the national weakness of peculation, and their position affords them ample opportunities for promoting their own personal interests. Generally far removed, in uninhabited regions, from the surveillance of superiors, no efficient check can be put on their doings. As a necessary consequence of this state of matters, all government mining works are very far behind private ones in machinery, and indeed in everything else essential to their efficiency, and are therefore unproductive. So far from being a source of revenue to the government, they are, for the most part, a constant expense. These mines are all private property of the Crown, and within the last five years the Emperor, despairing of being able to work them to a profit, has proposed leasing them out to private individuals, and would now gladly do so were persons of sufficient capital and enterprise to come forward.

Private gold-diggings and mines, and, in a few instances, silver mines also, generally situated in entirely uninhabited parts of Siberia, are ceded by government to private individuals on certain conditions. The applicant must be either a hereditary nobleman, or he must have the right of doing business as a merchant of the second class, and must pay the dues of the second guild. The portion of ground ceded to him is seven versts (nearly five miles) in length, and one hundred fathoms in breadth. The place always chosen is along the margin of a stream flowing through the mountains. Hence the elongated form of the allotment is adopted, in order to include as much water privilege as possible. The claimant may, however, if he chooses, take a greater breadth, but in that case the length must be reduced so as to give the same area. The river, or stream, is always included in the claim, as the richest gold is often found in its bed. The land, once allotted, is the property of the claimant only until it has been entirely worked out, or has been thrown up and abandoned, when it reverts to the Crown. Or, if not worked by the claimant at least one out of every three years, the claim is forfeited to the government, who may let it out to another applicant. The object of the government is to promote the working of gold, in order to secure the revenue from it, which is of some importance, as all gold must be delivered to the mint at a fixed price, which leaves a good profit to the government.

Then, as to the manner of working the mines. To get at the gold-sands an upper layer of earth, varying in depth from five up to thirty-five or forty feet, must be carted away. On the depth and extent of earth necessary to be removed principally depends the value of a gold-digging, and the first business of the speculator is to discover whether the gold-sands are rich enough to pay for the removal of the upper strata. To ascertain this, shafts are sunk at various distances over the ground where the works are proposed to be opened, and the exact depth of the upper layer taken. Then the gold-sands are bored through, and their depth ascertained. The proportion of gold contained in a given quantity of sand is next ascertained. With these *data*, an easy calculation will show the practical miner whether the claim will be remunerative.

The outlay in buildings and machinery necessary to start the work is very heavy, the expense of conveying the materials to the spot being alone a considerable item. For what are considered small works, employing from four to five hundred workmen, at least ten thousand pounds must be laid out in buildings and machinery. The works require a constant expense to keep up, and alterations and additions are frequently needed. After all, the works must be abandoned as valueless when the claim is worked out, or given up as unremunerative, as the cost of removing them to an inhabited region would far exceed the saleable value of the materials.

Many diggings employ as many as two, and even three, thousand workmen. The largest item in the working expenses is the wear and tear of horseflesh, and one horse for every two men employed is considered necessary in the calculation of the year's expenses. Provisions for the men, and corn and hay for the cattle, are brought during the winter months from distances of four or five hundred versts, and do not cost much. The free peasant seldom goes to work at the diggings, for, if at all industriously inclined, he can earn much more by agriculture at home. The workmen employed at the diggings are generally convicts sent to Siberia for theft and minor offences. Bad characters of all sorts, drunkards, vagabonds, men who will not settle to any steady work, convicts who have paid the penalty of the law, but have not found homes of their own—these are the kind of men who find a refuge in the gold-diggings. When all his money is gone, the digger engages himself to a proprietor for three roubles per month (equal to nine shillings). This looks a small sum for an able-bodied man to earn, but his regular wages is a matter of minor importance to the scapegrace who thus engages himself. His primary object is to obtain the *hand-money*, amounting to five or ten pounds sterling, which is paid him by his employer on making the contract. Out of this sum, as much of his debt is paid as the authorities are cognizant of, and with the whole of the balance he proceeds deliberately to get drunk, the extent and duration of his *spree* depending solely on the amount of money in his possession. He is then ready to proceed to the gold-works, and with one or two hundred comrades, under the charge of a couple of clerks, he is despatched to the scene of his labours. On arriving there, the digger has invariably to be clothed from head to foot by his master, and generally by the opening of the summer months, the beginning of the gold-washing season, the workman has contracted a debt to his master equal to twenty or twenty-five pounds sterling. The working-season lasts about 110 days in the year, and terminates invariably on the 11-23 September. To enable the workman to reduce his debt, and possibly have some money in hand on receiving his discharge at the end of the season, he is handsomely paid for all extra work he may do, over and above the daily task assigned to each. No holidays, Sundays, or Saints' days are allowed to a workman who is in debt. The law compels him to work on these days. What with compulsory and voluntary labour, a workman has it in his power to earn from five to seven pounds sterling per month. But he must work very hard to do it. The bell is rung at half-past two in the morning; by three o'clock he must be at work, all weathers. He seldom can leave off before nine in the evening. He is allowed half-an-hour for breakfast, an hour for dinner, half-an-hour for tea, and he takes his supper after the labour of the day is finished. The task generally set for the day is the breaking up and carting away of two cubic fathoms of earth to every five men and two horses. Extra work is allowed up to one-half of the daily task, and for extra work the workman receives pay at nearly ten times the rate of his contract wages. If a workman finds a piece of gold he is also paid extra for that according to its value. When not working "extra," the five men are allowed to leave the field as soon as their task is done, whatever hour of the day it may be.

The workmen at these gold-diggings are well fed, as indeed their excessive labour renders it necessary they should be. Each man is allowed from one pound to one pound and a-half of beef *per diem*. This is a luxury to him, for the Russian peasant at home seldom can afford to eat meat except on great holidays. Salt, buckwheat or other grain, and as much bread as he can eat, are daily issued to the workman. His lodging is made as comfortable as possible, every care being taken to have the barracks dry, warm, and well ventilated. Their health is also in a general way well-cared for. Every gold-digging has a fully equipped hospital, with a superintendent in charge, who must have some medical knowledge. A qualified surgeon either resides on the premises or on a neighbouring establishment, his services being paid for jointly by two or more proprietors. The surgeon has then the general superintendence of hospitals, and the care of the sick over the district. The proprietor of these works in fact takes as much care of his workmen as he would do of his horses, knowing well that unless they are kept healthy and contented, it would be impossible to exact the desired amount of work out of them. Besides the fixed rations of food, large stocks of corn-brandy (*vodka*) are kept for the men, who each get a tumblerful of the liquor two or three times a month, by way of counteracting the effect of the rawness of the climate. Of clothing also, large magazines are kept by the proprietors, and the workmen supplied with them as required for winter or summer wear. Tobacco is also considered a necessary, and is extensively consumed by all Russians. It is thought to be anti-scorbutic, and good for the climate. Supplies of brick tea are kept on hand, and of this article every workman consumes at least one pound per month. All these articles are supplied to the labourer in advance of his wages, and reckoned up when he gets his discharge. But even should he be deeply in debt the supplies are not withheld, the proprietor wisely considering that one sick man would be a dead loss far exceeding the cost of the few extras he might need.

The proprietor obtains all the goods he requires at wholesale prices, in the principal commercial and manufacturing towns, and they are supplied to the workmen at lower prices than they themselves could purchase them. The goods are always of the best quality, and it would not be considered respectable for a proprietor of gold-diggings to take a profit from his workmen on the articles supplied to them. To the original cost is added the expense of transit, and at the most an interest of three or four per cent. on the outlay. Even the latter item is not always charged.

When the gold-washing season is all over, the majority of the workmen find their way to some of the large towns with the balance of wages in hand, and spend the winter in riot and wantonness, often no doubt in great misery, until the next season comes round. They seldom or never think of saving money, or of bettering their condition.

CHAPTER XVIII.

TOMSK TO OMSK.

WHILE waiting for our servant to come up with the tarantass, we had sundry matters to look to in Tomsk before committing ourselves once more to the road, of which we continued to hear shocking accounts. Our portmanteaus were so smashed by the concussions the hard rough roads had exposed us to, as to be unfit for further service, and it was necessary to replace them with Russian *chemadáns*. This is an excellent contrivance for rough travelling; being constructed of soft leather, hard knocks have no effect, and it is capable of being so tightly lashed up as to be practically waterproof. It has also this advantage over an ordinary trunk or portmanteau, that whether it is full or not, there is no empty space left in it to block up the carriage where there is no room to spare.

A few accessories, in the way of fur gloves and such like, completed our wardrobe so far. To replace a broken thermometer we were led into an optician's establishment, managed by some clever Germans. Here we were surprised to find as good an assortment of instruments as is usually to be met with in any similar establishment in this country. Telescopes, microscopes, transit-instruments, theodolites, and all kinds of surveying instruments, of excellent workmanship, were there for sale. Everything, except the very simplest articles, was of foreign make, many of them German, but mostly French.

We had been strongly advised at the outset of our Siberian travels to provide ourselves with feather pillows, after the manner of the Russians, to use as buffers between our prominent bones and the hard substance of the carriage. Judging that our bedding would suffice, we, with the vanity of ignorance, rejected these good counsels in defiance of the well-known travelling maxim which inculcates the wisdom of taking your cue from the people of the country. Our carcases had been so unmercifully knocked about on the road to Tomsk, that we dared not go farther without pillows. It was not so easy to find them, however; for although Tomsk is said to be celebrated for them we could not hit on the right place to buy them. They are sold at about fourteen roubles per pood (36 lbs.). Our landlady was appealed to, but she avowed that there was not, and never could have been, any such thing in Tomsk, least of all had she any to dispose of. We were actually beginning to despair of pillows when a young Russianised German introduced himself to us, and, as usual in such *rencontres*, the conversation turned on civilisation. We happened to allude to the pillow difficulty, as proving the primitive state of society in Tomsk. On this our friend at once undertook to provide us. He went first to the old lady, and then to the younger members, none of whom he had seen before, and spent full half an hour ingratiating himself with them. The pillow question was in due time gently hinted at, and before very long one, and then another, and another, was produced, until we had pillows to our hearts' content. Delighted with his success, we begged our friend to tell us how he had achieved it. "First," he said, in very good English, "you must beat about the bush with these —— Russians; you must flatter them and humbug them. Then you must talk about everything but *the* thing. If you want to buy a horse, you must pretend you want to sell a cow, and so work gradually round to the point in view." He went on to tell us how he had coaxed and cajoled the good people into parting with their pillows, and how he backed up his requests by a touching appeal to their sense of hospitality. "You have two distinguished foreigners in your house, they are very good people, and you ought to treat them with the kindness due to strangers from distant countries. When Russians go to their country they are well treated. But if you refuse this small favour to these people, they will go home and tell their countrymen what beasts the Russians are," &c.

We were in a dilemma about the mode of travelling from Tomsk. Our tarantass was very much the worse for the wear, and on bad roads it might break down at any time. It would hardly be safe to leave the town with it. It would be equally imprudent to purchase a sledge, for there was very little snow; none fell during our stay, and there was reported to be none to the westward. We might of course use the post-carriages, but that mode of travelling has many inconveniences. It is uncomfortable in the extreme to sit in, and it necessitates changing at every station. The nuisance of turning out luggage, and turning out one's-self, every few hours, multiplies tenfold all the horrors of the road. Had we listened to the advice proffered to us on all hands in Tomsk we should have remained there till snow fell, which might be in one week or in six. We were entertained with terrible accounts of the road through the Baraba steppe, and the post had been six days coming from Kolivan, a town only 120 miles from Tomsk. The delay was attributed entirely to the roads, but making due allowance for Russian vagueness, we thought it just as likely to have been due to the difficulty of crossing some of the large rivers. In this uncertainty a diversion occurred in the advent of Schwartz, on the third day, minus the tarantass. He had been talked into the impossibility of getting it over the ice, and was induced to sell it for the small sum of ten roubles silver. The Russians designate their paper money by the high-sounding term "silver" roubles, *lucus à non lucendo*. This crowning act of folly, coupled with the fact of his having left behind (or sold) sundry articles which were in the tarantass, determined us to give Mr. Schwartz "the sack," and nothing but reflection on the probable consequences of his being left with no money, and a blighted character, to the "cold charity of the world," caused us to relent.

Old Barnaul left us a few hours after Schwartz's arrival. His destination lay nearly due south from Tomsk, a few stations beyond which town the road to Barnaul branches off from the Moscow road. The old gentleman refused to leave us entirely by ourselves, and had cheerfully sacrificed two whole days of his time, simply to keep us company until our own man came up. There was much genuine kindness in this, as in all his intercourse with us, and we parted with the pleasantest recollections on both sides (I hope).

Having made all necessary arrangements for resuming our journey, and armed ourselves with a pass from the Director-General of Posts for Western Siberia, we started on the 5th November in a post kibitka, with the intention of buying a sledge when we found an opportunity, and snow enough to use it. It was late in the afternoon before we got away from Tomsk, and dark before we emerged from the thick wood into which we plunged on leaving the town. The post-station had been at a village eighteen versts from Tomsk, but on arriving there we learned that it had been removed that very day to a place more convenient for crossing the river Tom, or on the other side of the Tom, for it was hard to deduce any positive conclusion from the various and partially contradictory statements we heard. At all events, be the new station where it might, our yemschiks refused to drive us any further than the old station in the village. To be cast adrift with our baggage in a village where no accredited officer of the government was located, would have consigned us to unknown troubles. We refused, therefore, to let the yemschiks go, but insisted on their proceeding to the next station, wherever it might be. The assistance of the starust, or village elder, was invoked, and he, with a few peasants, piloted us at our request to the river Tom, that we might examine for ourselves the state of the crossing. The ice was good, and apparently strong enough to bear the carriages, but the yemschiks lapsed into a state of mulish obstinacy, and refused to stir. The starust and his satellites, all speaking at once, held forth vigorously on general topics for the edification of the company, and went to bed. As for us, we had simply to keep possession of the carriages, and leave the rest to time. The yemschiks would get hungry, the horses would certainly have to be fed, and we might hope that when they got tired of waiting they would go on. With this idea we committed ourselves to rest in the kibitka. It was sadly deficient in comfort, as compared with our old tarantass. The kibitka is open in front, and rather over-ventilated everywhere. Cold kept sleep from our eyes for a time, while our ears were regaled with spasmodic bursts of indignation from the yemschiks, who now threatened to take us back to Tomsk, bag and baggage. To these attacks we offered nothing but passive resistance, and even the yemschiks wearied of a discussion so entirely one-sided. We were lulled to sleep in time by the chanting of some wild native airs by a Russian family in a neighbouring house. Their songs, many of them very sweet, are mostly, if not all, of the plaintive order. A drunken "brute of a husband," whom his poor wife was trying to decoy homewards, was the only incident that broke in upon the dead stillness of the night scene in the village of Kaltarskaya. There stood our wearied horses in the street that livelong night, bearing their sufferings from cold and hunger with resignation. How the yemschiks bestowed themselves during the night I know not. One at least must have kept awake to watch the horses. As morning approached the cold proved too much for my somnolence, and I was fain to turn out and grope my way into the house that had until the previous day been the post-station. On getting the door of a room open, the warm, fulsome exhalations of closely pent-up human beings that greeted the nostrils were enough to have produced a revolution in a sensitive stomach. The hard breathing of some, and the more sonorous articulations of others, enabled me to ascertain the positions of the heads of most of the sleepers, but still with every care I came into collision with sundry legs and trunks in my voyage across the floor in quest of a clear space where I might stretch myself. At length I discovered an unoccupied bench or table, and yielded to the luxury of sleep till daylight. When I again opened my eyes, my night companions had begun to stir about. Some were engaged in their toilet, which consists in stretching legs and arms, yawning a little, shaking up their clothes, and tightening the scarf which forms their girdle. By stooping low on entering the room I had escaped a broken head from a false ceiling which was used as a sleeping bunk. This is a common arrangement in post-houses, where the family of the post-master and all the yemschiks and hangers-on of the establishment are often jumbled up together, some climbing up to the top of the brick stove to sleep, and others lying on the boarded floor or ceiling which overhangs part of the room like a hay-loft. The Russian houses generally are built on traditional principles, the first thing aimed at being the exclusion of *air*, and consequently cold. They always feel warm, the temperature during the day being kept up to a pretty uniform scale by the large stoves. At night the fires go out, but the house retains its heat until about daylight in the morning, when it begins to feel a little chilly. There is scarcely one perfectly level floor in the country, and many of the houses, especially the old ones, are tipped up at one end so that the line of the roof makes a very wide angle with the level ground. Some indeed tumble over altogether, where the owners are too poor or too indifferent to take them down before they progress so far towards demolition. This phenomenon is not caused by the sinking of one end from the timbers rotting in the ground, but by the action of frost in the earth, which, unless the uprights are sunk deep enough, expands with cold so much as to heave up the foundations of the houses.

Early in the morning our yemschiks had made up their minds to take us over the river and to the next station. They had first to obtain the services of some peasants from the village, to pilot them over the ice. This local knowledge was necessary to enable them to avoid holes that had been only recently frozen, and other dangerous places. The Tom was here a fine broad expanse of ice, white with snow, very rough and lumpy. The crossing was satisfactorily effected, and we made the best of our way during the day through a flat, barren, and most uninteresting country, but still well wooded. A little snow fell, but only to tantalise us, for the ground never got covered more than half an inch.

Soon after daylight on the 7th, we arrived at a station on the right bank of the river Ob, which was the most formidable-looking obstacle to progress we had yet encountered. But as we had only ourselves and our baggage to get over, no serious difficulties were made, though we were threatened with trouble from a gang of drunken ice-men. The Ob, Obe, Obi or Oby, for all these spellings are used, is a noble river, and at the point where we crossed it is nearly half-a-mile wide. The current is rapid, and ice had only formed along the edges of the water. The difficulty in crossing arose from the huge masses of floating ice that were carried rapidly down by the current. To avoid being shut in by these small icebergs required all the dexterity of the adepts who manned the ferry-boat. Not only skill, but real hard work was necessary. Poles and boat-hooks were vigorously plied. The short paddle-oars were of comparatively little use; but by hooking on to the floating ice and hauling round them, then shoving off into clear water for a short space, and hooking on to the next lump of ice, we managed to thread our way through. The current had carried us down stream, but it was not nearly so strong on the left side of the channel, and there was a good breadth of clear water there which enabled the men to recover their lost ground. On reaching the landing-place, a rope was passed ashore, that is, to the solid ice, and the boat hauled up bodily far enough on the ice to enable horses to fetch the luggage. The sides and bottom of the boat being thickly coated with ice, enabled the men to slide her about with great facility.

From Tomsk our course had turned southerly, following the course of the river Tom, and striking the Ob obliquely. From the Ob we turned west again, and entered the great Baraba steppe.

Two stages from the Ob we reached the town of Kolivan, which is perhaps the most dreary, cold-looking town in Siberia, situated in a perfectly bare country, and exposed to every wind that blows. It possessed a peculiar interest for us, however, as being the then most easterly telegraph station in Siberia. The Tomsk station had been completed, but the manager had not arrived to inaugurate the opening when we left. Kolivan, being a second-rate station, only Russian messages could be sent; but having got a gentleman in Tomsk to write one out in that language, I was enabled to send a telegram from Kolivan to St. Petersburg, a distance of 2700 miles. Many repetitions were necessary in the transmission of this message, but it was delivered with perfect accuracy in thirty-six hours.

The Siberian telegraph, being now completed as far as Irkutsk, will no doubt be extended in time to the Amoor country. It is also probable that a branch will be formed from Irkutsk to Kiachta, and the Russians in Siberia confidently believe that their government will establish a line across Mongolia to Peking.

The Baraba steppe is, for the most part, one vast marsh, extending from the left bank of the river Ob westward to Tumen. It borders on the Kirghis steppe on the south, and is apparently a continuation of it. Its natural features are barren, being at the best a succession of wild prairies. The grass is long and coarse, but there is so much water on the ground that, in the summer season, the grass can hardly be available for pasture. The steppe is bare of wood, with the exception of strips here and there of dwarf birch-trees, which struggle for existence. In some of its more elevated parts, trees grow to a good size, but these spots are like oases in the desert. The inhabitants of the steppe are few, and lack the comforts enjoyed by the natives of other parts of Siberia. Villages are thinly scattered, and poor and mean-looking. The principal subsistence of the people consists in their cattle, and at every village a large tract of common land is fenced in for pasture.

At the stations in Baraba the post-master is seldom found at home, the domestic part of the establishment being generally left in charge of women, and the posting-department in that of the senior yemschik. The women in the steppe, we were informed, are mostly Kirghis, called by the Russians by the generic name of Tartars. The Kirghis women are physically superior to Russian women of the same class,—cleaner, better dressed, and handsomer. They have, in many instances, blue eyes and fair complexions, in marked contrast to the Kalmuks and Mongols. In manners they are more cheerful than the Russians.

Game abounds in the steppe. Blackcock were in some parts met with in great numbers. Pure white pheasants and *ryabchik* are plentiful, and, I have been told, though I did not see any, that the ptarmigan and capercailzie are also to be found.

The most conspicuous objects in the steppe are the windmills, a number of which are to be found round every village. These are the only marks that exist in the country, and they indicate the positions of the villages long before any other evidence of habitation is visible. They are primitive in construction. In order to face the wind the whole fabric is moved round on its axis by means of a clumsy, but powerful lever.

The road through Baraba looks like a strip of ploughed land in a desert, and was frozen so roughly that if solely depended on, traffic would soon have been brought to a stand. As it was, the heavy cart caravans were stopped for a time, and very few travellers were met with on this part of the journey. We rarely travelled on the road at all, only crossing it occasionally in quest of tracks through the open country. The frozen marsh greatly facilitated our progress. There was enough grass overspreading the ice to enable the horses to keep a footing, and by taking advantage of every sheet of ice we came to, we managed, by circuitous paths, to keep clear of the main road.

The weather was mild in the steppe. The sun was strong enough in the middle of the day to melt the thin covering of snow that lay on the ground; and even the nights were not so cold as we had experienced to the eastward. Snow fell occasionally, but not enough to make a sledge-road.

Slow as our progress was, it was quicker than we could have anticipated, and it was some satisfaction to keep ahead of the post which left Tomsk at the same time with us. Our yemschiks in the steppe were an unusually drunken set, but though often in jeopardy, we escaped without accident, saving one upset.

Passing Kainsk on the 9th, we reached the town of Omsk at midnight on the 11th, putting up at the Hôtel Moscow, an establishment of the same empty, comfortless character as other Siberian hotels.

Omsk is built round a hill at the junction of the Om river with the Irtish. It has a population of about 12,000; and is at present the residence of the Governor-General of Western Siberia. This functionary had recently made a tour to the Kirghis frontier, where some disputes had occurred between the Russian soldiers at the outposts and the Kirghis tribes. These *émeutes* are of constant occurrence. The Cossacks at the Russian stations make raids on their own account on the Kirghis people, and subject them to very rough treatment. An outbreak among the Kirghis occurs, which requires a military force to subdue. An expedition for this purpose is sent every year to the Kirghis steppe—the Russian outposts are pushed further and further south—more disturbances occur, and so the frontier is, year by year, extended, on the pretext of keeping the peace. That has been the system pursued by the Russian Government in all its aggressions in Asia. Siberia is dotted all over with old forts, which have become obsolete as the country has become quiet and settled under Russian sway. One of the strongest of these works is on the hill that stands in the middle of the town of Omsk. It is almost intact, and still kept up after a fashion. On the Kirghis frontier forts continue to be planted as footholds on the soil, and centres from which outlying territories may be subjugated.

A great deal of injustice, oppression, and cruelty have unquestionably attended the aggressions of Russia among the various Asiatic races, but in the long run the results have been rather beneficial than prejudicial to the tribes. The Kirghis who live as Russian subjects in the province of Omsk, are probably more comfortable than their semi-nomad brethren who feed their cattle on the southern steppes. The Mongol tribes who dwell under the auspices of Russia under the name of Bouriats, are more cultivated, and lead a more civilised life than the Mongols proper. They enjoy some degree of comfort, and have undoubtedly improved by their contact with the Russians. The wild hunting tribes, again, who inhabit the forests of Northern Manchuria, recently annexed to Russia, are said to have longed greatly to be transferred from allegiance to the autocrat of China to that of the Tsar. On the whole, the ambitious projects of Russia have been the means of spreading the benefits of civilisation and Christianity (in a much diluted form, it must be confessed) to many savage tribes. Highroads have been opened through deserts, and commerce has followed in the wake of conquest. The tribes who have become Russian enjoy, under the shelter of a strong government, immunity from war with neighbouring tribes, to which they were in former times constantly exposed, and have at least the opportunity of giving more attention to the arts of peace. Of course many bad, as well as good, results have flowed from the contact of Russians with these barbarous people. Those who were too low in the scale of humanity to bear the shock of a superior order of life, have been demoralised by it. The Tunguses and Ostiaks, who live in the northern parts of the provinces of the Irkutsk and Yeniseisk, are of a very low order of savages. The Tunguses are thievish, treacherous and cowardly, and live solely by fishing and hunting. The Ostiaks live almost entirely on and about the water, eat little else but fish when they can get it. They wander as far north as the Frozen Ocean. When deprived of their usual food in winter, they are reduced to eating carrion and garbage of all kinds. In their habits they are filthily dirty. Small-pox and drunkenness together make frightful havoc in their numbers. These tribes have been greatly injured by their contact with Russians. Naturally addicted to drunkenness, they have been supplied with ardent spirits to their heart's content by the invaders. The use of money being unknown to them, they only receive brandy in exchange for their services and products. They supply the gold-diggings with game, which brings them in return large quantities of spirits. They also act as guides to exploring parties, and such services are invariably requited with brandy. To obtain this liquor seems indeed to be the main object of their lives, and they have recourse to the most extraordinary expedients to gain their purpose. They are low idolaters, but they know how to turn to account the solicitude of the Russian Church for proselytising. They will allow themselves to be baptised in consideration of a bottle of brandy, but on the next favourable opportunity, they will pass over to another part of the country, and again offer themselves as candidates for baptism, if a similar inducement be held out. Brandy is fast ruining these people, and in a few generations they are likely to become extinct—a catastrophe which will have been greatly accelerated by the Russian settlers.

The reverse of this is the case with the nomad tribes who are spread over the steppes of the southern districts of Siberia. Their nomad habits have been so far circumscribed that they remain for many years together in the same places, moving only to suit the seasons and the pastures for their horses. They have a fixed place where they live in spring, but move off for the summer months, then again to winter quarters. At each of these encampments they leave their tents of felt or skins standing, thus evincing great confidence in the security of life and property. These tribes use tents of the same construction as those of the Mongols; but, unlike them, they care little for the rearing of horned cattle or sheep, their wealth consisting in horses, of which they keep large herds. They do not practise agriculture, but live a great deal by the chase, and a few of them carry on a kind of wandering trade. They obtain bread and other necessaries of life in barter for the skins of wild animals, but never part with their horses until hard pressed by necessity. If they have no skins, they will rather want bread than sell their horses. These tribes respect themselves, and command the respect of others by the strict sobriety of their habits, their general honesty, and cleanliness. They are mostly Mahometans. In many respects these people stand higher than the Russians, and are not likely to be demoralised by them.

Another Mahometan tribe may be mentioned in this category—the *Yakuts,* who occupy some of the northern part of the province of Irkutsk. They are no longer nomads, although they still live in tents. The Yakuts are very industrious people, rear large herds of horses and cattle, occupy themselves with trade, are skilled in ironwork, and have more recently taken to agriculture. They bear the character of sobriety, and are much more cleanly in their habits than any neighbouring tribes. The Yakuts have a tradition that they were once settled in the province of Kazan, whence they were expelled during the great irruption of Tartars into Russia, and wandered to their present habitat before they settled.

The wildest and most unmanageable of all the Siberian aborigines are the *Khargasses,* who live about the Altai mountains on the Chinese frontiers, in the south of the provinces of Yeniscisk and Irkutsk. The Khargasses are quite nomad, carrying tent and all with them when they move. They are said to be fierce and treacherous, perfectly uncivilised, and idolaters. It is a common practice with them when the time for the collection of their *essak*, or poll-tax, comes, to strike their tents, and cross the mountains to Chinese territory. There they remain until some similar claim is made on them on behalf of the Emperor of China, when they again pack up and return to Siberia. The Khargasses are great hunters, and live on the produce of their guns. They own no cattle, their riches consisting of reindeer and guns, like the Tunguses.

We saw two small tug steamers and six huge barges frozen-in at the junction of the Om with the Irtish. These barges go as far as Tumen with their cargoes, but of this more hereafter.

As there was still too little snow on the roads to warrant us in buying a sledge, we were obliged to continue undergoing the torture of a small kibitka, changing at every station. Sleep had now become out of the question, and if we could get a nap once in forty-eight hours we had to be satisfied. Eating was almost equally irregular, for the steppe afforded but few opportunities of enjoying a good meal. And yet this rough mode of life rather improved my health than otherwise. The constant exposure to the clear bracing Siberian air was certainly most beneficial, and I am convinced of this, that with all its ice and snow, there is no finer—that is, more salubrious—climate in the world than Siberia.

CHAPTER XIX.

OMSK TO OCHANSK.

ON the 11th November, we bade adieu to Omsk at an early hour in the evening. At the end of the second stage, forty-four versts from Omsk, we came to the river Irtish. At the station we found an officer travelling with a courier's *padaroshna*, who had failed in an attempt to cross the river in the dark. This was a sufficient hint that *we* had no chance, so we quietly lay by till morning, spending the night in the station in the company of the officer aforesaid. He was bound to the town of Tara, some distance north of the place we met him. His mission was to convey recruits thence to St. Petersburg. They are marched at the rate of thirty versts a day, which was slow enough to make us feel grateful for the moderate progress we had ourselves been making. Recruiting was going on very extensively in Siberia at this time. In Russia proper, and in the territories subject to it, recruiting is carried out on similar principles. The empire is divided into two zones, southern and northern. In each zone recruits are levied every alternate five years. They are chosen from among the free peasants and agriculturists, and when levies are made, every proprietor tries to get rid of a bad subject. The usual levy is one in every thousand of the men; but the government always takes into consideration circumstances that may entitle certain provinces or districts to partial exemption,—such as a bad harvest, or other similar misfortunes, to which agriculture and cattle-breeding are liable. When these circumstances occur, the suffering districts frequently have the term of the levy postponed a certain number of years, and in many cases they are wholly exempted. All that is applicable to times of peace. In war time, the frequency, as well as the per-centage of the levies, depends entirely on the exigencies of the government. For instance, during the Crimean War, recruiting in Eastern Siberia occurred twice in one year, and beginning at one man in a thousand, it increased gradually to seven in a thousand. The peasants on the rivers Lena and Yenisei are exempted from furnishing recruits on certain conditions, such as providing horses for travellers, and conveying the post, for which services they are of course paid besides. The peasants on the Angara enjoy similar exemption in consideration of their providing pilots for that very dangerous river.

Next morning we crossed the Irtish on the ice, without difficulty, and re-entered a frozen marsh, exactly similar to that part of the steppe which lies east of Omsk, windmills and all. Late in the evening, we passed through the town of Tukalinsk. At daylight on the 15th, passed Ishim. It snowed steadily all that day, and we soon had practicable sledge-roads, which enabled us to travel 160 miles a day. Early on the 16th, we passed through Yalootorofsk, and the same evening arrived at Tumen.

Finding at Tumen a very comfortable covered sledge for sale at the post-station, we immediately purchased it, as well as a smaller one for the accommodation of Mr. Schwartz and the baggage. The posting from Tumen westward is better organised than in Eastern Siberia. It is managed, not by government, but by a private company. No scarcity of horses is ever complained of in the company's line; for government takes care that the work is well done. But not the least of the improvements we experienced was, that we no longer required to pay the fare at every station. At

From a photograph. VIEW OF EKATERINBURG, SIBERIA. (Page 207.)

Tumen we paid our *progon* through to Ekaterineburg, and had no more trouble about it. In consideration of these facilities, double the government rate of fare is charged by the company from Tumen to Perm. Eastward the rate is about three-farthings per mile per horse. Westward from Tumen it is three-halfpence per horse.

We are now fairly through the great marshy steppe. The country from Tumen is undulating, and thick pine forests reappear.

We were in thorough condition to enjoy the soft luxury of travelling in a warm sledge, gliding so smoothly over the snow that at times we could not tell whether it was in motion; and it is not very surprising that we slept the greater part of the way to Ekaterineburg. Hunger even could not seduce us out of our snug retreat. The distance from Tumen to Ekaterineburg is 240 miles,—time occupied thirty-five hours. This is far from being a quick rate for sledge travelling, but the roads had not yet been properly formed, and in many places even the ground was quite bare of snow, the little that had fallen having been blown away by the wind.

Ekaterineburg is first sighted at some miles' distance through the vista formed by the road. A few scattered streets of small log houses form the outskirts of the town, and give one a poor opinion of the place. On emerging from the forest the town itself bursts on the view, and produces an impression of elegance, comfort, and even grandeur. It is spread over a large surface, and is divided into two parts by the river Irchet, which, though a small stream, widens out here to the dimensions of a lake. The situation of the town shows it off to better advantage than the other towns we had passed through as more of it can be seen at once. The proportion of brick-built houses to wooden ones is much larger, and the array of handsome churches and public buildings is more imposing. The bridge which connects the two portions of the town enhances considerably the beautiful effect of the whole. Although an improvement on the rest, especially in the matter of stone houses, Ekaterineburg presents a strong family likeness to the other large towns in Siberia, and is a fair specimen of the general type. The population is about 19,000.

The government mint is the most important building in Ekaterineburg. The principal coinage is copper, and I think I am right in stating that all the copper currency of Russia and Siberia is coined there. The Ural (pronounced by Russians *Oo-rál*) range, at the foot of which stands the town, is rich in precious stones, the cutting and setting of which is a standing occupation for a great number of people. The government lapidary establishment was formerly celebrated, but through neglect or mismanagement it has sadly fallen off of late, and very little of interest is now to be seen there. Strangers in Ekaterineburg are beset by little boys of most agreeable address, regular walking polyglots, who bring for sale amethysts, topazes, and other stones, with heaps of malachite, which latter is the most abundant in the neighbourhood.

There are several large iron-foundries in this place, the best one belonging to an Englishman who has been many years resident in Siberia. The mention of this gentleman recalls pleasing recollections of the kindness we received from him and his family on the day we rested there. It is refreshing to meet a countryman in such a far-off region, and this circumstance greatly enhances one's appreciation of true hospitality. There is a fair sprinkling of Englishmen scattered over Siberia, and there is considerable scope for their enterprise, both in private undertakings and as government servants. One gentleman who preceded us a few days in the homeward journey had lived some years at Stretnoi, the head of the Amoor navigation, in charge of the government machine-shop there. His salary is 3000 roubles silver (*i.e.* paper) per annum, with the perquisites of a house, fire, and light. He was so well satisfied with his post that he was then travelling to England to return with his family to Stretnoi, some 2000 versts beyond the Baikal lake. This instance out of many shows first that the English skill in machinery is prized by the Russian government, and also that even the most remote districts of Siberia are not very disagreeable as places of residence.

But to return to Ekaterineburg. The iron mines now being worked are at the convenient distance of 100 miles from the town, and the cost of transit of the pig-iron is comparatively small. This town is therefore advantageously situated for iron-work, and a large quantity is turned out every year. Most of the iron-work for Siberia goes from this place. The boilers and engines for the Baikal steamers are made in Ekaterineburg, and transported nearly 2400 miles to their destination. The workmen in the English foundries are chiefly Germans and Russians, with English foremen. Experience has proved the remarkable fact that English workmen deteriorate in Siberia. The native Russians are excellent workmen under skilful superintendence. Some few of them have intellect enough to be trusted with the more responsible departments of their business, but such cases are quite exceptional. They are in general mere imitators, exhibiting no power to think for themselves.

A large fish-curing trade is carried on here. The fish is brought from the great rivers, chiefly the Ob, near its mouth. About 50,000 poods, equal to 1,800,000 lbs. avoirdupois, are salted annually in this town.

Recruiting was going on actively here also. Having occasion to call on the master of police on a little matter of business, we drove up in a sledge to his office, but found the doorway and the portion of the street immediately adjoining it, so crowded with rough-looking moujiks wildly vociferating, that we could neither get in, nor even make our presence known, for some time. These were recruits who were being registered, passing one by one into the bureau, and coming out again by the same crowded doorway. It seemed to be quite an understood thing that each recruit should drop kopeks into the hands of the *gendarmes* who acted as door-keepers. By dint of hard pushing we succeeded in insinuating ourselves into the passage, but only to find a yet more impenetrable crowd inside. Sickened by the exhalations of so many unclean animals in sheep-skins, half suffocated in the frowsy atmosphere within, and crushed in the living mass till we had to fight for breath like a person in a nightmare, we were glad to escape into the fresh air, and abandon the purpose of our visit. The moujiks were followed to the rendezvous by their wives, who made confusion worse confounded by their frantic yelling and pushing, each one eager to get her own *protégé* into a good place. There were many hundreds of them, and one day would not suffice to register them all at the rate they were then progressing.

The temperature was ominously high on the 18th of November,—only one degree of frost. Some days previously it had been down to —15° Réaumur (—2° Fahrenheit). We were fairly committed to sledge travelling, and there was so little snow on the ground that a few hours' thaw would have melted away our charming sledge road. The frost set in about the usual time at Ekaterineburg, October $\frac{1}{13}$, but the snow there as elsewhere was late.

The hills and forests in the neighbourhood are well stocked with game. Black-cock, white partridges, *ryabchik*, reindeer, elk, and hares, are more or less abundant. Wolves are also common, but there are no wild boar. Game is plentiful in most parts of Siberia, but the Russians are no great sportsmen, except those who make a living by hunting. The nomad tribes are, however, expert in the use of the rifle.

Ekaterineburg is the most westerly town in Siberia, lying at the foot of the Ural mountains which separate Europe from Asia. I had formed great conceptions of this mountain chain, but the illusion was dispelled when, on inquiring for the Urals, I was pointed to densely wooded undulating hills, in appearance not more imposing than the Lammermoor range in Scotland. I know not why they are so darkly shaded on most of our maps, and made to look like a formidable barrier between the two continents. They certainly cover a broad expanse of country, but in elevation they are really insignificant, and rendered still more so in appearance by their very gradual rise from the level country. The elevation in the latitude of Ekaterineburg is little more than 2000 feet above the sea, and the plain on the Siberian side being between 800 and 1000 feet in elevation, the gentle slope of the mountains makes them look diminutive.

While settling about our horses at the post-station of Ekaterineburg, we fell in with an elderly German lady, who was going to start the same day for St. Petersburg. As she spoke very little Russian, it occurred to her friends that it would be a good thing for her to travel with us. There was plenty of room for her in our sledge, and we willingly consented to take her in. This was arranged accordingly. But old ladies (and young ones too) like to have their own way, and she discovered that she had too much luggage to go comfortably with ours in one sledge, besides little baskets of sweet cakes and knick-knacks, of which she had laid in a store for the journey, and which were likely to come to harm lying under our feet. She therefore determined to travel in her own sledge, where she could munch cakes at pleasure, but keeping company with us for the sake of the collateral protection our escort afforded.

At six in the evening of the 19th we left Ekaterineburg with our convoy, and about ten at night we reached the highest point of the road on the ridge of the Ural. In a heavy fall of snow we turned out to see the obelisk which has been erected there, as the boundary stone between Europe and Asia. It is a plain stone with no other inscription than the word "Europe" on one side and "Asia" on the other. It is said to have been erected in honour of Yermak, the Cossack robber-chief, who atoned for his other offences by discovering, and partly conquering, Siberia for the Russians in the end of the sixteenth century.

It is quite unaccountable that the vast country of Siberia should have been left to be discovered by Yermak at such a late period. It was well known to the Tartars, for the dynasty of Genghis had extended their conquests there, and yet the Russians, during their communications with the Mongols of the Golden Horde which subsisted for two hundred years, had never learned what was beyond the Ural mountains.

Yermak compelled by some accident to "leave his country," *i.e.*, being outlawed, found his way, with some two hundred adventurers, across the Ural. After pillaging the Tartars for some time, his handful of troops, *i.e.*, robbers, became so wasted with constant fighting that he could no longer maintain himself among his numerous enemies. It then occurred to Yermak to return to Moscow, announce his discovery, and make his peace with the Tsar. The robber was promoted to the rank of a hero, and was appointed to command an expedition for the conquest of Siberia. Yermak first crossed the Ural in 1580, and in 1660 nearly all the Siberian tribes were subjugated by Russia.

After a night's travelling we were still among the outlying spurs of the Ural range, well wooded with pine and birch, the former in greater variety than on the eastern side of the chain. On the road to Perm we passed through many cleared spaces, with villages and farms at short intervals.

On the 21st we reached Perm, a very flourishing manufacturing and commercial town on the left bank of the river Kama. Perm is the first (or last) town in Europe, and a little earlier in the season it would have been our last stage of road travelling. But we were too late and too early all the way through. The river Kama was not frozen, but so much floating ice was coming down, that the steamers which run between Perm and Nijni-novgorod had been taken off and sent down the Volga to Astrachan for the winter. Only a few small craft were left for repairs to their machinery. We met some more English workers in iron in Perm, and they seemed to have a good winter's work before them. A few weeks earlier, we should have embarked on one of the passenger steamers at Perm, steamed down the Kama as far as Kazan, where it joins the Volga, then up the latter from Kazan to Nijni-novgorod. This voyage would have been accomplished in five days, the whole of which time would have been available for sleep, but no luck fell in our way. Not only must we continue our journey by land, but it was very doubtful whether we could even cross the Kama at all, owing to the velocity of the current and the weight of ice that was borne downwards. The ferry is not at Perm, but at a point fifty versts lower down.

The navigation of the Russian and Siberian rivers is making astonishing progress. There are now no less than 370 tugs on the Kama and Volga, and new steamers are being added every year. One company runs steamers from Nijni to Perm, and two from Nijni down the Volga to Astrachan. The Volga Steam Navigation Company is managed by an Englishman at Nijni-novgorod, and in his hands has proved a very remunerative undertaking. Under Russian direction it had been quite the reverse. Nearly all the steamers are of foreign construction. Many come from the German ports, and many from England. They are usually sent to Russia in pieces, but several have steamed across the North Sea, and have made their own way into the very heart of the country by means of the canals in communication with the rivers.

The facilities enjoyed by Russia and Siberia for inland navigation are so vast, as to afford almost unlimited scope for capital and enterprise in introducing steam. It is, of course, a serious disadvantage that vessels have to be built in foreign countries, but there is no good reason why this should continue. If the authorities had encouraged the working of their own iron and coal mines with half the zeal they have misapplied to the gold-diggings, the country would have been further advanced in real wealth than it is. The Russian statesmen must sooner or later learn that mere gold no more constitutes wealth than tallow or any other article that has a mercantile value. The capital and labour consumed in procuring a given quantity of the precious metals would have probably produced a higher marketable equivalent, if coal and iron had been the object. At any rate, iron would have proved a surer basis for the propagation of wealth than gold. When steamers, for example, are built in Siberia, the manufacturing profits will, in the first instance, be disseminated in the country, and the gold that would, as now, be sent abroad for their purchase, may lie in the bowels of the earth, and no one be a loser by it. A good deal has already been done on the Siberian rivers, and the heavy traffic between Irkutsk and the west is conveyed for the most part in barges, which on the Om and Irtish are towed by steamers. The mere navigation of rivers in the Russian dominions is not new, but in former times the barges were incapable of ascending the rapid streams. They were constructed merely for the one trip down stream, and on reaching their destination and discharging their cargoes, they were broken up for fire-wood. The water communication between Eastern Siberia and Western Russia is necessarily very circuitous from the circumstance that the great rivers in Siberia run from south to north, and fall into the Frozen Ocean. For example, the distance by water from Omsk to Tumen is 3000 versts, and by land only 632. The Amoor and its tributaries form an exception, flowing eastward and falling into the Sea of Ochotsk. To begin at the extreme east; the grand water-route now used for goods is from the Pacific up the Amoor as far as the Shilka. Thence to the Baikal land carriage is at present used, but the Shilka itself is capable of navigation much higher up. The London and China Telegraph, August 15, 1864, reports that a steamer has lately ascended this river and its tributary the Ingoda as far as Chita, the government town of Trans-Baikal. From the Baikal the communication is by water down the Angara to Irkutsk, and 1400 miles beyond that town, to the junction of the Angara with the Yenisei, in the north of the province of Irkutsk. The water-route on the Angara below the town of Irkutsk is only used for traffic to the north. Goods in transit for Europe go by land from Irkutsk to Tomsk.

From the west, the Siberian water-route begins at Tumen, proceeding down the Irtish from Tobolsk, then up the Ob and the Tom as far as Tomsk. Then, if for the northern part of Eastern Siberia, land carriage from Tomsk to Krasnoyarsk; from the latter town down the Yenisei to the towns of Yeniseisk and Turukhansk, beyond which the country is inhabited only by wandering Tunguses and Ostiaks. There are other important water-routes in Siberia, such as that from Tumen by the Ob and Irtish to Semipalatinsk on the Kirghis steppe; and from Irkutsk down the Lena to Yakutsk,

but the lines of greatest traffic are those running east and
west. The ice interposes a serious difficulty in the navigation of these rivers, especially in the more northern parts,
where the summer is very short, and frost sets in early.
Goods are frequently caught in the ice, and in some parts
of the rivers, they may be frozen up for six, or even eight
months together. This risk would, of course, be greatly diminished were steam in more general use. The duration of
a voyage could then be calculated with tolerable certainty,
and a convenient port reached after the premonitory indications of freezing-up had shown themselves. Steam would
also afford the means of expediting goods so much quicker,
that the heavy part of the year's traffic might be conveyed
by the rivers during the open season.

A project for improving the water communication in
Siberia was set on foot by an enterprising Russian in 1859.
The scheme was revived in 1862, and the projector was supported by a Hamburg banker, and assisted by a Russian
colonel of engineers. Their intention was to form a complete
water route from Tumen to Kiachta, first by the rivers Ob,
Tom, Tchulim and Ket. From the last-named, a canal
thirty to thirty-five miles in length would have to be cut into
the river Yenisei. From the Yenisei, the Angara would be
used to its source in the Baikal lake. From the lake the
route would be up the Selenga to a point about eighteen
miles from Kiachta. Thus, by one cutting, of, at the most,
thirty-five miles, clear and uninterrupted water conveyance
would be established from near the Ural mountains to the
frontier of China. But the difficulties in the way of this
enterprise are very serious. The river Angara is, in its present
state, not navigable except down stream. In a distance of
800 miles below Irkutsk, there are no less than seventy-eight
rapids and dangerous passes, some of which it would be impossible even for a steamer to ascend. Native craft shoot

the rapids when the water is high, and effect a passage down the river, but of course never return. To render that part of the river fit for navigation, rocks would have to be blasted and cleared away. Above Irkutsk also, there are one or two places on the Angara that would have to be cleared before the steamers could ply with safety on the river. But supposing all that accomplished, to carry out the water communication with efficiency, steamers of various classes suited to the depth of water, and the nature of the different rivers, would be necessary, thereby adding greatly to the expense. On the whole, the cost of clearing out the channel of the Angara, and other minor items of expense, would be so enormous that it is highly improbable the scheme will ever be carried out; certainly not for some generations to come. All that can now be done is to improve the water communication at present in use in so far as steam traffic is practicable. Before the Angara is cleared of rocks, railways will probably traverse Siberia. Not that I consider the construction of railways in that region nearer than a remote possibility. For, although Siberia would be no exception to the general rule that railways make traffic for themselves, yet the cost must bear some proportion to the return. The length of railway necessary to connect the traffic of the various distant parts would be enormous, and as these matters are managed in Russia, would probably cost three times the amount that would be required in any other country. There is no capital in Russia available for such a purpose, and foreign capital will find many more attractive investments than Siberian railways.

From Perm we were driven by "Tatárs," who are capital coachmen. We first met these Western Tatárs at Ekaterineburg, where they live in peace and good will with the Russians. They have no apparent affinity with the Mongol races, but yet they betray, in their manner of life, their descent from nomad tribes. Many of them are engaged in trade, but they prefer hawking to settling in a shop; and even when they have opened shops they like to sally forth with a " pack " on their shoulders and roam about the great towns with their merchandise.

The general and sweeping misapplication of the name of Tartar, or Tatar, to the various wandering tribes of Asia, has led some persons to doubt whether there ever was any one tribe properly entitled to the appellation. The name has been too widespread—say from China to Russia—not to have had a foundation in fact, and there is not much doubt that an insignificant tribe of the Mongol family was known to its neighbours, and called its people by the name of Tatars. But the dominant tribes, even of the Mongols, have always repudiated the appellative; and although the Russian-speaking "Tatars" of the west acknowledge the name as applied to them, it is much in the same sense as an English-speaking Chinese calls himself a Chinaman (*Cheen*aman) to accommodate himself to western phraseology, although the term has no equivalent in his own language.

It is indeed curious to trace old names of countries and races to merely accidental circumstances. The name of China in use among the Mongols and Russians, is still *Kitai*, which is the *Kathay* of Marco Polo, and the name of the northern part of China during the reign of the Mongol dynasty. The name originated with a northern tribe, also called the *Liau*, who pushed the frontiers of their empire into North China, and held sway there from the tenth to the thirteenth centuries, and who, defeated by the Niu-ché, retired into the desert, and at a later period founded the formidable empire of Khara Khitan, or the Black Khitan, near the source of the river Obi.

But the name of Tartar has been liberally bestowed on all those Asiatic tribes who led a roving life, and of whose history little or nothing was known. The Chinese, for reasons somewhat similar, term all "outer" nations "barbarians," just as the Jews grouped all who were beyond their own pale under the comprehensive title of "gentiles;" and the ancients gave the name of Scythians to all the barbarians of Asia, of whom they could not give any more definite account.

Arriving at the last station before crossing the Kama, late at night, we were compelled to wait till morning, as no inducement would prevail on the men to attempt the ferry at that hour, although there was a bright moon. The truth was the men were all so hard worked during the day as to be unfit for anything at night. In the morning, however, we got across with our sledges, and proceeded to Ochansk, a small town three versts from the right bank of the river, where we breakfasted.

During the 22nd the frost disappeared for a few hours, and to our confusion the snow vanished so rapidly during the short time as to leave us in many places bare ground to drive our sledges over. The sight was really appalling, for all our hopes of ease and comfort for the journey rested on the snow. It was absolutely essential to us, seeing we were committed to sledges, and when we saw the black patches appearing here and there, we could sympathise in the despair which a fish must feel when abandoned by its native element and left panting on dry land. A westerly wind got up, and increased to a gale in the afternoon, coming round to north in the evening. This brought cold weather back again, and that night was one of the most severe we encountered in the whole journey. With the extreme cold the wind fell, and a dead calm ensued, which lasted a night and a day. The hard frost converted the soft, melting snow into a magnificent sledge-road, so far as it went; but all the way to Kazan we were plagued with bare places where the wind or sun had been most powerful.

CHAPTER XX.

RUSSIAN AND SIBERIAN PEASANTRY.

WE had not travelled far into Russia proper, before the difference in the condition of the peasantry there, and in Siberia, forced itself on our attention. The houses in Russia are decidedly inferior to those in Siberia. They lack the air of rude comfort peculiar to the latter. Windows are broken and stuffed with straw, and roofs are out of repair. Women and children are ill-clad and squalid. The men are haggard, abject, and degraded. Everything is suggestive of poverty, negligence, and misery. In remarkable contrast to these phenomena are the outward circumstances of the peasants in Siberia. As I have intimated in the course of this narrative, these latter are well clad, well housed, and at least adequately fed. They have something of independence in their bearing, and the condition of their families, as well as the tasteful decorations often met with in their houses, evince a certain amount of self-respect. The difference is easily accounted for—the explanation lies in the words *serf* and *no serf*, and it illustrates the inevitable effects of slavery on a people. And if slavery, in its modified form of serfdom, can so deeply mark the character of the subjects of it, what may be expected from the pure, uncompromising "institution?"

The Siberian free peasant is the descendant of a convict. This applies to almost the whole Russian population of Eastern Siberia, as also to the great proportion of that of

Western Siberia. In the latter region there are still the descendants of many of those Cossacks who followed the renowned Yermak in his victorious march across the Ural, and who continue in the enjoyment of certain privileges granted to them by the Empress Catharine. But Eastern Siberia, by far the richest of the two, may be said to be entirely peopled by the descendants of convicts. These belong to two categories—those who are condemned for capital crimes, and those who are expatriated for minor offences. The criminal who belongs to the first category, when he has undergone the corporal punishment allotted to him, and served his term (generally mitigated) of hard labour in the government mines, has a portion of land granted him, on being released from his confinement. He may cultivate as much ground as he chooses to clear, using the timber for building purposes or fuel. He is exempt from the payment of taxes, and from the conscription. The children of these convicts, born in Siberia, enjoy the same privileges, but they are still what are called *minors*, and do not possess the rights of a free peasant. For example, they are disqualified from holding any honorary appointment in the village or community where they may reside. Such disabilities may be, and frequently are overcome by means of money; for an industrious peasant has an opportunity of saving, and it is not an unusual thing for them to become rich. Many of the most wealthy men in Siberia at the present moment—large gold-digging proprietors, merchants, &c., are the descendants in the second or third generation of convicts who have undergone the penalty of the law. These men generally manage to "write themselves up," by a judicious application of their money, and then by paying the dues of one of the three guilds of merchants, they obtain a status in society, and enjoy the right of trading; they often make fortunes, either in trade, gold-digging, or other enterprises.

The other class of criminals is composed of those who have been exiled for minor offences such as theft; and of serfs, who, before their great emancipation in 1859, were liable to be sent to Siberia for any offence against their masters, or even for no offence at all, but from sheer caprice. I met an old woman in Tomsk who had been exiled on the latter count. She had inadvertently stuck a needle into the wall, and her mistress, with the nervousness that a bad conscience produces, took it into her head that the serf intended to bewitch her. For this offence the old wretch (though I dare say she was young then) was sent to the police, to be despatched to Siberia with the next batch of government exiles, and the official record stated she was so sent "by the will of her master."

Well, these convicts not possessing the rights of free citizenship, are, on arriving in Siberia, appointed to reside in, or registered as belonging to, a certain district of the province where the Governor-General may determine to colonise them. After three years' residence, certain advancement is held out to these people, if they can produce a certificate of good behaviour. They are allowed to marry, to become settlers, to clear and cultivate land at pleasure. They are exempt from taxes for the space of twelve years; and after that they only pay a trifle. These convicts are, however, legally dead, can never hold property in their own name, and of course can never return to Russia. But so far from this latter restriction being a real hardship, if a return to their native air were permitted them, it is highly improbable that any would avail themselves of the privilege. Siberia is really the land of promise to them. The descendants of these convicts become free agriculturists, and live in independence. They pay to government a tax of from three to four pounds, sterling, per head,* per annum, which is very much higher

---

* This tax is levied on every male above 18 years of age.

than the tax levied on the peasants of Russia proper. But
there the peasant had, in addition to the small tax to
government, an' *obrok* to pay to his master, amounting
on an average to about four pounds sterling a year. The
Russian peasant, before the emancipation, got nothing in
return for this tax, but was bound body and soul to his
master, and unable to do anything to better his condition
that was not entirely agreeable to the arbitrary will of his
owner. The peasant in Siberia, on the other hand, is absolutely free in all things to follow the bent of his own will.
He has no master to dread and serve, and owes obedience to
nothing but the law of the land. The Siberian peasantry
are treated with every liberality by the government, whose
ruling purpose with respect to that country is to colonise
it with industrious communities, who will turn its natural
wealth to account, and become an arm of support to the
state. For the single tax above-mentioned, the peasant receives as much land as he can clear, as much timber as he
chooses to fell, and no rent is required from him. The land
he has worked is his own. No other person can disturb his
possession, and the government even cannot claim from him
any portion of the land so acquired without his formal re-
nunciation. The primeval forest may be said to cover the
whole of Siberia—the cleared spaces are as drops in the
bucket, and the bare steppes, where timber is scant, bear
but an insignificant proportion to the whole. In the immediate vicinity of some of the large towns, where the people
have been burning wood for two hundred years, a palpable
impression has been made on the forest, and there it has
been found necessary to restrict the cutting of wood to
certain limits, both as to the quantity consumed, and the
boundaries within which trees may be felled. These restrictions are enforced with a view to securing the growth
of young wood within a convenient distance of the towns.

There is but one Siberian nobleman and proprietor of serfs in existence,—Mr. Rodinkoff, Counsellor of State and Vice-Governor of the Province of Yeniseisk, a kind-hearted, good old man. His grandfather received from the Empress Catharine a grant of lands and peasants in Siberia on the terms of Russian serfdom. But neither he nor his successors ever attempted to exercise proprietary rights over their peasants, who lived very much as the free peasants do. One of the family, the brother of the present proprietor, broke through the custom of his fathers, and paid the penalty of his life for his imprudence. He attempted to put in force his full signorial rights, and to levy contributions on his peasants, as in Russia proper. The consequence was that he was murdered in one of his excursions to visit his estate, within thirty miles of the town of Krasnoyarsk. The present proprietor seldom interferes with, or visits his peasants, but contents himself with the modest imposts of wood for winter fuel for his town residence, and hay for his horses, with which they cheerfully supply him.

In the matter of recruiting, the Siberian peasants have always been leniently dealt with. In many parts of the country they are exempted altogether for certain considerations. Those who settle on the rivers Lena and Yenisei, are exempt from all taxes and recruiting, on condition that they supply travellers with post-horses, and convey the government post, for both which services they are, moreover, paid at a higher rate even than in other parts of the country. This privilege extends from near Irkutsk to the frozen ocean on the Lena, and from the town of Yeniseisk to the frozen ocean on the Yenisei. The extreme severity of the climate, and the inhospitable nature of the soil in these regions render it necessary to encourage settlers, and so to secure uninterrupted communication through the country. There is no spring, and no autumn in these parts. Three months, and in some districts less, of summer, is all the time allowed them for cultivation of the soil. The rest of the year is winter, during which snow lies to the depth of from seven to upwards of twenty feet. The temperature then falls to 30°, 40°, and in some parts 50° Reaumur of frost (equal to $-35°$, $-58°$, and $-80°$, Fahrenheit). No corn grows, and but few vegetables, but the country abounds with wild animals such as bear, elk, deer, sables, foxes, squirrels. The inhabitants become expert hunters, and make a good living out of the furs they obtain.

The settlers in the river Angara are also exempted from taxes of all kinds, and from recruiting, on condition of their supplying government and private travellers with skilful pilots and guides, for which they are of course likewise well requited by those who employ them. This is necessary on the Angara, that river being one of the most dangerous in the world. Being the only river that runs out of the Baikal Lake, a heavy volume of water is forced down into it, and during its course from the lake to its confluence with the Yenisei, it is full of falls and rapids, which can only be passed with safety under the guidance of pilots of local skill and knowledge.

The amenities of free life enjoyed by the peasants of Siberia have produced the unmistakeable effect of, in some measure, eradicating the impress of slavish degradation which centuries of servility had stamped on the whole race of moujiks. The hereditary marks of the yoke are still too plainly to be seen, and many generations will probably pass from the scene before even the Siberian Russians can claim to be really civilised. But it is a great thing to have made such a good start on the road to improvement. The progress made is not likely to be lost; each stage of advancement rather becomes a guarantee for still greater, and more rapid progress in the future. The feeling of independence has taken deep root in the minds of these freemen, and it would be no longer possible to enslave them, without causing a revolution. Their ideas have been enlarged. Industry and economy are seen to have their full reward. The security of life and property, and the liberation from the arbitrary dictates of a superior will, give the people encouragement to cultivate their talents in the full faith that their labours shall not be in vain. Unlimited wealth is open to all who have the energy to seek it. Great numbers of the Siberian peasants have amassed fortunes already. Other tastes naturally flow from worldly prosperity, and already among the merchants who have enriched themselves from the ranks of the peasants, education is beginning to attract attention. In due time mental culture will, no doubt, spread downwards, and the distinction of classes, which has so greatly retarded the progress of civilisation in Russia, may gradually be smoothed away. The amalgamation of classes will consolidate and strengthen the whole body politic, and should that happy consummation ever be realised in Russia, Siberia will have the honour of leading the way. The barriers that obstruct free intercourse between the different strata of society are already partially broken down, greatly to the advantage of all. For slavery or serfdom exercises a demoralising influence on masters and slaves alike. The institution in Russia crushed the energy of life out of the serfs, and almost destroyed their thinking faculties—so much so that centuries of freedom may be inadequate to enable the emancipated to rise to their proper level of intelligence.

While the serfs were thus degraded and kept down to a position but little superior to that of domestic animals, their masters, having no community of feeling with them, were actuated by the single motive of extorting the maximum revenues out of their human property. The cares of management devolved on the serfs, and the masters, being for the most part almost as much as the serfs shut out from their legitimate share in public affairs, abandoned themselves to extravagant pleasures and dissipation, or to mischievous intrigues. Without any healthy occupation for body or mind, a highly artificial mode of life developed itself in the ranks of the wealthy serf-proprietors, the sole refuge from which was in the military or civil appointments of the government. Practical education was wanting in the great body of them, so that when their source of revenue was taken away by the liberation of their serfs, they broke down from the want of any resources within themselves by which they might have maintained their standing in society, and even have improved their pecuniary condition in other careers. There were very many exceptions to this, but such was the necessary tendency of the institution of serfdom, and such was the actual fate of those proprietors who allowed their energy to be sapped by the unnatural life to which they were born.

It was probably the growing prosperity of Siberia, and the marked superiority of the condition of the population there, that induced the government to emancipate the serfs of Russia proper. The importance of this great measure can hardly be over-estimated, and I doubt whether the Emperor Alexander II. has received the full credit due to him for the enlightened liberality which dictated, and the noble courage which carried into execution, this truly magnificent conception. It is well known that the most determined hostility of the great majority of the nobles was arrayed against the measure, which, from their point of view, threatened to sweep away at one blow their whole worldly wealth. The Emperor stood almost alone, being supported by a small, and not overwise minority. His life was several times in jeopardy. But he maintained his purpose with singular pertinacity through three years of discussion and deliberation, during which the ill-timed zeal of his supporters raised serious difficulties in his way by trying to drive matters too fast. At the end of three years the ukase was signed, and in two years more twenty-three millions of male serfs, with the corresponding number of females, were set free. Whether we consider the vast numbers of men and women whose destiny was involved, the radical character of the change effected, the formidable opposition which had to be borne down, or the germs of expansion which it implanted into the Russian people, moulding the whole future history of the nation, this act of the Emperor of Russia stands unrivalled as a measure of reform in the history of the world. Many other reforms have been introduced during the present reign, but the emancipation of the serfs is an achievement in itself worthy of a lifetime.

Peter the Great did much to promote the progress of the material prosperity of his country, and considering the barbarous character of his education, and of the age in which he lived, more than established his claim to the title of *Great*. Catharine made her reign "glorious;" Nicholas made his name terrible; but to Alexander II. belongs the immortal honour of liberating his people from slavery. The full results of this great work will only be manifested in future ages. The serfs have now, as it were, been born to political life—their education is but beginning. With freedom, industry will grow; the comforts of life will be enjoyed; intelligence will spread, and higher aspirations will be infused into the servile millions. In course of time the Russian population will be capable of exercising the rights of freemen, and the day may come when even the despotism of the government may yield something to the claims of the people for representation. Already a change for the better is observable among the liberated serfs. Each had a piece of land allotted to him, varying from eight to twenty acres, with the right to farm or purchase more. Residents in Russia have noted an increase in the productiveness of many parts of the country, in consequence of the improved system of agriculture that has been initiated since every man began to grow his own crops, instead of slaving his life away for behoof of a master whom he seldom saw, and who took little interest in the management of his property. Even the character of the people is already sensibly ameliorated. They show more self-reliance and self-respect than formerly, and their increased industry is implied in the greater production of the country.

The effect of the emancipation on the nobles has been various. The spendthrift portion of them have been ruined by it, as also those who had not the ability, foresight, or resolution to take timely measures to meet the consequences of the social revolution. Others lost heavily, to the extent of half or two-thirds of their incomes; but, facing the emergency in a practical spirit, they betook themselves to useful employments, with a view to improving their circumstances; and many of these have regained by such means all that they had lost. The more prudent and economical proprietors, who devoted themselves to the improvement of their estates, and were fully prepared for the change, have been positively gainers by the movement; for, besides making more out of their property by efficient management and free labour than they could extort from their serfs, they have the indemnity paid by government to the credit side of their accounts.

The highly exasperated feelings displayed by the majority in the first instance cooled down considerably during the five years which elapsed between the first notice of the intended reform and the actual consummation of it. The Russians are tolerably well accustomed to arbitrary measures, and their feelings are not naturally very deep. But the nobles were still far from being satisfied, and the mutterings of general discontent that were heard long after the inauguration of the new regime, continued to be a cause of anxiety to the Emperor. The dissatisfaction of the nobles was fed from various causes apart from the serf question. A pretty general reform of abuses was instituted about the same period. Many time-honoured privileges and monopolies were invaded, to the prejudice of those who were battening on the spoils of office. Matters continued in a critical state until the perpetration of the infamous deeds of incendiarism which preceded the Polish insurrection. These occurrences brought all the best part of the population to the side of the government, and restored the wavering loyalty of the nobles and military officers; and the malcontents, whose nefarious gains in public offices of trust and otherwise were put an end to, were fain to sink their grievances in oblivion.

CHAPTER XXI.

KAZAN—POLISH EXILES.

WE passed through a great deal of bare, flat and uninteresting country on the road to Kazan. The ground being covered with snow, we could not judge of the soil, but farming villages were tolerably numerous, and a fair amount of population seemed to find a subsistence there. Oaks, of which we saw none on the Siberian side of the Ural range, now began to appear. The birch trees grow straight and tall, and pines were less conspicuous in the woods.

The number of Polish prisoners we found on the road threatened seriously to impede our march. We had met them occasionally in Siberia, but between Perm and Kazan we encountered companies of them on the way, and at almost every station. The resources of the posting establishment were severely taxed to provide horses for so many travellers at once, and we had frequently to wait till the Poles were gone, and then take the tired horses they had brought from the last station. The Poles travelled in the same manner as we did, in large sledges containing three or four people, sometimes more. Those who could not be accommodated with sledges had carts, or *telégas*, which were more or less crowded. None of them travelled a-foot. All were well clothed in furs. On the whole I was surprised to find such a number of people travelling with so much comfort. When we met a party of them in a post-station we were very short of room, unless when we happened to be there first. Then the cooking establishment was entirely monopolised by the exiles when it pleased the officer in charge to dine them. On such occasions we postponed our repast to the next station. The prisoners are invariably treated with kindness and consideration by the officer in charge and by the *gensdarmes*. They are under close surveillance, but I did not see any of the prisoners in irons, though I was informed that some of them were so. I remember one fat, jolly fellow in charge of one of the detachments of prisoners. He was a captain in the army, and had hard work to console himself in his forlorn situation. He did not at all like the service he was engaged in; indeed he seemed to feel his banishment to Siberia more than the exiles themselves. He envied our destination homewards, and took occasion to bemoan himself a little. "Ah! you are happy," said he; "in a few days you will be in Moscow, but I, poor devil, must go to Tobolsk with *gensdarmes*"— accompanied by an expressive shrug of the shoulders, and downcasting of the eyes. He made companions of some of the prisoners; one in particular he seemed to be on cordial terms with. The officer told us this prisoner had held a commission under Garibaldi, and had been lately captured leading a band in Poland. He was a handsome young fellow, with a wild look in his eye. As for the rest of the prisoners, there was nothing remarkable about them. They ate well and talked loudly; the din of their voices at a post-station was intolerable. They joked and laughed a great deal, by way of keeping their spirits up I suppose; but no indication whatever was given that they were exiles undergoing the process of banishment. If one might judge from appearances, I should say they rather liked it.

On the 24th of November, late at night, we reached Kazan, a fine old town, the name of which is closely bound up with the ancient history of Russia. I found a letter waiting me at the post-office there, in answer to my telegram from Kolyvan, which was a comfort. How I got into the post-office at eleven o'clock at night, and how the men happened to be there in their places at that hour, I was not very clear about. But it was explained that two posts were then expected, one from the east and one from the west, and that when I hammered at the door they thought it was at least one of them. Arriving in Kazan very late, we took up our quarters for the night at the station hotel, where we were half suffocated as usual by the close fusty atmosphere of a room kept up to + 16° Reaumur (68° Fahrenheit), no air being ever allowed to enter.

In the morning we began to hear ominous warnings about the Volga. The ice was coming down in big lumps, and our sledge could not be got across—so we were informed. It was seven versts from the station to the ferry. We might drive there and see for ourselves, but then it would have been excessively disagreeable to have to return defeated. We consulted a Russian gentleman to whom we had a letter of introduction, but no comfort was to be got from him. The state of the river was as bad as it could be, and he strongly advised us not to leave Kazan until the Volga was hard frozen. The voice of the tempter had been saying "wait, wait," at every point of our journey from Kiachta to Kazan, but as we had not listened before, we were not likely to do it now, when so near the end of our journey. I could not help remarking how singularly we had been baulked by contumacious rivers during the two months that had passed since we encountered the Tolla in Mongolia. They were always just in the impassable crisis when we happened to reach them, and last of all the Volga gave us trouble, a river that we never reckoned on crossing at all. A little earlier we should have passed up the river in a steamboat. A little later we should have driven up the Volga on the ice, for that is an almost direct road to Nijni-Novgorod. But of course we hit the wrong time, just betwixt and between. The river must however be crossed if we would proceed.

An offer of twenty roubles being made for the sledge, we sold it to the post-master. It was he who persuaded us that we could not take it further, and of course we thought ourselves "done" in consequence. We got our traps stowed in two post-chaises and drove towards the ferry on the Volga. In leaving the main town of Kazan we crossed over a causeway, or embanked road, through a marsh which connects the town with a kind of suburb. The view of Kazan from the other side of the swamp is very fine. It is built on high ground, and its spires and domes show to great advantage from a distance. In the summer season, when tree leaves and green grass are out, the environs of Kazan must be very pleasing to the eye; for even in November, when the country was one great snowy waste, bleak and cheerless, the town looked really handsome. The best houses, as well as public buildings, are built of brick, indeed a wooden house is rather the exception there. Having crossed a flat tract of country, we reached the Volga at a point about five miles from Kazan, and as many above its confluence with the Kama. It is truly a noble river, and the high banks enable one to get a sort of bird's-eye view of the broad sheet of water. I should rather say a compound of water, ice, and snow, for the surface of the river was covered with large blocks of ice, loaded with snow, moving rapidly down the stream, with a few open spots of clear water here and there. There was great commotion at the ferry among moujiks, Cossacks, and Tartars. Several boats were busy conveying passengers across, but they made slow work of it. The men refused to start from either side until they saw, or thought they saw, sufficient space clear to hold out some hope of their being able to effect the passage.

They would wait an hour or more for a favourable opportunity to start, and even then they were just as likely to be carried down by the driving ice as to fetch the opposite landing. One boat was jammed in mid-channel and borne down in a perfectly unmanageable condition for two or three miles, until the moving icebergs voluntarily released her, when she was got to land at a place where it was impossible to get horses or sledges near, owing to the precipitous nature of the bank. The model of these boats is beautifully adapted to this kind of iceberg navigation. Their sides are cut away, so that a straight line is drawn from the gunwale to the keel. A section of the boat is represented by the letter V, but the angle formed by the two sides is much greater than that in the usual form of that letter, so that the boats are very flat. They may be nipped between two fields and no damage be done, as there is nothing for the ice to get hold of. Did the boats present a perpendicular side to the edge of it, they could not escape destruction. We unfortunately had ample time to make observations on the navigation of the Volga and other matters that came under our notice, for we were compelled to kick our heels about the whole day, without finding a boat disengaged. Long before dark the men stopped work for the day, to make sure they would not be caught in the dusk of the evening essaying a passage which demanded all their wits in broad daylight. The first hour or two passed pleasantly enough while we entertained ourselves watching the process of a river freezing. A margin of thick ice had already formed along the bank, strong enough to arrest the progress of the "pack" in its downward course, when borne against the projecting points. The floating ice-fields crashed with great impetuosity on the fixed ice, were shattered by the shock, and, urged by the force of the current, the fragments were piled up one above another in huge chaotic masses. When left still for a short time the pile congealed, and in a few hours was ready to serve as a barrier to stop more of the pack and annex it to the mass. During that one day the solid ice was extended six or eight feet, and with continued frost a very few days would suffice to freeze over the whole river.

The military were in great force on the banks of the Volga, and carried everything their own way, regardless of the interests of the general public, as represented by the few civilians who presented themselves as candidates for the middle passage. We had seen some of the soldiery before this time, but they were so-called " Cossacks " of the old type. Those we encountered at Kazan, and on the Volga, were smartly set off with French military caps, and had really a soldier-like bearing. The traditional grey over-coat was universal, but there was enough of innovation in their get-up to mark the recent improvement that has taken place in the Russian soldier. I shall probably allude in the sequel to the army reforms introduced into Russia during the present reign.

A good many Tartars were sprinkled among the crowd that infested the landing-place at the Volga ferry. They usually wear a round fur cap, somewhat different from that worn by the Russian moujik. Their physiognomy is widely removed from the Sclavonic type. They have the flat features of the Mongol races, but are not to be confounded with any of them.

The ferry-boats were engaged the whole day in conveying Polish exiles across the river, bound for Siberia. It is a sad sight to see so many people in captivity, and still more so to see a number of women accompanying the exiles. It is quite common for the wives, daughters, and mothers of the political convicts to follow their relatives into Siberia. This is not discouraged by the Russian government; on the contrary, every facility is granted to enable the families to emigrate, and they have always the means of travelling in company. The object of the government is to colonise Siberia, so that the more people go there the better. Besides, the residence of families in exile offers some guarantee against any attempt at a return to their native country. Two old ladies I particularly noticed coming out of a boat, accompanied by two soldiers. They were both well dressed in black silk and warm fur cloaks. One of them was extremely old, and unable to walk. She stooped a great deal, and leaned on a crutch while standing on the ice. The other was also very frail. We pitied these old creatures, exposed as they were day after day in such inclement weather, compelled to undergo the hardships and privations inseparable from all Russian and Siberian travelling. They were treated with great kindness by the soldiers, who lifted them carefully out of the boat, carried them to their sledges, which were in waiting, and put them in as tenderly as if they had been their own mothers. After carefully wrapping them up with their furs, a Cossack got in beside each of the ladies, and they drove off to Kazan. A girl who was with them was equally well attended to by the officer in command of the party, who seemed to consider the Polish maiden to be his especial charge.

Much has been said and written on this Polish question, and an unusual number of distorted and exaggerated statements have gained currency in Europe on the subject. It is certain that neither the oppressors nor the oppressed are to be implicitly trusted as regards their veracity, and it is not easy, in consequence, to sift out the bare unvarnished truth. But, leaving out of sight for a moment the actual merits of the question, as between the Russian government and the rebellious Poles, the fate of the exiles is by no means such a hard one as is too commonly supposed. I have taken pains to inquire into this, and the more I have heard about it from persons well able to judge, the more have I been convinced that the Poles in Siberia are very much better off than the average of those in Poland. The Russians to a man condemn them, and justify their government in the measures that have been adopted to put down the insurrection. But their feelings of loyalty to the Emperor may possibly warp their judgment. The foreign residents who have no such influence to sway their opinions, may be considered impartial in the matter; and they, on the whole, indorse the Russian views as regards the Poles. Those English residents in Siberia with whom I have conversed, assert that the Polish exiles enjoy a degree of peace, comfort, and prosperity, that they were altogether strangers to in their own country. Wealth, talent, industry, and education have the most ample scope in Siberia, and are set free from those distractions which sap healthy enterprise in a country torn with civil wars. I have already given some hints of the position occupied by Russian political exiles in Siberia, and I need not dwell on the subject now, further than to say that the Poles are treated with still greater leniency and consideration.

That the exiles are, on the whole, dissatisfied, there can be no doubt. But the more sensible of them admit that their worldly circumstances are improved by going to Siberia. Many of them are pleased at the change, and would not willingly return home if it were open to them to do so. So long as they remain in Poland, they say, they are at the mercy of every band of malcontents, who have nothing of their own to lose. In revolutionary times they are constrained, in spite of themselves, to take part in the proceedings, and to sacrifice their time, property, and everything else to schemes of which they may strongly disapprove. They never feel secure from the consequences of the folly of their hot-headed countrymen. They have no heart to work, when they are liable, at any moment, to be involved in ruin by the rashness of some insurrectionary party. But Siberia offers an escape from all this strife and endless conspiracy, and some of them hail with delight the sentence that exiles them to a more congenial soil. No one, indeed, who has observed, in an impartial manner, the conditions of life in Siberia and Russia respectively, will be disposed to doubt that the former is really the more attractive residence, and although it is remarkable, it is not incredible, that many Poles should deliberately prefer it to their own country.

As a precautionary measure, the Russian government has always studied to scatter the exiles over Siberia, to prevent any large communities of them from congregating in one place. The governor-general of Western Siberia has the power of distributing them as he may see fit. All the exiles are taken to Tobolsk as a rendezvous, and are there told off to the various districts they are destined to reside in. In their final distribution there is great room for favouritism, as well as for the gratification of malevolence on the part of the governor; some of the exiles may be sent to the large towns, and others to wild, uninhabited regions, and inhospitable climates. Oppression and cruelty have doubtless been in former days practised on them, and may possibly still, to some extent, exist. But, in the main, they are treated kindly, both while travelling, and in their appointed residences. Whatever sentence may have been awarded (speaking of criminals), it is invariably mitigated in practice. The stigma of exile is no bar to their well-doing in Siberia. Everything combines to make their lives pleasant, except that one element of bitterness, the ever-present consciousness that they are under the ban of the law, and doomed never to return to their own unhappy country. That one consideration is, no doubt, powerful enough, in ardent and sensitive minds, to neutralise all the elements of happiness that their banishment affords; but time mellows it down to a vague, latent feeling of oppression, and sympathy with those of their countrymen who may still be engaged in the hopeless struggle for independence. Those of the exiles who have sense enough to accept their lot in a philosophical spirit, and do not weary their lives out in chafing under their fate, have comparatively little cause for dissatisfaction. The object of the Russian government is not so much to punish the insurgents, as to colonise Siberia with people of education and intelligence. Attempts to escape are punished with the utmost severity; but these attempts are rare.

Mrs. Atkinson relates a story of a Pole who was caught in a desperate effort to return to Europe, and sent to the mines. The same is still the stock-story served up for the entertainment of travellers, the ten years or more that have elapsed not having apparently supplied another instance.

There cannot be much difference of opinion on the question of the spoliation of Poland by the three great powers. Although the vices inherent in the Polish constitution rendered the subjugation of the country by its powerful neighbours almost inevitable, nothing can justify the unscrupulous proceedings of Russia and her two satellites in seizing it. But in the immediate causes that prompted the recent insurrection, and the measures adopted by the Russian government to quell it, the Poles have perhaps received more sympathy, and the Russians more odium, than they deserved. It is certain that the Emperor was liberally disposed towards the Poles; but they aspired, not to greater liberty, but to absolute independence of Russia. As was well shown by the correspondent of the "Times," no reform, however radical, would conciliate them while they were connected with Russia, and the easy rule of Alexander II. was the very thing that enabled the Poles to rebel, which, under the iron hand of Nicholas, was impossible.

It is, doubtless, a legitimate grievance that a highly cultured people, as the Poles are, should be governed by semi-barbarous Russians; but, on the other hand, the superior intelligence of the Poles found its full value in Russia. They were rapidly gaining posts of trust and emolument in the imperial service, and I have heard it said, by a person eminently qualified to judge, that if they had but postponed their insurrection for ten years, they would then have had no cause to rebel, because by that time they would have virtually governed Russia as much as Russia governs Poland. If the Poles had possessed the practical philosophy of the Chinese, they might have overcome their conquerors by a process somewhat analogous to that by which the latter people have successively out-civilised the various Tartar powers, and overrun their territories. But they cast to the winds their opportunities, and committed their destiny to the hazard of a desperate venture, in which success was, humanly speaking, impossible. The only result, indeed, that could reasonably have been expected from this fatal enterprise was that the old relations between the two countries should be replaced on the footing of a rigorous despotism on the one hand, and absolute subjection on the other.

Without attempting to extenuate the severities, often arbitrary, and cruelly unjust, that have been practised on the Poles by the Russian officials in the later stages of the insurrection, due allowance should be made for the exaggerations inseparable from one-sided accounts, especially in times of great excitement. And it is reasonable that their fair share of responsibility for the blood that has been needlessly shed, should be borne by the leaders of the movement, who with suicidal rashness plunged their country into a war, which a little calm reflection might have shown them was hopeless from the beginning.

It is well also to note that, since the rebellion has been finally put down, the Russian government has evinced no vindictive feeling towards the subjugated Poles; but, on the contrary, has set itself to improve their condition by the establishment of many liberal measures, social and educational, the progress of which was interrupted by the outbreak of the insurrection.

But supposing even that the insurrection had been successful, what substantial advantage would have accrued to Poland? A return to the conditions existing before the partition, the hostile factions and the confederations more tyrannical even than Russia, would not have been a great improvement. And Poland would then have been a small, weak, and poor kingdom, surrounded by three powerful enemies, who would never want a *casus belli*. How long would the kingdom have been likely to maintain its existence under such conditions?

CHAPTER XXII.

KAZAN TO PETERSBURG.

WHEN, far on in the afternoon, we saw no prospect of effecting a crossing of the Volga that day, we were glad to pack our traps into the first sledge that offered, and make our way back to Kazan. We were not the only disappointed ones, but the other westward-bound travellers, having more practical knowledge than ourselves, took the precaution to drive down in a town sledge, without their baggage, to reconnoitre the ferry. With our bulky *impedimenta*, we were in a condition eminently favourable for being victimised by the rapacious rascals who repaired to the spot with horses and sledges, attracted thither by the same instinct that brings the eagles to the carcase. In the first instance, we had been charged the fare for fourteen versts, for a stage that was acknowledged to be only seven—no better reason being alleged for the charge than that it was "necessary." The sledge had been sent back to the post-station, after being discharged of our persons and appurtenances, and at the end of the day we found ourselves at the mercy of a set of wide-mouthed moujiks, with the most exalted ideas of the value of their services.

The hotel "Ryazin," where we took up our quarters, had the reputation of being one of the most fashionable in Kazan, as was made apparent to us by the thick atmosphere of stale tobacco-smoke that pervaded the long narrow corridors, and close pent-up rooms. Deeming ourselves to have

entered a country so far civilised that we could get anything
for money, and feeling greatly in need of consolation under
the defeat we had sustained, we mustered courage to order a
bottle of wine with our dinner. We had carefully eschewed
liquor at the hotels in Siberia, not expecting great things
there, and from a desire to discourage a taste which we
should rarely have the means of gratifying. In old Kazan
we had more confidence, and the classical names and aristo-
cratic prices on the " wine card" of the Ryazin gave promise
of something good. But we were only tantalised—the wine
was not only of no recognisable species, but positively
nauseous. We did get good fresh butter, however, an
article, strange to say, scarce in Siberia, notwithstanding
the abundance of milk. It is worth notice that the Russians
have but one word, *maslo*, to signify butter, cart-grease, and
oil in general. Can it be possible that the confusion of ideas
frequently caused by this circumstance has given rise to the
exaggerated, but generally believed, reports of the foul
feeding of the Russians ?

A diorama was being exhibited in a distant part of the
huge building of the hotel. The pictures were mostly copies
of originals in the Hermitage at St. Petersburg, and their
merits were extolled after the usual fashion by the exhibitor
in French and Russian. The attendance was fair, but the
entertainment very so-so. The only impression I carried away
was that the Russians of Kazan were easily amused.

On the following morning we again proceeded to the
Volga to try our luck. The river had totally changed its
appearance during the night. The thick masses of conglo-
merated ice and snow had disappeared. The open water had
shifted from the right to the left bank, and the middle of
the river was covered with a thin sheet of new ice, floating
downwards. A boat was soon loaded by ourselves and a few
other passengers, and half-a-dozen lusty moujiks tracked us

slowly up the stream by means of a rope. Sometimes a towing path on the high bank was used, and sometimes a path was extemporised on the margin of solid ice, which in places was piled up in high sharp peaks that entangled the towing-rope. The master of the boat urged on his team, familiarly addressing them as "dogs," which I am bound in charity to consider as a term of endearment, when applied to Russian moujiks. When we had gained a position whence we could cross the river easily, the crew was brought on board, and the boat launched into mid-stream. The thin ice was easily broken up by poles and boat-hooks, and no great difficulty was experienced in effecting this passage. The Russian ferrymen have a very inconvenient habit of stopping to cross themselves, and mutter invocations to the saints while in the most critical situation. They do this sometimes at starting, but invariably when in the middle of the river. I frequently felt that we were put in peril by this ultra-superstitious practice, for often at the moment when the greatest care is needed to pilot the boat through treacherous ice-fields, the whole crew lay down their oars, take off their hats, and perform the ceremony. The Chinese sailors beat gongs and burn joss paper to ensure good luck on their voyage, but they are too sensible to endanger themselves by such superstitious observances, and on the whole, show less confidence in supernatural aid than in the appliances within their own control. "Prayer and provender never hinder a journey," is an excellent maxim within reasonable limits, but the practice of Russian ferrymen shows how the best of rules may be abused.

A number of small steamers were frozen in on the right bank of the Volga, as also a fleet of hulks elegantly fitted up with rooms on deck. These were the floating steam-boat and other offices, government offices, &c. In the season, when the navigation is open, and passenger steamers, tugs, and barges are plying to and fro, this part of the Volga must be a busy scene.

A sledge was sent for us at the farther side, and we were once more *en route*. A tap-room, kept by a very low kind of Jew, is conveniently situated near the ferry on the right bank. Here the boatmen indulge themselves freely in liquor out of the proceeds of the harvest they make while the ice is forming. We got slightly warmed with tea in this house, but the publican objected to our drinking our own brandy "on the premises." The law was on his side, and we could say nothing, but the alternative of drinking the poison which he was licensed to sell was too repulsive, even had our need been greater than it was.

At Kazan and the Volga we observed that the Russian *pourboire* changed from *na vodku* ("for brandy") to *na tsai* ("for tea"), the latter being the common expression in Russia proper, and the former the current phrase in Siberia. Tea drinking is considered a matter of superlative importance in Russia. When a cab is hired for the day, the driver will ask for a quarter of an hour "to drink tea," and a little money on account to provide the means of doing so. People repair at stated times to a *trakteer*, or tavern, in Moscow and Petersburg to drink tea. After the opera, parties retire for the same purpose. It does not follow that tea is always the beverage patronised on these occasions. The tea drinking at midnight is more likely to consist of caviar, ryabchick, and champagne.

Our road lay parallel with the general line of the Volga, occasionally approaching near to some of the elbows of the river. The country is flat and marshy, but well cultivated, and farming villages are numerous. The villages and small towns are built on raised ground, whether naturally or artificially raised, I am uncertain. The most remarkable feature in the towns is the extraordinary number of churches. In one very small place I counted eight.

Oaks are abundant in the country between Kazan and Nijni-Novgorod, and the beech trees grow to a good size, and in beautiful form. The forest has been cleared away to make room for agriculture, and the bare flat is only relieved by the clumps of gnarled oak and the fine avenues of birch, which are planted in double rows on each side of the post-road. In winter, they looked handsome in their nakedness, and in the summer heats they will afford a grateful shade to travellers on the road for some hundreds of miles.

The roads were bad; but habit had inured us to that. The postal arrangements were, however, worse than anything we had experienced. The reason was obvious. This part of the road being only used for a few weeks, between the closing of the Volga navigation and the complete freezing of the river, no provision is made for the comfort of travellers in the way of covered conveyances. Having parted with our own sledge, we travelled *peracladnoi*, that is, changing at every station. No covered sledges could be procured for love or money, but so long as we could use sledges, the discomfort was not intolerable, although the snow became gradually scantier as we advanced westward. On the 28th, however, the little snow that remained melted, and some rain and sleet fell. Sledge-travelling was discontinued, and we had to resort to the *telega*, simply an open cart without any springs. For the whole day we did dreadful penance in these lumbering vehicles, over the most atrocious roads that can be imagined. Our progress was, of course, slow in the extreme, and to complete the catalogue of our miseries, a heavy shower of sleet fell, which soaked our furs and wraps to such an extent that we could hardly bear their weight. In this pitiable condition we reached the last station before Nijni at 10 o'clock at night. We had resolved to pass the night there, and get our clothes dried before morning, deeming further exposure to the cold dangerous to our health. The surly brute of a postmaster, whom it was our misfortune to meet, put his veto on our intentions. I shall never forget his face, nor his blue coat and brass buttons. He was one of those slaves, dressed in a little brief authority, whose sole experience had been the iron heel of tyranny planted on his neck, and whose one idea, when not licking the dust himself, was to make others do so if possible. It is a necessary result of a slavish education in some minds, that they cannot conceive of any other relation in life, than that of oppressor and oppressed. For the honour of Russian postmasters in general, I am glad to say that such specimens as the jack-in-office at Kstavo are rare. He refused us a fire, or a room, or any means of making ourselves decently comfortable, so after shivering for an hour we determined to resume our journey to Nijni. A hard frost had set in, accompanied by a keen wind that cut us to the bone. The misery we suffered during the last stage of our journey, was beyond all description. Never was I more grateful than when we gained admission to the hotel "Russia" at Nijni-Novgorod, at four o'clock next morning. Under the genial influence of a warm room and a dry bed, our miseries were soon forgotten, and the horrible experiences of the night dissolved into a dream that helped to intensify present enjoyment. "Sweet is pleasure after pain." There is no rest without labour, and happiness itself would be insipid without a seasoning of misery. Life, to be really enjoyed, must be chequered with light and shadow. The bright passages remain vivid in the memory, while the darker shades fade into forgetfulness.

The time to see Nijni-Novgorod is during the great fair which is held in July, and which attracts to the spot people of every race and language. The Nijni fair is one of the great commercial events in Russia. Goods are brought to it from vast distances, and as much business is done there in a few days as in many months in the larger cities. There are several other great fairs still held in Russia, such as the one at Irbit, in the west of Siberia. They are relics of an unsettled state of society, and will no doubt gradually give way before modern civilisation. The enormous cost of transport necessarily incurred in bringing merchandise to the fair, and in carrying it away again to its destination, does not equal the guild dues, and other charges, which the traders would have to bear, in order to do the same business in Moscow or Petersburg. The consuming population are, therefore, taxed out of all reason, with no advantage to the merchants, or to the government revenue. One merchant may, for example, take his wares from Moscow or Kiev to the fair at Nijni, and sell them to another, who carries them back to the point whence they were originally despatched, and the double expense of carriage may still be less than the cost of transacting the same business in the towns.* It cannot be that such a state of affairs can long withstand the inevitable march of enlightenment.

We of course saw Nijni-Novgorod at a disadvantage. The town was comparatively empty; the steam traffic which keeps the neighbourhood alive during the summer was all over for the season, and the rivers Volga and Oka looked deserted. The snow was melting fast, and the streets were a mass of slush. This, with a leaden sky and drizzling rain, rendered the town as miserable as can be imagined. The Oka joins the Volga at Nijni, and the town is situated on a high peninsula between the two rivers. The suburb in which the great fair is held is opposite the town, on the other side of the Oka, and there also is the terminus of the railway. At the time we passed, there was but one train a day to Moscow. It started at about four o'clock in the afternoon, and was calculated to arrive at Moscow—three hundred miles— about six or seven next morning.

* "Russ. Shores of the Black Sea."—L. Oliphant.

Our journey virtually terminated with our joining the railway, for though still some 2500 miles from London, we had no more hardships to look forward to, no toilsome days, or sleepless nights, no hard fare, and no struggles with the elements. It was hard to realise the superlative comfort of a railway carriage in our shaken and shattered condition. It seemed too good to be true. The varied incidents of our four months of travel crowded on the memory, and we soon dropped into a delicious sleep amid confused visions of drunken yemschiks, broken wheels, diabolical roads, icebergs, and ferry-boats, with deserts and strings of camels dimly shadowed in the back ground. In the grey of the morning, we found ourselves in Moscow the Holy, and were soon comfortably settled in M. Billet's hotel. Our progress towards civilised comfort culminated here, and the luxury of bed and board at M. Billet's seemed a full compensation for the miseries of the road.

To do justice to the delights of Moscow would require a higher inspiration than I am blessed with, and all I could say about the Kremlin, its palaces and churches, the theatres, operas, &c., has been much better said already. The few days spent there seemed very short. Should I ever be tempted to revisit the fine old city, however, I hope the municipal council will have made some arrangement for lighting the streets with gas. In this respect they are sadly behind the age; and in a gay population like that of Moscow, which lives mostly at night, it is surprising that illumination has not before now been demanded by the popular voice. The portable gas which is carted about the streets in hogsheads, is a wretched makeshift. The sudden exhaustion of the supply of light frequently causes a theatrical performance to be interrupted until another hogshead of gas is procured; and during the interregnum young Russia delights in electrifying the audience by yelling and whistling, as if they would bring the house down.

A large building on the outskirts of Moscow was pointed out to us as the foundling hospital, a great institution in Russia, one of whose chief uses seems to be to rear ballet-girls, and most efficiently does it perform its functions.

From Moscow to Petersburg by railway is a monotonous and uninteresting journey, especially in winter. The country is flat and bare; here and there a patch of winter wheat struggled through the thin covering of snow, but the general aspect in the month of December was that of a desert. The only town of note on the line is Tver, on the Volga, where the railway crosses that river. In the construction of the line, the convenience of the various small towns has not been consulted. It was a purely imperial project to connect Moscow with Petersburg. It is said that when the engineers, who were engaged in the construction of the line, applied to the Emperor to know what curves they should make so as to pass through the most populous towns, he laid a ruler on the map, drew a straight line from Petersburg to Moscow, and bade them follow it.

Railways, like all other public works in Russia, have been constructed at enormous expense, from the peculations of the officials who had to do with them. It is related of the Emperor Nicholas, that when he had failed to impress certain Persian ambassadors with the magnificence of his capital, he turned in despair to Prince Menschikoff, and asked him whether there was nothing that would astonish them. The prince suggested that they might be shown the accounts of the Moscow railway.

We were not so favourably impressed with Petersburg, as a place of residence, as we had been with Moscow. It is a magnificent city, no doubt; its quays, bridges, "perspectives," palaces, and squares present a faultless exterior, and leave an impression of grandeur on the memory that makes other things small by comparison. But the chill of officialism rests on the place; it was created out of a swamp by the fiat of an emperor, and the imperial will is all-pervading still; you cannot shake off the idea. Looking down the "Nevsky," you take in at a glance miles of street laid out with mathematical accuracy, and the effect is very striking; you admire the magnificent Nicholas bridge that spans the Neva, a work that made the fortune of others besides the architect; in short, you admire everything separately and collectively about the capital, but the reflection always crops up that this fine city and the glory of it exists by the will of the emperor. Moscow is antiquated; its streets are not so straight, nor so wide, nor so regular; its buildings are not so imposing; but it is a natural and spontaneous growth; there is a more homely and comfortable air about it than Petersburg; and it was not built for the admiration of the world, but because people wanted houses to live in. Petersburg lacks the historical interest that invests the old capital, and it will be long before it displaces the holy city in the affections of the Russians, who one and all have a kind of superstitious reverence for Moscow. The Czars also hold the old city in high esteem, and are said to regard the Kremlin as the focus and ultimate asylum of their power.

The season was late in Petersburg. Up to the middle of December the little snow that fell melted. The temperature varied from a little above to a little below the freezing point. Some days the Neva brought down masses of floating ice from Lake Ladoga, and on other days the river was quite clear. I fear the pork-butchers of the interior were premature in sending in their supplies of frozen pigs, for they seemed very likely to get thawed in the mild atmosphere of Petersburg. The sky was constantly overcast, and the few hours of daylight were consequently cut short at both ends. Everything conspired to throw a gloom over the place, and the people were longing for their snow roads and their sledges, their races and games on the Neva, and the pleasures of their winter season. The "Court" was at Tsarskoe-selo, writing despatches, while the Polish insurrection, the proposed congress of Paris, and the financial difficulties of the government, supplied food for gossip to all circles in the city. The reply of the Emperor to the invitation of his "good brother," as published in the *Journal*, excited universal admiration. And as for the currency crisis, everyone had some nostrum of his own which would infallibly put things right, but none of them seemed to touch the essential point, the supply of bullion.

Great activity prevailed in the government dockyards, where a number of iron-clads were being built. One of these building yards was close to Miss Benson's, where I lived, and we got the full benefit of the clanging of hammers, from a very early hour in the morning, till the latest hour at night at which we happened to be awake. I believe they worked day and night, as if busily preparing for war. Some vessels had been hurried out of England unfinished, and enormous quantities of iron-plating, and other materials, had been imported from England for vessels to be constructed in Russia. The yards we were shown through were all under the superintendence of English firms, and Englishmen occupy responsible positions in the admiralty. The number of iron-cased frigates in progress at Petersburg and Kronstadt, is sufficient to account for the abstraction of bullion from the government treasury in such amounts as to derange the paper currency of the country.

But the financial disturbance is of some years' standing, although it has gradually been getting worse. It dates from the Crimean war, which drained the resources of Russia, both in men and treasure, to an extent which the government has been reluctant to admit. The difficulty was met at the time by the increased issue of paper-money,

A A

which government has never been able to redeem. The crisis was not much felt until the Polish insurrection again taxed the energies of the government, while it was still languishing under the effects of the Crimean war, and unprepared for this fresh demand on its resources. This was probably the real reason why the government was so slow to meet the emergency in Poland with adequate means. More paper-money had to be issued, unrepresented by bullion, and unconvertible. The paper currency became depreciated twelve to fifteen per cent. below its ostensible value, and in the uncertainty that prevailed as to the future, business was for a time brought almost to a stand. All the financiers of Russia have been labouring to restore the equilibrium, but as yet their best laid schemes have failed, for none of them has discovered the means of replenishing the bank treasury.

The most casual observer cannot fail to mark the respect in which all classes in Russia hold the Emperor. In the most distant provinces, indeed, the peasants regard the Czar as a kind of demi-god who, if he could only be informed of their grievances, would set all to rights. But in Petersburg, where his majesty may be seen any day in the street, divested of ethereal attributes, the people love him. The contrast between the reign of the present emperor and that of his father is very striking. Formerly the interests of agriculture, manufactures, and commerce were sacrificed to the ambitious schemes of the Czar. The military glory of the empire, and the imperial projects of aggrandisement absorbed the energies of government; and to promote these ends the substance of the country was wasted. That is all changed now. The Emperor Alexander II. from the time of his accession has devoted his energies to the amelioration of the condition of the people, to the encouragement of native industry, to the economising of the national resources, and to promoting the efficiency of the executive. Reforms have been set on foot in all departments of the state,—military, legislative, financial, and social. Success has attended many of these new measures; many are still in progress; but the great work is only begun. It is an important step gained, however, that the government has become alive to the need of administrative reform, and if the life of the present monarch be spared to the age of his father, he will have left his country a century in advance of where he found it.

The Russian soldier is now smart and well equipped, well armed, well fed, and well treated. Military discipline has been greatly improved, and the men have now to go through regular courses of gymnastics. The army is undergoing a transformation. Recruiting is more regular. The term of service has been reduced to fifteen years, but practically it is much less. The soldiers begin to look like civilised beings, and to acquire self-respect.

Important reforms in the legislature of Russia have also been introduced. The term of penal servitude has been greatly reduced. A project of law-reform which will include trial by jury is under deliberation. This, if carried, will be a startling innovation in Russia; and will no doubt be the precursor of many other popular measures.

A budget is now published yearly, which, though it is not of much practical utility, is nevertheless in some sort a recognition of the political rights of the people.

The police, customs, and the navy are all being subjected to improvements more or less important; in short, the spirit of reform has been so active, that its influence pervades every institution, except perhaps the Church. Some evils have necessarily attended the recent changes. For example, the abolition of the brandy farm, and the substitution of a system of excise, by reducing the cost, has increased the consumption of spirits among the peasantry. The fatal consequences of excess threatened to be alarming in some parts of the country, and I heard great complaints in Siberia of the increase of drunkenness. But as a financial measure it has been very successful. The excise duty on spirits in 1863 gave the government 117,000,000 silver (*i.e.*, paper) roubles, which is more than one-third of its gross annual revenue.

The revenues of the Russian government are still susceptible of great development. The system of corruption that prevailed so long that it had become almost respectable, has been attacked, but it must be rooted up before the government can reap the full harvest of its own financial resources. This is not a matter of easy accomplishment, however, as the men from whom the Emperor is entitled to look for support are themselves directly interested in the continuance of the old system of universal peculation. The vast extent of territory also over which the government executive is diffused, adds greatly to the difficulty of the radical reform of time-honoured abuses.

No annoyance of any kind, either about passports or luggage was experienced by us in arriving at, or departing from Petersburg; but the pleasantest impression the Czarish capital left on my mind was that of the kindness and hospitality of my own countrymen, and of all others whom I happened to meet there.

CHAPTER XXIII.

RUSSIA AND CHINA.

ONE cannot travel for four months through the two largest empires in the world, without reflecting on the analogies and contrasts which they mutually present, and trying to figure out the causes which have been working such different results in each, since they first became acquainted with one another. Analogies in the manners, customs, and modes of thought of the two races are constantly turning up; and their resemblance to the Chinese has become a proverb among the Russians themselves.

Both empires were subjugated in the thirteenth century by the Mongol-Tartar hordes under the descendants of Genghis; and both succeeded in expelling the invaders from their respective territories.

From that time the histories of Russia and China have been closely interwoven; their frontiers have been gradually approaching each other, as Russia extended her conquests eastward, and China westward; and for the last two hundred years the advancing wave of Russian aggression has impinged on the whole northern line of the outlying deserts and wildernesses which own the sway of China.

The triumphal advance of the Russians over the aboriginal tribes of Siberia was checked when it came in contact with the superior civilisation and higher military organisation of the Chinese; and, after a five years' war, China was in a position to impose conditions on Russia, which was done by the treaty of Nerchinsk, 1689. But the Russian schemes have never been abandoned. With the patience of the Asiatic, combined with the determination of the European, Russia has contested the frontiers of China with slow and fluctuating, but ultimately certain, success. Sometimes by force of arms, sometimes by diplomatic craft, by every device that cunning could suggest, Russia has made good her progress in Chinese territory from point to point, until the last grand *coup* of General Ignatieff in 1860 crowned all her endeavours with success. By making dexterous use of the victory of the Anglo-French troops at Peking, he, with a stroke of the pen, transferred to Russia the whole coast of Manchu-Tartary, from the mouth of the Amur river to the frontier of Corea.

When China first encountered Russia in the debates about the frontier, every advantage was on the side of the former. China was in the position of a powerful, wealthy, populous, and civilised nation, dealing with barbarians. If men were wanted, the warlike Manchus were ready at call. If money was wanted, the resources of China, with her vast producing population, were immeasurably superior to those of Russia, and perhaps to any country in the world at that time. The Chinese were acting on the defensive, and near home. The government was vigorous and intelligent, and naturally confident of its own superiority. The Russian people were, on the other hand, ignorant, servile, and degraded. Their government was not much better; and their military resources could only be drawn from vast, thinly peopled, unproductive steppes.

Peter the Great infused new life into Russia by the energy of his own character, and the judicious encouragement of foreigners, by which means he tried to graft civilisation on his unpromising stock. Amid his varied cares he did not forget his supposed interests in the far east; but both he and his successors found China too hard a nut to crack. The Manchu emperors had consolidated their power in China, and from the days of Kanghi, who drove the Russians from the districts they had occupied on the Amoor in 1688, till the early part of the present century, China was strong and prosperous. The Czars could do no more than send embassies, chiefly charged with mercantile questions, to the "Khan of Khans," at Peking.

The Russian ambassadors were treated as suppliants at Peking; their reception was such as was accorded to the missions from subject states—in Chinese phrase, "tribute bearers."

But Russia was all the while making rapid strides in her own internal progress; foreign inventions, and foreign enterprise, were largely subsidised, and Russia became a great military power.

The passion for aggrandisement was strongly developed in Peter, in Catherine II., and in Nicholas; but still Russia could only knock at the gates of China by means of peaceful missions, and China could still afford to be supercilious. But while Russia progressed, China at the best was stationary; and, since the first English war in 1839—41, the germ of decay which the effeminate luxury of the Chinese court had implanted into the Manchu dynasty, born in a hardier climate, has rapidly spread over the whole complex machine of Chinese government.

The degenerate Manchu emperors, forgetting the wisdom of their fathers, abandoned themselves to flatterers, discontinued the manly sports to which their predecessors attached so much importance, neglected the affairs of government, and wallowed in sensuality.

The last emperor, Hienfung, died almost in the prime of life of the grossest debauchery. A wide-spread corruption was the natural result of the demoralisation of the court, and injustice and oppression pressed heavily on the people. Brigandage on a gigantic scale appeared, and soon wasted the fairest provinces of China, running riot for ten years almost unchecked by the imbeciles who ruled at the capital and in the provinces. The whole fabric was ready to fall to pieces, and only waited for some determined will to take the reins out of the hands that were no longer able to hold them.

Up to the last, however, the self-blinded rulers of China refused to believe in their vulnerability, until the fatal delusion was rudely dissipated by the capture of Peking itself by the Anglo-French forces in 1860.

The empire lay prostrate at the feet of her conquerors, whose moderation in the hour of victory was the marvel of the vanquished. But China's extremity was Russia's opportunity; and the subtlety of Russian diplomacy was never exhibited to greater advantage than on this occasion.

The Russian minister had affected warm friendship to the Chinese government in its troubles, and volunteered indirect assistance to it in the impending struggle with the foreigner. But the moment he saw the Chinese government at its wits' end, he swooped down on it with unscrupulous demands, which included the cession to Russia of the whole sea-coast of Manchuria, and the large tract of country from the Usuri and Amoor rivers to the Sea of Japan. The Chinese were in no condition to demur, and to aid them in coming to a conclusion, they were gently told that in the event of non-compliance, the vengeance of the Czar would be more terrible than the chastisement they were then smarting from. The treaty was made, and Russia triumphed.

The substantial loss to China of the Manchurian forests was inconsiderable; but the importance of the gain to Russia can hardly be over-rated. Up to that time, Russia had possessed no harbours on the Pacific that were not closed by ice for half the year. This new accession of maritime territory gives to Russia many excellent harbours, particularly towards its southern extremity, which are open several months longer than the harbour of Nikolaefsk at the mouth of the Amoor. The new harbours in Manchuria are moreover of easier access, not only shortening the voyage from Europe or China by some 600 or 700 miles, but affording great advantages over Nikolaefsk in the simplicity of navigation.

The present helpless condition of China is in a great measure owing to the contempt of military affairs which a long peace had engendered. The Chinese people are eminently averse to fighting, and consequently to all military matters. They have a proverb which illustrates this:

> " Haou tih pu ta ting ;
> Haou jin pu tso ping."
> Of good iron you don't make a nail ;
> Of a good man you don't make a soldier.

They are too intent on industrial pursuits to waste men, time, or money in feeding armies. Hence they are at the mercy not only of foreign armed powers, but of any band of native ruffians who may organise a pillaging expedition. An enlightened and energetic government, alive to the progress of other nations, would have seen that an efficient standing army was not only compatible with the prosperity of the country, but absolutely essential to its existence ; and would have made a military nation of the Chinese in spite of their more peaceful proclivities.

But the government of China has for half a century been the reverse of this. Blind and deluded, it has wrapped itself up in false security, trusting to ancient prestige and adroitness in negotiation to keep the wolf from the door, and has let the military element slip through its fingers. The paper wall collapsed at the first touch of the hostile foreigner. The government lost the respect of its own people, and became more than ever a by-word among the nations.

The ascendancy of Russia, on the other hand, is due directly to her military organisation. Her frequent struggles in Europe compelled her to look well to her armies; and the ambition of universal dominion, deeply rooted in the Russian autocrats from Peter downwards, and probably even long before Peter's time, was a powerful stimulant to military enterprise. The constant wars of aggression in Asia gave employment to large armies, wasted them, and called for continual drafts of new troops. Everything combined to make Russia a great military nation. The absolute despotism of the Czars, allied to projects of vast ambition, was eminently favourable to such a result. This very despotism and lust of conquest probably grew up under the all-pervading influence of the Mongols. Genghis bequeathed to his successors the sovereignty of the world, just as Peter the Great did five centuries later. The Mongol khans taught the Russian princes how to oppress the people. The extortion which these vassals practised under the sanction of the dreaded Mongol name, inured the rulers to tyranny, and the people to submission. When the invaders were expelled, therefore, it was natural that the arbitrary habits of the Russian princes should be retained. It was also a natural reaction of ideas for the Russians, when their time came, to turn the tables on their late conquerors. They had seen Tartar hordes, moved by one strong will, overrun Asia, and rule a large portion of Europe. Why should not emancipated Russia issue forth from Europe and subjugate Asia ? But whencesoever the idea of the conquest of Asia had its origin, the history of Russia for the last two centuries shows how persistently it has been followed up through each successive reign, and how remarkably it has ruled the policy of the Czars from Peter to Nicholas.

It was no small advantage to Russia, considered as an Asiatic nation, and not the least barbarous among them, to live on the confines of European civilisation. The Czars have been wise enough to avail themselves of the advanced knowledge, and the energy to apply it, which their European neighbours possessed. They cannot be said to have civilised Russia by this fusion of foreign materials, but they have certainly succeeded in making her a powerful nation. It is not probable that the Russian government could ever have held its head so high in the counsels of Europe without this extraneous aid; and although they might, from their native resources, have overcome the nomad tribes of the Asiatic steppes, they could hardly have been in a position to dictate terms to China.

The Chinese government has had similar opportunities of using foreign science, and mechanical and other inventions, though in a less degree. But it has, till lately, despised and rejected them, and has paid dearly for its mistake.

In one respect the two empires greatly resemble each other, and that is in the general venality of their officials, high and low. The fact is recognised, to a certain extent, by the governments, and being probably considered irremediable, they seem to make the best of it by placing men in responsible positions, with salaries ludicrously inadequate to provide for the ordinary necessities of life. This has proved one potent cause of the decline of China.

In Russia the vigour of the government has risen superior to the evil. Official dishonesty may have done incalculable injury to the prosperity of the country, but the will of the Czars makes its voice heard to the remotest corner of their unwieldy empire. The provincial officers have great latitude for defeating the ends of justice and good government from sordid motives, and, in a general way, the government will not scrutinise their conduct very closely. But nothing is allowed to obstruct the execution of an ukase from Petersburg, and the government is, on the whole, well served. Everything in Russia has been made subservient to the glory of the Czars and the military status of the country, and every consideration is sacrificed to the furtherance of that one object.

It cannot be denied that the warlike and aggressive policy of Russia has been productive of much good. The hidden wealth of desert regions has been to some extent at least developed, and highways of commerce have been opened up through forests peopled with wild animals and their hunters. The plough has been driven over old battle-fields, and populations have been settled where all was desolation before. These, and such like, have been the good results which may be considered as a set-off against the evils of war. How different have been the issues of the infatuated " peace at any price" policy of China, where fertile plains are being daily converted into battle-fields!

These, however, are but some of the external or accidental circumstances which have modified the characters of the two empires, and variously influenced their destinies. The essential causes of the progress of Russia and the decadence of China lie much deeper. Some people would tell us that Russia is in the young, vigorous and growing stage of its national life, just emerging from barbarism, when every step must be towards improvement, because, from their low starting point, deterioration would be impossible; while China, on the contrary, has long since reached maturity, has outlived the natural term of national existence; its industries, arts, learning, social life, and all that constitutes civilisation, have reached a point beyond which they cannot advance; that the zenith of its glory has been passed; and that, in the natural course of things, the only advance it can now make must be towards decay and dissolution.

But that theory of the decline of China does not hold good. The mass of the people have not degenerated; they are as fresh and vigorous as ever they were. It is the government only that has become old and feeble; and a change of dynasty may yet restore to China the lustre which legitimately belongs to so great a nation.

The indestructible vitality of Chinese institutions has preserved the country unchanged through many revolutions. The high civilisation of the people, and their earnestness in the pursuit of peaceful industries, have enabled them to maintain their national existence through more dynastic changes than, perhaps, any other country or nation has experienced.

"La nation (chinoise)," says De Guignes, "s'est trouvée renfermée dans des bornes naturelles et fortifiée, jusqu'à un certain point, contre les étrangers. D'ailleurs ces étrangers ont toujours été barbares; ainsi lorsque quelquefois ils ont été assez puissants pour pénétrer dans la Chine et pour s'emparer de cet empire, l'attachement inviolable des Chinois à leurs anciens usages a forcé les vainqueurs d'adopter les lois des vaincus. L'empire a changé de maîtres sans changer de lois. Lorsqu'un jour les Tartares, qui le possèdent à présent, seront chassés par une famille chinoise, il n'y aura que le nom de Tartare d'aboli; le gouvernement sera toujours le même, et la nation se retrouvera dans l'état où elle était il y a deux mille ans."*

The barbarian invaders had nothing to substitute for the institutions of the Chinese, and they made no permanent impression on the nation. So far from being able to grind down the people, the result of their successive conquests has been rather to open up new fields of enterprise to the industrious Chinese, who have gradually appropriated to themselves the

Hist. des Huns, tom. iii. p. 93.

territories of their conquerors. Thus the Manchu Tartars have been edged back into the forests by the energetic Chinese colonists, have lost their influence, become absorbed in many parts of their country, and are now almost extinct as a nation.

The unprecedentedly long existence of the Chinese nation, of their language and literature, their laws and their philosophy, has naturally produced in the people a high veneration for antiquity. Their geographical position isolated them from all the rest of the world, excepting the rude nomads of Tartary. So, for many ages, they saw no people equal to themselves in education and intelligence, and no laws like their own. They were constrained to despise the barbarism, even while they feared the power, of their neighbours or their enemies. Their intercourse with the Romans was not sufficiently close to give them much idea of the culture of that people, and they judged of mankind at large by their experience of the Tartars. It was therefore in the nature of things that an overweening self-satisfaction should spring up among them, which would ripen into arrogance. They came to think themselves *the* nation, the "middle kingdom," the centre of the world, and to look upon all foreign races as " outer barbarians." Whatever *we* may think of this national conceit now, there can be no question that, up to a recent period, the Chinese were justified in their high opinion of themselves, and their contempt for all other races, languages and laws.

It is necessary to keep this in view, in order rightly to appreciate the character of the Chinese. They are very generally supposed to be so proud and bigoted that they cling with blind affection to the traditions of the past, insensible to excellence of any kind that is new, or of extraneous origin. But this notion of their character is wide of the truth. As their own greatness comes from ancient times, and they have passed the culminating point of their civilisation, so their reason dictates to them reverence for the past, just as their experience has taught them to despise everything external.

The intercourse between the Chinese and the civilised nations of Europe has, in the first instance, brought out the weak side of the Chinese character into prominent relief, and held it up to the derision of the world; but as that intercourse has become more intimate and thorough, it has afforded a rational explanation of some apparently anomalous traits of character, and has produced among those of the Chinese who have come within its influence, modifications in their views of relative superiority. Ideas that have grown with the growth of a people, through many ages, are not likely to be eradicated in a day; but, if founded on reason, they will yield to reason, when it has shown them to be erroneous; and the adoption of new ideas is likely to be permanent in proportion to the slow and gradual nature of the transition.

The Chinese first encountered modern Europeans in small numbers, and in the outposts of their empire. They naturally applied to these visitors the rules whereby they had from time immemorial been taught to manage strangers or barbarians. The Western adventurers who repaired to the shores of China were actuated by purely utilitarian motives; and to promote their own objects they were not above pandering to the arrogance of the Chinese. Had their policy been different, indeed, they had but slight opportunities of exhibiting their superiority in culture and civilisation; and their numbers were too insignificant to have made any marked impression. The result of the earlier intercourse between Europeans and Chinese was, therefore, rather to confirm than destroy the self-esteem of the latter, who continued to regard the new tribe as belonging to the category of barbarians. The East India Company did its share in perpetuating the Chinese conceit, by submitting to every indignity that was offered to it for the sake of trade. The natural tendency of this course of action, so soon as the controlling power of the company was removed, was to bring on quarrels, the history of which everyone knows. In these wars, which succeeded each other between 1839 and 1860, the superiority of European civilisation asserted itself in China ; the government was first compelled to acknowledge the power of the foreigner, and it is now learning something of the moral qualities of nations whom it had affected to regard as beasts.* For the first time in their history, the Chinese came into contact with a people superior to themselves. No precedent could be found to guide them in the great emergency, and hence the aggression of Europeans inevitably entailed disaster on China, which experience alone could have enabled them to avoid. The ascendancy of Europeans in China is now a fact accomplished and irrevocable, accepted by the natives themselves, and therefore destined to work important changes on the condition of the people and their government.

The people have been quick to appreciate the advantages which foreign appliances offered to them in the conduct of their business. For many years their merchants have been employing European vessels in the coasting trade, induced by economy, despatch, and the facilities for insurance thus secured. The extension of sea-board opened to foreign enterprise by Lord Elgin's treaty, and the free navigation of the great river Yangtsze-Kiang, have attracted a large fleet of

* Soo-tung-po (a celebrated Chinese classic author), says, "The E and the Teih" (the former term being used to designate foreigners), "are like the brute creation, and cannot be governed by the same rules of government as those of the central nation. If liberal rules of government were applied to them, it would infallibly give rise to rebellious confusion. The ancient kings knew this well, and therefore ruled them without laws (or by misrule). This is therefore the most judicious mode of governing them."—*Amherst's Voyage; Lindsay's Report.*

steamers to the coast and rivers of China. These are chiefly employed, and in many instances owned, by natives. In everything the Chinese have exhibited a remarkable freedom from prejudice. They are much too practical to allow any freak of fancy to influence them in matters in which they have a tangible interest.

The Chinese government also has shown, in the most emphatic manner, the high value it sets on European aid, both in civil and military affairs. The alacrity with which it has adopted the modern engines of war at the dictation of foreigners in whom it had confidence, proves conclusively that the conservative government of China is not so wedded to its own traditions as to reject innovations indiscriminately. It may be slow in coming to a conclusion, and is naturally jealous of any reform which is imperfectly understood. But it only wants convincing evidence of the utility of any measure that may be suggested to ensure its adoption. And on those occasions when the government may appear most reluctant to leave the beaten track, there may be other motives for this besides mere obstinacy. Its prestige is in peril; indeed, may be said to be already to a great extent lost. The wholesale introduction of foreign improvements would place the government at the mercy of its foreign *employés*, and its existence as an active and responsible power would be virtually destroyed. The attempt to amalgamate foreign ideas of progress with ancient precedent and stagnation is at best a hazardous experiment, if any value is to be attached to the preservation of the integrity of the government. Great allowance must therefore be made for the difficult position in which Chinese statesmen find themselves. Reforms they know to be necessary; but their duty is so to temper them that they may be adopted with the least possible shock to indigenous institutions. And, even if they foresee the ultimate collapse of these institutions, still their prudence would load them so to restrain the influx of new ideas, that changes might not be too sudden or sweeping.

The Chinese nation is at present in a crisis of its history, in which it is peculiarly susceptible of external influences; and as its foreign relations become more and more consolidated, these influences are brought to bear from various quarters and in constantly increasing force. Great Britain having by far the largest stake in the country, and the largest share of the responsibility attaching to the necessary interference in its affairs, the state and prospects of China demand from us a little more attention than is usually bestowed upon them; for the destiny of that great empire, and our own future interests, will be to some extent moulded by our present policy.

The problem that is now being worked out in that country is one of which history affords no clue to the solution. The nation has been convulsed for fourteen years by a great insurrection. That is nothing new to the Chinese; but the conditions are vastly altered. According to precedent, some powerful Tartar or Chinese prince would have appeared to aid the government in quelling the rebellion, and then seat himself on the throne. Or the empire might have been dismembered between two independent dynasties. Some such solution may still be found, though it is not easy to see whence the movement is to come. Were the other European powers out of the way, Russia would be almost in a position to grasp at the sovereignty of China. Had the crisis occurred a hundred years ago, and our interest in the country been as great as it is now, China might have become a second India. But none of these contingencies is now feasible. The integrity of China, and the independence of its government, are sufficiently hedged round by the jealousies of rival powers.

The cause of the insurrection, and the great difficulty in

the way of a settlement of Chinese affairs, and of the re-establishment of order, lie in the utter prostration of the Imperial government. This circumstance, which would have been the strength of the insurrectionary party had they possessed the elements of cohesion or administrative capacity, tends only to prolong the weary struggle. The rebels have forfeited the respect of all classes, except the most profligate, or the most ignorant. Their dynastic ambition has been made a convenient battle-cry to cover their crimes. They have no policy but devastation, and have neither the disposition nor the ability to govern. Even if they succeeded in crushing the existing government, they would still have to be subjugated in their turn by some other power, before tranquillity could be restored to the country.

The Imperial government has been at last awakened to the importance of quelling the rebellion, which for many years was only trifled with. The division of authority in the provinces prevented that combined action which alone could have met the exigencies of the situation. It was considered a great success, if a body of insurgents was merely chased out of one province into another. The efforts of the Imperial government were, and are still, constantly nullified by the private interests of the provincial authorities. That is one of the greatest abuses that their peculiar system of government is liable to. The armies that are levied from time to time to defend the provinces are mere local bands, under the control of the governor or his deputies, over whose acts the Imperial government has little or no check. If left entirely to itself, it is doubtful whether the present government would ever have been able to make head against the rebellion at all. What has been accomplished towards that end has been mainly due to the moral support of foreign powers, and the active services of European military officers. The necessity of centralising the government more and more has been made obvious to the Prince Regent. That is one of the reforms most urgently needed to secure efficiency and economy in the administration. The old system worked well enough in quiet times, and as long as there was no disturbing element. But the extension of foreign influence along the coast, and in the interior of the country, is constantly stirring up questions of Imperial interest, the inevitable result of which is to sink local customs, and to place foreign relations at all the ports on one level. The embassies at Peking have helped to bring all local and provincial questions home to the Imperial government in a more direct manner than ever was done before. The British minister, deeply impressed with the advantages that must result to China from the centralisation of the government, has striven by all legitimate means to promote it. He has only been partially successful, it is true, and in his despatches of June last he betrays disappointment at the result of his efforts. But still a good deal has been done, and every day's experience must teach the government the necessity of strengthening its own authority, and of exercising a more direct and active control over the provincial governors than heretofore.

The attitude of France and England towards the belligerents in China is anomalous. Their principle at first was strict neutrality, but the rapid extension of commercial intercourse has rendered this course impracticable. The Imperial government has been tamed into granting us a treaty advantageous to us, but much more so to China herself. By this treaty several new ports of trade were opened on the coast; access to Peking, and the residence of foreign ministers there, were secured. But above all, the Yang-tsze-Kiang was thrown open to foreign trade and navigation. That noble river had been closed to commerce for about eight years. The rebellion had devastated the country on both sides; the cities on its banks were in ruins, and their populations dispersed or destroyed. From a point five hundred miles from the sea, downwards, to Chin-Kiangfoo, scarcely a sail was seen on that vast expanse of water. Such was the state of things in 1861, when the navigation was opened to foreigners. Now the muddy waters are ploughed by a large fleet of steamers; the greatest activity prevails everywhere; cities are being rapidly rebuilt, and populations are returning. The products of the interior are freely interchanged with those of the sea-board, and a new life has been imparted to great tracts of country. The lion's share of this new trade has as usual fallen to the natives. It is they who chiefly supply cargoes for the foreign steamers, and native trading craft everywhere crowd the river.

These events brought us into contact with the rebels, who held, and still hold, Nanking as their head-quarters. From that point they commanded the river on both sides, and it became necessary that the British authorities should make arrangements for the protection of commerce. Amicable relations with them were attempted to be established, but, as was natural, it soon appeared that our interests clashed with the assumed rights of the insurgents, and that our close alliance with the Imperial government was incompatible with similar relations with its enemies. But the programme which the Taepings announced touched us more nearly than that. The conquests which they proposed to themselves included some of the very ports which were then being opened on the river, an event which would have nipped the root of that new development of trade.

Our interest in China, as politicians are constantly telling us, is purely commercial. But peace is essential to the prosperity of commerce, and the present state of confusion and civil war is inimical to it.

Early in 1862 the rebels menaced Shanghae in great force, drawing a cordon of forts round the city, and cutting off the supplies from the interior. Provisions rose to famine prices, and the vast population of the city and suburbs was forced to undergo a siege. Some years before that time circumstances had compelled the British government to undertake the protection of the treaty-ports, and more especially Shanghae, as being the most important of them, and the most open to attack from the rebels, who held the whole country in rear of it. But, in 1862, it became imperative to do more than that. The little garrison placed there for the defence of the city, might be kept under arms for months, or even years, ready to repel an attack when the invaders should come within range of the city walls; the population would live in a chronic state of panic, many of them would leave (as they did); trade would be paralysed; the city and foreign settlement would be a mere fortified camp, cut off from all communication with the interior of the country.

In this crisis Sir James Hope, then naval commander-in-chief, came to the front. That officer was well acquainted with the character of the Taepings; he had had a great deal of communication with them, and had tried every means in his power to induce them to change their manners, so as to secure the respect of their countrymen and of foreigners. He had also repeatedly warned them of the disastrous consequences which would follow any demonstration on their part against the consular ports, Shanghae in particular.

The state of affairs in Shanghae, in the beginning of 1862, made it clear to Sir James Hope that the effective protection of the city involved the necessity of such aggressive operations as would clear the country in the immediate vicinity. Without waiting for instructions, therefore, he assumed the responsibility of immediate action, and commenced a campaign against the Taeping strongholds, which extended over a space of nine months, and ended in the dispersion of these marauders from that portion of country included in a radius of thirty miles from Shanghae.

This is a practical illustration of what the policy of the British government has been, and how it has from time to time submitted to circumstances. At first we have the theoretical principle of strict neutrality broadly asserted; then we are compelled to violate that principle in our own defence; an emergency arises in which the officers on the spot have to choose the alternative of an armed protection of British property, necessarily including a portion of the territories of the Imperial government, or the abandonment of British interests to destruction. Our own government confirms the decision of its officers—hence, first the ports themselves, and then the arbitrary thirty-mile radius are placed under foreign protection. At such a distance from the scene of operations, amid such rapid changes in the posture of affairs, and with such important interests at stake, it would be impossible for Downing Street to frame a code of instructions for officers in China which would apply to all possible contingencies, and impolitic to frame them on the pattern of the laws of the Medes and Persians. The abstract principle of non-intervention is very excellent in itself, but to adhere to it when our own material interests are directly assailed, would be pure infatuation. Expediency and self-interest must, after all, be our rule in China as elsewhere.

Our government at home, and its officers abroad, have always had a dread of complications in China, but much as they have studied to steer clear of them, they have step by step been sucked in, and the end is not yet.

The disturbances that have ruined so many of the richest districts in China are incompatible with the free course of trade. We have, therefore, a direct interest in the restoration of peace. The present government of China is on friendly, and even confidential, terms with us; it has shown great readiness to cement still closer our mutual relations. It is, moreover, such as it is, and with all its rottenness, the representative of order, and the rallying point for whatever remains of patriotism in the country.

The insurgents, on the other hand, are hopelessly given up to their propensities for desolation. If, therefore, peace is to be restored to China at all, within the present generation, it can only be by the subjugation of the insurgents, and the ascendancy of the Imperial government. With this view Admiral Hope first supported the American, Ward, a soldier of fortune, but a man of energy and genius, who disciplined and led a Chinese force in the service of the Imperial government. Following up the same line of policy, men and material were subsequently lent to the force, and, after Ward's death, a great number of her Majesty's officers and men were permitted to join it, and the little army was placed under the command of Captain (now Lieutenant-Colonel) Gordon of the Engineers. Under that officer the force grew to be a formidable power. Its career during the twelve months or so of Gordon's command was, with one or two exceptions, a series of brilliant successes.

It can no longer be said that the Chinese do not make good soldiers. Under leaders in whom they have confidence, they exhibit the highest military qualities. Gordon was, perhaps, the first who taught Chinese troops to overcome a repulse.

The result of Gordon's campaign has been to recover from the rebels the whole of the province of Keangsoo, between the Grand Canal and the sea. He has cut the Taeping rebellion in halves. The capture of Soochow, last December, gave him the command of the Grand Canal, and enabled him to interrupt communications thereby between the rebel garrisons of Nanking and Hangchow. Leaving the latter point to be acted on by the Franco-Chinese, who had Ningpo for their base, Gordon followed the Grand Canal towards Nanking, and captured all the cities that lay between. Nanking itself would probably have fallen an easy prey to him, but at that juncture he was compelled to resign his commission in the Chinese army. The service was, from the first, distasteful to him, from the position he occupied in relation to the Chinese officers with whom he had to act. The treachery perpetrated by the foo-tai, or governor of the province, at the capture of Soochow, in putting to death the rebel chiefs who had surrendered to Gordon, disgusted him; and, failing to obtain satisfaction from the government for this outrage on his own good faith, he determined to quit the service. The Queen's order in council which permitted him to serve the Emperor of China was withdrawn, and the "ever victorious" army has been disbanded, with what consequences the future will disclose.

It will be always a difficult thing for an officer with a high sense of honour, and with proper self-respect, to serve the Chinese government on its own terms, though it would be comparatively easy for a military adventurer, who is less particular, to build up his own fortunes in such a career. The system of management which places the forces of the empire under the control of local authorities, whose interests are frequently antagonistic to those of the nation and the Imperial government, precludes foreign officers from attaining their proper position. They are liable to be called upon to participate in proceedings of which their humanity disapproves. They have to listen to the constant complaints of disaffected troops in arrears of pay. They never can calculate with certainty on next month's supplies, and their men are always on the verge of mutiny. The disbursements for troops are provided out of the provincial treasuries, and hence the provincial authorities have a direct interest in levying as small a number of men as possible, and in doling out their pay in such measure only as may suffice to prevent a general rising. The scheme of supplying the Chinese government with a steam fleet failed for this, among other reasons, that Captain Osborn declined to serve under any mere provincial authority.

Whether the Chinese government will now of itself be able to give the *coup-de-grace* to the Taepings, or whether, through the incapacity and venality of local officials, anarchy will again distress the newly-conquered districts, is a question of serious import both to them and to us. The policy to be pursued by the British government in China, in any emergency that may arise, will demand honest consideration. It has been too much the fashion of political agitators to treat the subject flippantly, and to make the "China question" a parliamentary shuttle-cock. The general indifference to the subject which prevails in and out of Parliament, affords ample scope for misrepresentation, and some of the men to whom the country looks for sound views are often guilty of hiding their light under a bushel.

To go no further back than the last debate on China, as reported in the "Times," June 1st, 1864, we there find ample illustration of the fallacious arguments advanced by a certain class of politicians when dealing with this subject. Mr. Bright is very solicitous to clear his friends, who had preceded him in the debate, from the imputation of party motives, that their statements may carry the more weight. The disclaimer will naturally apply *à fortiori* to himself. But "*qui s'excuse s'accuse.*" How does Mr. Bright treat those who ventured to express opinions at variance with his own? An honourable member, desirous of obtaining light on the question, sought for it in the prosaic region of fact. Applying to the most authentic sources within his reach, he had collected opinions from a number of persons who had a practical knowledge of the country. These various opinions were remarkably concurrent, but they did not suit Mr. Bright's argument. He therefore considers them "uninteresting," and accounts for their unanimity by insinuating that the honourable member had concocted them all himself!

The ponderous speech of Mr. Cobden is as remarkable for what it omits as for what it contains. His object seemed to be to show, first, that our commerce in China was not worth protecting at all; and, secondly, that he had an infallible scheme of his own which would secure the ends that the policy of the government had failed in attaining. The facts he adduces in support of his argument are judiciously selected; the inferences he draws from them are framed to suit his foregone conclusions, but have no kind of reference to the relation between one fact and another. Causes and effects are blended in a fantastic medley, well calculated to throw dust in the eyes of the unwary, but fatal to the elucidation of truth. Mr. Cobden excludes from his view of the China trade the most important part of it, selecting the smallest item—the direct exports from this country—as a criterion of our commercial progress in China. His deductions from such a partial view of facts must necessarily be worthless. But, even on the narrow ground he has chosen, his conclusions are all forced. He avoids saying so in plain language, but the only inference that can be drawn from his line of argument, is that the successive re-actions that have occurred in the advancement of our export trade to China have been the result of our war policy there, and of the closer intimacy of our political and social relations with that country. If Mr. Cobden means anything, he means that. Now what do the facts say, even as Mr. Cobden himself has stated them?

After the peace of 1842, our exports increased steadily up to 1845, in which year they doubled the value of 1835, the year that followed the abolition of the East India Company's monopoly. For ten years, after 1845, the value of our exports fell to a lower level. Yet during that time we were at peace with China. A marked falling off occurred in 1854, but that was caused by the prostration of trade consequent on the outbreak of the Taeping rebellion, a circumstance wholly overlooked by Mr. Cobden. The wars of 1856—60 were followed by an unprecedented increase in our exports in 1859, 1860 and 1861. Mr. Cobden is perfectly right in saying that the trade of these years was vastly overdone, and a recoil was inevitable. But even in the two following years, when the re-action was operating in full force, the export returns showed a vast increase beyond the highest point reached in 1845, or in any year previous to 1859. At this point, Mr. Cobden, probably discovering that he had *proved* too *much*, shifts his ground to the single article—cotton. If, as the member for Portsmouth said, Mr. Cobden considers Manchester as the centre of the world, the cotton test is probably to his mind the most infallible. The exports of cotton goods to China fell from 243,000,000 yards in 1861, to 80,000,000 yards in 1862; and to 46,000,000 yards in 1863. "That," says Mr. Cobden, "is the character of the business you are transacting in China."

A word from Mr. Cobden would have explained the diminution of the export of cotton goods on an hypothesis, not at all involving the general decadence of our trade with China. The cotton famine had raised the value of the raw material to two shillings per pound, and the enhanced price which the manufactured goods cost to the Chinese naturally diminished consumption. Again, the Chinese happened, at the beginning of the cotton famine, to be over supplied with cheaper and better goods, and old stocks had to be used up before a response to the exorbitant prices paid in Manchester or an active resumption of business could be looked for.

While surveying our relations with China from the

"cotton" point of view, Mr. Cobden might have had the candour to acknowledge the handsome contributions of the raw material which Lancashire has received *from* China during the last three years.

Sir Frederick Bruce is a better authority than Mr. Cobden on Chinese affairs, and he says, in a report to the Foreign Office, dated Peking, June 7th, and published in the "Times," September 7th, 1864, "The import trade has increased from 41,000,000 taels (about 13,000,000*l.*) in 1860 (the last year before the opening of the Yang-tsze and the northern ports), to 81,000,000 taels (about 27,000,000*l.*), in 1863. The increase is due in a great measure to the large and increasing trade from the ports on the Yang-tsze in Chinese produce of all descriptions."

The vastly increasing trade in imports into this country from China, compared with which the exports are a bagatelle, Mr. Cobden passes over as having no bearing on the question. The opium revenue to the Indian government is also overlooked. The large shipping interest engaged in the China trade goes for nothing in Mr. Cobden's estimate, but it is nevertheless of great importance to the country, even though the vessels are not all owned in Lancashire, and do not all carry cotton. The amount of capital that British ship-owners find employment for in connection with China, is not limited to the large fleet of vessels engaged in the direct trade with this country, but is spread all over the coast and rivers of China. In the dispatch above quoted, Sir F. Bruce states that the entries of foreign shipping in China have increased from 293,568 tons, in 1860, to 996,890 tons in 1863.

The interest which British merchants, and through them the nation at large, possess in the prosperity of China is widely ramified. They are closely involved in the local and coasting trade; large amounts of British capital are sunk in fixed property of various kinds at all the open ports; and such investments are increasing at a rapid rate. These things lie under the surface, and are not generally considered in estimates that are formed in this country of the actual stake Great Britain has in China. But they are none the less real on that account. Theorists may say what they will, but our establishment on the territory of China is a great and important fact; and whether the process which led to it was theoretically correct or not, it will be impossible to undo it.

Not only are we fixed in China ourselves, but large native populations at the treaty ports have thrown in their fortunes with ours, to abandon whom would bring calamities on the Chinese for which it would baffle Mr. Cobden to find a remedy.

To reverse our progress is, however, the policy or the hobby of Mr. Cobden. He would not only undo what has been done, but he would urge the Government on to a new career of conquest in China, without even a pretext for war. He would seize two more islands on the coast in order to make free ports which would draw trade away from those now established. "Get two other small islands .... merely establish them as free ports; I don't ask you to do more." Mr. Cobden does not commit himself to say how the islands are to be acquired, but he knows very well there is but one way of acquiring them. And supposing we took possession of two islands, how many would France take? and if England were to lead the way in such schemes of aggrandisement, would the ambition of France stop short at islands? Many high-handed proceedings have been laid to the charge of this country, but this scheme of spoliation would surpass everything else of the kind. Mr. Cobden would probably suggest purchasing the islands, which would be, at least, a civil way of putting it.

But the whole scheme is so purely utopian that one marvels that a practical thinker could have shown such contempt for his audience as to propound it. Hong-Kong is the model on which Mr. Cobden would shape his new colonies; very flattering to Hong-Kong, perhaps, but betraying an incredible forgetfulness of the whole history of that colony. The "London and China Telegraph," of 13th June last, in commenting on Mr. Cobden's speech, shows clearly that the advancement of Hong-Kong as a port of trade was due to purely adventitious circumstances; and that for many years, when it rested on its own merits for success, it was an absolute failure, and a constant expense to the country. If Mr. Cobden aspires to be a second Stamford Raffles, he is beginning at the wrong end. Our policy in China will be more safely left to the chapter of accidents than to visionaries. We have hard facts to deal with, and not phantoms of a lively imagination.

The suppression of the Taeping rebellion cannot fail to produce remarkable effects on the condition of the Chinese people. They are ripe for great changes, not in the government or social institutions (the first is of little or no importance to the people, and the second are stereotyped), but in their relation to the progress of the world. Amid all political convulsions the people have remained unchanged, and that mainly because they are a non-political people. They are indifferent to affairs of state, but intent on their own business. Yet they have the faculty of self-government developed in an eminent degree. They are quiet, orderly, and industrious; averse to agitation of any kind, and ready to endure great sacrifices for the sake of peace. Such a people are easily governed, and their instinct of self-government is one important element in their longevity as a nation; it has enabled successive dynasties, often weak and vacillating, arbitrary and corrupt, to control three hundred millions of people. This constitutes the elasticity by which they regain lost ground after any temporary disturbance. Let the present reign of brigandage be destroyed, and the people will soon rise again; like pent-up waters they will flow into their former channels, and in a few years scarcely a trace of desolation would be left.

In this prediction we have the experience of various episodes, even of the present rebellion, to guide us. The rapidity with which the city of Shanghae was re-built, after its destruction during the rebel occupation of 1853—5, was astonishing. Other cities have been re-built and re-peopled with equal rapidity. Han-Kow, on the great river, has been several times sacked and destroyed by the rebels, and in a short time after each visitation it was worth plundering again. The important city of Soo-chow, captured from the rebels last December, is reported in June following to be showing signs of commercial life, although the surrounding country was still the theatre of war.

The Chinese people have, however, little cause for confidence in the efficiency or the stability of their own government; they have on the other hand implicit faith in foreigners. It is obvious, therefore, that any guarantee from Western powers that peace should be maintained in the districts once recovered from the rebels, would stimulate the commercial and industrial energies of the people, and materially contribute to the renewed prosperity of the country.

The prosperity of China is, then, intimately interwoven with our own, for vast fields of enterprise would now be opened out to Europeans which have heretofore been closed. Its resources have been developed to the utmost, perhaps, that a fossil civilisation, unaided by modern invention, is capable of. The Chinese have been ahead of the world from time immemorial in agriculture, commercial economy, manufactures, and all industries; in short, in everything that constitutes material wealth; but now in these later days the world has in some things got a little ahead, and is waiting to impart its new accomplishments to them. The vast mineral wealth of the country has been but partially taken advantage of. Its coal, iron, gold, and silver have hitherto been worked by the most primitive and inadequate machinery. But we are prepared to teach the natives how to economise their forces, and to make the most of the natural resources of their country ; and they are being prepared to receive the lesson.

The avidity with which the Chinese have grasped at the advantages offered to them by the steamers that now ply on the coast, and on the great river, is an earnest of their readiness to appreciate any other western inventions that are commended by their practical utility. The favourable introduction of steam on the Chinese rivers, and the popularity with which their earlier career was attended, were indeed due to fortuitous circumstances. On the Yangtsze Kiang steamers had not to compete with an old-established native trade— that had been for many years dead—but they reopened a commercial route that had been closed, and, at the time, they offered the only feasible means of navigating the great river. Under different conditions they would have had to work their way slowly into the favour of the Chinese; but now, having established a foothold, they will certainly maintain the position they have assumed, and the Chinese would be sorry to return to their former *régime*, under which they could hardly hope to accomplish in a month what is now easily performed in three or four days.*

There is still great room for the extension of steam traffic

---

* "Owing to the violence of the winds, and the rapidity of the current in certain places, the application of steam to navigation was required before the Yangtsze could be made available as a highway for transport. The decks of the steamers are now crowded with Chinese passengers, and their holds are filled with produce destined, not for foreign export, but for Chinese consumption. The practical advantages of foreign inventions are thus brought home to masses of the population in the very centre of China, and they can now avail themselves of the natural outlet for the productions of those rich internal

in the interior of China, and great need of it. For the present, however, foreigners are limited by the provisions of the existing treaties, to the ports formally opened by those treaties. Steamers may penetrate as far up the great river as Hankow, 600 miles from the sea; but the upper Yangtsze, which is navigable by steamers for 500 miles above that, must still be left to the monopoly of uncouth barges, which are slowly tracked up-stream by men who labour like beasts of burden. The navigation of the Poyang and Tung-ting lakes which communicate with the Yang-tsze; the Peiho river between Tientsin and Tungchow; the western river from Canton to the province of Kwangsi, and many other water routes—all practicable for properly constructed vessels—are equally excluded from foreign enterprise. The native traders on these routes are deprived of the aid which steam has afforded them in other quarters, and that by a decision of their government which, from a cosmopolitan point of view, is arbitrary and unjust. Inexperience may excuse the Chinese government for this narrow and pernicious jealousy, but what shall we say of European diplomatists who, in full view of the advantages which, as the past has shown, must accrue to natives and foreigners alike from the spread of foreign intercourse in China, would diminish "the points of contact" from a nervous, and not very rational, apprehension of possible complications?

Much has been said of the ruffianism that our newly established commerce on the Yangtsze Kiang has let loose on the great river. It cannot be denied; but it would be singular indeed if, with a weak government, a deplorably inefficient executive, and a timid people, outrages should not be committed. In every community there must be lawless charac-

provinces, instead of being driven to the slow and circuitous method of artificial water communication, and exposed to the exactions of the officials of the different provinces they had to pass through."—SIR F. BRUCE.

ters whom physical force, or the dread of it, alone can restrain from criminal acts. Under existing circumstances in China, it is the duty of each foreign state to control its own subjects; but it is manifestly unfair to circumscribe the legitimate privileges of a whole community, in order to punish a few unworthy members of it. Such a policy can only be dictated by indolence in seeking out and punishing offenders. But the instances on record of piracy and other crimes on the Yangtsze Kiang, although authentic, are apt to engender exaggerated views of their relative importance. They are made unduly conspicuous by rhetoricians, who, on the other hand, ignore the smooth under-current of affairs which is silently conveying blessings to many thousands of people. These occasional outrages are, after all, mere excrescences on a system that, in an essential manner, ministers to the well-being of whole populations who would otherwise be in penury. At the worst, the good vastly outbalances the evil; and, to take the lowest view of the matter, it were better even that the lawless proceedings of a few rowdies should go on unchecked, rather than that the remedy for them should be found in the curtailment of a trade of such great promise. It must never be forgotten that it is the natives of China who derive the chief benefit from foreign commercial intercourse; and that, while arbitrary restrictions on the plain meaning of treaties, by which it has been sought to limit the application of their provisions, are unjust to foreigners, the refusal to extend foreign intercourse is an injustice of which the Chinese people have a right to complain.

The unexampled success of steamers in China, within the three past years, has paved the way for a similar result for railways. The Chinese, having satisfied themselves of the advantages that accrue to them from the former, will be perfectly ready to avail themselves of the latter. They are not naturally given to travel, that is, they travel for profit and not for pleasure. But the facilities for locomotion which steamers now afford them have created a large and increasing passenger traffic. The steamers on the coast and on the rivers are usually crowded with Chinese passengers, who seek very moderate accommodation, and therefore can be carried economically. The shortening of a month's journey to one of a few days has induced many thousands to travel who did not think of it before. It is, therefore, a fair inference that the greater economy of time which railways would secure would enable millions to travel who are at present excluded from it. The mere monopolising by railways of the revenues of the present passage-boats, and other means of passenger communication, in certain districts, would be but a trifle compared with the new traffic which railways would create for themselves in such a populous and eminently commercial country.

And, perhaps, no other country of equal area presents fewer natural obstacles to the construction of long lines of railway. This has been shown by the investigations of Sir Macdonald Stephenson, who has lately published a full report on the subject. The labour, and many of the materials, are to be found in the localities where they would be wanted.

It may safely be assumed, also, that in no other country would railway investments be more remunerative, if organised on a uniform and comprehensive plan, such as that proposed by Sir M. Stephenson.

The most populous parts of China are alluvial plains, either fed by great navigable rivers, or intersected in all directions by networks of canals. With regard to the great water routes, which are open to large vessels, it is very problematical whether railways could supersede, or even compete with, navigation in the carrying of bulky goods. It could not be expected, for example, that on the proposed line from Hankow to Shanghae, following the course of the great river for 650 miles, goods should be conveyed as economically as in steamers that can navigate the river easily, carrying 2000 tons of cargo.

But in those parts of the plain where very small craft only can be used, a railway may easily supersede the present means of transport.

The saving of time would, perhaps, in all cases attract the passenger traffic to the railways, and that alone would probably be amply sufficient to support them remuneratively.

There are many large tracts of country in China less thickly peopled than the rich plains, and which do not possess the same facilities of water communication. In the north the traffic is conducted by means of caravans, necessarily slow and expensive; and in some parts of central China, goods are transported on men's backs. In such regions railways would not only be highly remunerative, but would be an inestimable boon in opening up those parts of the country which, being less favoured by nature, have been kept far behind in wealth and prosperity. To compensate for these natural disadvantages of the north, the Grand Canal was cut to connect the city of Hang-chow with Peking. That stupendous work required constant repairs to maintain its efficiency, and a considerable annual outlay of money. In the disorders of the last ten years the necessary funds for this purpose have either not been raised, or have been misappropriated, and the Grand Canal has consequently gone to ruin. The importance which has been attached to this great line of communication by successive dynasties for 900 years, point to the track of the canal as favourable for a line of railway. Of all the branches of Sir M. Stephenson's scheme this is the most obviously desirable. A railway that would restore, and vastly increase the old traffic on the Grand Canal, would do for the forty populous cities it would touch at, what steam navigation has done for the marts on the banks of the great river. Although Peking and the commercial cities of North China are accessible by sea for eight months in the year, and in the direct communication between them and the southern coast ports, there is less urgent need of improvement, yet the time now occupied in travelling from Peking to its nearest shipping port is as great as the whole journey to Nanking or Shanghae by railway would take. The benefits which the railway would bring to the inland cities, more remote from the sea or from navigable rivers than Peking, would be incalculable.

In the correspondence published by Sir M. Stephenson, to show the prospective results of the introduction of railways into China, rather too much stress has been laid on their bearing on foreign trade, and especially on the transport of tea from the interior to the shipping ports. There is nothing in the saving of a few hundred miles of a long sea voyage to compensate for the cost of transporting goods by railway. And the conveyance of tea would be a more insignificant item in the whole traffic of railways than it has already become in that of the steamers that trade in the heart of the tea districts.

The whole question of the foreign trade of China may be put on one side so far as the railway scheme is concerned. The success of railways, and the need of them, rest on a much broader and surer basis. The internal trade of China; the interchange of the products of the diverse climates and soils that are included in the limits of the empire itself— is what really gives life and activity to the people. It is to that source alone that the promoters of railways ought to look for a guarantee of their success. The whole foreign trade in tea does not probably exceed one tenth of the native; and yet tea forms but a small proportion of the inland trade of China.

In the consideration of the railway question, therefore, the more such irrelevant matter is kept out of account, the more likely are sound general conclusions to be arrived at. The lines to be established should be determined solely with a view to supplying the wants of the Chinese in the broadest sense. But if a desire to benefit this or that port, or this or that party, be permitted to influence the direction of the undertaking, it will probably be at the expense of its ultimate success.

The political advantages that would flow from the use of railways would be no less important than the commercial. It would bring the distant provinces within reach of the government, and enable it more effectually to centralise its authority, without which it it is no longer possible to govern China well.

Peking is in the worst situation that could have been selected for the seat of government ; that is, from a Chinese point of view. It was convenient as a citadel for the Tartars while they were consolidating their power, as its vicinity to their native wilds kept open for them an easy retreat in the event of revolution. And, while their vigour remained fresh, the enfeebling influence of distance from the provinces was neutralised by the energy of the executive. But in the process of degeneracy which the Manchu dynasty, like its predecessors, has undergone, the remoteness of the capital has been a fertile cause of misrule, corruption, and distress in the provinces. The natural capital of China is Nanking or Hang-chow, or some other easily accessible point in the central provinces.

The railway scheme, by connecting all parts of the empire in rapid daily communication, would bring the government face to face with its officers ; local abuses would be exposed, if not corrected, and imperial and national interests would cease to be at the mercy of corrupt, mendacious, and treacherous provincial authorities. Nothing would so surely save the existing government from the annihilation which threatens it; restore order throughout the country; and promote the well-being of all classes.

The local famines and inundations to which China has in all ages been liable, and which, from the absence of proper communications, have occasionally entailed great suffering on the people, would, under the reign of railways, lose their horrors. The brigandage with which the government keeps up a desultory and unsatisfactory struggle over an area too wide for rapid or decisive results, would die a natural death, were railways in operation. Their moral effect alone would do much to keep down local risings, and the facility they would afford for the transport of troops would enable the government to act with promptitude at the point required; and instead of keeping up half-disciplined, disaffected, and idle hordes, often worse than useless, and yet very expensive, a small, compact, well-equipped force, with the power of motion which railways would supply, would do the work better, and at a mere fraction of the expense.

Railways would be very popular with the Chinese people, whose readiness to support them is proved by their capitalists offering to invest in shares. But will the consent of the Imperial government be granted to the project? Without its co-operation nothing can be done; and this therefore is the question which will have to be primarily decided.

In the first place there is the *vis inertiæ*—the aversion to innovation—to be got over. That can be accomplished if the government can be convinced of the advantage of the proposed scheme. Then, on the other hand, the representatives of foreign powers at the court of Peking may, from national jealousy, influence the government against any reform emanating from Great Britain. But the determination of the Chinese government will depend most of all on the view which the British minister or *chargé d'affaires* may happen to take of it ; and he may meet the projectors with active or lukewarm support, or with positive opposition. The conciliatory and upright spirit which has ruled Sir Frederick Bruce's intercourse with the Chinese government has inspired it with unlimited confidence in the British minister, whose counsels have in consequence acquired great weight in Peking. It is earnestly to be hoped that his successor will avail himself of the good impressions Sir Frederick leaves behind him to promote with all assiduity those reforms and improvements which, while subserving the best interests of China, will also redound to the honour and the profit of our own country.

It is the duty of our ministers to maintain the legitimate influence of this country in China. Our actual interest in that empire greatly outweighs that of any other people ; but we are in some danger of losing our prestige, and allowing other powers to rival us. We failed in the telegraphic scheme through Mongolia, but the Russians will certainly accomplish it. The Lay-Osborn fleet failed, but the French and the Americans will supply its place. We have withdrawn British officers from the Chinese service ; but the French and Americans remain. Railways will, some day, be established in China ; the people are as ripe for their introduction now as they ever will be ; if we miss the opportunity, some other nation will seize it, and, with or without us, China will have railways.

The electric telegraph would of course accompany railways, if, indeed, it does not precede them. I am not prepared to speak of the adaptability of the Chinese hieroglyphics to telegraphy, but the Chinese people and government have a keen appreciation of the importance of the rapid transmission of intelligence. This is shown by the admirable system of government expresses, and the extent to which carrier-pigeons have been used to influence the exchange markets of China. The vast area of the Chinese empire would render telegraphic communication more than ordinarily acceptable, and, in the present age of the world, even necessary.

It needs no great stretch of imagination to predict that the free use of machinery in China will yet do much to enrich the nation, and to ameliorate the condition of the poorer classes. Many parts of the country are suffering from over-population. Their economy in food, clothing, and housing, together with the great fertility of the soil in such districts as the plains of Che-kiang and Keang-soo, enable an incredibly large population to find a subsistence there. But 800 persons on the square mile is too much, even for the richest part of China, to support efficiently. A large proportion of these people is consequently underfed, poorly clad, and miserably lodged; they suffer the penalties of civilised life without its comforts, and their physical and mental development are seriously impaired. The Chinese do not possess within themselves any remedy for this state of things; economy of their means and moderation in their desires have already been cultivated to perfection. Their manual industry is unexampled, and leaves no room for improvement. Their diligence in taxing the resources of their soil cannot be exceeded. The surplus population might certainly find an outlet in foreign lands, but the Chinese people as a whole are singularly averse to emigration.

The greatest boon that could be conferred on these people, and the only feasible means of raising many thousands of them from the lowest depths of poverty, would be the introduction of new industries which would give them profitable employment, which at present they are excluded from. A promising field is open for this. The perseverance of the Chinese is proverbial, and the perfection they have attained in making the most out of the means at their disposal has been the admiration of the whole world. But they are still strangers to the modern mechanical appliances of Europe and America for economising human labour. Compared therefore with the attainments of western nations, the material resources of China are wasted. The division of labour, as practised in the agricultural districts of China, is diametrically opposed to the principle advanced by Adam Smith. Each family grows, spins, weaves, and wears its own cotton; and so with many other products. This system has the advantage of keeping the people employed all the year round, and there may no doubt be a great deal to be said in its favour.

But to what purpose—with what results—is all this labour spent?

The practical answer to this is, that it has happened that England has imported raw cotton from China, manufactured it, returned it to China two years afterwards, and sold the cotton cloth cheaper than the article could be produced by domestic labour on the spot where it is grown. It is, of course, to a small extent only, that England can compete in manufactured cotton with the native product of China. But that it should be possible at all, first to buy the raw material at such an enhanced price over the cost to the natives as will induce them to part with it, then to send it 15,000 miles across the sea, and the same distance back again, and spite of the enormous expenses incurred in the operation, still to supply the manufactured article at a lower cost than the natives produce it at, proves that a vast amount of labour is misapplied in this branch of Chinese industry. And yet their manufacture of cotton has, perhaps, been brought to a higher state of efficiency than any other.

Their coal and iron are worked in the most primitive

manner. Both articles are supplied from abroad, although existing in great abundance in the country. The native coal that is sold in the markets of China costs from thirty to forty shillings per ton, and is so poor in quality that English coal is more economical at double the price. By proper appliances, and a better system of working, the quality of Chinese coal might be greatly improved, and the cost diminished.

It would be endless to enumerate the various departments in which steam and machinery might be advantageously applied in China. Sugar and paper may be mentioned, as also the various oils used by the Chinese, all produced and consumed in the country in enormous quantities, and all susceptible of great improvement both in the cost and quality of the preparations.

In everything that constitutes the wealth of the country we see the same disproportion between the power expended, and the results obtained, as has been instanced in the case of cotton. The waste of human labour is multiplied by the vast and varied products of the country; and the field offered for the expansion of new enterprises is commensurate with the size and population of the Chinese empire.

The introduction of machinery into the interior of the country, and its application to the manufactures that now employ the people, will only be secured by a slow and gradual process. Great opposition would be met with, particularly at the outset; for, though we may claim for the Chinese a freedom from prejudice equal to any other people, it would be absurd to expect of them more enlightenment than our own countrymen have shown, when put to the test by innovations which threatened to supersede manual labour. The Chinese will be convinced, as usual, by results. When they find the materials of wealth which they now possess multiplied to them by the cheapness of the necessaries of life, they will not be slow in following up the idea. The elevation of the poorer classes, when profitable occupation is supplied to them, will create new wants, while it provides the means of gratifying them. The benefits accruing to China will naturally react on this country precisely to that extent to which a commercial nation must always profit by the increasing wealth of its customers.

In small matters also, the social condition of the Chinese people is in a fair way of being improved by their contact with restless and progressive foreigners. Gas, which is now being introduced into Hong-Kong and Shanghae—a simple thing in itself—may nevertheless do something towards elevating the Chinese, and preparing them for more important advances. The erection of water-works, for the supply of the large cities, would be a boon of no ordinary value to those populations who live on the alluvial plains. The impure water, drawn from turbid rivers and canals which are the receptacles of filth, is a fertile cause of disease in many localities. These communities might be supplied with pure filtered water at a lower cost than is at present paid for the mere carriage of the unwholesome compound now obtained from sources as putrid as the Thames. One successful experiment would probably demonstrate the necessity of extending water-works to most of the populous cities in the empire.*

* Shanghae, from its situation and over-crowded population, is one of the greatest sufferers from the want of pure water; and there cannot be a doubt that this circumstance has contributed, in no slight degree, to the sickliness that has prevailed there for several years past, as the increase in the population tends more and more to the defilement of the river,—the only source whence water is obtained. The question of water-supply for that settlement having been submitted to practical and experienced engineers in London, the result of their calculations is, that a system of water-works, with reservoirs beyond the influence of sewage, would provide each household with an unlimited supply of pure, filtered water, at about one-fourth of the expense which is at present incurred in merely carrying water from the river to the houses. Messrs. Simpson and Giles have further demonstrated that, at the

Nor is the influence of European intercourse with China limited in its scope to the mere commercial, manufacturing, and other material pursuits of the people. Their notions of good government must be inevitably modified by it, and no one can estimate the extent to which a few Europeans, by their superior force of character, may impress the huge multitudes of China. Circumstances have rendered Shanghae the great focus from which these external influences are brought to bear on the natives. The distracted state of the surrounding country first brought numbers of fugitives, both rich and poor, to seek shelter under the ægis of foreign flags, until an enormous population has accumulated on the ground set apart for the residence of foreigners. The kind of small republic which the Europeans set up for their own protection, and for the due regulation of the natives who crowded into the settlement, became popular with the Chinese; its functions became more and more important; and accessions of power were from time to time added to it, but always inadequate to the efficient discharge of its constantly increasing duties. The Chinese like the municipal administration of Shanghae, because, although heavily taxed, they at least know how the revenue is applied, and they enjoy more or less personal protection, and immunity from extortion. The system has worked with more harmony than could have been expected, considering that it to a certain extent rivals the provincial government. It has at any rate taken deep root, and may possibly be the precursor of similar growths at other commercial towns. In any disruption of the Chinese power that may result from the present disorganised condition of the empire, these anomalous foreign " settlements "

proposed rate of one shilling per 1,000 gallons, a large return would be secured on the capital necessary to be invested in the works. We may therefore hope that at no distant day the inhabitants of Shanghae, at least, will enjoy this great blessing.

will certainly play an important part. The weakness of the government of the country and the disorders which accompany it, while impairing the prosperity of the settlements as commercial *emporia*, tend to strengthen their political influence. The prestige which naturally accompanies a European residence, and the guarantee of security to life and property, with or without armed protection, which it holds out to the Chinese people, render these consular ports asylums of authority in times of anarchy, and will naturally maintain them as commercial centres when the government of the country has crumbled away. In them a nucleus of power will be preserved, which will facilitate the reconstruction of a government, should the present one be broken up, and in this way these commercial settlements may yet prove of essential service to the Chinese nation. They may possibly grow into free, independent republics, an issue which the leading journal has more than once predicted. In an article of June 2, 1864, the "Times" says:—"The free cities we hope to see are those which grow of their own accord, and which arise out of the circumstances of an abundant commerce and an unsettled country. If the nations of Europe would agree to stand aloof, we should very soon see little commercial republics intrenching themselves and extending themselves upon the shores of China; just such cities as arose upon the coast of Africa, and in later history upon the coasts of Italy, when similar dangers compelled traders to draw together for defence and self-government. We believe that our cheapest and our best policy is not to establish, but to favour the growth of such communities as may develop themselves into free cities. Nor can we expect that this development will be the work of a day, or that so great a ruin as that which is mouldering over the heads of one-third of the human race can fall, and be reformed into modern habitations, without many clouds of dust and some terrible catastrophes."

Should such be the destiny of these trading ports, no class will have more cause for satisfaction than the body of Chinese who may reside in them, who regard with pleasure every advance of foreign influence, and would be glad to live in peace under any power strong enough to maintain it.

POSTSCRIPT.

EVENTS have progressed rapidly in China since the foregoing chapter was written. Lieutenant-Colonel Gordon, after resigning his commission in the Chinese army for the reasons I have mentioned, apparently considered that it would be too hazardous at such a juncture to leave the Government entirely to its own devices. He accordingly remained, with the approval of Major-General Brown, to instruct and advise them, and he has had the satisfaction to witness the crowning success of all his labours, in the fall of Nanking, and the extinction of the Taeping rebellion.

The two provinces of Che-Kiang and Keang-soo—the richest and most populous in China—are now freed from rebels, and have had peace and order once more restored to them. It may require some little time entirely to reassure the populations of these provinces of the security of life and property in districts that have so long languished under the devastating effects of civil war; but there is now every reason to suppose that the reign of anarchy has been banished for many years to come, and that the pacified region will soon enjoy the prosperity which its natural advantages must bring, enhanced, as it must inevitably be, by the extended intercourse with foreigners which has not yet had an opportunity of bearing its full fruit.

This success of the Imperial arms has naturally resulted from the acceptance of foreign Ministers at the Court of

Peking, and the introduction of China into the family of nations, which is the great triumph of the policy inaugurated by Lord Palmerston twenty-four years ago, and steadfastly followed up by that statesman through good and evil report.

Whether the scattered remnants of the Taepings will again become formidable from their concentration in the province of Kiang-si, beyond the reach of the immediate foreign aid which has led to their dispersion, will depend very much on the vigour of the Imperial Government at Peking. If it realises the gravity of the position, and the truth of the maxim that prevention is better than cure, it will adopt timely and energetic measures to anticipate a reorganisation of the Taepings.

But, however that may be, it is pretty certain that if the provisions of the Treaty were carried out in the broad sense evidently contemplated by the framers of it; if the Poyang lake and the rivers which communicate with it were freely opened to foreign trade; if Europeans were permitted to reside at the commercial marts of Kiang-si, their moral weight alone, especially after the campaign just concluded in Keang-soo and Che-Kiang, would go far to prevent any further demonstration of the rebels in that quarter. The authorities at Peking may yet find cause to regret that their suspicion of friendly foreigners has deprived them of such important auxiliaries at many of their most vulnerable points.

October 27.

THE END.

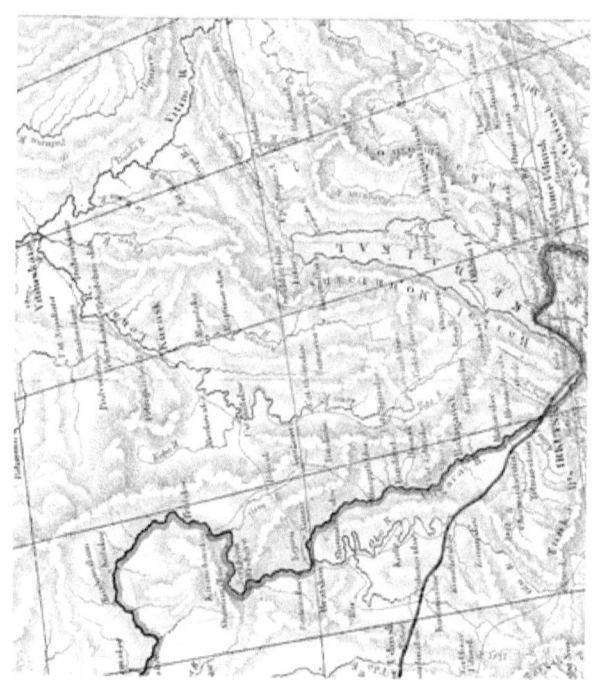

www.ingramcontent.com/pod-product-compliance
Lightning Source LLC
Chambersburg PA
CBHW022148300426
44115CB00006B/403